TALKING BOOKS

Talking Books

Readings in Hellenistic and Roman
Books of Poetry

G. O. HUTCHINSON

OXFORD
UNIVERSITY PRESS

OXFORD

UNIVERSITY PRESS

Great Clarendon Street, Oxford OX2 6DP

Oxford University Press is a department of the University of Oxford.
It furthers the University's objective of excellence in research, scholarship,
and education by publishing worldwide in

Oxford New York

Auckland Cape Town Dar es Salaam Hong Kong Karachi
Kuala Lumpur Madrid Melbourne Mexico City Nairobi
New Delhi Shanghai Taipei Toronto

With offices in

Argentina Austria Brazil Chile Czech Republic France Greece
Guatemala Hungary Italy Japan Poland Portugal Singapore
South Korea Switzerland Thailand Turkey Ukraine Vietnam

Oxford is a registered trade mark of Oxford University Press
in the UK and in certain other countries

Published in the United States
by Oxford University Press Inc., New York

British Library Cataloguing in Publication Data

Data available

Library of Congress Cataloging in Publication Data

Hutchinson, G. O.

Talking books : readings in Hellenistic and Roman books of poetry / G. O. Hutchinson.

p. cm.

Includes bibliographical references and indexes.

ISBN-13: 978–0–19–927941–8

1. Greek Poetry—History and criticism.   2. Latin poetry—History and criticism.   I. Title.

PA3092.H88 2008

881'.0109—dc22   2008004126

Typeset by SPI Publisher Services, Pondicherry, India
Printed in Great Britain
on acid-free paper by
Biddles Ltd., King's Lynn, Norfolk

ISBN 978–0–19–927941–8

1 3 5 7 9 10 8 6 4 2

In memoriam F. C. Downing soceri carissimi
et M. Downing socrus carissimae

Preface

This volume collects some recent pieces which concern books of poetry from the third century BC and the 'long' first century BC, and adds four new chapters. Of these the first is a relatively lengthy creation of context, by way of prologue, the last, by way of epilogue, a relatively brief attempt to assemble and advance some of the argument. An appendix has been affixed to chapter 9; the first part of that piece has been expanded. 40 per cent of the book is new. Various changes have been made in the rest; but there has been no systematic attempt to update since the original publications. The whole package, though dealing only with some authors and periods, aspires to broaden and deepen the study of poetry-books.

The idea of such a volume was not mine, but Professor A. Barchiesi's; I am deeply grateful to him for his heart-warming encouragement. The articles had at any rate been written with connected lines of thought in mind. Though I have long been interested in poetic books (cf. Hutchinson (1984)), the papyrus of Posidippus engaged me in the subject afresh (cf. ch. 4). If other subjects come into some of the pieces, that is not altogether unfortunate: it is part of the point that this subject must be considered like and together with other critical questions. ('Books' in the title is accusative as well as nominative.) The conclusions suggested to particular problems do not matter so much as the general approach. The work is meant to encourage, among other things, the active study of Greek and Latin together, and involvement with actual ancient books—papyri—in considering books of poetry.

The work has been written during a period encumbered with major administrative jobs in Faculty and College, and enlivened by the fourth book of Propertius. This may serve as an excuse for some of its shortcomings. Besides the many debts acknowledged in the text, I have further debts to Dr D. Colomo, Dr R. Daniel, Dr G. F. De Simone, Dr R. Dekker, Professor J. Diggle, Professor M. Étienne, Professor F. Ferrari, Professor K. J. Gutzwiller, Professor P. R. Hardie, Professor S. J. Harrison, Ms J. Himpson, Professor N. Holzberg,

Professor R. L. Hunter, Professor Sir Hugh Lloyd-Jones, Professor R. T. MacFarlane, Professor D. J. Mastronarde, Dr D. Obbink, Professor J. I. Porter, Dr F. Reiter, Professor D. Sider, Dr S. E. Snyder, Professor V. M. Strocka. I am obliged to the Verlag Dr. Rudolf Habelt GmbH, Bonn, for permission to republish chapters 2, 4, and 9 (original versions: *Zeitschrift für Papyrologie und Epigraphik* 145 (2003), 47–59; 138 (2002), 1–10; 155 (2006), 71–84); to the Cambridge University Press for permission to republish chapters 5, 6, and 7 (*Classical Quarterly* 53 (2003), 206–21; 52 (2002), 517–37; S. J. Harrison (ed.), *The Cambridge Companion to Horace* (Cambridge, 2007), 36–49); and to the Oxford University Press for permission to republish chapter 3 (M. J. Clarke, B. G. F. Currie, R. O. A. M. Lyne (edd.), *Epic Interactions: Perspectives on Homer, Virgil, and the Epic Tradition Presented to Jasper Griffin* (Oxford 2006), 105–29). Hilary O'Shea and others at the Press have been kind and helpful as ever. Dr D. McCarthy and Dr K. M. Fearn have assisted indefatigably with production, and Ms S. Newton has copy-edited vigilantly and sympathetically. My wife and daughter have given cheerful support and have endured my cooking, jokes, and papyri with meritorious patience.

Gregory Hutchinson

Exeter College, Oxford
September 2007

Contents

List of Illustrations

The following gives the sources of the images in chapter 1, and some additional images of the same papyri or inscriptions: the aim is both to acknowledge permission and to enable the reader to view images independently.

Abbreviations

Periodicals are cited roughly as in *L'Année philologique*. Ancient authors, papyri, inscriptions, etc., are usually cited as in, or more fully than in, Liddell and Scott[9], with *Revised Supplement* (1996), and the *Oxford Latin Dictionary*. Roman numerals after epigrams refer to the numbers in Gow and Page (1965, 1968); 'AB' after epigrams of Posidippus denotes Austin and Bastianini (2002).

AE   *L'Année épigraphique* (Paris 1889–).

ANRW
H. Temporini and W. Haase (edd.), *Aufstieg und Niedergang der römischen Welt* (Berlin and New York, 1972–).

ARV[2]
J. D. Beazley, *Attic Red-figure Vase-Painters*[2] (Oxford, 1963).

ASR
C. Robert *et al.*, *Die antiken Sarkophagreliefs* (Berlin, 1890–).

CCSL
Corpus Christianorum. Series Latina (Turnhout, 1954–).

CEG
P. A. Hansen, *Carmina epigraphica Graeca*, 2 vols. (Berlin, 1983–9).

CMG   *Corpus Medicorum Graecorum* (Leipzig and Berlin, 1908–).

CPF   *Corpus dei papiri filosofici greci et latini* (Florence, 1989–).

FGE   D. L. Page, *Further Greek Epigrams* (Cambridge, 1981).

FRP   A. S. Hollis, *Fragments of Roman Poetry*: c.60 BC–AD 20 (Oxford, 2007).

GDK[2]   E. Heitsch, *Die griechischen Dichterfragmente der römischen Kaiserzeit*[2], 2 vols. (Göttingen, 1963–4).

GLK   H. Keil *et al.*, *Grammatici Latini*, 7 vols. and suppl. (Leipzig, 1857–80).

GMAW[2]   E. G. Turner, *Greek Manuscripts of the Ancient World*[2], rev. P. J. Parsons, BICS Suppl. 46 (London, 1987).

II   *Inscriptiones Italiae* (Rome, 1931–).

ILS	H. Dessau, *Inscriptiones Latinae selectae*, 3 vols. (Berlin, 1892–1916).
LIMC	*Lexicon iconographicum mythologiae classicae*, 10 vols. (Zurich and Munich, 1981–99).
LTUR	E. M. Steinby (ed.), *Lexicon topographicum urbis Romae*, 6 vols. (Rome, 1993–9).
ORF[4]	E. Malcovati, *Oratorum Romanorum fragmenta liberae rei publicae*[4] (Turin, 1976–9).
RAC	Th. Clauser *et al.* (edd.), *Reallexikon für Antike und Christentum* (Stuttgart, 1950–).
RE	A. Pauly, G. Wissowa, W. Kroll (edd.), *Real-Enzyklopädie der classischen Altertumswissenschaft* (Stuttgart and Munich, 1893–).
RRC	M. H. Crawford (ed.), *Roman Republican Coinage*, 2 vols. (Cambridge, 1974).
RS	M. H. Crawford (ed.), *Roman Statutes*, 2 vols., BICS Suppl. 64 (London, 1996).
RVAp	A. D. Trendall and A. Cambitoglou, *The Red-figured Vases of Apulia*, 3 vols. (Oxford, 1978–82).
SGO	R. Merkelbach and J. Stauber, *Steinepigramme aus dem griechischen Osten*, 5 vols. (Stuttgart, 1998–2004).
SH	H. Lloyd-Jones and P. J. Parsons, *Supplementum Hellenisticum* (Berlin and New York, 1983).
SSH	H. Lloyd-Jones, *Supplementum Supplementi Hellenistici* (Berlin and New York, 2005).
SVF	H. von Arnim and M. Adler, *Stoicorum veterum fragmenta*, 4 vols. (Leipzig, 1905–24).
Tab. Vind.	A. K. Bowman, J. D. Thomas, and J. N. Adams (edd.), *The Vindolanda Writing-tablets (Tabulae Vindolandenses)*, ii–iii (London, 1994–2003).
TrGF	B. Snell, R. Kannicht, St. Radt, *Tragicorum Graecorum fragmenta*, 5 vols. (Göttingen, 1971–2004).

1

Doing Things with Books*

This chapter will concentrate on the reading and writing of Greek books in the third century BC and of Latin books in the first century BC. How novel the third century was is not easily ascertained, thanks to our ignorance of papyri and poetry in the fourth century; but we can see in the third century significant developments away from literature of the fifth, whether or not these are new, and can gain some idea of areas that will prove important in the rest of the book. From the third century on, papyri and other sources give real opportunities to attempt some history of reading and to view the presentation and structuring of books; issues about poetic books can be seen in the context, however complex and incomplete, of material evidence and concrete practice.

Divisions are a common feature of literature. Many in Greek literature are created by performance: for instance the act-divisions of New Comedy, where a choral song separated the parts of the main play. But the circulation of literature in books leads to other divisions, based on the book itself. There are two main types. Separated entities, for example distinct poems, may appear within a book; or an entity larger than one book, for example Herodotus' work, may be divided into books. In the second case the book divides; in the first, it could be thought to unite. Thus Pindar's odes for Olympic victors

* A version of this chapter was tried out at a conference on literary papyri at Austin, Texas; I am grateful to Professor D. Armstrong, Professor T. K. Hubbard, and others for their comments. Dr D. Obbink has read the piece with his immense expertise. The chapter has many points of contact, and concurs on many issues, with Don Fowler's brilliant unpublished work, which Peta Fowler has kindly enabled me to read.

are made to belong together as they might not have done before they were collected. In both these types we have division and a larger entity, parts and some kind of whole.[1]

These examples were not, it is supposed, directly part of their authors' conceptions, although they may relate to those conceptions. Thus breaks between books may correspond to significant articulations within the apparent continuum of Herodotus. Pindar's victory odes, or Sappho's or Anacreon's poems, may in their succession build up a sense of the author's role as celebrator of victory, or of the narrator's identity as lover or voice; such a sense seems to be aimed for, in other ways, by the poets themselves. The books may also express the interpretation of the person who assembled them; this too will shape the reader's reception. When the author himself or herself unites shorter works into a book or divides a longer one into books, those forms become a mode of authorial meaning. This is not to say that only authorial meanings matter; and indeed the specific meanings here are most often left inexplicit and depend on the reader's interpretation. But if the forms are part of the original context in which the books are written and, particularly, read, it is the more imperative to incorporate the forms in interpreting the works. To give an analogy: we know that the *Agamemnon* and *Eumenides* were performed together in a connected tetralogy; this obliges us to explore their relationship more pressingly than if we knew they had been performed in different years. (And even if they had, authorial meaning in the relationship should still be investigated.) Both types of authorial book multiply meaning: in a single poem of several books the book-divisions add precision and shape to our understanding of the whole; when there are many poems within one book, the meanings can multiply more dramatically, as individual poems relate to each other and a larger structure, and the reading of the book becomes a dynamic process.

---

[1] On Pindar, see Rutherford (2000), 137–65; Negri (2004); W. S. Barrett (2007), 164. Many of the papyri discussed in this chapter have been examined at first hand. Bibliographical reference has been kept slender in this introductory chapter; for a detailed bibliography on ancient books, see <http://www.ulg.ac.be/facphl/services/cedopal/pages/bibliographies/Liber%20antiquus.htm> accessed 30 Nov. 2007. The immense literature on modern books, though it has given inspiration to what follows, cannot be summarized here. McKenzie *et al.* (1999–) surveys the book in Britain; Eisenstein (2005), a classic text, well illustrates the questions of revolution so prominent in this whole area, and particularly difficult for the ancient world.

The division of works into several books can be followed as a historical process, but is hard to observe in papyri. The most celebrated instance supposed for pre-Hellenistic literature is the division of Homer; but the resulting units are until a much later period always thought of not as books but as 'rhapsodies'. The physical size of books is unlikely to have dictated a division in which *Iliad* and *Odyssey* have the same number, and the number is that of the letters in the alphabet, used as a way of referring to the rhapsodies. Some Ptolemaic rolls contained more than one rhapsody, though the beginning or end of rolls appears always to fall at a division of rhapsodies. Within the roll, such division is not strongly marked in third-century papyri.[2]

Outside Homer, the unit is normally conceived of as a 'book'. These will commonly coincide with the physical rolls, as is indicated by labels attached to the outside of rolls (cf. P. Oxy. 2433, 3318), and probably by postings of specific books (cf. e.g. *CPF* 6 (P. Mil. Vogl. 11, ii AD), including in the list Posidonius, *Protrepticus* 3 (F3 Edelstein–Kidd); Cic. *Att.* 13.32.2 Dicaearchi περὶ ψυχῆς utrosque uelim mittas). But original books could be divided into two rolls (cf. e.g. P. Herc. 1538, which unlike the other papyrus of Philod. *Poem.* 5 indicates a division into two; if the form τῶν εἰς δύο implies a subsequent division, note the label P. Oxy. 2396). More doubtful is the inclusion of two original books in one roll. If the 'book' of these divisions is commonly physical but ultimately conceptual, that only strengthens its significance as an entity.[3]

The historian Ephorus, we happen to hear, divided his own work into books (Diod. 5.1.4). It cannot be known whether the division by

[2] On 'book'-division in Homer, see S. R. West (1967), 18–25. On the origin of the division, cf. Heiden (1998) (division original); Van Sickle (1980) (Ptolemaic); Nünlist (2006) (made by γραμματικοί, in ancient views). ῥαψωιδία is standard in the scholia, notably the A-scholia to the *Iliad*, e.g. 6.348a (ἐν τῆι Α ῥαψωιδίαι), 12.213a, 18.105–6a (cf. with letters e.g. Σ Eur. *Or.* 356, Apoll. Soph. *Lex. Hom.* 9.4–5 Bekker; with ordinal numbers e.g. Philo, *Cont.* 17, Hermog. *Dein.* 27); titles for particular ῥαψωιδίαι Σ *Il.* 8.1, 9.1, 10.1 (a style of reference probably older than this division, cf. Hdt. 2.116).
[3] Ohly (1928), 45–8, gives no non-Homeric instances where rolls combine two numbered books. I have noticed no instance myself; note that P. Oxy. 698 (iii AD) contains the opening sentence of Xen. *Cyr.* 2 (as in the MSS), but puts it as the last sentence of Book 1 (Canfora (1974), 16, sees a *reclamans*, presumably wrongly placed). See Canfora (1974), 9–16, for books divided between rolls and the normal identity of roll and book. Requests for particular books do not actually exclude non-coincidence of books and rolls; they remain significant for books as distinctive entities. In P. Oxy. 2396 the α is clear under the microscope.

peoples was as strict as Diodorus suggests; nor do we actually know that each book had a proem. However, the use of a separate title for Book 4 (Εὐρώπη) may, for all Diodorus' imitation, take us to an early stage, where the books are more self-contained entities, with their own names. Timaeus' proem to his sixth book (a significant point in the work), may take us nearer the series of numbered books so clear in Polybius. The works of philosophers come to be spoken of as 'books' rather than λόγοι, including particular works: so ὅπερ ἐν τοῖς περὶ φύcεωc βιβλίοιc δείκνυμεν (Epic. *Pyth.* 91), or Euphemus' ἄδικα βιβλία (Call. fr. 191.11 Pfeiffer). Even poets can be spoken of as filling books rather than singing (Hermes. fr. 7.25, 45 Powell; *SSH* 985.13). Despite convention, the practices of reading are starting to make an impact on the very language of literature. The development and organization of Hellenistic prose works in several books is considered in chapter 10; mention is made of Apollonius of Perga's *Conica*, explicitly divided into eight books, grouped into halves of four books each. Apollonius' *Argonautica* exploits a related approach to division, and displays an emphatic new beginning at the start of the third and fourth books of four, together with a division of the whole series into two halves; there is a clear resemblance here to the books of the *Aetia*, though these are subdivided into smaller entities. The connection with the approach in prose subsists, whether or not the poets are directly inspired by prose, or by earlier authorial division in poetry.[4]

The collection of different poems or works into one roll is harder to trace historically, but the papyri illuminate the position from the third century on. Earlier authors were already being collected, as we shall see, with principles of arrangement (P. Köln Inv. 21351 + 21376). Zenodotus must have produced, or at least used, an edition of Pindar. Callimachus' classifications for his Catalogue would have implications

---

[4] Say, in Antimachus (*Thebaid* at least five books, *Lyde* at least two (fr. 85 Matthews))? It should be noted that the fourth book of the *Aetia* may well be much shorter than the books of Apollonius (*if* the *aitia* of 4 have the same average length as those of 3, 26–8 (say) = 70% of 1360 = 952; shortest book of AR (2) 1285; others 1362, 1407, 1781: more like a Euripidean tragedy). On references to books, etc., in poetry, see Bing (1988), ch. 1. Aristotle's extant works pose interesting questions for division and presentation; for doubts on their being lecture notes or lectures cf. Burnyeat (2001), 115 n. 60. But the place of books and reading before the third century falls outside the scope of this chapter; Yunis (2003) contains much interesting discussion.

for subsequent editions (Call. fr. 450 Pfeiffer; P. Oxy. 2368; cf. also *Σ* Alcm. fr. 3 Davies for related disputes). But papyri offer us a much richer and closer picture, and enable us to see an attitude which is the essential context for the making and reading of poetic books. Some Ptolemaic papyri will be surveyed in what follows. The following possibilities need to be borne in mind: a papyrus may contain a collection of pieces by one author or several; in the former case, the collection may have been made by the author or made subsequently (in the latter case only subsequently); the book may be a home-made and unique production, or may be written by a professional scribe, and in the latter case may be one of many copies sold and circulated.[5]

P. Petrie 49b (Oxf. Bod. MS Gr. Class. e. 33 (P); iii BC; Fig. 1) presents in two columns a series of mostly four-line epigrams on particular tragedies or satyr-plays: it looks as though the title character or characters speaks in each (*SSH* 985.19 ἐμός; in 16 ἀείδομαι is plausible; 26 | ἡμεῖς is followed by | 28 ἐξ ἡμέων ϲτ[(so Hutchinson; .ε.μεων ϲτ[Maltomini; κεῖϲαι? ἐάν ed. pr.; supplement ϲτ[εφαν?). It is a reused papyrus: there is writing under the last poem, and under 10. The first poem, which seems general, is probably an introduction to the series. The last poem has only two lines (presumably because it is last); it is followed by a blank space. It does not look particularly as if a new series follows on. We seem to have a whole, and perhaps single, series. The series shows an interesting self-consciousness about form and about history. Homer's work is regarded as books and there is some play on staging (3, 37), spectacle, and the present format. Old and recent seem to be contrasted (23, contrast 5, 10, 15 (Sosiphanes is iii BC)). There can be no doubt that this is a sequence by one author. The presentation is noteworthy, in view of the spareness of Ptolemaic books. Each poem has an inset title, ἐπί + work + author, a space after the title, and a paragraphos; the hand is literary, the layout is quite neat. This could be a version made for an individual and taken from a published book (possibly with more series).[6]

---

[5] On *Σ* Alcm. fr. 3, see Hutchinson (2001*a*), 104–6. The date of the first collections of short items by Simonides or from Theognis is very uncertain; cf. M. L. West (1974), 40–59; Hubbard (2007); Sider (2007). Woudhuysen (1996), 153–73, offers interesting analogies on verse miscellanies in 16th- and 17th-cent. England.

[6] On this difficult papyrus, see Maltomini (2001), a fine piece of reading. I have used ultra-violet and infra-red light; they did not greatly help. In 24 κερτομεω seems

Figure 1 P. Petrie 49b.

Figure 2 P. Mil. Vogl. 309, col. xiv.

The famous P. Mil. Vogl. 309 (iii BC; Fig. 2) presents, probably, epigrams of Posidippus; these are arranged in series which are themselves subdivisions of familiar types, but are collocated to create striking changes. (See chs. 4 and 11.) A title is given to each series; the poems are separated by paragraphoi. Within the series, there are impressive openings and deviant closes (see ch. 4); both may develop practices in editions of earlier poets, such as Pindar. Some of the series, e.g. the οἰωνοσκοπικά, are likely to be authorial and unlikely to assemble pre-existing epigrams; indeed the whole collection looks likely to be of one author by the author. It is not a complete works of Posidippus, but a selection organized for variety, not just system. It is a professional copy; but some items, mostly within one series (ἱππικά), have apparently been marked for later and private excerption.[7]

P. Köln 204 (Mnasalces) (ii BC; Fig. 3) looks at first sight similar; but here a heading (Μ[ν]ασάλκου) implies an anthology, or a one-off collection within the roll (the series begins at the top of a column). The hand seems more documentary than literary. The epigrams do not fall into types like those of Posidippus. The fourth epigram appears to be one ascribed to a different author in the Palatine Anthology.

BKT v.1.77–8 (P. Berol. 9812; iii BC; Fig. 4), *SH* 974, presents an anthology of epigrams without authors' names, in a literary hand. These epigrams concern dedicated 'works of art', and must deliberately set the crude club against the small and artistic work that follows; perhaps Apelles' Aphrodite is also set against more masculine work.[8]

---

clear (satyr-plays should be borne in mind). In 32 οὐϲ looks promising. *SSH* should not be misunderstood to suggest that the first epigram is in a different hand.

[7] If τον is indeed τοῦτο. An interesting, but somewhat problematic, alternative in Ferrari [2004] (τοῦ short for τοῦ δεῖνα, 'by...'). On openings and closes cf. Rutherford (2000), 159. The closes in Posidippus would be an aesthetic development of an originally classificatory practice, deviant instead of miscellaneous. The vast bibliography on Posidippus can best be approached through Acosta-Hughes, Kosmetatou, Baumbach (2004), and Gutzwiller (2005). A bibliography and progressively updated text can be found at <http://chs.harvard.edu/chs/files/posidippus 9_0.pdf> accessed 30 Nov. 2007. Professor Ferrari is working at a commentary on the whole papyrus, Ms S. Rishøj Christensen at a commentary on the first section. On collections of epigrams see further Pordomingo (1994); Argentieri (1998); Gutzwiller (1998); Parsons (2002); Ferrari [2004].

[8] For this papyrus see Gronewald (1973); Ebert (1974). It is notable that in the *Theognidea* there are significant links between items, even in the earliest part (cf. e.g. 39, 52, 53; 69, 74, 75, 77, 80; 117, 119; 151, 153).

Figure 3 P. Köln 204.

A highly interesting book is the early third-century P. Köln Inv.
21351 + 21376 (Fig. 5). This shows two poems by Sappho, in the
same metre but not with the sequence of poems found in later
papyri. The poems probably come from a metrical edition, and the
sequence may result from selection. Sappho's poems are thus already
arranged by metre. Another hand, after a small interval, presents a
lyric poem later than Sappho, but influenced by her. The hands look

Figure 4 P. Berol. 9812.

Figure 5 P. Köln Inv. 21351 + 21376.

Figure 6 P. Berol. 9771.

professional; the copying of the final poem need not be part of a unitary plan, but shows a wish to juxtapose related items.[9]

P. Hamb. 118 (+ 119?) (iii–ii BC) offers an anthology of prologues from Euripides, written in a documentary hand. *BKT* v.2.79–84 (P. Berol. 9771; iii BC; Fig. 6) presents the parodos of *Phaethon* as an excerpt, with ἐμ Φαε[centred (top of column). It is written in a literary hand. There is frequent punctuation by dashes. The text is not even divided into stanzas; since the first line is considerably shorter than most (probably 31 letters as against 36–43), and the first two lines contain one metrical period each, the scribe may have been copying from a text with colometry (two written lines at first combined into one?).[10]

---

[9] See, among other writings, Gronewald and Daniel (2004a and b, 2005); M. L. West (2005); Rawles (2006a and b); A. Hardie (2005); Bernsdorff (2005). The texts of Sappho will appear as P. Köln 429, the other poem as 430, in *Kölner Papyri* xi; I am grateful to Dr R. Daniel for showing me the edition in advance of publication.

[10] Line 16 has 32 letters, with a dash; the other countable lines have 36–40. In fr. 773.80 Kannicht there must have been serious miscopying, as the antistrophe indicates (cf. Kannicht's apparatus on fr. 773.80). See for the papyrus: Schubart (1911), viii and pl. 4b (revising date from *BKT*); Diggle (1970), pl. v; Kannicht (2004), 805. On P. Hamb. 118–19 see Harder (1985), 139–43.

Figure 7 P. Tebt. 1 *recto* col. ii.

Figure 8 P. Tebt. 2 frag. (a) *verso*.

P. Tebt. 1 and 2 (late ii BC; Figs. 7 and 8) seem to imply the general circulation of an anthology. Both the papyri, from the same archive and possibly by the same hand, present the same lyric and other extracts (or pieces), with a difference in order, and with more than one transcription, notably in 2, which extensively exploits both sides of the papyrus. 2 marks the pieces with ἄλλο, as in an anthology. This may make it less likely that the original anthology was straightforwardly a set of party pieces for the symposium. 1 ends the series with a piece which was not included in 2 (see below); the last extant piece of the series in 2, marked by ἄλλο, was not included in 1. The next column in 2, and fr. (d) *verso* (mime), present material, not in 1, that appears distinct in character; it is thus more likely that the shared items are an extract from an anthology, or mini-anthology, which has been used differently in these two intriguing papyri. 1, the more neatly written, has before the series of pieces a column, which then stops, of decrees by Euergetes II, in the same professional-looking semi-uncial hand. Like *BKT* v.2.56–63 (P. Berol. 13270, early iii BC, also a collection of pieces), it marks change to a different metrical or generic category with eisthesis (and paragraphos), and it uses a long line for its uncolometrized lyric (*c.*54 letters; P. Berol. *c.*62). At the end of the series, which is followed by a blank, it follows three pieces on love with a fourth indecent and jocular piece, not in 2, on the dying instructions of the φιλοπυγιϲτήϲ. It could have been added to the original. The change and surprise at the close of a series is a strategy we see Posidippus using, in a more elevated fashion.[11]

P. Köln 242 (ii BC; Fig. 9) contains two texts, a hymn with author's name above, and before it an evidently popular extract in anapaestic tetrameters (comedy? *TrGF* 646a), in a documentary hand ('popular' because it appears also on P. Fackelmann 5, i BC). They seem to deal with related subjects: the birth of gods.[12]

---

[11] On P. Tebt. 1 and 2, see Pordomingo (1998). For full photographs of both, see on Apis <http://www.columbia.edu/cu/lweb/projects/digital/apis/search/> accessed 30 Nov. 2007, berkeley.apis.262, 284, 383 (P. Tebt. 1) and 283 (upside-down), 308, 337 (P. Tebt. 2). Note the non-Maasian drift to the right in P. Tebt. 1: perhaps the scribe was holding the papyrus in an unusual way. The left-hand and perhaps the lower margin of P. Berol. inv. 13270 suggest a mini-series rather than a whole roll.
[12] So M. L. West *ap.* Maresch (1987), 31.

Figure 9 P. Köln 242, frr. a, b, c, d, j.

Figure 10 P. Hibeh 7.

P. Hibeh 7 (Oxf. Bod. MS Gr. Class. d. 78 (P), iii BC; Fig. 10) contains an anthology including Euripides, marked by name, with division by paragraphoi, and space between and before heading and text. It is written on the back of a speech of Lysias, in two hands with cursive features, different from the hand of the Lysias.[13]

A papyrus published by Barns (1950) (Egypt Exploration Society, ii–i BC) provides a probably professional text of a gnomological sequence; many of such sequences from the third and second centuries look home-made, and some are written on ostraca. This papyrus consists of quotations on fortune, marked by inset names, and with paragraphoi. Variant readings are included in the ample lower margin. The product looks commercial, and the variants suggest an interest in the texts and sentiments beyond use for adorning one's own prose.[14]

A similar view could be suggested of a patently home-made item: P. Hib. 17 (Oxf. Bod. MS Gr. Class. d. 79 (P), iii BC). The text is written in a documentary hand; the other side presents accounts, in a different hand. The text gives an extract from a work on Simonides (δ' line 3, καί line 4); it is headed [περὶ] ἀνηλωμάτων | Cιμωνίδου (the latter in ek-thesis). The layout is neat; gaps and paragraphoi punctuate. It looks from the right-hand margin as though there may have been no other text written; this extract could itself be extracted from a gnomological work. Interest in the sentiments (possibly not unrelated to the accounts!) seems more likely here than work for a composition using them.[15]

This varied and colourful material shows how lively interest was in the relation between items in a sequence. This interest is apparent at an authorial level (P. Petrie 49b; P. Mil. 309?). It is naturally unclear to what extent readers, i.e. producers of the actual papyri, are drawing from

---

[13] The extract before Eur. *El.* 367–79, a gnomic passage, is *TrGF* Adesp. 690, a mysterious text.

[14] In i. 28 of Barns's papyrus κατώρθουμεν not κατορθοῦμεν should be read, as is clear from the original (Sackler Library). On gnomologies (and other anthologies) see Barns (1950 and 1951); Messeri (2004); Chadwick (2006); Pordomingo (2007). Isocr. *Nicocl.* 44, Plat. *Laws* 810e–811a, [Isocr.] *Demon.* 51–2 are relevant to the early history.

[15] Other series of quotations concern women (*BKT* v.2.129–30, *c*.ii BC) and wealth (P. Petrie 3, iii BC). P. Michaelid. 5 (iii BC; literary hand, with some cursive features), after iambics, and hexameters (some on the Persian Wars?), offers items (D and E) which are both clearly related to women and marriage; but the second, an unusual version of *Il.* 3.426–9, is not itself gnomic. The writing ends after the quotation (7 (at least) lines blank below)—perhaps this is the end of the collection. Photograph in D. S. Crawford (1955), pl. 1).

general circulated collections. We probably see this happening at least in P. Tebt. 1 and 2; cf. Barns's papyrus. On the other hand, P. Tebt. 1 and 2 also illustrate selection (cf. P. Hib. 17), perhaps insertion, rearrangement, and setting within a larger body of material; P. Köln Inv. 21351 + 21376 shows secondary addition. People are doing things with series of items. The frequent informality of hands and presentation indicates an active interest in appropriating or creating sequences of material, for a whole variety of purposes; readers do not just passively peruse books they have purchased. The sequences that confront us often look like small series of a column or two, rather than a continuous series which fills a roll (especially P. Petrie 49b, P. Tebt. 1 and 2, *BKT* v.2.56–63). The Posidippus itself may be seen as a combination of such series into a larger entity. That underlines the pervasiveness of a reading culture which relates items within a sequence. Twists and turns, especially at the end of a sequence, appear at different levels of production (P. Petrie 49b, P. Mil. 309, P. Tebt. 1 and 2). We see a vital context for the authorial ordering of collections across a whole roll in the third century. Callimachus' *Aetia* 3 and 4 and *Iambi*, and Herodas' *Mimamboi*, obviously order items significantly. They are written for readers highly responsive to collocation and connection.

The papyri give us some idea of the nature of reading in Greek from the third to the first centuries BC. Papyri of prose, not least, show a concern with articulating the text into divisions of sense. Punctuation by paragraphos and space is common: e.g. P. Hibeh 17 (above); P. Oxy. 2399, i BC (Duris?; *GMAW*² no. 55). The papyri of Philodemus show us abundant division in papyri of the first century BC read in Italy. In poetry P. Tebt. 4 (Homer, *Iliad*, ii BC) exemplifies larger division by sense: a diagonal stroke marks a new paragraph or the end of a speech at 147, 198, 207. Division by metre (between strophes, etc.) is marked e.g. in P. Lille 76 abc (Stes. fr. 222 (b) Davies, iii–ii BC), P. Oxy. 3716 (Euripides, *Orestes*, i BC).[16]

Papyri tend to offer more aid to the reader as time goes on; but much depends on the type of author: the most elaborate lectional aid (breathings, accents, etc.) is probably for lyric poetry, in its difficult dialects. Even so, the aid is often added by a second hand (P. Oxy.

---

[16] For punctuation in the Herculaneum papyri, see Cavallo (1983), 23–5; Scognamiglio (2005); Giuliano (2007).

Figure 11 P. Oxy. 3000.

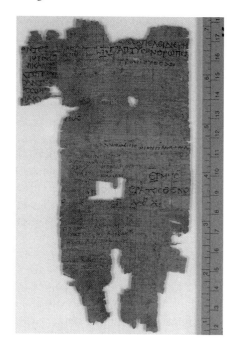

Figure 12 P. Sorbonne
inv. 2245A.

1790, i BC (Ibyc. S151 Davies; part in *GMAW* ² no. 20); P. Oxy. 1361 + 2081 (*e*) i BC–i AD (Bacchylides, *Scolia*)). There are notable variations among papyri of the same work, for example Callimachus' *Aetia*. So P. Lille inv. 76d, etc., *SH* 254–8, 260–3 (photographs Meillier (1976), 353–6; part in *GMAW* ² no. 75) already in iii (or ii) BC presents Callimachus' text together with a detailed explanatory commentary: lines of text in ekthesis are followed by comments. It has no lection signs. P. Oxy. 2214 (i BC–i AD), fr. 186 Pfeiffer, 97 Massimilla, has numerous lection signs; PSI 1092 (i BC?), fr. 110.45–64 Pfeiffer, is very neat, and has wide spaces between the lines, but no lection signs. No comment is visible in either.

In P. Oxy. 3000 (i BC–i AD; Fig. 11), Eratosthenes *SH* 397, there have been several moments of annotations, by at least two hands distinct from that of the main text. The relatively wide intercolumn for this date, and the abundance of the main set of comments, might suggest a plan of annotation (note the addition of the clarifying ὁ Ζεύς to the right of the main block of comment in Σ line 8). A different commentary has evidently been consulted for the note extended to the right in Σ line 5 (οἱ δὲ κτλ.). In general, it is difficult to know whether marginal additions to the text, often clearly from commentaries, were made by or for readers and were part of the production of the desired book, like correction. Sometimes notes seem to be written as part of the original production, as when text and comment are in the same hand.[17]

Textual variants are included e.g. in P. Sorbonne inv. 2245A (iii BC; Fig. 12; Homer, *Odyssey* 9 and 10; *Odyssey* þ 31 in S. R. West (1967), 223–56), a private copy (rather cursive hand, palimpsest). In this particular papyrus any variants are added, usually with deletion, by the first hand: the writer is seeking the most accurate copy. P. Oxy. 2387 (i BC–i AD) illustrates a more scholarly consultation of different editions (various hands). The common practice of correction

---

[17] Two lyric examples ch. 7 n. 3. In P. Louvre E 3320/R56 (i AD) recent scholarship is used, as the reference to Pamphilus indicates. For these scholia (in Hutchinson (2001*a*), 8–10), see Tsantsanoglou (2006); for Pamphilus, Hatzimichali (2005). On wide margins and planning cf. McNamee (1977), 9–11; the hand of the text in 3000 does not perhaps suggest a de luxe edition. On broader issues Cameron (2004), ch. 7; Cameron's relatively liberal approach to the possibility of planned comment might be extended further.

(*diorthosis*), most often by the original scribe, shows that the principle of textual precision was valued, however varied the execution.[18]

All this indicates that there were diverse ways of reading, but shows the existence of an intensive and careful approach; this is particularly apparent with difficult texts. Understanding of what it could involve is taken much further when we confront directly the many metatexts, works which are read to help the reading of other works. Commentaries (hypomnemata) are indirectly attested through marginalia and through signs that point to commentaries in primary texts; there are also direct references, and actual copies. Hipparch. 1.1.3 indicates that there had already been numerous commentaries on Aratus by the second century BC, basically exegetical. Cf. e.g. Theon's commentaries (i BC) on numerous Hellenistic poets. P. Louvre E 7733 (ii–i BC; Fig. 13), *SH* 983–4, presents a riddle about the oyster, followed by an extensive commentary. It seems a relatively informal copy: it has been made on the back of a neatly written philosophical papyrus; it is not perhaps part of a more extensive transcription. Both text and commentary are written in a hand with numerous cursive features.[19]

Figure 13 P. Louvre E 7733 *verso*.

[18] On *diorthosis* see McNamee (1977), 17–25; Turner (1987), 15–16.
[19] Lasserre (1975); the other side is pl. IX in Bingen, Cambier, Nachtergael (1975). For commentaries on Aratus in later papyri see Obbink (2003), 53; add now P. Köln 400 (iii AD), cf. also 401. For commentaries on papyrus see quite recently Dorandi (2000), and the edition by Bastianini *et al.* (2004–).

The most striking example of close and scholarly study is provided by the most popular poet: Homer. An early papyrus of a commentary is P. Lille inv. 83 + 134 + 93 b + 93 a + 114 t + 114 o + 87 (iii BC), from the same mummy as the commented text of the *Victoria Berenices*; see Meillier (1985). A more substantial example, based on Aristarchus, is P. Oxy. 1086 (B.M. Pap. 2055, i BC, on *Il.* 2.751–827; photo in Erbse (1969–88), i (pap. II), part shown at *GMAW*² no. 58); P. Oxy. 4451 is probably part of the same commentary. It has huge columns, with forty very wide lines; the hand is small and informal. There are frequent abbreviations, of a type particular to commentaries. This illustrates how commentaries are seen as aids to reading literary works rather than literary works themselves. The commentary includes quotes from Pindar, Anacreon, Alcaeus. The comments are as often connected to critical signs marked in the text to facilitate cross-reference.[20]

Philitas' and other collections of glosses illustrate a further form of aid to reading, and interest by scholars; cf. e.g. P. Freiburg 1 c, a glossary to Homer (ii/i BC, photograph Naoumides (1969), pl. II after p. 184). Related ancillary works in third-century papyri are seen e.g. in Berlin Ostrakon 12605 (*Odyssey* þ 120 in S. R. West (1967), 260–3; Cribiore (1996), 228, and plate XXV), extracts from a lexicon of obscure words in poetry with quotes, in a mature and literary hand, and P. Tebt. 695 (berkeley.apis.380; iii BC; Fig. 14), a list of

Figure 14 P. Tebt. 695.

[20] Cf. also e.g. P. Tebt. 4 (ii BC, on *Iliad* 2). On the Lille papyrus, see Pontani (2005), 135–6 (23–136 give an account of ancient exegesis and of the papyri).

tragedians with place of origins and number of tragedies, in a hand with cursive features (cf. the poems on dramas in P. Petrie 49b). Naturally with these works education will often be involved; but education can still inculcate ways of reading, and the wish that these ways should be learned tells us something about attitudes.[21]

We can also say something on the texts most widely read. Negative conclusions can only be made with great caution: a few new finds could easily alter them. If we look at the c.280 literary papyri from the third century BC, poetry is clearly more popular reading than prose. Homer, Euripides, Menander are much the most popular authors; epigrams are also frequent. Philosophy and oratory seem more popular than history; the oratory often has educational connections. Again there is no need to segregate reading experience at school from other types of reading experience, even if it is imposed by an adult. Practical books too make up a part of the papyri in prose.[22]

We come now to the Romans of the first century BC. The evidence for the Greek world and for the Roman world is strikingly asymmetrical; there are far fewer ancient books, but Cicero in particular, on whom we shall concentrate, gives us far more information on readers. We may begin, to facilitate comparison, with aspects of reading itself. There were notable differences for Romans in reading Greek poets, older Latin poets, and contemporary Latin poets, as regards metatexts. Commentaries and the like were undoubtedly far more abundant for Greek literature. It is notable how much of the interpretation even of Latin poetry was undertaken by *grammatici* trained in the traditions of Greek scholarship. So Pasicles from Tarentum, who changed his name to L. Crassicius Pansa, wrote a commentary on Cinna's *Smyrna* (Suet. *GR* 18.2), probably not long after Cinna's death. A commentary on Cinna's *Propempticon* was written by C. Iulius Hyginus, a freedman of Augustus (or Octavian) from Spain or Alexandria and a student

---

[21] For educational material see Cribiore (1996), and (2001). Naoumides (1969), 182–3, gives a dated list of lexica on papyrus. For Philitas, see Spanoudakis (2002), 347–92. On glossaries to particular authors, what looks like a glossary to Callimachus from a later period is of interest, PSI inv. 3191 (i–ii AD), in a hand with cursive features; see Menci (2004).

[22] The papyri are most easily surveyed through the Leuven database, <http://www.trismegistos.org/ldab> accessed 30 Nov. 2007. We naturally lack the rich material about consumers explored by, say, Fergus (2006); sometimes archaeology can help. Parsons (2007), esp. ch. 9, offers a valuable picture for the Roman period.

of Alexander Polyhistor (Suet. *GR* 20.1); he was in charge of the Palatine library. In the first half of the century M. Pompilius Andronicus, from Syria, wrote a treatise in more than one book on Ennius' *Annales* (Suet. *GR* 8.3). A work in more than one book on Lucilius was written by Curtius Nicia, perhaps the same as Cicero's learned friend Nicias, probably from Cos (Suet. *GR* 14.4; Cic. *Att.* 7.3.10, 13.28.4, *Fam.* 9.10.1–2, etc.).[23]

Much more scholarship will probably have existed in the first century BC on Lucilius and his predecessors than on more recent poets. Varro's work shows his intensive activity on the vocabulary, texts, and lives of older poets (cf. e.g. Cic. *Brut.* 60, Varro, *De Lingua Latina* Book 7). His *De Comoediis Plautinis* in at least two books (Gel. 3.3.9) concerned authenticity; there were at least five books of *Quaestiones Plautinae*. Already in the later second-century scholarly work on Latin dramatists, including work on authenticity, had been carried out by Accius (born *parentibus libertinis* in Pisaurum). Exposition of living or recently dead poets in schools was allegedly begun after 27 BC (Suet. *GR* 16.2: Epirota first taught on *Vergilium et alios poetas nouos*); authors may have envisaged such exposition in future, and the eventual writing of commentaries (as later of Asconius on Cicero, Cornutus on Virgil). But living authors will normally have been read with the scholarly tradition on their works not yet formed, the texts not yet elaborately annotated. The novelty would be exciting, all the more with classic status in the wings.[24]

Distinctive traditions lay behind the production of Roman books, traditions for the most part seen also in inscriptions; and inscriptions come to be marked up with particular elaboration in the last part of the first century BC. Literary texts, like inscriptions, usually divide

[23] See Kaster (1995) on the passages of Suetonius, and also Christes (1979), 25–7 (Andronicus), 67–72 (Crassicius), 72–82 (Hyginus). In general on writing about poets see Rawson (1985), ch. 18. See Deufert (2002), 50–3 for critical signs used by Republican scholars. Cavallo, Fedeli, Giardina (1989–91) deals with many aspects of the production and reading of Latin literature.

[24] For Republican scholarship on Plautus see Deufert (2002), chs. 2–3; 115–17 on the evidence, fairly slight, for commentaries. Gel. 2.24.5 suggests an ample tradition of commentaries on Lucilius; we do no know when they begin. Hor. *Sat.* 1.10.74–5, *Epist.* 1.20.17–18 (cf. Mayer ad loc.) are not good evidence for exposition of living authors to older boys, though the latter passage may glance at the possibility mock-modestly. Sen. *Ep.* 108.30–5 is interesting for work on Cicero's philosophical writing.

words with interpuncts, perhaps with increasing regularity in texts of poetry. This practice, though ultimately of archaic Greek derivation, is a Latin and Italian tradition; it is seen (with one or two dots) in Sabellian and some Etruscan inscriptions. Sen. *Ep.* 40.11 *nos etiam cum scribimus interpungere adsueuimus* presents it as national and part of a Roman tendency to deliberation, cf. Sen. Rh. *Contr.* 4 *pr.*7. Signs of length (*apices*) are common: they arise ultimately from a lack of differentiation in the basic Latin alphabet, but their use is not dictated simply by a need to avoid ambiguities.[25]

A striking difference from Greek texts of poetry is the large diagonal stroke which appears to mark the end of lines; the regularity of this use varies in poetic papyri. The punctuation is more frequent than we would expect in Greek texts of accessible poetry. No scholia have yet appeared. While even for earlier Latin, Roman readers had less scholarly guidance than for many Greek texts, Roman poetic texts were much more extensively marked up than Greek ones. Some of this marking aided grammatical understanding; it certainly gave Latin books of poetry a quite different appearance, and made the visual experience of reading them quite distinct.[26]

Space and material are more opulently used: on average, rolls are taller, margins bigger (especially upper and lower), letters larger. Virg. *Ecl.* 6.12 may imply a new column for a new poem; see also on the

---

[25] On interpuncts see R. D. Anderson, Nisbet, Parsons (1979), 131 n. 43. For Sabellian inscriptions see Rix (2002). On punctuation and related matters, see: R. W. Müller (1964), Wingo (1972); Habinek (1985), ch. 2; Parkes (1992), 9–12; Bowman and Thomas (1994), 56–61.

[26] The metrical role of the marks at the end of lines seems apparent from P. Herc. 78 (below). Their difference from the more compact internal diagonal stroke, a mark of punctuation, is seen clearly at *Bell. Act.* col. vi.5, where such a stroke is placed at the end of the line, and does not resemble the metrical marks two and three lines on (the punctuation after *uenéni*, though superfluous in modern terms, perhaps keeps *uolnere* and *ueneni* together). It may none the less be that continuity of sense was one factor that caused a metrical stroke to be omitted. Punctuation is not common in i BC texts of Euripides, or of Menander, save for changes of speaker (cf. e.g. *BKT* v.2.115–22 (P. Berol. 9767); only shown within line); there is some in P. Heid. Inv. G. 1385 (Eur. *Med.*; hand with documentary features; Seider (1982); image <http://www.rzuser. uni-heidelberg.de/~gv0/Papyri/Verstreutes/1385_Seider/1385_Seider_150).html> accessed 30 Nov. 2007. There are no punctuation or interpuncts in a pap. of Virg. *Ecl.* (i AD) P. Narm. inv. 66.362, Gallazzi (1982), with pl. II (a): but this is clearly not a normal commercial text. Contrast e.g. P. Herc. 1475, Costabile (1984), photograph 604, a papyrus with elaborately written letters and interpuncts (late i BC–i AD).

Gallus papyrus below. This approach to space adds to the firm differentiation from reading Greek texts. Writers often emphasize the smart presentation of books for distribution (Cat. 1.1–2, 22.1–8, Hor. *Epist.* 1.20.1–2 (booksellers), Prop. 3.1.8, Ov. *Tr.* 1.1.1–13, 3.1.13–14).[27]

Some particular literary papyri may now be mentioned: there are few of substance, but the number is likely to increase. It is possible that the script evolves from a more cursive style in the late Republic to a more elegant and monumental style in the early Empire. But this view, though it may in fact be correct, relies on the 'archaic' nature of these forms in epigraphy. The cursive scripts used in later documents e.g. at Vindolanda are seen at Pompeii e.g. in transcriptions on walls of Propertius and Ovid (*CIL* iv.1893–4, Fig. 15); different approaches to book-texts may have coexisted, and likewise different degrees of regularity with the interpunct.[28]

Three particularly interesting papyri of poetry use an 'Early Roman' script with cursive forms. P. Herc. 78, of Caecilius Statius' comedy *Faenerator*, gives a titulus to the right of the ending. Diagonals regularly mark line-end; interpuncts are often neglected. There are no visible marks of length, and no indications of change in speaker. In P. Herc. 21, of Ennius' *Annales*, Pezzo VII fr. 3, there are forked paragraphoi

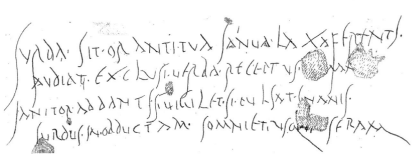

Figure 15 *CIL* iv.1893–4.

[27] On Latin papyri from Herculaneum cf. Del Mastro (2005). Inscriptions with both Greek and Latin highlight, and often accentuate, the difference in reading the two languages: cf. e.g. Degrassi (1965), nos. 292 (Delos, ii BC), 296 (Delos, 113 BC), 393 (Rome, 78 BC). Space between poems is seen already in Tiburtinus' series, *CIL* iv.4966–73 (Fig. 18). On changes of space in post-classical books, cf. Chartier (1994), 11.

[28] On scripts see Kleve (1994); the chronology of the few authors represented in the different scripts supports or is compatible with the proposed development. The capital hand used for the quotation from Virgil on *Tab. Vind.* 118 is interesting.

between lines, probably to mark a section or speech. They appear frequently. We might have the end of a book, with a mark (Pezzo VI fr. 2; perhaps not a coronis). The end of lines is often marked with diagonals. A papyrus probably of Lucretius is written in particularly large letters. The virgula in fr. N, like the diple in the Ennius Pezzi 7 fr. 1 and II fr. 2, would more naturally be thought a mark of punctuation than of line-ending; both instances in fr. N correspond to full stops in modern texts. Interpuncts appear normal.[29]

The papyrus of Gallus (P. Qaṣr Ibrîm inv. 78-3-11/1; Fig. 16) is probably from *c*.20 BC. It looks a luxurious volume. There is a wide upper margin: 3.4 cm. There is an elaborate sign after quatrains (in knowable cases), below the line; there is then a gap. The sign is perhaps more likely to separate (connected) poems than stanzas; even so, the generosity of space would be surprising in a Greek papyrus. There is interpunction, except often at the end of lines; there are no marks of length. Pentameters are indented; this is contrary to usual Greek practice, but is sometimes found with elegiacs at Pompeii. Again a visual difference from Greek poetry.[30]

P. Herc. 817 (Fig. 17), of an unknown epic poem on the war with Cleopatra, must precede AD 79. It is the most rewarding papyrus of Latin poetry. Of particular interest are the punctuation and the marks of sections. A short diagonal is used within or between sentences, not regularly but often: line 7 Courtney]ẹṣ ′ ṇec défuịt *impetus ill*[*is*], 25 . . . *im*[*per*]*ii′ quae femina taṇṭạ uirór*[*u*]*m* | *quaé series anṭiq*[*u*]*a* [*f*]*uit ′ ni gloriạ menḍax* . . . (the latter sign confirmed by the drawing in Scott (1885), pl. C), 35 *quid uẹlit inçertum est ′ terr*[*i*]ṣ *quibus* . . . (avoiding misplacing of *terris*), 43 *omne uagabatur leti genus ′ omnẹ timoris* (avoiding misplacing of *omne*?), 55 *haec régina gerit ′ procul han*[*c*, 67 *cónsiliis nox apta ducum ′ lux aptior armis*

[29] For P. Herc. 78 see Kleve (1996), (2001); for 21 and 'Lucretius', Kleve (1990), (1989), (2007) ((1989), 12, and (1990), 5, 6, 8, 13 take virgula and diple as marking the end of lines). On the coronis (Mart. 10.1.1–2), cf. Stephen (1959); Cavallo (1983), 24. P. Hamb. 167 (i AD; Seider (1972–8), ii.1. pl. VIII), is unlikely to be comedy; cf. Bader (1973).

[30] On the papyrus see R. D. Anderson, Nisbet, Parsons (1979); Capasso (2003). Indentation of the pentameter is seen already in *CIL* i².1732. Elegiac couplets written on walls in Pompeii vary both on indentation and on the use of interpuncts. Cf. R. D. Anderson, Nisbet, Parsons (1979), 130. *CIL* iv.1893–4 are indented, but not 1895 on the same wall. *CIL* iv.4971–3 were not indented, though Republican.

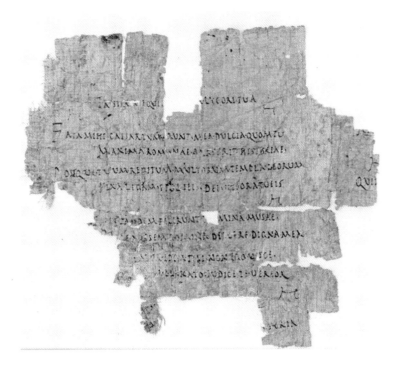

Figure 16 P. Qaṣr Ibrîm inv. 78–3–11/1, with detail of col. i.9.

(others look likely in the lesser fragments). A new paragraph is marked by a forked paragraphos between 51 and 52 and between 64 and 65 (the final paragraph of the book has only three lines). The end of the book is marked, with a sign to the right of the last line; the meaning of the X below and to the left of the last line is disputable.[31]

[31] Certainly not the *beginning* of Book 10 (Courtney (2003), 340). I am much indebted to Professor R. T. MacFarlane for excellent multispectral images of the original and of the Neapolitan *disegni*. Note that Wingo (1972), 56, remarks the

Figure 17 P. Herc. 817, *cornice* 6.

We may now survey briefly series of books and touch on collections, and then proceed to aspects of publication, consumption, and reading. Ennius' *Annales* were firmly divided into books, to judge from what appear to be proems in books 6, 7, 10, and 16 (164 Skutsch with Quint. *Inst.* 6.3.86; 206–12; 322–3; 401–6 with Plin. *NH* 7.101; note also the apparent summary at the beginning of Book 3, 137 Skutsch). The self-praising attack on predecessors in 7 and the change of plan and connection with the author's life in 16 show links to Hellenistic prose and poetry, and conjoin the series of books with the idea of the author.[32]

absence of punctuation after *imperii* in 25, which is actually present. For frequent punctuation of prose by diagonals, and mark of a new part section (with *K*), see P. Iand. 90 (i AD, Cic. *Ver.*; photograph in ed. pr. and in Seider (1972–8), ii.1. pl. I), and also P. Heid. Lat. 1 a, b (i AD, technical text, Seider (1972–8), ii.1. pl. VI).

[32] Cf. ch. 11 below. Cf. also Call. frr. 1 Pfeiffer, Massimilla and 203 Pfeiffer, Hdas. 8.66–79.

Lucilius evidently produced books himself, but may well not have numbered them. He will presumably have perceived the impact of an accumulated series. In book '1', the change to a new metre may interplay with the grandiose hexameter beginning on cosmic beginnings (1.1 Charpin). One book (16?) had for its title the name of a girl-friend *Collyra* (Porph. Hor. *C.* 1.22.10): a device exploited by later poets, and perhaps following poem-titles like that of Antimachus' *Lyde* (T 10–17 Matthews; at least two books).

Early in the first century came Laevius, who wrote at least six books of *Erotopaegnia*; presumably the title was Laevian. The unusual prefix Ἐρωτο- indicates a theme, apparent in the last *ode* of the last book (fr. 22 Courtney). But metrical and formal range seems to have been cultivated, even within single books (frr. 2–3, 22; cf. his *Polymetra*). The title suggests 'light' pieces and Hellenistic precedent (cf. esp. Philet. fr. 25 Spanoudakis); it may have included named treatments of myths (cf. also fr. 4).[33]

Further on in the century, Parthenius wrote a three-book work in praise of his dead wife; the extension of the series showed his love. The work is called the *Arete* (fr. 1 Lightfoot); perhaps to be compared is Valerius Cato's single book *Lydia*, doubtless named after a woman rather than a country (Tic. *FRP* 103 (Suet. *GR* 11.2); Ov. *Tr.* 2.436). Catullus disperses his poems about Lesbia across two volumes; these volumes compare with each other, while neither has priority. (The opening poem of *a*, the polymetrics, sets one book against Nepos' three.) Meanwhile, many-booked epics are in production; Furius Bibaculus' *Annales* on (Caesar's?) Gallic War had at least eleven (*FRP* 78–9). Lucretius' six will be influenced by Empedocles and developments in Hellenistic didactic, as well as by Hellenistic prose (see ch. 10). Cicero's *De Consulatu Suo* and *De Temporibus Suis* each encompassed three books. The third of the *De Consulatu*, which perhaps had a specific character in content and tone, ascended to give the Muse's climactic instruction to the author and hero Cicero (*Att.* 2.3.4, fr. 11 Courtney). Caesar comments on the first book of

---

[33] Ael. *NA* 15.19 applies the term to Theocritus, contemptuously. Even if Mnaseas author of Παίγνια was probably a writer of prose (Bain (1997)), the explanation that he was called after a diversely coloured fish διὰ τὸ ποικίλον τῆς ϲυναγωγῆϲ (Athen. 321f) remains interesting for the title and presuppositions about books.

De Temporibus to Cicero before reading (or being able to read) the rest, *QF* 2.16.5.[34]

In the triumviral period and beyond it, Gallus' love-poetry on Lycoris covered a range of time and a number of books (*FRP* 139 (*a*); *FRP* 145.6–7 may be pertinent). A few years after *Satires* 1, Horace proceeds to a sequel; the same will happen with the *Epistles* (whatever the dating of *Epistles* 2). The *Odes* also extend themselves unexpectedly, certainly in Book 4, and perhaps in Books 2 and 3. Propertius and Tibullus centre themselves on the developing series, focused in Propertius' case on one woman (2.1.1–2 *Quaeritis unde mihi totiens scribantur amores*...; 2.3.3–4; 2.24.1–2 *cum sis iam noto fabula libro,* | *et tua sit toto Cynthia lecta foro*). The question of final closure to his series is to intrigue the reader, whose interest is partly in the author and the gossipy biography (cf. Ov. *Tr.* 2.427–40). Tibullus' shift from Delia (and Marathus) to Nemesis is no less calculated to pique the reader's curiosity (cf. Ov. *Am.* 3.9.53–8). Quite different is the *Georgics*, a structure fixed at one point in time, and envisaged by reader and author from the start. Ovid presents series separated in time, like the original *Amores*, the *Tristia*, and the *Remedia* in relation to the *Ars Amatoria*; the three books of the *AA* are at least presented as an entity unseparated in time like the *Georgics*. The *Metamorphoses* and, in their notional projected form, the *Fasti* present a grand simultaneous entity like the *Aeneid*; the *Fasti* here contrast with the *Aetia*, whose final version absorbs an earlier version of the first two books. The interest in series and exploiting them is apparent.[35]

The comments of Cicero on books, his own and others', provide detailed background for series of books and for books within series as distinct entities. His own works are significantly and effectively divided, as we shall see. It is notable that he can wish to impose

[34] For Cicero's poems, see Harrison (1990*a*); Kurczyk (2006), ch. 3. The title of each can be viewed as *de* or as a nominative, cf. *QF* 3.1.24 *secundum librum meorum temporum* (which he is revising); cf. *Att.* 16.11.4, Courtney (2003), 156. We cannot tell from Charis. *GLK* i. 101 *Caluus in carminibus* (in contrast to the prose works, also cited by Charisius) that the poem on Quintilia's death did not have its own title or fill a whole book (cf. Cat. 96). The first of the two quotations (*FRP* 27) need not come from this poem.

[35] On closure to Propertius' love-elegy in and after Book 3, cf. Hutchinson (2006*b*), 7–10.

coexistence retrospectively. He wishes his consular speeches to be seen and denoted as a body (cῶμα), like Demosthenes' *Philippics*, *Att.* 2.1.3; it is unclear how wide a circulation of the set is in view, but the conception is significant.[36]

Within planned series, the individual books are often approached as distinct entities. Balbus took one book of the *De Finibus*, the last, to transcribe (*Att.* 13.21*a*.1). The speaker at *Tusc.* 5.32 tells Cicero *legi tuum nuper quartum de finibus* (he is aware of the pairing with the third book). At *Att.* 15.2.4 the *prima disputatio Tusculana* seems a separate entity, but others are of course presupposed. The books of the *Academica* are four *admonitores non nimis uerecundos*, not one (*Fam.* 9.8.1); the books of the *De Officiis* are like three *hospites*, not one (*Off.* 3.121; cf. Ov. *Tr.* 1.1.115–18, 3.1.65–6, 14.17–20 (*Ars*, *Metamorphoses*)). Cicero very commonly refers to works as his 'six books on the *res publica*', his 'three books on the orator', etc. (*Att.* 13.19.4, *Tusc.* 4.1; *Fam.* 1.9.23; *Tusc.* 5.120; *Div.* 1.7, cf. 9). The number sometimes underlines structure or quantity: cf. e.g. *ND* 1.11, *Div.* 1.7, with 9, and the preface to Book 2.[37]

The relation of items within poetic collections will be seen many times in this book. Virgil's *Eclogues* and Horace's *Satires* 1 and *Epodes* provide relatively early examples of collections palpably designed to be read as a sequence. Early too is the Gallus papyrus, which has already been mentioned. Even earlier is the sequence of apparently connected poems written on the wall of the Sullan theatre at Pompeii, perhaps all by Tiburtinus, *CIL* iv.4966–73 (Fig. 18; cf. 4966–7; 4967 and 4970). Later *CIL* iv.1893–4 (Fig. 15), found in the Basilica, puts together a couplet of Ovid and its probable model in Propertius (Ov. *Am.* 1.8.77–8, Prop. 4.5.47–8); even on a relatively informal level, the interest in collocation and intertextuality is clear. Varro's *Hebdomades* (first book of at least ten, 39 BC) gave 700 portraits of

---

[36] See Cape (2002); cf. *Brut.* 2.3.4, 4.2 (on the title *Philippicae*, not as an arrangement, but as a conception). Cicero's numbering of the items is notable.

[37] *Att.* 4.16.3 comments on the planning and distinctness of books in the *De Oratore*. The books of philosophical and rhetorical series have separate proems unless they have dialogue continuous in time; even so cf. *Rep.* (*Att.* 4.16.2) and *Div.* 2. Relevant to the structure of distinct conversations in distinct books of a series is M. Iunius Brutus frr. 1–3 Huschke (Cic. *Clu.* 141, *De Orat.* 2.223–4). The sending of specific books or pairs of books suggests distinctness in content, cf. p. 3 above and *CPF* 5 (P. Getty Mus. acc. 76.AI.27.5–7, i AD).

Talking Books

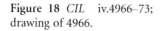

Figure 18 *CIL* iv.4966–73; drawing of 4966.

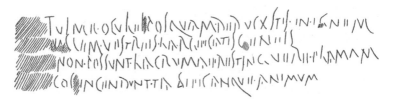

the famous with short poems, seemingly not all his own, and some scholarly prose (frr. 106–24 Salvadore, Symm. *Epist.* 1.2.8; two-line non-dactylic poems: frr. 109, 111 Salvadore). Atticus produced a single volume with portraits of politically distinguished Romans, and a poem of four or five lines (so not all elegiac couplets), Nep. *Att.* 18.5–6. The relation to P. Petrie 49b is apparent; to be noted in the Roman works are the large scale, the opulence of production, and the expansion beyond the literary.[38]

---

[38] On Tiburtinus see Solin (1968), 118–21; Courtney (2003), 79–81. On Varro and Atticus see Geiger (1985), 81–2; Courtney (2003), 184–5.

The evidence for anthologies and personal combinations is far less abundant than for Ptolemaic Egypt; but the popularity of Meleager's anthology, with its pointed combinations, is clear. A significant passage is *Ad Her.* 4.7, where the conception of an individual excerpting *sententiae* from Ennius or messenger speeches from Pacuvius is evidently a familiar one. As in the comic Catullus 14, we see a creative handling of books which suggests an interest in cohesion within the new collection. A further illustration of relatively private activity is the collection of witticisms in several books which Caesar (b. 100 BC) compiled when young, but evidently did not circulate publicly (Cic. *Fam.* 9.16.4, Suet. *Jul.* 56.7; cf. Cic. *Fam.* 15.21). Beside these moves from public to relatively private (excerpting texts) and relatively private to relatively private (collecting *mots*), we may set Cicero's idea of moving from relatively private to public with a collection of his own letters (*Fam.* 16.17.1, *Att.* 16.5.5). The posthumous *Ad Familiares* (published by Tiro?) exhibits a strong division of material by book. Design and connection are seen in Roman literary culture, as in Greek, at various levels of formality; the Greek scene helps to illuminate the Roman.[39]

We may now turn to how books made their appearance in the world. Scholars have stressed the importance of a genial circulation among friends; but it is essential to see a decisive stage which, for the author, discloses the work for the possibilities of criticism and of fame and, for the public, offers the excitement and interest of a new work (note at Cic. *Div.* 2.5 the incitement for the author of readers' enthusiasm). Even friends who are shown the work in advance of circulation can professedly be feared as critics: even that departure from privacy holds risks and rewards. But one point in showing them the work is to enable 'correction' which will arm them against the critics more strongly feared. Recitation seems to have been a growing practice for various genres (see below); but the evidence favours viewing both it and general distribution as risky moments of publication, the latter more serious and permanent.[40]

---

[39] For other evidence on Roman anthologies see Vardi (2000). On the publication of Cicero's letters see Hutchinson (1998), 4–5; on the books, Beard (2002), cf. Leach (2006), 250–1.

[40] Cf. for correction and criticism e.g. Gall. *FRP* 145.8–9 (Fig. 16), which on re-examination of the papyrus (Capasso (2003)) clearly reads *non ego, Visce,* |]*m̨*

Cicero's letters show working in detail the process which poets often describe. The friend is an 'Aristarchus' both at Cic. *Att.* 1.14.3 (criticism before delivery of speeches) and at Hor. *Ars* 450–2 (criticism before recitation). At *Att.* 15.1*a*.2, for example, Cicero reports that Brutus wanted him to correct unsparingly (*ne ambitiose corrigerem*) a speech Brutus had delivered *ante quam ederet*; difference on oratorical fundamentals prevented this. Cicero will look at and correct the letters for his proposed collection; *tum denique edentur* (*Att.* 16.5.5).[41]

The antagonism and drama of literature making its public appearance forms a topic inherited from the Hellenistic period and earlier; but the intensity of accounts in letters, poems, and treatises must correspond to some reality. Hor. *Epist.* 1.19 and 1.20 both vividly present the passage of the works into the hands of strangers, and the spread of fame. (Recitation appears in the pair of poems as a showier but more limited means of gaining celebrity.) Cicero must be actually concerned at the possibility of criticism about verisimilitude when his dialogues appear: cf. *De Orat.* 2.1–11, *Att.* 4.16.3; *Ac. Pri.* 7 (claims actual criticism), *Att.* 13.12.3, 16.1, 19.5. In the case of the *Academica*, the question becomes interwoven with worries about the reaction of one person, Varro; but those worries themselves are connected with the visibility of public appearance, in a laudatory dedication (by Varro) and in a speaking part (for Varro). Cicero has

---

plakato iudice te uereor (*quemqua*]*ṃ* Capasso; *plakato* had been suggested by Hutchinson *ap.* R. D. Anderson, Nisbet, Parsons (1979), 146, cf. Hutchinson (1981)); Ov. *Pont.* 3.9.1–32. In Cat. 22 the criticism of acquaintances appears alarmingly after publication and in a publication. On revision and friends cf. Gurd (2007). On 'publication', cf., among other works, Sommer (1926); Starr (1987); Habinek (1997), ch. 5; Murphy (1998); Goldberg (2005), e.g. 40 (the emphasis on friends here particularly strong). For 'publication' used of written circulation even in the age of printing cf. Love (1993), esp. ch. 2; cf. R. Thomas (2003), 182, where the word is used of sophistic epideixis.

[41] 'Corrections' of form and content before wider circulation are planned at 13.21*a*.1, 22.3 (cf. the exaggerated *incohatum*), 16.3.1. Cf. e.g. Ov. *Tr.* 3.14.21–4. Cicero wishes urgently to have corrected in *omnibus libris* after wider circulation a single factual error noted in *Lig.* 33 by its beneficiary and transmitted by a friend (13.44.3). These are copies circulated to individuals by Atticus (cf. 13.12.2 (preliminary promotion); 12.6*a*.1; contrast 13.21*a*.1 2nd para.). However, the error got through to the MSS. Like the *Academica Priora*, it shows the rapid diffusion of the text beyond the author's control; cf. *Att.* 13.20.2 (*ad Ligarianam … neque possum iam addere (est enim peruulgata) …*). It also suggests a line of circulation independent of Atticus.

an alternative to Varro if need be (*Att.* 13.25.3): so important to him is readers' criticism on credibility.[42]

Other forms of personal offence were feared, precisely because the work would be in the public domain, and so the offence would be the greater; for this reason Cicero does not allow the *De Temporibus Suis* to escape (*effugere*) into general circulation (*edi*), but will show it to friends (*Att.* 4.8a.3, *Fam.* 1.9.23 (itself an advertisement); cf. *Att.* 13.20.2). Hor. *C.* 2.1.1–8 depicts graver and more political peril for Pollio. Offending those in power presents greater risks in even minimal circulation; but 'correction' would even here be one solution (*Fam.* 6.7.1, 6 (from A. Caecina), cf. 6.5.1, 6.6.8–9): all these problems of circulation are seen as connected.[43]

The authors are writing in part for those who do not know them personally. So at *Tusc.* 1.6 Cicero haughtily dismisses those who *suos libros ipsi legunt cum suis* (the wording implies a few philosophical cronies), *nec quisquam attingit* save other would-be authors. (Cf. *Cat.* 95.5–8 for the underlying contrast.) On a more modest note, the name of its addressee especially will make the *Orator* be spread abroad (*diuulgari, Orat.* 112); everyone else (*ceteri*) will come to know Cicero (*cognoscant*) in his lifetime from Lucceius' work (*Fam.* 5.12.9; cf. Hor. *C.* 2.20.17–19 *me…ultimi* | **noscent** *Geloni*). Atticus' copyists are to help Hirtius' flattering riposte to Cicero's book *diuulgari* (*Att.* 12.40.1, cf. 44.1, 45.2, 48.1; Hor. *Epist.* 1.19.33 (sc. *Alcaeum*) *Latinus* | *uulgaui fidicen*, with a play on books and notional performance). With a neat twist, Cicero's books themselves form a *turba* which have obscured what was once the most famous Roman speech; the *turba* matches the *plerique* who by implication now read only his speeches (*Brut.* 122–3; cf. Ov. *Tr.* 3.14.18).[44]

---

[42] Lucilius contemplates possible readers with some show of anxiety; a wider circle, and an actual lack of control, are implied (cf. 26.16–17 Charpin; note that fr. 2 Krenkel is probably not Lucilius). It is notable that he benefits from the dedication of a book by the Greek (Carthaginian) philosopher Clitomachus (Cic. *Ac. Pr.* 102; fr. 4 = Carn. fr. 5.102 Mette).

[43] Cf. *Att.* 15.13.1–12, 13a. 3, where general circulation of *Philippic* 2 is in question (*proferendae, edendam, foras prodiature*). Fear of Atticus' own evaluation is set against the fear of the consequences were the speech circulated.

[44] In *Tusc.* 1.6, *legunt cum* and *allicere* indicate a very different point from that made at 4.6, where the publication of Amafinius' books (*editis*) won a *multitudo* for Epicureanism (*Tusc.* 4.6). The point at *Tusc.* 2.7–8 is also differently conceived, even if

The awkwardness of claiming and desiring general fame is often mitigated by referring to 'youth', a humble audience, and one whom it is public-spirited to help. So Cicero writes published versions of speeches *adulescentulorum studiis excitati*, though they delight even Atticus (*Att.* 2.1.3); his philosophical works aid the *res publica* by instructing youth, though his adult fans are more numerous than he thought (*Div.* 2.4–5). Poetry can likewise stress its utility to the young, and so the state (e. g. Hor. *Epist.* 2.1.124–9). The theme can be made more forceful in attack: no one will read Piso's pamphlet speech replying to Cicero's, unless he in turn replies (cf. Ov. *Rem.* 366), whereas *meam in illum pueri omnes tamquam dictata perdiscant* (*QF* 3.1.11). The generality and importance of renown matters acutely.[45]

The sale of books seems a much more flourishing trade than is sometimes implied, and not restricted to bookshops. If neither Cicero nor Pliny refers to his using booksellers, one cannot exploit only Cicero's silence to infer that the book trade has mushroomed in the first century AD. There is simply much less evidence apart from Cicero in the late Republic. Cicero early in the correspondence is attempting to buy a particular Greek library through Atticus: cf. *Att.* 1.4.3, 1.7, 10.4, 11.3. (Latin books concern him much less, but cf. *Att.* 1.20.7, 2.1.12.) We see him gaining many books through gifts and legacies, and using friends' collections; on the last point, Cato is made to express surprise *cum ipse tantum librorum habeas* (*Fin.* 3.10). Cicero has libraries in various locations. He will scarcely need a *taberna libraria* like that casually mentioned in *Phil.* 2.21. So Catullus in 14 pretends that Calvus, as orator, has received the frightful anthology from a client; he himself will have to use the bookshops (even if this is only a joke, others would use them). In 54 Quintus, who already has lots of Greek books (cf. Cic. *Att.* 2.3.4), wants to buy more and build up a Latin collection (*QF* 3.4.5, 5.6).

the underlying target is the same. With the *delectatio* needed to *allicere* the (unknown) reader, cf. Virg. *Ecl.* 6.9–10 *si quis tamen haec quoque, | si quis captus amore leget* (where the modesty has a youthful colouring; cf. Cat. 14*b*.1–3, contrast Ov. *Tr.* 3.14.27). Caelius can tell Cicero *tui politici libri omnibus uigent, Fam.* 8.1.4; cf. Cavarzere ad loc.

[45] Cf. n. 24 above on Hor. *Epist.* 1.20.17–18. On Hor. *Epist.* 2.1.124–9 see Brink (1982), 156, 165–71. For the *utilitas* to the young on a more personal level, cf. *Fam.* 1.9.23, 6.18.4.

Buying direct from a seller is clearly an obvious resource in Latin, though the present quality of transcription does not satisfy Cicero (*ita mendose et scribuntur et ueneunt*, 3.5.6, cf. 3.4.5).[46]

In Horace, later in the first century BC, the significance of book-sellers as an index of fame is clear; it is linked with geographical and temporal range. Cf. *Ars* 345–6 (*hic meret aera liber Sosiis*, etc.), 373. Greek philosophical books again seem to be bought through agents (*C.* 1.29.33–4). Horace's alleged unwillingness, in his first book, to be sold in bookshops (*Sat.* 1.4.71–2) takes modesty and snobbery to an ostentatious extreme; but the trade is obviously thriving.[47]

We may turn now to the various practices and environments of reading. In Cicero and elsewhere different kinds of reading are encountered; these show us possibilities and conceptions rather than norms. Outside ordinary adult life, boys are spoken of as learning literature by heart; the educational task becomes a non-literal expression of youthful enthusiasm in reading. Cicero's contrast of Piso and himself above (*meam . . . tamquam dictata perdiscant*) is sadly turned round at Sen. Rh. *Contr.* 3 *pr.*15 in a contrast of Cicero and Cestius (the anti-establishment youths *ediscunt* Cestius' declamations, and do not read Cicero's speeches save those which Cestius wrote counter-speeches to). The youths can be separated from the adult authors they could one day become (so the young Lepta against Cicero, *Fam.* 6.18.4–5). Future old age can be imagined as a time of unbroken reading, unlike the present (cf. e.g. *Att.* 1.10.4); in actuality, that reading can be tainted by circumstance (*Fam.* 5.15.3).[48]

---

[46] The importance he attaches to accurate texts is notable. Legacies and the like: *Att.* 1.20.7, 2.1.12; use of collections: 4.14.1. Pliny, while not speaking of buying books, wishes to tell the public of his own success with the *bibliopolae*, 1.2.6 (start of collection), 9.11.2 (last book).

[47] *Sat.* 2.1, like the opening references to critics in some of Cicero's treatises, carefully indicates that Horace's work is now widely known and discussed.

[48] Hor. *C.* 2.20.19–20 pointedly imagines foreign and grown-up readers learning him (by heart): *me peritus | discet Hiber Rhodanique potor.* On Roman reading see Cavallo (1999); the whole volume (Cavallo and Chartier (1999)) presents an important diachronic treatment of reading. Darnton (1984), ch. 6, for example, presents a paradigmatic study of one French reader in the later 18th cent. Some valuable material and ideas for various periods: Flint (1993); Baggermann (1994); Johns (1995); J. Coleman (1996); Kintgen (1996); Bickenbach (1999); Blaak (2004); St Clair (2004); Fergus (2006); Waller (2006).

The reading we see Cicero and others currently engaged in suggests a particular interest in new books, especially as regards Latin. So he and Quintus read and discuss some Lucretius (*QF* 2.10.3), he and Atticus some Varro (*Att.* 16.11.3). Friendship is sometimes plainly involved (Sallustius, *QF* 2.10.3; Caesar reading Cicero not generally circulated, 2.16.5; Brutus reading Cicero, *Brut.* 2.4.3); but the appeal of newness is clear.⁴⁹

The form of reading to which Cicero is most deeply attached is the study of philosophy (cf. e.g. *Fam.* 4.4.4: philosophy his special delight *a prima aetate*); and philosophical works are his usual requests. He often opposes his two modes of life in uneasy tension: sustained reading in villas and the activity and disappointment of politics (cf. e.g. *Att.* 1.11.3, 2.16.3 (the tension becomes itself a philosophical controversy), 4.10.1). Sustained reading is best practised in country villas, for reasons of time (society) more than space (libraries).⁵⁰

The public libraries supplied for Rome by Pollio, Octavian, and Octavia created a particularly scholarly milieu for reading (cf. e.g. Plin. *NH* 7.115, Dio 53.1.3, Plut. *Marc.* 30.11; Suet. *Jul.* 44.2). But individuals had already built up, through expenditure or plunder, magnificent libraries of their own; these displayed culture, taste, and specific interests (like philosophy). Sculpture and other decoration (Cic. *Att.* 4.5.4; Pompeii VI 17 (*Ins. Occ.*) 41) proclaimed enthusiasms and also created an environment for reading; Cicero fondly imagines reading in Atticus' library beneath the bust of his admired Aristotle (*Att.* 4.10.1; cf. e.g. *Fam.* 7.23.2; Plin. *NH* 7.115, Isid. *Etym.* 6.5.2; *Tab. Heb.* 1–4, Tac. *Ann.* 2.37.2). Book-rooms, though books could always be read there, were of different sizes and bore different relations to connected spaces, where one could also read, and discuss one's reading. So at the Villa dei Papiri at Herculaneum the small rooms where papyri were stored contained tables; one adjoined an elaborate portico. The Roman section of the public library on the

⁴⁹ Cf. Ov. *Pont.* 3.5.11–14, more generally Sen. Rh. *Contr.* 4 *pr.*1; Hor. *Epist.* 1.20.10 *carus eris Romae donec te deserat aetas*, Cic. *Brut.* 123; even at Hor. *Epist.* 2.1.53–4 note *paene recens*. The poet Alexander of Ephesus (*SH* 19–39) may be a Greek contemporary; but Cicero is reading him with a purpose (*Att.* 2.20.6, 22.7). On *QF* 2.10.3 cf. Hutchinson (2001*b*), 153–4.
⁵⁰ Cf. Hor. *Sat.* 2.6.60–2, *Epist.* 1.2.1–2 (books and country); 2.2.65–86 (distractions in city); Cic. *Fam.* 9.1.2, Cat. 68*a*. 33–6 (books in Rome).

Palatine was large enough for official meetings (P. Oxy. 2435.29–40; cf. Suet. *Aug.* 29.3).[51]

Greek and Latin books were often, perhaps usually, kept distinct in libraries. The Palatine library and the Porticus Octaviae stored Greek books separately from Latin (cf. P. Oxy. 2435, *CIL* vi.2347, etc.); at *Att.* 1.20.7 the presumption seems to be that the late Ser. Claudius' collection had distinct Greek and Latin parts, both desirable. Such separation in place heightens for the consciousness of readers the difference that we saw in Greek and Latin papyri themselves. The exclusively philosophical character of the Greek books so far discovered in the Villa dei Papiri makes clear a further division (there must have been Greek poetry too), and a deep special interest. This instance also indicates at the least that in some areas some collections will not have represented the languages equally. Cicero fantasizes that Greek libraries could eventually be dispensed with in philosophy (*Tusc.* 2.6–8), if Latin authors follow his lead and produce well-written philosophy (cf. *Div.* 2.4); he presupposes a present preponderance of Greek in many Roman philosophical collections. The symmetry of structure in the Palatine library suggested by the *Forma Vrbis Romae* fr. 20b (cf. P. Oxy. 2435.29–40) may have presented wishful thinking, ambition, and a challenge to authors (cf. Hor. *Epist.* 2.2.92–4).[52]

[51] For sitting and working in *bibliothecae* cf. e.g. Cic. *Top.* 1, *Fin.* 3.7, *Div.* 2.8. On public libraries see Strocka (1993), Gros (1993), 55; Coarelli (1993), 134; Viscogliosi (1999), 141; Haselberger, Romano, Dumser (2002), 68, 206; and esp. Nicholls (2005). (An ancient passage like Pasternak, *Doktor Zhivago, Čast'* 9.10–12 would be welcome.) On the Porticus Octaviae see also Gorrie (2007), 4–5. For Greek public libraries cf. Platthy (1968); note the public library at Tortona in Liguria built or rebuilt in 22 BC (*CIL* v.7376). For important private libraries cf. e.g. Varr. *Hebd.* fr. 106.17 Salvadore, Plut. *Sull.* 26.1, *Luc.* 42.1–2 (social aspects); Strocka (1981), 298–302, 307; Rawson (1985), 39–42. For the library at the Villa dei Papiri see Sider (2005) (diagram p. 62). For the library in the house Pompeii VI 17 (*Ins. Occ.*) 41 and its decoration (second style), see Pugliese Carratelli and Baldassarre (1990–2003), vi. 37; Strocka (1993), 341–51; De Simone (2006), 60–5; jacket illustration of this book. It is doubtful whether the House of the Menander contained a library, with a portrait of Menander: see Ling (1997), 61, 137.

[52] See Horsfall (1993). But it is notable that even more officials are attested for the Latin libraries of the Palatine and Porticus Octaviae than for the Greek (Latin: *CIL* vi.2347, 4431, 4435, 5189 (× 2), 5191; Greek 2348, 4433, 5188). Nicholls (2005), 137–42, urges general caution on such a division, though with little positive evidence for other systems. A forceful contrast may be made between the division now possible and the Greek library at Tauromenion in Sicily (ii BC?), where Fabius Pictor's Greek writing on

Reading could be done almost anywhere. Cato unusually read books, Greek books, in the senate-house before meetings (Cic. *Fin.* 3.7, Val. Max. 8.7.2). Poets imagine women reading in the bedroom (Hor. *Epod.* 8.15–16, Prop. 3.18–19). In the Ciceronian world alone there are many modes and circumstances of reading. One can read with scrolls piled all round one, when ardently involved (Cic. *Att.* 2.2.2; *Fin.* 3.7 (Cato again)). One can explore someone's collection; one can have another person there, pursuing his own interests (*Top.* 1). One can read with an expert or friend, or enjoy joint study (*Att.* 4.11.2, 5.12.2; *Fam.* 16.21.4, 8 (the younger Marcus)). One can read for relaxation (*Arch.* 12–13, 16; *Att.* 1.20.7). One can read at night (*Fam.* 4.4.5, *Arch.* 16, Hor. *Ars* 268–9). One can reread a good work (*Brut.* 71; cf. e.g. Hor. *Sat.* 1.10.72–3, *Epist.* 1.2.1–2, *Pont.* 3.5.9–14); one can read repeatedly to gain technical expertise (*Fam.* 9.25.1, playful). One can look up arguments, or details, for one's own writing (*Att.* 8.11.7, 13.30.2, 32.2). A proper collection of books could be claimed vital to writing poetry, both for material and for inspiration: cf. Cat. 68a.33–40, Hor. *Sat.* 2.3.11–12, Ov. *Tr.* 3.14.35–8 (addressed to a public library official?) ... *non hic librorum, per quos inuiter alarque,* | *copia*, cf. 7.4, *Pont.* 3.3.45.[53]

In addition, works could be imbibed by ear. This mode of reception is significant; but the evidence does not justify making it the prime mode for the élite. They could be read to by an *anagnostes*, a slave—with Greek designation—kept for this purpose; Cicero has one, Atticus several (Cic. *Att.* 1.12.4, *Fam.* 5.9.2 (from Vatinius); Nep. *Att.* 13.1, cf. Cic. *Sest.* 110, Philod. *Rhet.* 4 col. xviii[a].4–5). One could be read to at dinner-parties (e.g. *Att.* 16.3.1, Nep. *Att.* 14.1). Authors, friends, perhaps girl-friends could read aloud to one (cf. e.g. Ov. *Tr.* 3.7.23, 4.10.43–6, *Pont.* 3.5.39–42; Prop. 2.33b.36–8, Ov. *AA* 3.333–46). Special cases are formed by reading to Augustus (e.g. Ov. *Tr.* 2.77–8, 557–60) and to children (369–70). Public recitation

Roman history, elaborately summarized in the wall inscription, was simply placed among the other Greek books. Cf. Battistoni (2006), 175–7. The philosophical papyri (i BC and earlier) in the Villa dei Papiri must go back to a Republican arrangement, whatever the relation of the villa to the Pisones.

[53] The last passage offers a useful addition to the perspective supplied by Cameron (2004), ch. 10. On Cato, see Hutchinson (1998), 88. The primary focus of Johnson (2000) is rather different; but the cognitive element is important.

seems to begin, and to increase, in this century for prose and for poetry (for prose cf. Sen. Rh. *Contr.* 4 *pr.*2, 7, 7 *pr.*1, 10 *pr.*4). Horace implies the popularity of public recitals of poetry, sometimes in a hall (*theatrum*), which he himself modestly refuses to give (so *Sat.* 1.4.21–5, 10.37–9, *Epist.* 1.19.33–45, 2.1.223; cf. Ov. *Tr.* 2.519–20, 5.7*b*.1–4 (25–8) (not performed by poet), *Pont.* 1.5.57–8). Greek influence lies behind most of these modes and fashions.[54]

The range of readers we know about in detail is very limited; early Latin papyri do not have the same social scope as the far more numerous Greek papyri. Female readers, though variously marginalized, appear sufficiently in the evidence to make them seem a significant proposition. Their interests include philosophy.[55]

Cicero's ardour for philosophical reading (*Att.* 4.10.1 *pascor; sustentor; recreor;* 11.2 *uoramus*) will have been matched by others in other types of writing. He mentions, incidentally, his own repeated reading of Xenophon's *Cyropaedeia* (*Fam.* 9.25.1 *contrieram legendo;* cf. *Sen.* 30, 79–81). He depicts, and shares, a widespread enthusiasm for historiography (*Fin.* 5.51–2, cf. *Fam.* 5.12.4–5). Nepos envisages a strong response among historically-minded readers to Atticus' austere accounts of Roman families (Nep. *Att.* 18.4 *quibus libris nihil potest esse dulcius iis qui aliquam cupiditatem habent notitiae clarorum uirorum;* Horace, *Odes* 3.17 and 19 are related).

Among readers of poetry Cicero mentions, for example, Ser. Claudius (d. 60 BC), with his constant reading (*consuetudine legendi*) and acute critical judgement (*Fam.* 9.16.4). The prominence of poetry in literary culture and in papyri, the emotional engagement poetry demanded (cf. e.g. Ov. *Pont.* 3.4.9–10), the multitude of poets (cf. e.g. Hor. *Epist.* 1.3.1–25, 19.19–20, 2.1.108–10, Ov. *Pont.* 4.16): all make it clear that the eager readers of philosophy seen in Cicero and his circle will have been more than equalled in this century by the

---

[54] For Greek poetry cf. A. Hardie (1983), ch. 2; Cameron (1995), 48–53. For Latin poetry, cf. Gaertner on Ov. *Pont.* 1.5.57. Words like *populus* and *uulgus*, as opposed to invited friends, need not take one far down the social scale. For the relation of oral performance and written circulation in a later period, one could see Hutchinson (1993), 146–8. The Elder Seneca's dubious claim on Pollio at *Contr.* 4 *pr.*2 (Dalzell (1955)) is hard to relate to the chronology of Pollio's activities; but the claim is of interest as a perception.

[55] Cic. *Att.* 13.21*a*.2, 22.3; Hor. *Epod.* 8.15–16, with Watson's note. Cf. also e.g. Prop. 3.3.19–20, Ov. *Am.* 2.1.5, 11.31, *Tr.* 2.253–64. See Hemelrijk (1999).

eager readers of poetry. The potential relation of philosophy to the reader's life finds various counterparts in poetry, not least in a type of poetry greatly built up in this period, love-elegy: the poets' self-presentation entangles reading this poetry with the reader's own amorous life (e.g. Prop. 1.7.13–14, 23–4, Ov. *Am.* 2.1.5–10). But the attractions of fiction and narrative were manifest too (cf. e.g. Cic. *Fin.* 5.52).[56]

We can discern something, especially through Cicero, of the reading lives of some Romans. Here the impact of Greek reading culture is plainly significant, both for the place of reading in existence and for the keen, close, and accurate approach to reading which formed at least one possibility for Romans. This applied to Latin literature too, for all the distinct traditions of Roman books and all the difference in reading Greek classics and contemporary Latin productions. It is apparent that in Latin reading too the book is a vital literary entity, even in works of several books, and that readers would give attention to the relation of items within a single book. The Hellenistic and Roman evidence together gives us essential and rewarding context for the consideration of books as a central form in ancient poetry.

This chapter, then, has prepared for the detailed discussions of particular works in the ensuing chapters. Various themes have emerged which can be considered in the specific works and drawn together in the final discussion; others will emerge. To pursue our original categories, we will consider books made up of smaller entities; these entities may be arranged into larger blocks. In general, such books often present dynamic structures, and thus relate to books which form part of a narrative or exposition. Those books are only one form of connected series; books may be separated in time of composition and without overt narrative connection, and yet form a significant sequence. They may even be notionally simultaneous but unrelated by plot. It will be explored how far books of narrative are

---

[56] Cicero's own reading in poetry, though obviously considerable, can only be judged to a limited extent from his quotations; positive and negative inferences are precarious. Some quotations in Greek especially are standard. The paucity of Hellenistic poetry will be partly a matter of convention; it might still make us pause before ascribing Call. *Hec.* fr. 165 Hollis to Callimachus (*Att.* 8.5.1). The consciousness of abundant poetic activity in the 1st cent. BC is interestingly deployed at the end of Pulci's *Morgante*, esp. 28.148–51.

distinct entities. Contrasts between books will be important—and contrasts within them. Framing devices will relate both to internal structure and to structure over more than one book; so will questions of the narrator's role, of lives, and of perspectives. The whole question of small and large is thematized and vital to the apprehension of internal and external structures and their relation. Although poetic books are our concern, the relevance of prose structures has already been seen, and will prove significant in the penultimate chapter particularly. The total effect of the following explorations will be to show the wide range with which the elements of book-structure are exploited, and their richness in meaning.

2

The *Aetia*: Callimachus' Poem of Knowledge*

Our own knowledge of the *Aetia* is based on many documents and various types of source. These themselves bear witness to the phenomenal popularity of the poem for a thousand years. We have summaries, commentaries, a translation into Latin poetry, close adaptations in Greek prose. The papyri of the poetic text, of very varied kinds, range from the third century BC to the sixth or seventh AD, and frequently overlap. For all the complexity, unevenness, and incompleteness of our information, it is worth attempting to say more than has been said so far on the whole conception and thematic network of this hugely influential and important poem.[1]

Two structural features of the poem are conspicuous: it is made up of what we shall call different sections (to call them poems would

* This piece was originally delivered to a seminar I conducted on the *Aetia* in the summer of 2003; the present version has benefited from a magnificent paper delivered to the seminar by Professor M. A. Harder, and from contributions by Mr E. L. Bowie, Dr J. Burbidge, Dr P. J. Finglass, Dr P. G. Fowler, Professor P. R. Hardie, Dr M. Hatzimichali, Dr W. B. Henry, Dr S. J. Heyworth, Ms R. Hughes, Dr Chr. Kaesser, Professor R. O. A. M. Lyne, Mr C. Parrott, Professor P. J. Parsons, Ms M. Reedy, and others. In writing the piece I have inspected the eighteen papyri of the poem in Oxford (whence some small divergences from Pfeiffer and Massimilla), and the papyrus of Posidippus in Milan; I am extremely grateful to Dr N. Gonis, and to Professors C. Gallazzi and L. Lehnus, for their kind assistance. Professor R. Kassel has made some characteristically learned observations.

[1] Aristaenetus, who in 1.10 and 15 closely reworks *Acontius* and *Phrygius and Pieria*, is dated to the 6th cent. AD by Vieillefond (1992), pp. ix–xi. On the *Diegeseis*, see van Rossum-Steenbeek (1998), 74–84. It is interesting that two commentaries on the prologue should have such different contents: P. Lit. Lond. 181 (i AD) and P. Oxy. 2262 (ii AD). We hear of commentaries by Theon and Epaphroditus (frr. 49, 61–2

be to beg questions); and the relation of these sections differs between the first two books and the last two. As is well known, Books 1–2 seem to have presented a sustained conversation between the poet-narrator and the Muses, in which at least most of the particular *aitia* are set; in Books 3–4 the *aitia* are not so joined. This difference immediately presents a challenge to anyone who views the whole poem as an entity, all the more so as there are apparent grounds for dating Books 3–4 later than Books 1–2, excluding the prologue on brevity.[2]

A couple of preliminary observations may be made: first, the papyri present a new section in the same way for both pairs of books, with a coronis and forked paragraphos; the *Diegeseis* likewise display for both pairs the first line of each section, in ekthesis. One possibility is that the unified presentation of the poetic text goes back to the author: the more elaborate presentation of poems under

---

Massimilla = 42, 52–3 Pfeiffer). For further types of aid to readers, one may notice for comparison PSI inv. 3191 (i–ii AD): probably a glossary to an elegiac, conceivably epinician, work by Callimachus (Bastianini (2002); Menci (2004)), cf. P. Oxy. 3328 (glossary to *Hymn* 3, ii AD). The poem is not much quoted in works of literature, but that is because it is too late to seem an apt ornament of literary prose. Imitations confirm its importance: Propertius Book 4, Ovid, *Fasti, Heroides* 20–1, and e.g. the Salmacis inscription (*SGO* 01/12/02, ii BC; Isager (1998); Isager and Pedersen (2004); Lloyd-Jones (2005*a*)). Some important works on the structure of the poem: Parsons (1977); Krevans (1984), ch. 4; Harder (1993). But these footnotes make no attempt to include even the most important books and articles on the *Aetia*.

² If Books 1–4 were first published (generally circulated) together, it would be strange that royal events should receive conspicuous treatment at the beginning of Book 3 and at the end of Book 4, but nowhere, so far as is known, in Books 1 or 2, certainly not at beginning or end (a possible inexplicit allusion to Arsinoe is something different, *Σ* Lond. on fr. 3.1 Massimilla = 1.41 Pfeiffer). The speaker of the prologue claims to be oppressed by old age like Enceladus by Sicily; if there are two publications of the poem, one might incline to put the prologue with the later, which appeared roughly thirty years after his first known court poetry. *Σ* Flor. (*Dieg.*) on frr. 2–4 Massimilla, 2 Pfeiffer, says that Callimachus claimed to have had the dream of Books 1 and 2 when he was ἀ]ρτιγένειος. This does not demand, though it would suit, a wide interval in time between the versions. Cameron (1995), a very important book, makes an elaborate effort to plane the wood against the grain, and date the prologue to the two-book version; on his reasons, in my view inadequate, see Harder (2002). The term 'poem' for sections of the *Aetia* creates problems of expression too: in ordinary usage, a 'poem' does not usually consist of 'poems'; but Eliot's *Four Quartets* shows how complicated the question can be. Critics do not normally think of the sections of Ovid's *Fasti* as separate poems; but the difference from *Aetia* 3–4 is by no means so great as this might suggest.

headings in the papyrus of Posidippus may be the author's and is
certainly third-century BC. Second, the criticisms which are answered
in fr. 1 Massimilla, Pfeiffer have much more point in relation to the
four-book version: this consists of two halves of different structure,
and in the second half the sections are formally unconnected. οὐχ ἓν
ἄεισμα διηνεκές and ἐπὶ τυτθόν (fr. 1.3, 5 Massimilla, Pfeiffer) would
thus relate to salient aspects of the poem. Such a defence would be
closely paralleled by *Iambus* 13, which also answers objections to
surprising features in a work as a whole.[3]

Callimachus' choice to continue the work but not the frame is made
the more notable when one considers what an effective idea that frame
had been. The device of separate stories joined in a framework lies
behind some of the most spectacular successes of mediaeval and
Renaissance literature. For *Aetia* Books 1–2 the form develops out of
προβλήματα: prose questions and answers in various fields of knowledge. We cannot say whether the form already embraced cult, as it
certainly does later; that seems at least a plausible possibility. The
dialogue form has further connections with prose: already in Xenophon it has extended into areas other than the philosophical. Whether
or not there is a genetic relationship with Plato's dialogues, the contrast with *Aetia* Books 1–2 is arresting. In Plato, the dialogue is mostly
driven by the wish of the superior partner to work out ideas; in
Callimachus it is driven by the inferior's desire for knowledge. Ardent
though that desire is, its objects are not philosophical but scholarly and
entertainingly abstruse. The very subject-matter of the *aitia* comes
largely from prose, from local historians; to treat it in a dialogue with
the Muses increases the complexity of the relationship in the work
between prose and poetry.[4]

---

[3] If we stressed instead that the prologue should reply to actual criticisms, the
four-book version still has the advantage, as the two-book version would already have
been published. The two aspects could be reconciled (actual criticisms sharpened for
presentation of four-book version). Coronides (sometimes missing in lost margin) +
paragraphos: fr. 50.17, 83 Massimilla = 43 (i.e. 43.17, 83) Pfeiffer; between frr. 66
and 67 Pfeiffer, 92 and 93 Pfeiffer, 95 and 96 Pfeiffer; cf. comm. on fr. 2
Massimilla = 1a Pfeiffer, line 30 (coronis probably at end of prologue proper).
Coronides are used in various ways in papyri, and do not themselves indicate that
the sections are conceived as 'poems'. For a new section in the *Diegeseis* of Books 1–2,
cf. esp. P. Oxy. 2263 col. ii.9–10 (with ekthesis of 2.5 letters).
[4] For cultic προβλήματα cf. Hutchinson (1988), 41 n. 31. On the frame and its
connection with early poetry cf. Harder (1988). The contrast with Platonic dialogue

There may have been specific reasons for the change in Books 3–4; but in any case, Callimachus turns it to literary advantage. He expands and intensifies the thematic and formal concerns of Books 1–2 to create a much more intricate poem. Something comparable happens in the later two books of Apollonius. Central to Callimachus' enlarged conception are knowledge and the relations between the narrator and his characters.[5]

The prologue, so often discussed, has various functions here. First, like many prologues, it is written to be read from two perspectives: before and after reading the rest of the poem. From before, it sets up surprises, like many other prologues. The work turns out to be a much bigger, more interconnected, and more ambitious entity than the prologue had led us to think. One need only contrast the work with the popular books of epigrams to perceive this point. Most poems in the Posidippus are 4–8 lines, and the longest are 14; the average length of the twenty-four to twenty-six sections (poems) from after fr. 75 Pfeiffer to the end of the *Aetia* was 52–6 lines, and some sections in the work were much longer (*Victoria Berenices* over 213, with PSI inv. 1923; *Acontius* very considerably over 107; *Argonauts* over 120). The involved position of the work in regard to length and brevity is already indicated by the prologue itself: it is not an embodiment of laconic compression, but exuberantly accumulates images and restatements of its thesis. The prologue prepares us to be struck by a large if far from straightforward design.[6]

is strikingly illuminated by Dante's *Paradiso*; here, though the form descends from Plato via Boethius, the dialogue is driven by the inferior's pressing desire for knowledge and the solution to puzzles, no doubt in the light of scholastic conceptions of man. For Callimachus' antecedents, cf. Krevans (1984), ch. 3.

[5] For new information on the contents of Book 3, see Gallazzi and Lehnus (2001); see now also Bulloch (2006). It is interesting to compare, from a later period, the expansion of design presented by Rilke's *Der neuen Gedichte anderer Teil* of 1908, after the 'Gedicht-Kreis' *Neue Gedichte* of 1907 (*Briefe*, 2 vols., Frankfurt and Leipzig, 1991), i. 249). The addition of the second volume creates a new and elaborately interrelated whole, although the full idea may be late and even provisional (cf. *Briefe an seinen Verleger*, 2 vols., Wiesbaden, 1949), i. 46–7). Phelan (1992) is much more responsive to the total entity than Bradley (1976), 14–15.

[6] Lucretius' prologue notably misleads from the perspective of before; so too Propertius 4.1 (both halves). Horace, *Epode* 1, perhaps even Luc. 1.33–66, are more complex examples. Euripides too is relevant. On books of epigrams, see Gutzwiller (1998); Argentieri (1998); Parsons (2002), esp. 115–28. After fr. 75 Pfeiffer, there were 186–152 (page-numbers in P. Oxy. 1011) × *c*.40 lines = *c*.1,360 lines. Note that this

Second, the prologue parades the figure of the writer. His activity of writing is mapped on to a life: childhood and old age are contrasted and connected. Themes are planted, and so is the possibility of seeing them on two levels: outside and inside the narratives of the poem. From after reading the poem, we see that the Telchines, with their muttered spells, are figures from Book 3 (fr. 75.64–9 Pfeiffer); βροντᾶ‸ν οὐκ ἐμὸν ‸ἀλλὰ‸ Διός (fr. 1.20 Massimilla, Pfeiffer) includes a warning of their mythological punishment. Sicily, from Book 2, becomes an image of old age. Apollo gives guidance, as so often in the poem. One crucial theme is planted in the first word of the second line, νήϊδε‸c: the idea of knowledge appears in the critics' ignorance, and the author's implicit understanding, of the art of poetry.[7]

Knowledge is fixed as a central theme of the poem by the framework of Books 1–2. We shall first look at knowledge as something which people wish to acquire, knowledge of specific things. We will proceed from this point of view through the best-preserved substantial sections of the poem; there alone certain thematic interactions can be properly observed. In particular, we should notice an opposition between searches and struggles by characters for knowledge of information,

---

sequence comes later than two particularly lengthy sections in Book 3. Aristaen. 1.10 shows that a lot is missing from the *Acontius*; it was preceded, probably for contrast, by two *aitia* which between them occupied the length of one page in P. Oxy. 2211 (cf. n. 24). In each of Books 1 and 2 there may have been nine speeches by the Muses (this does not allow for double *aitia* or *aitia* from the narrator). On brevity and the relation to epigram, cf. ch. 4, pp. 102–7. Fr. 1.4 Massimilla, Pfeiffer, suggests that epic should still be seen as a foil, even though the stress on elegy in the prologue by Cameron (1995) is important; cf. Kerkhecker (2000). To view the prologue as a defence, there are two levels, which between them assure satisfaction. The charge is reduced to propositions *p* 'this work is (and Callimachus' works are) short (and made up of little bits)' and *q* 'this is bad'. Callimachus replies overtly by accepting *p* and arguing against *q*. But the reader should actually see that *p* is unfair; if so, the acceptance of *p* will seem admirably understated. In any case, the reader will not accept both *p* and *q*.

[7] Contrast ἐπιcτάμενον line 8, of the 'skill' they do possess; and τέχνηι | . . . coφίην | in 18–19. βαcκαίνοντεc (cf. βάcκανοι in the gloss on line 1) is used by Xenomedes of the Cean Telchines, fr. 4 Fowler. For the magical suggestion of ἐπιτρύζουcιν cf. Theoc. 2.11, 62, with Gow. (It should be said that the space does not well suit πολλάκ]ι; ὡc πολλάκιc could be part of the scholiast's words in the original which has been abbreviated to the interlinear note in U⁵ on Hom. *Od.* 2.50. Cf. Pontani (1999).) The use of Sicily rather than the expected Etna in lines 35–6 emphasizes the link with fr. 50 Massimilla = 43 Pfeiffer. Some important recent works on fr. 1 Massimilla, Pfeiffer: Asper (1997), chs. 1–2, 4–6; Schmitz (1999); Acosta-Hughes and Stephens (2002).

tactics, and so forth, which are of great practical importance to them, and the narrator's searches for obscure scholarly facts; the opposition is often complicated, or infringed. Even at this stage, we will often see how the idea of knowledge involves not only information (knowing that something is the case), but also active skill (knowing how to do something) and passive experience (knowing of something because it has happened to you). At the same time, we will be exploring some connected aspects of the relation between narrators and characters.

The second *aition* of the poem, already ambitiously enlarging on the first, consists of a double *aition*, to which is attached yet a further *aition*, spoken by the narrator. This structure itself raises questions about knowledge in the frame (the poet really knows it all). The first part of the double *aition* teases the narrator and reader by beginning from a distant point, the Argonauts' departure from Colchis; only after much digression, literal and literary, does it reach, almost as an appendage, the rude exchanges which give rise to the rude language of the rite at Anaphe—and so answer the narrator's question. (Note fr. 17.6 Massimilla = 12 (i.e. 12.6) Pfeiffer.) Within the narrative, much more dramatic searches for knowledge occur, in situations of life and death. First the furious Aeetes' subjects search for the Argonauts (fr. 12 Massimilla = 10 Pfeiffer (Colchians) μαϲτύοϲ ἀλλ' ὅτ' ἔκαμνον ἀλητύϊ); later the Argonauts are trapped in darkness, and the skilled Tiphys himself is ignorant of how to direct them (fr. 19.8 Massimilla = *SH* 250 ἔνθ' ὁ μ‿ὲν ἠδμώλει πῆ[ι ... |Τῖφυϲ ἄ‿γοι πομπ[). The Argonauts are rescued by divine aid, which Jason beseeches in anguish (fr. 20.5–6 Massimilla = 18 Pfeiffer). This contrasts in intensity and significance with the Muses' satisfying the narrator's curiosity (fr. 9.19–21 Massimilla = 7 Pfeiffer). When Jason reminds Apollo how his oracle guided them at the start of the expedition, it is easy for the reader of the final version to make a link and a contrast with Apollo's witty instructions to the poet at the beginning of his career. The stories of Heracles provide an antithesis to the story of the Argonauts at Anaphe: the singular god-to-be, unlike the plurality of Argonauts, can help himself—and the mood has much more humour, the subject-matter much less dignity.[8]

---

[8] For the narrator's contribution of a story, cf. Hollis (1982), 118. For Σ Flor. (*Dieg.*) 51–2 π(αρα)τίθεται ('adduces, brings in') δ(ὲ) κ(αὶ) αλλ[ὅ]μοιον, ἡνίκα..., cf.

In the second book, it looks reasonable to accept the combination which places fr. 89 Massimilla = 178 Pfeiffer before fr. 50 Massimilla = 43 Pfeiffer. Perhaps it is more likely that the author should include an excursion at the start of the book, before the frame resumes, than that the very focused narrator should chat to the Muses in quite so casual a fashion (fr. 89.1–14), or expatiate so sententiously (fr. 50.12–17). If this is correct, there is much to connect these two consecutive sections (the second beginning at fr. 50.18). For example, both the narrator in fr. 89 and the founders in fr. 50 receive invitations, though their tastes in drinking contrast (ἐϲϲ δαίτην ἐκάλεϲϲεν fr. 89.5, ἐρ]χέϲθω μετὰ δαῖτα fr. 50.82; ὀλίγωι δ' ἥδετο κιϲϲυβίωι fr. 89.12, οὐκ ὀλίγωϲ ᾳ[ῖ]μα βοὸϲ κέχυται fr. 50.83). It thus seems plausible to notice other connections.[9]

In fr. 89, the narrator, though not particularly entering into the festival, passionately desires information on a seeming oddity in the rites of Icus (fr. 89.21–2 ὅϲϲ[α] δ' ἐμεῖο ϲ[έ]θεν πάρα θυμὸϲ ἀκοῦϲαι | ἰχαίνει, τάδε μοι λ[έ]ξον [). The subject seems the more incongruous after the apparent building up of friendship between him and the Ician. The narrator, unlike the Ician, has a life without *knowledge* of seafaring (ναυτι λίηϲ εἰ νῆϊν ἔ χειϲ βίον, fr. 89.33); he is collecting his information at a party in Egypt. In fr. 50, the narrator, by way of priamel, swottishly reveals his knowledge of Sicily (| οἶδα... | οἶδα... fr. 50.46, 50): in view of fr. 89, we associate his knowledge with histories of Sicily rather than with travel. He has not even travelled to Helicon, but has reached it in a dream. Within the narrative, two characters have travelled to Sicily (fr. 50.60). They dispute (fr. 50.72–74) who is to be reckoned the founder of Zancle, and travel to Delphi: ἐϲ Ἀπόλ[λωνα δὲ βά]ντεϲ | εἴρονθ' ὁπποτέρου κτίϲμα λέγοιτ[ο (fr. 50.74–5; the first supplement fits the space). The answer to their question is purely negative—neither of them; the

---

Dieg. on *Ia.* 4 (VII.6–7) καὶ γὰρ τὸν αἶνον παρατίθεται ἀκόλουθον, ὡϲ..., and further *Σ* Flor. 12–13; *Σ* AR 2.314; *Σ* Arat. 1, pp. 41–2 Martin. For the accounts in Conon, see now M. K. Brown (2002), nos. 11 (Anaphe) and 49 (Lindos).

[9] For papyrus invitations ('*x* calls you to feast...', etc.), cf. e.g. P. Köln 280, P. Oxy. 2678, 3202, 3693, 3694 (all ii–iv AD). The hating in fr. 89.11 recalls *Ep.* 28 Pfeiffer. The view above on how fr. 89 fits in is much the same as that of Zetzel (1981), 33, though fr. 50.2–6 makes against supposing further stories after the Ician. The paragraphos below fr. 50.17 should be taken as the sign of a new *aition*; the larger letters in 8–9 are an unlikely sign of this in a literary papyrus. The size of letters varies in this hand; cf. P. Oxy. 2210 fr. 17.

narrator's question, which was presumably 'why?', thereby receives a satisfactory answer. The characters, then, unlike the narrator, wish to know for practical reasons. (Feasting, we observe, is an end for the heroes but only a means for the narrator.) They journey to gain an answer; he acquires knowledge without literal journeys.[10]

The visit to Delphi for knowledge is a recurring motif in the work (see below and frr. 84–5 Pfeiffer (*Dieg.* II.1–4); fr. 187 Pfeiffer = 111 Massimilla (?)). More broadly, the idea of dynamic movement, probably already apparent in the first *aition* of Book 1, is graphically embodied in the great mythological travels of the Argonauts and Heracles. The *Aetia*, like the *Argonautica*, sweeps across the whole range of the Greek world; but its narrator is a static and intellectual figure.

The *Victoria Berenices* which opens Book 3 is still very much in contact with Books 1–2. In *SH* 264 = fr. 57 Pfeiffer Molorcus is promised he will learn the answers to most of his questions at a feast ($\overset{\text{\textasciiacute}}{o}cca\ \delta'\ \overset{\ast}{a}\nu\epsilon\iota\rho o\mu\acute{\epsilon}\nu\omega\iota\ \phi\hat{\eta}[c]\epsilon\ldots\text{‘}\ldots\tau\grave{a}\ \mu\grave{\epsilon}\nu\ \overset{\ast}{a}\lambda\lambda a\ \pi a[\ldots\ldots\delta]a\iota\tau\grave{\iota}\ \mu a\theta\acute{\eta}c\eta\iota\ (\text{-}\epsilon\iota\ \Pi,\ \text{edd.})\ldots\text{’}$). Molorcus' actual question was evidently omitted; it may be this that the reader is asked to imagine, in the interests of brevity ($\tau\acute{a}\mu o\iota\ \delta'\ \overset{\ast}{a}\pi o\ \mu\hat{\eta}\kappa o c\ \overset{\ast}{a}o\iota\delta\hat{\eta}\iota$). The section is evidently playing with the unabridged dialogue of Books 1–2, its own length, and the concerns of the prologue. Heracles proceeds to pass on aetiological information (though about the future), learned from a goddess (*SH* 265 = fr. 59 Pfeiffer).[11]

---

[10] For the language of knowledge (and the idea of home) in relation to the sea, cf. 'The Seafarer' 5–6 (I have) 'gecunnad in cēole cearselda fela, | atol yþa geweolc'. The narrator's catalogue in fr. 50 Massimilla = 43 Pfeiffer has the air of epitomizing or selecting from a history of Sicily, somewhat as in fr. 75 Pfeiffer, since histories were of the whole of Sicily (Jacoby *et al.* (1923–) III b. 488). The fragments of Antiochus (*FGrH* 555, mostly on Italy) and Thuc. 6.3–5 indicate this well. See further Fabian (1992), 171–87, and also, for the material and the historians, Th. Miller (1997); Sammartano (1998). Thuc. 6.4.5 shows that Callimachus must at least have had to select in order to find his anomaly on Zancle. Discord between political groups, with the reading $\delta\iota\chi o[c\tau a c\acute{\iota}\eta\nu$ in line 73, is suggested by Iannucci (1998).

[11] The point on the feast is owed to Dr P. J. Finglass. A feast would certainly be related to frr. 50 and 89 Massimilla = 43 and 178 Pfeiffer, and possibly to the frame of Books 1 and 2, if the dreaming narrator feasted with the Muses: cf. fr. 3.16–17 Massimilla = 2a.64–5 Pfeiffer. The cutting short of the section is ironic in view of its length; the Posidippus brings out more strongly how the section is from one point of view a vastly expanded epigram (cf. Parsons (2002), 130). The first part of the section, on the victory, now seems longer (PSI inv. 1923, Ozbek (2005), esp. Bastianini (2005)). Affinities appear with the *Victoria Sosibii*, which extends further the

We should also see thematic significance in a two-fold struggle to solve a problem within the narrative. Heracles' problem in dealing with the unwoundable Nemean Lion is parodied by Molorcus' problem in dealing with the mice. Heracles' wrestling requires παντοίαιϲι τέχναιϲ in Bacch. 13.49, and mousetraps are crafty devices which need know-how. One of the two mousetraps is itself metonymically ascribed knowledge of a skill: ἀνδίκτην τε μάλ᾿ εἰδότα μ‗α‗κρὸν ἀλέ‗ϲθαι (*SH* 259.33 = 177 Pfeiffer). The narrator, it may be added, has an easier time. Knowledge of the fact of Berenice's victory he acquires painlessly in Egypt: the news simply arrives there from Argos for him to sing of (*SH* 254.1–6).[12]

The arrangement of the story of Acontius brings close together the quest of Cydippe's father and the research of the narrator, both for

speeches, first-person elements, and geographical perspectives. (In PSI inv. 1923.10 read not ἔνεπ[ε but ἐνέπ[ων vel sim., cf. *SH* 259.15, fr. 384.28, 46.) PSI inv. 3191 (Menci (2004)) may also be germane material. The first part of the section, strangely, looks a more promising object for comment in P. Oxy. 2258 B fr. 2 'back' and 'front' than the first conversation with Molorcus (so Krevans (1986)), with horse(s) (?), running, a bronze statue (?), Perseus (?) or Persians (?), and the adj. 'royal' (ἀνα]κτορίηιϲι, Σ 'front'). ('Back' 4–5 are not easily made a comment on *SH* 257.26, cf. Σ (*SH* 258), esp. as (on my reading) the upright after α᾿, followed by δ‗ ἱπ[, excludes ὁ δὲ ἱπ[πικὸϲ ἀγών, or οἱ δὲ ἵπ[ποι.) If so, the narrative would virtually begin from Molorcus (cf. the *Hecale*): the 'front' contains *SH* 259.4–6. But *SH* 259.14 seems to indicate that Molorcus is already entertaining Heracles (though if one doubted D'Alessio's φέρο[ιϲθε in 13 and read φέρο[ντας | ξ]είνοιϲ, ξ]είνοιϲ could be the mice's 'hosts'). In any case, since Σ 'back' cannot be commenting on *SH* 259.7–37, the 'back' must be the front; and *SH* 257.21–43 (cf. fr. 176 Pfeiffer) + *SH* 259 = fr. 177 Pfeiffer make an unlikely column in the papyrus PSI 1218 + P. Oxy. 2170 (61 lines + any missing).

[12] The games had been moved from Nemea: see S. G. Miller (2001), ch. 5. The cunning of mouse-trapping is stressed at Opp. *Hal.* 2.156–61. For the relation of Heracles' and Molorcus' struggles see Livrea (1979). Mythology makes the contrast significant even if Heracles' fight was completely elided; but there is some difficulty with this interpretation of *SH* 264 = fr. 57 Pfeiffer (for which see Seiler (1997), 29, 31–2). It would be a little awkward that the excuse for the absent narrative should come *after* the recent mention of Molorcus, and that specification of the question should be omitted. As to background, the figure of Heracles encourages parodic refractions of the hero; cf. e.g. Dionysus in Aristophanes' *Frogs*; Pherecr. frr. 21, 163 Kassel–Austin, Men. frr. 409–16 Kassel–Austin, esp. 416; P. Oxy. 2331 (iii AD: γρύλλοϲ papyrus); even Eur. *HF* 465–6, 470–1. The miniaturization of lion to mice brings in the crucial theme of size. The appearance of a lion-*cub* in the comparison at *SH* 259.10–11 = fr. 177 Pfeiffer is significant, all the more so in the light of the connection now visible with the story of Phalaecus later in Book 3 (Gallazzi and Lehnus (2001), 7–13).

truth (cf. fr. 75.39 Pfeiffer ἐτῶς, 76 ἐτητυμίηι). Ceyx goes to Delphi to save his daughter's life—and get her married—whereas the narrator finds an interesting story by reading an old writer's history of Ceos. Yet the story interests him not only as a scholar but as someone with a very different kind of knowledge: that of love (fr. 75.49 Pfeiffer). The gods enter the thematic network too. Ceyx is enlightened by Apollo; but the poet's Muse, now an ostentatiously vestigial fiction, receives her information from Xenomedes.[13]

The complicated relation of the narrator with the character Acontius may be mentioned at this point. The two are connected in their knowledge, their experience, of love; they are also connected by writing and their skill with it. The playful link is taken far. A god has taught Acontius, much like the narrator, τέχνην (fr. 67.1–3 Pfeiffer, with an allusion to Eur. fr. 663 Kannicht, cf. Nicias *SH* 566, on Love teaching poetry; cf. fr. 1.21–30 Massimilla, Pfeiffer). And what Acontius writes, or contemplates writing, is exceedingly brief (apple: *Dieg.* Z 3 and Aristaen. 1.10.39–40 Vieillefond; trees: fr. 73 Pfeiffer ἀλλ' ἐνὶ δὴ φλοιοῖσι κεκομμένα τόσσα φέροιτε | γράμματα Κυδίππην ὅς' ἐρέουσι καλήν). But Acontius' craft is merely practical cunning. Like Cydippe he has knowledge of writing in the basic sense of literacy (Aristaen. 1.10.37–40); he can also exploit the simple convention involved in reading as quoted speech. But his use of writing is unaesthetic: he aims to affect reality, or contemplates venting his emotion with the ubiquitous graffito Χ καλός. One may contrast with such a graffito the narrator's own elaborate descriptions of Cydippe's, and Acontius', beauty (frr. 67.9–22, 68, 69 Pfeiffer). The apparent connection between the narrator's and the character's writing and skill breaks down for a further, and humorous, reason. The narrator, and the *Acontius* as a whole, are extremely loquacious. Most notably, in fr. 75.4–9 Pfeiffer the narrator is almost led by his implied great scholarly knowledge (πολυιδρείη) into impious revelation; his uncontrolled speech instead leads him into a digression on uncontrolled speech.[14]

---

[13] The reading of a written work (cf. fr. 75.54–5, etc.) shows clearly through the lightly conventional language of listening (fr. 75.53). A new text of fr. 75, and the other material relating to Xenomedes, appears in R. L. Fowler (2000), 370–4. On fr. 75 see esp. Harder (1990).

[14] Fr. 75, and probably the whole of the *Acontius*, teases the reader by repeated deferral of the happy ending and of the expected *aition*. The treatment of πολυιδρείη

The narrator himself is absent from the *Lock of Berenice*. He does appear immediately after in the *Epilogue*. There he makes a closing address to a divine queen parallel to the Lock's (fr. 112.7 Pfeiffer, cf. fr. 110.94ᵃ); alludes to his own contact with immortal beings (fr. 112.5–6, cf. esp. fr. 110.71–4, and note the link to Arat. 216–24); and announces a purposed 'movement' from the *Aetia* to prose (see below). Within the *Lock*, Conon appears as a sort of refraction of the narrator. The Lock is his discovery, owed to his learned research-ing in his drawn charts (fr. 110.1 Pfeiffer) and to his seeing the Lock in the sky. The fixed figure of the observer is set against the Lock, which travels dramatically, without wanting to, from Berenice's head to the sky. (Contrast Ptolemy's purposeful and warlike travelling, Cat. 66.11–12; the first sentence, cf. fr. 110.1, 7–8, brings all these figures together.) The Lock has had various drastic and unacademic kinds of learning and new experience, passively undergone rather than actively sought, as by the human travellers in quest of informa-tion. It has known Berenice's courage (Cat. 66.26 *cognoram*), which was exemplified in her having Demetrius killed; it has seen Berenice's bridal night, where it has learned the truth about brides (Cat. 66.15–20). The movements of the constellations are, for the Lock, not astronomer's data (fr. 110.1) but its new life and social world (fr. 110.69–74, 93–4, Cat. 66.65–74, 93–4). What it most wants ex-perience of, however, is the married woman's hair-oils (fr. 110.69–78); yet it cannot return to Berenice's head, without cosmic displacements (fr. 110.93–4).[15]

---

evokes Presocratics on πολυμαθίη; cf. esp. Heraclit. fr. 16 Marcovich (with Hesiod as first example), Anaxarch. B1 Diels–Kranz. For *kalos*-names see Dover (1989), 111–24. One might wonder if fr. 69 Pfeiffer (note the proper name) picks up fr. 68.9, despite Aristaen. 1.10.7, 13. Acontius' oath: cf. Barchiesi (2001*b*), 119, 120. Ariosto's handling of writing on trees, which ultimately descends from this passage, shows related exploration of physicality, language, etc. So the actual letters are of great importance: *quante lettere son, tanti son chiodi* | *coi quali Amore il cor gli* [Orlando] *punge e fiede* (*Orl. Fur.* 23.103.3–4; the names embody the people 103.1–2, cf. 19.36.7–8); and the writing on trees and cave deprives the polyglot Orlando of the ability to use language (recovered 39.60.3, with a quote from Virgil).

[15] See the end of the appendix below for some questions relating to fr. 110 and its last part. For the events behind fr. 110 see esp. *OGI* 54, 56.7–20, *FGrH* 160 ('Gurob' papyrus), P. Haun. 6.15–17 (Bülow-Jacobson (1979)), Just. 26.3.28, 27.1 (and 2–3), Porph. *FGrH* 260 F 43.18–30 (Jerome, *Dan.* 3.11.7–9, *CCSL* 75a pp. 904–5). Cal-limachus' 'down-to-earth' approach to the social world of stars as to that of trees and

Experience of events or of sensations, and other kinds of learning and knowing, are interwoven with the interests of the poem in various primary moments and emotions that belong to particular sub-divisions of mankind. The universe of the poem rests on divisions between young and old, male and female, mortal and divine. The first of these divisions, however, involves a dynamic process (growing older), which humans normally undergo; the other two involve firm boundaries, which an individual does not normally cross. Progress through the stages of life, especially for women, involves experiencing particular fundamental happenings and emotions; these greatly concern the poem.[16]

The large thematic scope of the poem in these respects is much clearer and more pointed in the four-book version than in Books 1 and 2 alone. The prologue itself strongly establishes and thematizes the idea of young and old, as we have seen. We may perhaps add that women and goddesses are significant there, on the metapoetic level (fr. 1.9–12 Massimilla, Pfeiffer; cf. with $\Theta\epsilon\epsilon\mu o\phi\acute{o}\rho o[\epsilon$ 1.10 fr. 63 Pfeiffer, esp. 10 $\Theta\epsilon\epsilon\mu o\phi\acute{o}\rho o\upsilon$, also at the end of the pentameter). The difference between gods and mortals often appears implicitly in the prologue (so fr. 1.20; 29–34 myth of Tithonus; Apollo, Muses); in any case the frame of Books 1 and 2 confirms this difference as a theme for the poem in general.

A starting-point is offered by male experience of love and sex (i.e. emotion and event). We have seen love presented as the object of

bushes (*Iambus* 4) is very typical of him. The connection with the narrator in fr. 112 Pfeiffer is enhanced if we see his removal to Helicon too as divine abduction (Crane (1986), 270–1; cf. now the new Sappho P. Köln Inv. 21351 + 21376, relevant to the whole prologue). There does not seem a sufficient case for the view that the *Epilogue* has been moved by a scribe from the end of Book 2: cf. Knox (1985 and 1993), and Cameron (1995), 145–62. A reference back from the end of Book 4 to the frame of Books 1 and 2 emphasizes the whole large structure. The positive evidence deployed by Knox and Cameron is exceedingly fragmentary (Σ Flor. on frr. 2–4 Massimilla = on fr. 2 Pfeiffer and *SH* 253 (b), the latter hardly an argument even if it did come from the close to Book 2). The *Diegeseis* may never have included the probably very short *Epilogue* (what was there to say?); and the *Diegesis* of fr. 110 in P. Mil. Vogl. 18 is slight. The end of a poem would be oddly presented in any case by P. Oxy. 2258, and one might even consider an accidental omission, caused by the initial $\chi a\hat{\iota}\rho\epsilon$ of frr. 110.94[a] and 112.7 and 8 Pfeiffer.

[16] The boundary of god and mortal is crossed more often in the *Aetia* than that of male and female: so, besides Heracles, frr. 85, 91–2, 110 Pfeiffer. In Posidippus play between male and female appears more prominently: cf. 36 AB, 74.9, 88.

painful knowledge in fr. 75.48–9 Pfeiffer (ψήφου δ' ἂν ἐμῆϲ ἐπιμάρτυρεϲ εἶεν | οἵτινεϲ οὐ χαλεποῦ νήϊδέϲ εἰϲι θεοῦ). The description of Acontius' love and his monologue conveyed the experience in detail (Aristaen. 1.10.15–23, 49–84). Acontius falls for Cydippe when he is still a παῖϲ (frr. 67.2, 75.76 Pfeiffer): an unusually early age, which shows that the relation of categories and experience is not invariable. Intriguingly, his liking for solitude in the country made his companions mock him with the nickname 'Laertes'—an infringement of the opposition in this section between young and old. In fr. 48 Massimilla = 41 Pfeiffer, from Book 1, love lingers into old age. Old age is lightened by love from boys, of a quasi-filial kind; ἐλαφρότερον there links up with the heaviness of age in fr. 1 Massimilla, Pfeiffer. Acontius' experience of the wedding-night is set against the boyish pleasure of athletic success (fr. 75.46 Pfeiffer). The singing of Cydippe's unmarried companions (fr. 75.42–3) obliquely reminds us, even in this male-centred narrative, of the momentous experience for her, of the new stage of life which it marks, and of its ritual setting. There is a similar point to the sexless prenuptial sleep in fr. 75.1–3, and to Hera's unmentioned experience (premarital sex with Zeus). The latter further becomes the *object* of different kinds of knowledge: sacred knowledge, and learning (fr. 75.8).[17]

Mention at fr. 75.6–7 of Demeter's mysteries creates a connection with the female-centred fr. 63 Pfeiffer shortly before (the length of one page separated that *aition* from this). In fr. 63.9–12, sight of the rites of Demeter Thesmophoros (ἐπ' ὄθμαϲιν o[ἶ]ϲιν ἰδέ[ϲθ]αι) is not lawful for Athenian girls πρὶν νύμφια λέκτρα τελέϲϲαι. A link is made in these lines between decisive moments of sexual and of religious knowledge; τελέϲϲαι itself suggests a rite. We may notice the contrasting ages involved in the narrative (old woman 4, girl 8, etc.; cf. fr. 26 Massimilla = 24 Pfeiffer below).[18]

The *Lock*, in emphatic contrast with fr. 75 Pfeiffer, portrays the experience of the bridal night from the female perspective. The account implies complex feelings, to which is surprisingly added,

---

[17] For knowledge of love cf. e.g. *Ep.* 43.5–6 Pfeiffer (where it is comically equated with a thief's active skill); AR 3.932–7.

[18] On τελέω cf. F. Williams on *H.* 2.14; the stem acquires further resonance in the present context. For ὀργι- (fr. 63.10) used metaphorically of sex cf. Ar. *Lys.* 898–9 τὰ τῆϲ Ἀφροδίτηϲ ἱέρ' ἀνοργίαϲτά ϲοι | χρόνον τοϲοῦτόν ἐϲτιν. Directly before *Acontius* come frr. 65–6 Pfeiffer, another female-centred section.

for Berenice, the pain of sudden separation from her husband and fear of his death. Berenice was abruptly changed by love, the Lock implies (*quis te mutauit tantus deus?* Cat. 66.31); she did not behave like her heroic self (Cat. 66.23–8). The Lock's detached knowledge *about* Berenice and brides (see above) is set against Berenice's direct experience. At the same time the Lock mimics her experience, in another refraction. It too is forced to be absent *a caro corpore* (Cat. 66.31–2, fr. 110.75–6 Pfeiffer); it left its sisters, rather like a bride (fr. 110.51), and entered a new world, possibly like Berenice leaving Cyrene (note the emphasis on 'new' in the Latin text in relation to both Berenice and the Lock: 11, 15 (Latin idiom), 20, 38 (45 *nouom* not in Greek), 64 (ἀρχαίοις at least in Greek)). However, the snatching off of the Lock is a kind of divine abduction, as of a beautiful boy or girl, which contrasts with the proper ritualized marriage of Berenice. This contrast is enhanced by contrasts and connections with other *aitia* in Books 3 and 4. In two *aitia* near to each other in Book 4, marriage is horribly perverted in the punishment for fornication (Leimonis shut into the bridal chamber with a horse) and in the rite imposed by the hero at Temesa (frr. 98–9). In Book 3 the armed man as part of the marriage rites at Elis recalls the forced mass union there of widows with soldiers (frr. 77–77*a* Pfeiffer, *Dieg.* I. 3.3–9); in fr. 110 Ptolemy, by contrast, leaves his loving bride for war—though the Latin suggests language of violence and warfare for the bridal night itself (Cat. 66.13–14).[19]

Other sorts of knowledge come into the treatment of women in two probably consecutive *aitia* of Book 3. The reason that women in difficult labour call on Artemis is the *object* of the narrator's inquiry

---

[19] It is now very doubtful, one should note, that the *aition* of the Elean nuptial rite followed directly on *Acontius*: cf. Gallazzi and Lehnus (2001), 14–15. (The alleged π, for example, in Pfeiffer's reading of Εἶπ' (fr. 76.1) would certainly be too narrow for this hand; I have looked at the passage with infra-red and with ultra-violet light.) Berenice's distress at her husband's departure for war links up with the grief of the Spartan wives in fr. 100 Massimilla = *SH* 240 (Book 1 or 2). For the abnormal combination with the wedding cf. AR 3.656–64, with Hunter's note. The Lock provides more specifically, when a lock, a miniaturization of Berenice; big and small are vital to the poem (cf. e.g. fr. 110.45–6 Pfeiffer). Its ambiguous gender adds to the complexities of the relation: cf. Vox (2000). For divine abduction one may think particularly of Pind. *Ol.* 1.36–45 (Pelops): the parallel of Ganymede within the narrative indicates the poet's 'working' (cf. Ariadne fr. 110.59–60 Pfeiffer). Related is the evocation of Persephone at fr. 228.43–4 Pfeiffer (Philotera; cf. 228.6,

($T\epsilon\hat{v}$ δὲ χάριν [ ]ọ [ ]κουcιν . . . ;, fr. 79 Pfeiffer). The opening must have evoked to some extent a primary, and here an appalling, female experience; but the narrator's interest is in the anomaly of a virgin goddess being called on for such a purpose. A certain incongruity must have resulted. In *Phrygius and Pieria* Pieria, as an orator, much excelled even the most eloquent of men (Κύπ[ρι]ν ὅτι ῥητῆρας ἐκείνου | τ]εύχει τοῦ Πυλί[ου κρ]έccoνας οὐκ ὀλίγον, fr. 80.21–2 + 82.2–3 Pfeiffer, cf. Aristaen. 1.15.60–6 (embassies)). Her 'eloquence' is not chiefly a matter of verbal skill; but from the narrator—an old man like Nestor, a craftsman with words, and a victim of love—the comment gains extra force. In fr. 80.5–9 Pfeiffer Pieria's *wisdom* makes her transcend the boundary between men and women, as conceived by the narrator: she is not just interested in such trivialities as ornaments.[20]

One may see complicated use of knowledge again in the treatment of a category of males which is related to the progression of life: fathers. The second *aition* of Book 1 begins with the fury of Aeetes at discovering his daughter's deeds (fr. 9.27 Massimilla = 7 Pfeiffer). This moment of knowledge contrasts in mood with its setting (fr. 9.19, 23–5): it starts the answer to the narrator's inquiry concerning an oddity. In the preceding *aition*, Minos was informed of terrible news about his son (cf. fr. 103 Pfeiffer in Book 4). This moment of knowledge will presumably have clashed with the Muses' and the narrator's erudite and impersonal discussions in this section on the parents of the Graces (Σ *Flor.* on frr. 5–9.18 Massimilla = 3–7

46); that poem, the Ἐκθέωcιc Ἀρcινόης, forms a fundamental intertext with this, and confirms the parallelism between Berenice and the Lock. The role of the wind in Psyche's abduction at Apul. *Met.* 4.35.4 probably draws directly on Callimachus (cf. fr. 110.53). Cf. further S. R. West (1985); Selden (1998), 340–4, argues for an Egyptian aspect to the scene. The possibility of a connection with Berenice's leaving Cyrene may perhaps be supported by the image of the moon and stars for the foreign bride at Sapph. 96.6–9 Voigt (a poet very relevant to this section). On frr. 98–9 cf. Currie (2002). ἀντὶ παρθέξ[ν]ου γυ[ναί]κα in the *Diegesis* might be thought to adapt part of the poetic text: cf. *IG* i³. 1261 = *CEG* i. 24 (c.540?), Soph. *Trach.* 148–9, [Theocr.] 27.65 (cf. Bühler (1960), 204; I am grateful to Professor R. Kassel for help here).

[20] At fr. 80.21 + 82.3 Pfeiffer, Aristaenetus' οὐκ ὀλίγον is Homeric with the comparative (*Il.* 19.217, *Od.* 8.187), and should be preferred to Barber and Maas's οὐκ ὀλίγως ((1950), 56); P. Oxy. 2213's ὀλίγους is a simple error of assimilation. The point on wisdom applies, thanks to πυκι[νοῦ, whatever the exact meaning of γ]νώματος; 'plan', 'thinking' both seem possible (cf. van der Ben (1995/6)).

Pfeiffer). We have seen the father's search for information about his daughter in fr. 75 Pfeiffer; in fr. 95 Pfeiffer, the end of the *aition*, the father's grief for the daughter he had killed may have been set against the author's neat explication of the toponym. On a lighter note, in fr. 26 Massimilla = 24 Pfeiffer the knowing father is amused by the childish anger of the hungry Hyllus pulling his chest-hair though he wants to help him. The fragment strikingly confronts males at different points in life: child, adult hero, and vigorous old man.[21]

The concerns of the poem with knowledge thus weave in with its large interests in different aspects of human life and human structures. This interweaving helps to confirm a positive and pointed interest in those aspects: we are not merely finding miscellaneous semblances in a random group of stories. So too with the divine. The gods as omniscient, and as sources of knowledge, provide obvious contraries to the humans searching for information. They clearly do this in the frame of Books 1 and 2; but the idea is equally evident, as we have seen, within the narrative of fr. 75 Pfeiffer. Some further points on the scene with Apollo there bring out the intricacy and subtlety that can attach to the divine giving of knowledge within the stories. First—a point we will return to—the giving of knowledge itself causes events to happen, and enables the narrative to achieve closure. Second, there is a complication: Apollo is speaking for Artemis, who is the deity actually offended and active. His own role as giver of information is thus accentuated and made genial; his information is combined with unexpectedly human-sounding advice to the father on the match. The opposition of Artemis and Apollo, and the more prominent role for the male, fit the divine level of the poem to its human level, with its opposition of boy and girl and its male emphasis. Finally, the effortless travel of Artemis (fr. 75.23–6) should be observed, in relation to the human theme of travel discussed above. It is mentioned to Ceyx, who has journeyed to find an answer. Artemis is like a walking encyclopaedia of her own cult and achievements.[22]

---

[21] Molorcus may very well have lost a son to the Nemean Lion: cf. Lloyd-Jones and Parsons on *SH* 257.20.

[22] Fr. 75.26 $\Delta\acute{\eta}\lambda\omega\iota$ δ' $\mathring{\eta}\nu$ $\mathring{\epsilon}\pi\acute{\iota}\delta\eta\mu o\varsigma$ gestures to Pind. *Pyth.* 10.37 $Mo\hat{\iota}\sigma\alpha$ $o\mathring{\upsilon}\kappa$ $\mathring{\alpha}\pi o\delta\alpha\mu\epsilon\hat{\iota}$ (of the Hyperboreans, inaccessible to ordinary mortals), and so to a distant cult-centre where Apollo can be (Pind. *Pyth.* 10.34–6, imitated at Call. fr. 97.10 Massimilla = 186

That scene at Delphi in Book 3 links up with two consecutive *aitia* in Book 1. In the first, Apollo's oracle shows the god resolving a situation in which he had fiercely and repeatedly punished the Argives (*Linus*, frr. 28–34 Massimilla = 27–31*a* Pfeiffer). In the second, Apollo's oracle again explains Artemis' thoughts: she actually likes the mortar that some insolent brigands have put on the head of her statue (*Diana Leucadia*, frr. 35–8 Massimilla = 31*b–e* Pfeiffer). Here the goddess, by contrast with the god, is behaving in a surprisingly unferocious and whimsical fashion. Apollo's εὔαδε τῆι κούρηι fr. 36.6 Massimilla = 31*c* Pfeiffer may even have shown some detached male amusement.[23]

The divine bestowal of important information is thus crucially connected to divine causality, but involves a variety of attitudes, tones, and arrangements from the gods. The connection between information and causality marks a difference from the role of the Muses in the frame of Books 1–2: they do not cause the events in telling about them. The same separation of speaking and causing may occur with other divine informants of the narrator: so the statue of Delian Apollo, if it is the narrator with whom the god is in dialogue (fr. 64.4–17 Massimilla = 114 Pfeiffer, from Book 3?). But the narrator cannot always be firmly distinguished from his characters as not himself directly affected by divine causation. Apollo's pronouncement in the prologue has had a causal effect on the nature of the poem, and also on the poet's art. The point is then reinforced (for readers of the final version) by the end of the first *aition*: there the Graces are asked to aid the art and ensure the longevity of the present poem (fr. 9.13–14 = 7 Pfeiffer). It may be added that in other respects too the gods spoken of by the narrative are not merely topics of discourse for the narrator. Some of the sections in Books 3–4, and probably even Books 1–2, and

Pfeiffer). Of course, the restraint of Apollo's advice in fr. 75.28–9 is full of irony; it is none the less striking how he considers the matter from the father's angle, and talks of family not beauty.

[23] The distance between the end of what is extant in col. i, which looks to come near the end of the first *aition*, and the beginning of what is extant in col. ii, which looks to come near the end of the second *aition*, is about eight lines less than a column (thus a probable maximum of *c*.32 lines). The second *aition* was therefore short, and almost certainly shorter than the first. The connection of the two stories is not of course affected, though perhaps enhanced, if the *aition* of Athena's statue followed (fr. 110 Massimilla = *SH* 276): cf. Hollis (1982), 118–19.

the *Epilogue* to the whole poem, present themselves as hymns, with a final χαῖρε to a god (fr. 25.21–2 Massimilla = 23 Pfeiffer, fr. 66.8–9 Pfeiffer, fr. 110.94ᵃ⁻ᵇ (Lock speaking), fr. 112.7–9 Pfeiffer; cf. fr. 9.13–14 Massimilla, already mentioned). They thus become themselves direct acts of homage, within the multiple fictions of the poem, to a god with power.[24]

There are many further aspects to the idea of knowledge in the poem, and to the relation of characters and narrator. One last area that may be briefly mentioned is that of historical and mythological time. Just as the poem covers the Greek world, so it also covers the whole of human time. This point is more acutely emphasized in the four-book version, where the outer poems of the second half bring us to very recent political events, in particular the Third Syrian War and the establishment of the new rulers, after a turbulent beginning. The whole idea of *aitia* bridges different times, and commonly involves the present; but the sense of range in time is intensified by sections like the *Victoria Berenices*, with its confrontation of news just received about Berenice and a story of Heracles, or the *Acontius*, with its sequence of history (fr. 75.54–77 Pfeiffer) and the distance between 'old' Xenomedes and Callimachus (ἀρχαίου fr. 75.54, cf. fr. 92.2–3 Pfeiffer]ανδρίδεϲ εἴ τι παλαιαί | ... ἱϲτορίαι). So too in Books 1–2 the distance between Hesiod and Callimachus forms part of the span of time created by the frame. In fr. 89 Massimilla = 178 Pfeiffer contemporary Alexandria (note the everyday 5–7) is set against the story of Peleus on Icus. The *aition* most likely following gives us the history of another island, Sicily, particularly in the eighth century.[25]

---

[24] Generically, one could see the whole poem as like a series of Homeric *prooimia*. For the dialogue in fr. 64 Massimilla = 114 Pfeiffer see Kassel (1991*b*). This quasi-epigrammatic dialogue is probably from Book 3 (cf. Gallazzi and Lehnus (2001), 17 n. 44); the large distinction of form between the two pairs of books still remains entirely apparent, though it is played with.

[25] The temporal span of the *Aetia* is now discussed by Harder (2003). The sequel to the Third Syrian War suggests that the *Lock* should ideally be published, even in the *Aetia*, relatively soon after Ptolemy's return (cf. Cat. 66.35–6). For the possible limits of Callimachus' activity, cf. Lehnus (1995). On the political role of Berenice II, see Hazzard (2000), 110–15; her place in poetry is another matter. Of course Heracles and his descendants the Ptolemies are in some senses brought together in art: so in the bronze statuette of Ptolemy II as Heracles (or rather as Alexander as Heracles), New York Metr. Inv. 55.11.11 (iii BC, h. 25 cm.).

In the above examples, we can already see past events and the range of time as objects of knowledge; we can also see writers as subjects of knowledge, people who learn and know. We might in addition consider the idea of knowledge growing in the course of history. The poem gives overall a sense of material progress and of movement in the direction of enlightenment. So a horrific custom is removed from Lesbos by the arrival of Greek colonists (fr. 91 Pfeiffer); or Heracles transplants the robber Dryopes (27 Massimilla = 25 Pfeiffer). But we may note some characteristic complications and twists. Athens οἰκτίρειν οἶδε μόνη πολίων (fr. 60 Massimilla = 51 Pfeiffer). The verb of knowledge (as if of a moral skill) is likely to be significant: the verb is not used casually or often in what we have of the *Aitia*, and this may well be the last line of Book 2. But Athens' moral knowledge looks more doubtful in the story of Leimonis (frr. 94–5 Pfeiffer), even if it is the father who weeps. The territory of Teuthis in Arcadia is so rocky as to nullify the advances in human technology presented by agriculture and viticulture: to attempt these activities would in fact be crazy (fr. 110.2 Massimilla = *SH* 276) rather than intelligent. The ground remains rich only in acorns, the Arcadians' δαῖτα παλαιοτάτην (fr. 110.11): progress is not to be seen here.[26]

Phalaris' brazen bull is an invention (εὗρε fr. 53.2 Massimilla = *SH* 252), but one of hideous cruelty; in a further twist on invention and innovation, Perillus πρῶτος ... τὸν ταῦρον ἐκαίνισεν, by being its first victim (contrast fr. 64.10 Pfeiffer; cf. fr. 110.49–50 Pfeiffer (iron)). The quasi-artistic model (cf. fr. 52 Massimilla = 45 Pfeiffer) for Phalaris' approach to ruling may have been Busiris. Busiris himself will have been dealt with by Heracles, a great civilizing force in the poem; but even Heracles shows deficiencies in his grasp of the polite arts (fr. 25.5–6 Massimilla = 23 Pfeiffer), not to mention politeness: stolen meals, he tells the victim of his larceny, taste sweeter (Σ on fr. 25.9–10).[27]

---

[26] Cf. R. F. Thomas and Mynors on Virg. *G.* 1.148–9 and 159; for a possible reason, cf. Hollis (1982), 120. The idea of progress in the poem was to be emphasized, I was glad to discover, by Professor Harder (now Harder (2003)); hence the essentially positive picture is not elaborated here. Professor Hardie suggests a link in the idea of progress with the *Theogony*. On the Dryopes, see Lehnus (2003), 32–3. For Athens in the *Aetia*, see Hollis (1992), 6–9, 11–15.

[27] Heracles' violent act here could be seen as a modification, at least in the source, of scenes where he takes a bull to sacrifice or cooks the sacrificial meat. Cf. e.g. Attic

For all these complications, in enlightenment and material progress Egypt under Busiris (fr. 51 Massimilla = 44 Pfeiffer) may be seen to present a contrast with Egypt at the present day (fr. 89 Massimilla = 178 Pfeiffer, probably earlier in the same book). Foreigners now abound, and presumably do so because business prospers (cf. fr. 89.6–7 Massimilla; no doubt the Ician is to be thought of as trading, cf. 32–3). At the end of the poem, the reign of Euergetes is good for Egypt (Cat. 66.35–6), his violence is against Syrians (11–12), royal sacrifice is of bulls (33–4).[28]

A question may be posed, very tentatively, which takes us to the level of the poet-narrator. Does the poem suggest and embody, purely implicitly, the possibility that there can be advances in the craft of writing, at least specific and limited advances? Progress in the art of sculpture is emphatically indicated in fr. 100 Pfeiffer, on the oldest Samian statue of Hera, later improved on by a named artist; the next *aition* (fr. 101 Pfeiffer) juxtaposed a newer Samian statue of the goddess. Posidippus adds to the interest here, with his presentation of recent progress in sculpture (62 AB), including indeed the avoidance of the heroic (63.4 AB, cf. Call. fr. 1.5 Massimilla, Pfeiffer). 1–20 AB make it inviting to see relations between artefacts and the poems describing them. The highly wrought lines of Callimachus in fr. 100 Pfeiffer, with ἐΰξοον in the hexameter matching the position of ἄξοος in the pentameter; words like ἔργον and ϲανίς (cf. Eur. *Alc.* 967), which could also be related to writing; the intertextual relation of δηναιόν to *H.* 1.60 on the false treatment of gods by δηναιοὶ ... ἀοιδοί: all this makes it tempting to think that pointed attention is being drawn to this poet's craft, and so in the context to the possibility of progress. After all, Callimachus writes with a metrical refinement not found in earlier poetry. The *Acontius* presumably displays Callimachus as making something more ambitious and impressive

---

bilingual belly amphora (type A), 530–20 BC, Boston 99.538, both sides (with essentially the same image) now attributed to the Andokides Painter, *ABV* 255, 6, *ARV*² 4, 12 (*LIMC* 'Herakles' 1332); Attic b.-f. olpe, early V BC, London B473, attributed to the Painter of Vatican G49, *ABV* 536, 37 (*LIMC* 'Herakles' 1340). He is sometimes seen actually playing the lyre, so Attic b.-f. neck amphora, 530–20 BC, Munich 1575, attributed to the Andokides Painter, *ABV* 265, 16 (*LIMC* 'Athena' 521).

[28] Even the Canopus Decree (239/8 BC) probably gives some idea of the actual problems for Egypt in the first years of Euergetes' reign (*OGIS* 56.13–15).

out of 'old' Xenomedes, by selection as well as style; this specific aesthetic advance on the prose of local historians must be implicitly present throughout the poem.[29]

Callimachus palpably claims an advance in sophistication on his model Hipponax in the *Iambi*; *Ep.* 27 Pfeiffer seems to indicate that Aratus as a whole is sweeter than Hesiod, through judicious selection in imitation. It might not appear too audacious for the reader of the *Somnium* and the *Epilogue*, with their neat ring-form, to observe an advance on the model Hesiod in elegance, particularly when his content is summarized in Callimachean elegiacs (fr. 4 Massimilla = 2 2 Pfeiffer). The point could be thought reinforced by Apollo's speech on graceful lightness in the prologue and by the prayer to the *Graces* (mentioning elegies) at the end of the first *aition*: both of these also allude to the Muses' inspiration of Hesiod in the proem to the *Theogony*. It is notable that the *Lock* takes us into the domain of Aratus; and reference to Hesiod follows in the *Epilogue*. It does not seem wholly out of place for the reader to bring *Ep.* 27 to bear as an intertext, and to sense the unspoken possibility that the *Aetia* too outmatches its model Hesiod in sweetness. There is innovation in poetry as well as in the skies. However, again there are some twists. The *Lock* actually dislikes its new position; and the poet who has transformed prose sources is off to write prose himself.[30]

---

[29] On the style of local historians see Hecat. *Test.* 17a–b Fowler. For selection in fr. 75 Pfeiffer see Fantuzzi and Hunter (2004), 63–5 (in a very valuable discussion of the *Aetia*). For Posidippus on statues, see Kosmetatou and Papalexandrou (2003). On the distinctive use of δηναιός in these two places of Callimachus, see Nikitinski (1996), 174–80. In fr. 64.9–10 Pfeiffer, Simonides introduces various innovations as an inventor, alphabetic and mnemonic; the reader will recall his (unmentioned) poetry, and may not unnaturally think of his innovative range in extensively cultivating separated genres. The section alludes in metre and subject to his elegiac poetry, and, through the particular story and other references, to his lyric poetry (11–14, cf. Quint. *Inst.* 11.2.11, 14). Innovation in range would perhaps be a subject of interest to readers of Callimachus; he used Ion as a precedent for it in *Iambus* 13 (41–9, *Diegesis*; cf. Kerkhecker (1999), 264–5).

[30] i.e. scholarship bearing on poetry. Fr. 112.9 Pfeiffer will hardly refer to the *Iambi*, as next in the collected works. Both the context and the need to point to the next roll in the τεῦχος (compare and contrast Crinag. VII) would demand that the *Iambi* should be defined with precision. 'The prose (pedestrian) pasture of the Muses' does not do this. It must be remembered that a codex, where the next work follows on the same page, presents a different situation for the reader. It seems unlikely that Callimachus could rely on being reproduced with the *reclamantes* seen in four Homeric papyri, even if they were suitable for his 'collected works'. Cf. S. R. West

The discussion has aimed to show how the four-book version of the *Aetia* enables a more complex and elaborate relation than in the two-book version between the level of the narrator in the poem and that of the narratives. This in turn makes possible a more complex handling of the poem's themes. These themes have been approached by following the thread of knowledge, which draws in the ideas of skill and experience as well as of erudition and information. This thread helps to bind, and to thematize, the large areas in which the poem interests itself: the divisions of human existence, the divine, and time. In its quirky way, the poem is exploring a cosmos. The absence of a single line of primary narrative in fact multiplies and makes more visible the interrelations of the sections. This is a very dense and rich design. It has mostly been considered by scholars either in small pieces or in its broadest structural outline. But so enterprising and imaginative a creation merits a fuller range of critical attention.

(1963). *pedester* is appropriate to Horace's *Satires* as it is not to the *Iambi* (choliambics of course depend on the idea of all poetry as having feet). The phrase would work even less well as the announcement of a forthcoming publication (Cameron (1995), 143–62). For Hesiod and the *Aetia* see Fantuzzi and Hunter (2004), 51–60. Gow and Page's (1965) understanding of *Ep.* 27 seems right; 'I fear' is because the speaker seems impolite about a classic. Fr. 110.59–60 Pfeiffer form a particularly obvious pointer to Aratus (71–3).

APPENDIX:

Catullus' Callimachean Book
and the *Lock of Berenice*

A recent piece (now chapter 5 below) discussed Catullus 65–116 as an authorial book in two parts ('*c*': composed of *c*1, 65–8*b*, and *c*2, 69–116). The two parts together displayed the writer's ability to match the supreme elegist Callimachus in his full range. A further aspect of the structure needs to be thought about. In counterpoint to these confident claims is the fiction of *c*1 whereby the poet, for reasons to do with his life not his skill, is notionally unable to write poetry.[1]

The first poem expresses—in elaborate poetry—the poet-narrator's inability to write a poem of his own because of his grief at his brother's death. This is a remarkable but striking way to begin a book: not 'I will write about *x*' but 'I cannot write'. The accompanying translation (66), though in poetry, is doubly removed from the poet's own voice: it is spoken, not by another author, but by the Lock. 67 is formally a dialogue with an object, which does three-quarters of the talking. 68*a*, supposing it to be part of the original book, presents another apology—in poetry—that because of his grief the poet cannot write poetry. (Poetry on love was requested.) 68*b* begins with the narrator's declaration to the Muses that he cannot refrain from praising his benefactor in love. This is a separate poem from 68*a*, but can now be seen as thematically related. Within 68*b* there is a significant opposition: *omnia tecum una perierunt gaudia nostra,* | *quae tuus in uita dulcis alebat amor* (95–6), against *lux mea, qua uiua uiuere dulce mihi est* (160). The relative clause in 96 may be defining, so that there is no formal contradiction; but even so, one can see love as now creating the ability to write. But 68*b* has already contained worrying suggestions about its unnamed mistress (135–48); these are extensively developed in *c*2. The 'happy ending' of *c*2 in regard to love (109) is even less closural and convincing than that in *c*1.

Thus Catullus' version of the last section in the *Aetia* (66) has a significant place in the whole process of finding a voice which *c*1 presents. 'Germanicus'' *Aratea* provides an interesting point of comparison for the movement

---

[1] Ch. 5. Add now to the works mentioned in n. 2 there Wray (2001), ch. 3; Claes (2002); Barchiesi (2005), 333–42; Hubbard (2005); Skinner (2007).

from translation to independence; in him it appears as a mark of growing assurance. In the first part the poet translates Aratus quite closely (though with various expansions); later, he gingerly considers the possibility of writing on the planets (444–5), which Aratus (*Phaen.* 460–1) had professed himself not bold enough to do. This plan 'Germanicus' actually carries out, whether or not in the same book or poem (frr. ii–vi Bain). Catullus' translation, then, plays an important part in the fiction and structure of *c*1. One might even find in this structure a rationale for Catullus' inclusion of a generalizing expansion in 66.79–88, if those lines are his addition. Near the end of the poem, his own writing would start to be seen. But to this particular problem there are many aspects. At all events, Callimachus emerges as ever more important for Catullus' design.[2]

[2] On 66.79–88 note recently Bing (1997), 92–4. One may essentially concur with Lobel's opinion that there was nothing to correspond with these lines in the papyrus. Later scholars have often been too definite about the number of lines to a page in P. Oxy. 2258, when this depends on the amount of scholia at the bottom (we do not have the very bottom of fr. 1 back); but C fr. 2 front seems to have the end of the scholia, so that the gap at the bottom of fr. 2 back will not have been great. One could imagine a very few extra lines, which Catullus expanded, but hardly ten; even a few, however, would somewhat spoil the neat connection of 78 and 89. Interpolation in Catullus' copy of Callimachus is another possibility; so is interpolation in Catullus, as Dr S. J. Heyworth points out. The case for a separate and earlier version of the *Lock* looks less attractive now that we know about the beginning of Book 3; it is also worth asking whether the place of the *Victoria Berenices* in the *Aetia* has something to do with its difference from the *Victoria Sosibii* (more aetiology, less victor). Cf. Fuhrer (1992), 217. One cannot say that the *Victoria Berenices* and the *Lock* must originally have been two occasional poems: a pre-eminent place in the second version of Callimachus' major work may have been a much more desirable kind of glory.

3

Hellenistic Epic and Homeric Form*

The main aim of this piece is not historical: it is not to discover, for the history of literature and culture, how the poets of the Hellenistic period made use of Homer. The hope is rather to illuminate Hellenistic poems by pursuing what they did with some aspects of Homer and with some ideas that were connected with Homer in the Hellenistic period. Accordingly, the inquiry will not consider the abundant and important evidence for poems that have been more or less lost; it will concentrate on one surviving epic, the *Argonautica*, and one partially surviving epic, the *Hecale*. Epic is the most obvious and natural category in which to place the *Hecale*. Its brevity may be provocative when set against the two famously lengthy Homeric poems; but even the provocation only makes sense from within the genre. The *Argonautica* itself may be thought strikingly short when likewise compared with *Iliad* and *Odyssey*. It is at any rate not evident that poems of twenty-four and four rhapsodies or books belong together and count as epics, while a poem of one book does not.[1]

---

* It gives me much pleasure to write in honour of Jasper Griffin, and about this subject: he has inspired me on Homer since my very interview at Balliol. Many thanks to Dr N. Gonis for assistance with papyri of and relating to the *Hecale*, and to Professor M. Fantuzzi for encouragement.

[1] Merriam (2001), 1–24, seems, despite 2, in practice to regard the epyllion as a genre distinct from epic; Gutzwiller (1981), 2–9, views it more as a subset. No argument could be drawn from Crinag. XI.1 τορευτὸν ('intensively crafted') ἔπος. The phrase may show surprise, cf. perhaps Antip. Sid. LVIII.2 (Erinna's βαιὸν ἔπος, with Anon. *Anth. Pal.* 9.190.2); but the point is not actually about length, cf. Dion. Hal. *Comp.* 25, ii. 132–3 Usener–Radermacher. It is more notable that Erinna's own poem of 300 lines is regarded as an 'epic', cf. *Suda* η 521.15–16.

This discussion will concentrate on form, but on form in its relation to meaning, and on form in different orders of magnitude. Especially when we are dealing with works of such varied size, different scales of form quickly begin to interact. The Hellenistic period, one may add, both pondered the large issues of structure which the Homeric poems exemplified and investigated the Homeric text in extremely close detail. The present discussion in fact begins, not directly from Homer, but from debate involving Homer. The procedure is not without value. When we are investigating the relationship of texts from different periods, we need not merely to look at the bare texts (i.e. as we see them ourselves), but at the critical ideas surrounding the earlier text at the later time. In looking at these critical ideas we also subject our own conceptions of the texts to scrutiny, in this case not because the critical ideas are unfamiliar but because they are all too familiar. Of course, the Homeric text itself remains crucial, especially with writers so intimately occupied by their model and with so deeply intertextual a genre. The line of argument will bring us back to the Homeric poems themselves, and to the Hellenistic poets' continuation of Homeric form and thought. Their relation to Homer will emerge as a complicated mixture of experimental divergence and profound connection.

At the beginning of the Hellenistic period, an account of the epic genre was produced which eventually came to possess fundamental importance, Aristotle's *Poetics*. The part of *Poetics* Book 1 that concerns the present paper is chapter 8, in which Aristotle discusses what constitutes one μῦθος, 'plot'. He claims that all those who have written a *Heracleid* or *Theseid* are much in error: the actions of one man do not make one action, nor does the agency of one man make the μῦθος one. The *Iliad* and *Odyssey* are contrasted with such productions: the *Odyssey* is not about all the things that happened to Odysseus but about one action.[2]

---

[2] The passage is discussed esp. by M. Heath (1989), ch. 4; the whole book gives a rich store of ancient material. Hunter (2001) includes the passage in his important discussion of Apollonius' structure; cf. Hunter (1993*b*), 190–5. Rengakos (2004) connects interestingly with some of the issues considered here (I am grateful to Professor Rengakos for showing me this admirable article before publication). Sharrock (2000) offers a thoughtful recent discussion of unity and disunity in literary works.

We must ask first whether these ideas and this formulation were known and important to third-century authors. It is completely uncertain whether or not the *Poetics* were current. Polymath cataloguers or librarians like Callimachus and Apollonius will have read any Aristotle available (cf. Call. fr. 407.XL Pfeiffer). Aristotle's three-book dialogue *De Poetis* was undoubtedly known (second in the list of works at Diog. Laert. 5.22–7). It seems to have had a general and argumentative element (Arist. *Poet.* 1454^{b}15–18). Certainly Aristotle's ideas were known to Philodemus (i BC), shaped and expressed in a way very similar to, but not identical with, that of the *Poetics* (P. Herc. 207 and 1581). Aristotle lauded and discussed Homer in 'many' dialogues (Dio Chrys. 53.1 von Arnim); *De Poetis* certainly said much more on individual poets than the *Poetics*. There is thus a high probability that Callimachus and Apollonius were familiar with not only the ideas in the *Poetics* on unity but the exemplification of those ideas through Homer. It is quite likely, for related reasons, that poems on Heracles and Theseus were familiar in this context. (Arist. fr. 70 Rose, from *De Poetis*, makes the same point on Homer and Empedocles as the *Poetics*.) It would in any case be likely that such poems would be drawn into discussion of these issues. Callimachus himself speaks of the huge number of Heracles' deeds, in a context of choosing subjects (see below); he also speaks of a poem on Heracles wrongly ascribed to Homer (*Ep.* 6 Pfeiffer).[3]

The importance of these issues for the period is also apparent. Hellenistic criticism was much concerned with the poet's choice and handling of plot, and with whether this was the most important of the poet's tasks (so Aristotle), or not really a specifically poetic task, and so forth. Homer was usually for critics the supreme exemplar of excellence. The handling of plots specifically in epic was probably discussed: cf. Andromenides (iii BC?) F 28 Janko = Philod. *Poem.* 1.15.21–6 Janko ἔϲτι [δὲ ἦθοϲ] καὶ τῆϲ ἐποποΐαϲ κ[ατὰ τὰϲ

---

[3] Theocritus writes an epigram for a statue of Pisander, whose *Heraclea* must be one of Aristotle's targets. On knowledge of Aristotle, cf. the sceptical treatment of Sandbach (1985); he cannot remove all significance (cf. (1985), 4–5), from the crucial passage of Epicurus (127 Arrighetti). At Diog. Laert. 5.26 note Bernays's ⟨Ἀπορήματα⟩ ποιητικὰ ά, printed by Marcovich (1999–2002), i. 324. On Philodemus and Aristotle on poetry see Janko (1991); Professors D. Armstrong and J. Fish have kindly shown me their new text of P. Herc. 1581 before publication.

ὁ]νομαcίαc, [καί], καθάπερ [ἐπὶ] τῆc μυθο[ποΐαc,... 'epic too has its own character with regard to vocabulary, and just as with the construction of plots...'. The detailed handling of the plot interests the exegetical Homeric scholia. In Polybius we seem to see a striking extension of Aristotelian language and ideas. His approach to the design of his work is governed by ideas of proper beginning and ending, and of reflecting the metaphorically aesthetic unity of Fortune's metaphorically teleological achievement in the events of his particular period: a unity as of a beautiful body, which his readers can perceive.[4] Other evidence suggests that Polybius' use of such language reflects wider historiographical debate. The criticism that Callimachus' *Aetia* is not 'one continuous song in many thousands of lines' (fr. 1.3–4 Massimilla) is in my opinion directed to the second edition, the second half of which was discontinuous in form. On this view the 'one' connects clearly with the discussion also seen in Aristotle.[5]

We have thus seen the significance for this period of these issues, of Aristotle's formulation, and of Homer and other epic in relation to them. We must now engage with Aristotle's ideas as ideas, in order to further our own exploration of Hellenistic epic, and of Homer.

Aristotle's use of the Homeric poems is a powerful persuasive weapon, in ch. 8 and elsewhere. The reader feels satisfyingly united with the author and Homer against the wretched poetasters. Yet Panyassis, whose *Heraclea* Aristotle must have in mind, was lauded

---

[4] 1.3–5, cf. 3.1–5.

[5] Cf. cυνεχοῦc καὶ μιᾶc at Arist. *Poet.* 1452ᵃ15, and continuity as a possible criterion for oneness at *Phys.* 1.185ᵇ7, *Metaph.* Δ 1015ᵇ36–1016ᵃ12, I 1052ᵃ19. See on Callimachus ch. 2 above, 44. For different views on μῦθοι, ὑποθέcειc, and the poet cf. Philod. *Poem.* 1.42.5–8 Janko (Pausimachus); 5.x.24–31 Mangoni; 5.xiv–xv (Neoptolemus). The scholiasts' οἰκονομεῖν, etc., of the plot is first attested in a related sense ('handle, arrange' literary features) at Arist. *Poet.* 1453ᵃ29; see e.g. Σ Hom. *Il.* 6.491, 18.312–3*a*, and *SH* 339A.14. (A somewhat different use in Alcid. fr. 29 Avezzù, note also 1.25.) On Polybius and other Hellenistic historiography cf. Walbank (1972), 67–8; M. Heath (1989), ch. 4, esp. 80–1. Heath emphasizes doctrine and denies a connection between Aristotle and Polybius; but the inspiration of language and ideas need not work so rigorously (one might think similarly e.g. at Dion. Hal. *Thuc.* 10, ii. 338.4–10 Usener–Radermacher). To doubt that Polybius read at least some Aristotle (Ziegler (1952), 1470), seems perverse in the light of 12.9.1 (very cautious Walbank (1957–9), ii. 330, 344).

for his οἰκονομία, his organization of the poem (Dion. Hal. *De Imit.* fr. 6.2.4, ii. 204 Usener–Radermacher).[6]

Aristotle's account of structure is much more elaborate and subtle than might appear. His view seems to be that any series of events, however long, which forms a causal sequence is in fact 'one'. But the tragic or epic poet must cut off for himself a sequence that is not too long to be *perceived* as a unity by the audience (note also 1459ᵃ30–4). The poet's sequence must be defined too by movement from tension to resolution and by a great change or changes in fortune. The emphasis on perception invites the question whether a sequence which was perceived as a unity but was not in fact so would be aesthetically acceptable. It seems hard to see how Aristotle could legitimately answer no. Indeed, he seems to countenance false and impossible actions which are made to seem probable (1460ᵃ11–ᵇ5). His account of causality seems to be weakened to suit either human events or, more likely, human perceptions;[7] his account of what constitutes a whole must make related compromises.[8] If, then, all that were suffered and done by Heracles could be subjectively felt by the reader as an entity, aesthetic objections to such a *Heracleid* might be unfounded. A voyage of Argonauts with an envisaged objective and end, with a limited time and a geographical sequence, might seem even easier.[9]

From this subjective point of view, the necessity of causal sequence for a reader's sense of 'oneness' may be doubted. One might further wonder about 'oneness' itself. If the underlying point were the reader's pleasure or satisfaction, the basic aesthetic need might be deemed, not a need to experience something that was one rather than two, but a need to avoid a lack of cohesion. If cohesion of experience

---

[6] Whence Quint. *Inst.* 10.1.54. Panyassis was not admired only in Halicarnassus: see the testimonia in Matthews (1974), 1–4, and M. L. West (2003a), 188–92 (for *SGO* 01/12/02 cf. ch. 2 n. 1).

[7] *Poet.* 1450ᵇ29–30, 1451ᵃ27–8 (1455ᵇ10); cf. *Rhet.* 1.1357ᵃ22–ᵇ1, 2.1402ᵇ 12–1403ᵃ10.

[8] *Poet.* 1450ᵇ29–30; cf. *Metaph. Δ* 1023ᵇ26–1024ᵃ10.

[9] *Poet.* 1451ᵃ16 ὥσπερ τινὲς οἴονται is probably a barbed reference to the poets rather than a disapproval in advance of a unity perceived but not actual. On the passages in the *Rhetoric*, cf. Burnyeat (1996). *Poet.* 1450ᵇ29–30 and 1451ᵃ37–8 might suggest that if the causal connection of elements in a πρᾶξις is not actual, it is not really one πρᾶξις. On πρᾶξις cf. Belfiore (1992), 83 with n. 2. The application of the term 'one' depends on perception at *Metaph. Δ* 1016ᵃ20–4.

is the aim, the ways of achieving it are enlarged; they might even go beyond plot, which is Aristotle's present subject. Aristotle's emphasis on oneness is not effectively justified (1451ᵃ31–2 seems to argue from the nature of imitation). An implicit justification may be found in the revealing analogy of a beautiful *creature* (1450ᵇ36–51ᵃ6): living beings, evident unities for Aristotle (cf. *Metaph.* M 1077ᵃ20–36), are the starting-point for considering beauty. This apart, some sense of structure or shape in the audience's experience, which Aristotle in practice demands, might be thought to presuppose the idea of a whole—or at any rate to be expressed by that idea. 'A whole' is naturally, if not perhaps necessarily, seen in singular terms (cf. *Metaph. Δ* 1023ᵇ26–36); but concepts like 'whole' and 'complete' (1450ᵇ24, etc.) may be aesthetically more revealing than 'one'.[10]

If we pursue Aristotle's approach, but emphasize perception, we can see aesthetic risks that are incurred by what can be called paratactic narrative (a sequence of parallel elements). The material might seem too diverse to cohere; the whole might have no shape; the whole might last too long to be grasped as an entity. But the last problem must also be faced by the poet following Aristotle's instructions, and the other two could self-evidently yield to poetic artistry. A less hostile approach might be needed to paratactic narrative, and, what frequently coincides with it, to narrative that coheres around an individual person rather than around a causal sequence of events.[11]

Interestingly, the *Odyssey* in particular shows signs of adapting paratactic sequences (adventures of Odysseus, returns from Troy) into a hypotactic structure. The work subordinates these sequences through *mise en abyme*, and generates a cohesive thematic network, woven round the idea of homes and hospitality. But it is not that a paratactic structure would have made such relations impossible. The specific form of the *Odyssey*'s hypotaxis, which sets true and untrue intradiegetic narratives in situations of hospitality, underlines this

---

[10] Cf. Ricœur (1983–5), i. 66. A crucial antecedent to Aristotle here is Plat. *Phdr.* 264c2–5, 268c2–9a3 (note Madvig's deletion of cυνιcταμένην in 268d5, not mentioned in Burnet).

[11] Even the ideas of romance discussed by Quint (1993) suggest a looseness of connection between episodes, however evaluated (so 34, 179). Immerwahr's post-Fränkelian use of 'paratactic' for Herodotus' structure ((1966), 47) should be kept separate from this discussion.

aspect of the narratives: their relation to hospitality and homes. A sense of accumulation, through a latent parataxis and through plurality, is actually necessary to the perception of Odysseus' and Penelope's experience; this is above all the case from their own perspective. Interestingly, too, the selectivity of the *Iliad*, praised at *Poet.* 1459ª30–7, involves centring the action around one predomin- ant figure (or, if we prefer, two). This could be thought positively to enhance the listener's sense of powerful cohesion, beyond the criteria of size and perceptibility which Aristotle emphasizes there.[12]

We are approaching a more positive conception of paratactic narrative. One may broadly distinguish between two extremes, which often blur. These are essentially: active and passive, a distinc- tion often implicitly deployed by Aristotle. In an active form, the deeds of the powerful hero mount up, and so as an entity enhance his glory. In a passive form, the sufferings of a person deprived of power mount up, and so as an entity create the sense of an unfortunate life. The two blend in a series of adventures, where suffering is as import- ant as achievement. It is notable that even the deeds of Heracles, the archetypal CV of success, are often viewed as a series of sufferings, from the *Iliad* on (8.360–9). Conversely, to endure numerous suffer- ings is in itself admirable. The passive model particularly lends itself to emotive or (from the sufferer) self-lamenting depictions, unified by the consciousness of the person afflicted. This consciousness may also give force to accounts of an individual's life too simple, or too lacking in internal parallelism, to possess the idea of a paratactic series. In Homer (and beyond), an individual's life is for him or her a primary and all-important narrative, necessarily an entity and nor- mally perceived as possessing a significant shape. A listener or reader can share or comprehend this perception through sympathy.[13]

---

[12] Some passages in the *Odyssey* stressing the multitude of Odysseus' and Penelope's sufferings: 1.1–5; 4.722–8; 5.221–4; 7.211–12; 8.155; 9.37–8; 12.258–9; 14.196–8 (Cretan tale); 19.129, 344–8, 483–4 (cf. 21.207–8, 23.101–2); 20.18–21; 23.300–9. Lowe (2000), 135–7, gives a good account of space in the *Odyssey* (while underexploiting homes); space should possibly be a more prominent element in the narratology of de Jong's valuable commentary (2001).

[13] For recent discussion of narrative and perception of one's own experience, cf. Fireman *et al.* (2003). The question of the totality of a narrated life becomes less central from this viewpoint; cf. Brooks (1984), 52, 60.

These ideas can form a way of looking at the story of entire poems, or aspects of it; they also often function on a smaller scale, no less important for the impact of the work. The *Iliad* itself can be seen as endless parataxis, of *aristeiai* and still more of inflicted deaths; the point, as in the Catalogue of Ships, is accumulation. (Catalogue—which virtually begins the *Argonautica*—is parataxis at its most elemental.) And crucial to the *Iliad* and its meaning are the evocation, not only of Achilles' life, but of a multitude of lives, each the thing that matters to its owner.[14]

We may add that visual art, not least in the classic century of tragedy, happily depicts paratactic narratives, including the labours of Heracles and Theseus. So the metopes of the Athenian treasury at Delphi, *c.*500–490 BC (both Heracles and Theseus, as in some other Athenian monuments), and the temple of Zeus at Olympia (Heracles), *c.*460 BC; and so (Theseus) the Attic red-figure cup, Ferrara T. 18 C VP (Beazley, *ARV*² 882.35; 72 cm in diameter!), attributed to the Penthesilea Painter, *c.*460–50 BC, or a calyx-krater, Oxford 1937.983, attributed to the Dinos Painter, *c.*425 BC (Beazley, *ARV*² 1153.13). The conception was continued for Heracles by artists of the stature of Praxiteles (Paus. 9.11.6), and on into the Hellenistic period. The synoptic possibilities of art are pertinent to these works; but so too is clearly delimited and balanced design. Art makes obvious the formal and cohesive possibilities of parataxis.[15]

The *Hecale* concerns itself with the life of Theseus. This was a well-known series of achievements, originally modelled as a structure on those of Heracles. The connection with Heracles is evident in the material and language of the *Hecale*, with its bull, its club (fr. 69.1 Hollis), and its explicit mention of the Nemean Lion (fr. 101). Callimachus' treatment of Heracles' deeds in the *Aetia* is in any case germane. In Book 1, after a Muse has told of one of his deeds (as befits the selectivity of the *Aetia*), there is some slightly two-edged praise of Heracles for the huge number of his actions. This leads to the irrepressible narrator telling of another deed. The *Aetia* is here

[14] On the Catalogue of Ships, see Visser (1997), who views it as simply part of the poem, not a pre-existing entity or the like.

[15] For the Athenian treasury, see de la Coste-Messelière (1957); there are problems of arrangement with both these metopes and those at Olympia. In general see Neils (1987); Boardman (1990); Neils and Woodford (1994), 925–9; further Froning (1992).

interested both in its own form and in the quantity of the actions. ἐπίτακτα μὲν ἑξάκι δοιά, | ἐκ δ' αὐταγρεσίης πολλάκι πολλὰ καμών, 'you performed six times two labours to order, and many times many of your own choice' (fr. 25.21–2 Massimilla), also distinguishes wrily between deeds inflicted and willed. The distinction has links with that between active and passive. Further deeds of Heracles appeared in later books. In the *Hecale* πάντας ἀέθλου[ς, 'all labours' (fr. 17.3), seems to view the series of Theseus' deeds in advance. But Callimachus has taken the striking decision to concentrate on only one deed of this one man, a hyper-Aristotelian solution: Theseus overcomes the Bull of Marathon. At the same time, other deeds are brought in hypotactically; and the lives of *two* characters are handled in the work. These lives interweave around the simple main action: Hecale, a poor old woman, entertains Theseus en route to the bull; he conquers it, and comes back to find her dead; his promised reward for her hospitality must now be posthumous honours.[16]

The main sequence seems in fact so simple, the surrounding material so abundant and so elaborately presented, that we may wonder if the Aristotelian reading of Homer's epics (a single action enlarged with episodes) has been pushed to a point of conscious and subversive play. It is noteworthy that Aegeus' *recognition* of his son Theseus and rescue of him from a plot by his stepmother was narrated by the poem, with powerful direct speech (ἴσχε, τέκος, μὴ πίθι, 'stop, my child, do not drink', fr. 7 Hollis).[17] This occurred either early in the main sequence or in a digression. In Aristotelian terms, one would expect such an event to form a climax. Presumably Callimachus' shaping or selection of the main action was made to appear unexpected. There seems also some toying in the poem with Aristotelian aversions: the poem suggests a narrative of the life not

---

[16] For the text of the *Hecale* see Hollis's very learned edition (1990), and his tireless later articles (1991*a*, 1991*b*, 1993, 1994, 1997*a*, 1997*b*, 1998*a*, 2000, 2004). On catalogues of Theseus' deeds see Hollis (1990), 209, with 289; the later hymnic catalogue at Ov. *Met.* 7.433–50 deliberately answers that of Hercules' deeds at Virg. *Aen.* 8.293–302. Attic vases often pair a deed of Theseus' with one of Heracles'. Diod. 4.59.6, Ov. *Met.* 7.434, etc., actually make the two bulls the same. On the club (commonly used in this exploit) see Hollis (1990), 216, 219; Neils and Woodford (1994), 927 no. 43, 937–9 nos. 185, 188–9, 199, 202–10, 214–15. In fr. 17.3 Hollis]νειν looks possible to me; cf. the first ν in line 4. Cf. Hollis (1997*b*) 47–8.

[17] Cf. fr. 79.

even of one person but of two. In fact the two contrasted lines of narrative, extended into the main action, gain cohesion precisely by their relation to each other. This relation may actually be compared to the relation in Homer himself of the lines of action concerning Odysseus and Penelope, or to the relation of the lives of old Priam and the young hero Achilles as they meet and take food together. But there are differences from Homer: Hecale and Theseus have hitherto existed in greater isolation from each other. The point of all this, however, is not purely metaliterary or ludic.[18]

The poem begins and ends with Hecale, and so implies the significance of her life. Her constant hospitality, despite her poverty, suggests in a way a succession of moral achievements (πάντες ὁδῖται, 'all travellers', fr. 2.1 Hollis; ἄπασιν, 'all' (travellers), 80.5); one might possibly compare the series of Theseus' heroic achievements (cf. fr. 17.3 (above) 'endure' (?) πάντας ἀέθλου[ς, 'all labours'). Hecale principally appeared in one central scene of dining and story-telling: a hypotactic setting that recalls the *Odyssey*, but also many a Heracles poem (and *Aetia* 3?). She narrates her fall, and successive disasters, which involved the loss of two or probably three loved ones. Fr. 49.2–3 bring out the terrible series of misfortunes, with emotive apostrophe: ἠρνεόμην Θανάτοιο πάλ̣αι καλέοντ̣ος ἀκοῦςαι | μὴ μετὰ δὴν ἵνα καὶ coὶ ἐ̣πιρρήξαιμι χ̣ιτῶνα;, 'Was I refusing to heed Death, who had long been calling, so that I should soon after rend my garment over you too?'. The paratactic sequence, and the narrative form, were more marked than in many pathetic Homeric speeches on the speaker's life; but two Iliadic life-stories in particular should be connected. Briseis tells (*Il.* 19.287–300) of enduring one woe after another (19.290): the death of her husband and three brothers at Achilles' hands, and then the death of Patroclus. Priam's story is told

---

[18] The centrality of aetiology for Callimachus may have affected the impact of the last part of the poem: that is in a sense the true τέλος. But it is noteworthy that Lehnus (1997) thinks that the poem ended with fr. 80; cf. also McNelis (2003). The order of events is not guaranteed by the 'Milan' *Diegesis* or by P. Oxy. 2258 A fr. 9 back: cf. frr. 98 and 198 Pfeiffer. The contribution of P. Oxy. 3434 is affected by whether one takes 6]α̣[β]`λ´ηι as work or character. (One might have some doubts about the putative kappa; but there are not many examples in the papyrus. Cf. e.g. P. Oxy. 2216.4.) On Callimachus and 'one' note the dispute of *Iambus* 13 (one metre). The relation to Aristotelian oneness is an aspect of the *two* actions in Theocritus 22 that could be enlarged on (cf. Hunter (1996), ch. 2).

mostly but not entirely by himself: how he was wealthy and then lost many sons, and then Hector, and endured to come and kiss his killer's hands (22.416–29, 24.493–506, 543–9).[19]

Those Homeric speeches show the validity of different viewpoints, and the importance of one's own story. Briseis' unexpected speech suddenly displays events from her perspective; it is revealingly followed by other women weeping notionally for Patroclus, but really each for her own woes (*Il.* 19.301–2). Just so Priam weeps for Hector, but Achilles for Peleus and Patroclus (24.509–12). In Callimachus' scene, two quite different perspectives combine and are contrasted, to moving and thought-provoking effect: the figures are contrasted in age, sex, fortune, and power. The contrast is more extreme than between Achilles and Priam. But also two lines of plot interlock: Theseus has killed (at least) a killer of one of Hecale's family. The interweaving of paratactic narratives here shows an ingenuity going beyond the straightforward designs of Aristotle.

We may interject here the characteristically Callimachean refraction by which a bird tells of its own (and its race's?) sad life, which combines with Hecale's; another tale of drastic peripeteia is thus brought in. In this case the proliferation of dubiously related but parallel material shows more a sense of sporting with narrative than an extension of the ethical point.[20]

The life of Theseus before the recognition was probably subordinated in various ways: by hypotaxis in the case of his previous great deeds, told to Hecale; relative brevity will have been another means of subordination (notice the fullness of description within the main action, as in the storm of fr. 18). However, direct speech appeared in the narrative both of the deeds (fr. 60) and of the childhood (fr. 10; 13?):

---

[19] Note Priam in Call. fr. 491 Pfeiffer. On the speech and story of Briseis cf. Dué (2002). Before Patroclus' death, her many woes were simultaneous rather than successive; cf. Andromache's account of losing at once her father and seven brothers, then her mother, soon to be followed, she fears, by Hector (Hom. *Il.* 6.407–39). In fr. 49 Hollis, it is probably the second son that dies, in view of the rhetorical preparation at the bottom of col. i in P. Oxy. 2376 (fr. 48). It seems papyrologically more natural to let fr. 47 follow fr. 49: it would be suspicious that there is no overlap between frr. 47 and 48 if 47 preceded 49 in the codex P. Oxy. 2377. If 47 is the later side, it is perhaps less likely that it concerns Hecale's husband (note fr. 49.2). On the opening of the poem cf. Hollis (1997*a*); πάντες in fr. 2.1 echoes Hom. *Il.* 6.15, but as she is poor unlike Axylus, the word stresses a more remarkable accomplishment.

[20] On 'refraction' in Callimachus, cf. ch. 2 n. 12, pp. 52, 55.

treatment of the childhood gives a strong indication that Theseus' whole life so far is being covered. The deeds are very much envisaged as a connected series: Theseus wishes, precisely, to be allowed to go on with the list (fr. 17.2–4).[21] These are not imposed labours but relished opportunities for glory. The active model of paratactic narrative is implied, by contrast with the passive model for Hecale. The death of Hecale brings a turn. It contrasts with Theseus' own escapes from death and reunions with his father (whom his heroism will eventually destroy); though a relief from sorrow to Hecale,[22] it causes sorrow to Theseus. The humanity and tenderness already seen in Theseus (fr. 69.4–9) now further enrich and limit the ethos of heroic triumph.[23]

Apollonius' *Argonautica* is longer, better preserved, and far more complicated than the *Hecale*. The narrative occupies the same number of books as the inset narrative of Odysseus' travels occupies rhapsodies, in the standard division (*Odyssey* 9–12). It concerns itself strictly with a series of ἄεθλοι. The word conveys the idea of toil and suffering; Pelias has inflicted on Jason the task, the ἄεθλος, of fetching the Golden Fleece, which itself involves innumerable ἄεθλοι. These make a paratactic series. The series forms a whole, a cumulative entity, both as an achievement and as suffering: the double aspect of active and passive is vital to the poem. The extent of the poem is entirely defined by the ἄεθλοι: after the briefest explanation of the single cause of the task, the poem starts to tell of how and by whom the task was executed. (The contrast with the narrative of Pindar's Fourth *Pythian* is extreme.) The ending of the series is looked forward to throughout, and is especially stressed in the last stages of the poem, where a close is almost lost (4.1275–6, 1307), and then realized.[24]

---

[21] Cf. AR 1.149–50.

[22] Frr. 49.2–3, 80.1–2.

[23] For the childhood cf. Arist. *Poet.* 1451ᵃ25–6; note the external analepsis of Achilles' childhood in Hom. *Il.* 9.485–95. The scene with the rock is sometimes included on depictions of Theseus' life (Neils and Woodford (1994), 928–9, nos. 50, 51, 57). On fr. 60 see Hollis (1965).

[24] In Homer, ἄεθλοι, save in an athletic context, often has the negative connotations of πόνοι, though endurance can be praiseworthy: *Il.* 3.126–8, 8.363 cf. 19.133 (Heracles), 24.734 (verb; servile work), *Od.* 23.248–50 (with stress on completion; more positive *Od.* 4.170, 240–3). Cf. S. Laser (1955). Hes. *Theog.* [992–1001] is important (though Apollonius probably had views on where the *Theogony* ended):

The ἄεθλοι are felt as a cohesive entity, despite their multitude; or rather, their multitude helps to constitute the entity. Their number is perceived as vast by the Argonauts and others (e.g. 4.1319–21, where Odysseus' experiences are evoked). They are said to be ἀπειρέςιοι, 'countless', but precisely in a context which defines their structural position. The prophet Idmon tells the Argonauts they are fated to come back with the Fleece, 'but countless are the sufferings that lie in between your departure for Colchis and your return here', ἀπειρέςιοι δ' ἐνὶ μέςcωι (lit. 'in the middle') | κεῖςέ τε δεῦρό τ' ἔαςιν ἀνερχομένοιςιν ἄεθλοι (1.441–2: the word-order expresses the protraction). One may compare the structure of Odysseus' lot: 'if he is fated to return, let it be late and wretchedly', etc. (Hom. *Od.* 9.532–5). The Argonauts' sufferings after the killing of Apsyrtus are planned by Zeus to be μυρία, 'innumerable', but in a context which defines their place: they are to 'return having suffered many woes first', πρό τε μυρία πημανθέντας | νοςτήςειν (4.560–1). The adjective, and the will of Zeus, make evident links with the plot of the *Iliad*.[25]

This numberlessness may be contrasted with the exact number of twelve labours that Heracles has to fulfil (1.1318). Heracles forms, it is well known, a constant counterpoint to the Argonauts; what matters here is not only his more active approach to his labours but also the structural comparison. Theseus highlights a different aspect. He appears at the start of the poem as one who would have significantly helped the Argonauts (1.104–5). But later only one adventure of his is brought in explicitly, and repeatedly: Theseus' encounter with Minos and, especially, his relationship with Minos' daughter Ariadne.

(Jason) τελέςας ςτονόεντας ἀέθλους (cf. Mimn. fr. 11.3 West, of Jason) τοὺς πολλοὺς ἐπέτελλε ... ὑβριςτὴς Πελίης (cf. Hom. *Od.* 11.622 of Heracles)...τοὺς τελέςας ἐς Ἰωλκὸν ἀφίκετο πολλὰ μογήςας. Cf. Pind. *Pyth.* 4.165 τοῦτον ἄεθλον ἑκὼν τέλεςον, and AR 1.15–16 (singular, as 469, 4.785), 362, 901–3, 2.615–18, etc. The discussion of Apollonius here is meant to complement that in Hutchinson (1988), ch. 3; for that reason, and because of the particular argument here, the emphasis is on Books 1 and 2, and little is said on Book 4. (That whole chapter has to be read for the argument on Book 4 to become clear.) Generally relevant are Nyberg (1992); Pietsch (1999); Wray (2000); Dräger (2001); Hunter (2001); Clare (2002). For Apollonius' use of Homer, cf., among much other work, Knight (1995); Fantuzzi and Hunter (2004), ch. 3 and 266–82; and the invaluable collection of M. Campbell (1981).

[25] The sufferings of Odysseus, like those of the Argonauts, have essentially a single cause. For the determination in Hom. *Od.* 9.526–36 of what ensues, see J.-U. Schmidt (2003); but note also 11.110–17, 12.137–41.

Ariadne freed Theseus, Jason persuasively observes to Medea, from the κακῶν ... ἀέθλων, 'grim trials', imposed by her father (3.997).[26]

For there is a crucial complication to the ἄεθλοι and the structure of the poem. The centre (in terms of the journey) presents an ἄεθλος/οι imposed by Aeetes in the midst of the ἄεθλος/οι imposed by Pelias. Aeetes' task, although consisting of two parts, is generally presented as singular: Jason must plough with bulls that breathe fire and sow a crop of warriors. The third book ends τετελεσμένος ἦεν ἄεθλος, 'the task was accomplished' (3.1407), as the fourth book ends with the κλυτὰ πείραθ᾿ ... ὑμετέρων καμάτων, 'glorious end of your labours', when there are no more ἄεθλοι (4.1775–6). The confrontation of a central ἄεθλος and surrounding ἄεθλοι is a challenging development of oneness in the plot and of parataxis. The separation of the poem into very distinct books (papyrus rolls) increases the complication. All this in fact enhances the shaping of the reader's experience, and the development of the poem as it proceeds.[27]

The surrounding episodes look forward or backwards to the central trial, for the reader; the Argonauts are in ignorance of its nature before Colchis. So the women of Lemnos, wearing armour and ploughing, evoke Jason carrying arms as he ploughs with the bulls.[28] This confusion of male and female roles links with the primary importance of the woman in the Colchian ἄεθλος.[29] The

---

[26] Cf. 1.255, 903. On Ariadne cf. Goldhill (1991), 301–6; Korenjak (1997). Note now P. Oxy. 4640 (hypothesis to a tragedy?) which suggests an elaborate treatment of relations between Theseus, Ariadne, and Minos. There are other possible or probable connections with Theseus in Apollonius, like the dragging of the bull by the horn in 3.1306–7 (cf. Call. *Hec.* fr. 68 Hollis, with Hollis's note). See further Hunter (1988), 449–50; Dräger (2001), 99–101. For the ἄεθλοι of Heracles in the poem, cf. DeForest (1994), 53, 66–7, 113–14.

[27] For πείραθ᾿ ... καμάτων cf. 2.424 κλυτὰ πείρατα ... ἀέθλου, of Colchis (411 is doubtful), 3.1189 πείρατ᾿ ἀέθλου (Aeetes thinks Jason will not accomplish it, cf. 4.1275–6, 1307 mentioned above); Pind. *Pyth.* 4.220 πείρατ᾿ ἀέθλων δείκνυεν πατρωίων; Hom. *Od.* 23.248–50 πάντων ... πείρατ᾿ ἀέθλων, not yet reached by Odysseus. For Aeetes' task as an ἄεθλος cf. also *Naupact.* fr. 6.4 West. At Pind. *Pyth.* 4.229–33 it is an ἔργον to be finished; on 220 see Braswell (1988), 304–5. On 3.1407, see Hunter (1989), 255.

[28] 1.627–30; 685–8 their ploughing; 867–8 ploughing by the Argonauts if they remain, with sexual suggestions.

[29] Cf. 1.637–8 Hypsipyle in father's armour, 742–6 Aphrodite with Ares' shield, 769–72 Atalanta's spear, 3.623–7 Medea yoking the bulls instead of Jason; cf. e.g. 4.1032–5 for Medea's all-important role.

men that spring from the teeth Jason sows are Γηγενέες, 'Earth-born', at one point actually γίγαντες, 'Giants' (3.1054). There could hardly be a clearer connection, or contrast, with the defeat of the Γηγενέες by Heracles and the other Argonauts (1.989–1011): a resumption of Heracles' participation in the Gigantomachy. (The episode contains much evocation of the warfare in the *Iliad*.) Imagery and other references greatly augment the connections and distortions. So cattle begin the second book (2.1); Amycus, the enemy of the Argonauts, appears like a Giant produced by the Earth (2.38–40), Polydeuces, in meaningful contrast, like a star of the sky.[30] Amycus and Polydeuces fight like two bulls (88–9, cf. 91). Or the Argonauts row like bulls ploughing (2.662–8): ἀϋτμή ... βρέμει, 'the breath' of such bulls 'roars' (2.665–6), as, conversely, the ἀϋτμή of Aeetes' bulls resembles the βρόμος, 'roar', of winds feared by sailors (3.1327–9). The central and other ἄεθλοι thus join together to form an elaborate and cohesive thematic texture, woven round ideas of heroic and less heroic achievement.[31]

Even in the apparently most paratactic books, Books 1 and 2, interconnections create a sense of cohesion, and form creates a sense of elegance. Some larger structuring elements may be briefly mentioned here; we will come back to explore them later from a different view-point. Phineus gives a detailed account in advance of the remaining trials to be faced on the outward journey (2.311–407); Jason summar-izes events so far to Lycus (2.762–71).[32] Both these lists make the totality easier to view as a whole, more εὐσύνοπτον. The encounter with the sons of Phrixus near the close of Book 2 (1090–227) helps to bridge the gap between the two halves of the poem.[33]

---

[30] Cf. also 2.1208–13 and 4.151, Aeetes' snake too as the offspring of Earth, γηγενέος.

[31] In further and more disconcerting extensions of the bovine motif, Heracles, who killed Hylas' father when he was ploughing with a bull (1.1213–17), runs distraught at Hylas' loss like a bull pursued by a gadfly (1.1265–72—a male Io). Jason kills Apsyrtus like a great bull (4.468–9): Aegisthus' killing of Agamemnon in Hom. *Od.* 4.534–5 and 11.409–11 is plainly recalled. The motif may already be exploited by Pindar, cf. *Pyth.* 4.142 (very unusual), 205.

[32] Cf. 4.730–7.

[33] Their warnings end with Aeetes' snake, like Phineus' main prophetic speech, 2.404–7; cf. Pind. *Pyth.* 4.244–6.

The distress of Jason's parents at the start (1.247–305) helps to establish the ἄεθλοι (cf. 1.255) as an entity, a lamentable whole.

The most important of all the structural elements is the division of the two books. The first is closed through a device that makes it seem like a distinct Attic tragedy: the sudden appearance of a god to intervene and settle (1.1310–28). The separation of the books groups the material into two differentiated units, with contrasting episodes. In Book 1, things tend to go sadly wrong. The Argonauts dally with the Lemnian women, who had half-heartedly taken male roles; they are themselves temporarily made soft and amorous. By contrast, in Book 2 the Argonauts do not even meet the warlike Amazons, of whom we hear much; if they had, they would have fought them (2.985–95). The Argonauts are hospitably entertained in Book 1 by Cyzicus, but then by accident engage in Iliadic yet pointless and disastrous warfare with their hosts. By contrast, in Book 2 their Iliadic fighting against Amycus' people is entirely justified, and the hospitality of Lycus has no calamitous sequel. In Book 1 they lose their greatest hero, Heracles, in awkward circumstances, which lead to a strife that is characteristic of the book. The loss of Idmon in Book 2, by contrast, is a death in the arms of friends (833–4), which underlines the harmony more characteristic of this book, and recently affirmed (715–19). The Boreadae urge against returning for Heracles; this is part of a quarrel, and will in the future cause Heracles actually to kill them (1.1298–1308). In Book 2 the Boreadae rescue Phineus by pursuing the Harpies: a heroic deed, at the limits of human power. Book 2 is generally marked, until the blow of Tiphys' death, by heroic achievement. Polydeuces kills Amycus, and the Argonauts pass through the Plegades. Temporary despair at their helmsman's death (2.858–63, cf. 885–93) marks to some extent a change of direction in the narrative; but it is evident how the division of books shapes the material into large masses and patterns. The separate rolls of Books 1–4 are fundamental to the organization and perception of the poem.[34]

The structure of the poem is elegant and formalized. The strong divisions between books, episodes, scenes, not only disrupt and express but also, as in, say, metopes, articulate a design. The design

---

[34] On the nature of Book 1, cf. Clauss (1993).

focuses on the Argonauts and their deeds and experiences: not one man but many, not their lives but a tightly delimited action and period. As has become apparent, the structure creates complex ideas of the Argonauts themselves, as regards heroic achievement. But the poem also looks beyond the Argonauts, and in doing so broadens its vision and deepens its thought. All the structuring moments that were mentioned from Books 1 and 2 in fact also display this looking beyond. The way they combine structuring the poem and enlarging its meaning demonstrates strikingly the importance of both these aspects. In complicating the focus of the poem, these passages do not only show structural daring and experiment; they also lead the poem, through Homeric forms, into Homeric, and especially Iliadic, complexity and emotional profundity.

Let us look at how other people and lives are developed in these passages; some Homeric connections will also be mentioned. Phineus' itinerary particularly recalls Circe's (*Od.* 12.37–110); but Phineus has a more elaborate life-story than the Odyssean Circe (*Od.* 10.135–9). His speech presents the future and a new beginning for the Argonauts; about the end of their task, they fail to learn (2.408–25). (πείρατα ναυτιλίης ... ἄνυσίν τε κελεύθου (310), 'the end of the voyage and accomplishment of the journey', only refers to the outward voyage, it transpires.) Phineus himself, as juxtaposition brings out, has now had his peripeteia: the Harpies have gone for good. No further change to his blind old age is possible, and he would like to die (444–7). The irreversible blindness links him to Polyphemus (*Od.* 9.542–5): that scene, while determining Odysseus' future, also opens unexpected and pathetic vistas on the Cyclops' ruined life (9.447–60). The stages reached by Phineus' and the Argonauts' stories and lives are opposed. Phineus is an archetypal old man; the specific designation ὁ γεραιός, 'the old man' (254, etc.), summons up Iliadic figures. Phineus contrasts with the youthful Argonauts (327).[35] He joins up with the old people at the beginning of the poem, especially Jason's father.[36] The speech of the old man *Phoenix* in *Il.* 9 (434–605) may be

---

[35] Cf. 1.341, etc. νέοι, 'young men'; 1.448 κοῦροι, 'youths'; 2.419–20.

[36] 1.263–4, cf. 253–5; δυσάμμορος, 'most unfortunate' is used in the first two books of Jason's father at 1.253, his mother at 286, Phineus at 2.218, and in connection with old age at 1.685.

compared: Phoenix's life, and those of others, are set against Achilles'.[37]

In the Phineus episode, the narrator's and Phineus' own accounts, and first-, second-, and third-person perspectives, produce a vivid and elaborate idea of Phineus' story. The contrast with his previous reign and good fortune, before the earlier and unhappy peripeteia, recalls Priam.[38] The general technique too is Iliadic: the Lycaon episode gives a conspicuous example of perspectives in different persons on the same narrative (*Il.* 21.34–114). In the case of Phineus, for all his and the Argonauts' mutual goodwill, we see his distinct and separate viewpoint; the separation is grounded in biography and biology.[39]

Jason's summary to Lycus is immediately followed by Lycus' own reminiscences of his youth (2.774–91), in rather Nestorian vein (cf. Hom. *Il.* 1.260–72). When Lycus saw Heracles he was just leaving boyhood (2.779), but now he has a son of his own (homonymous with his own father),[40] who is old enough to be sent with the Argonauts. He and his people have their own reasons to be delighted at the Argonauts' defeat of the Bebryces, with whom they have always

[37] The name of (a different) Cleopatra at AR 2.239 may sharpen the connection with Phoenix's speech (cf. Hom. *Il.* 9.556–65, 590–5). That speech is itself very much an expansion of the *Iliad*'s usual world. On the narrative of Meleager there and its relation to Achilles, cf. Alden (2000), ch. 7; Grossardt (2001), 9–43. For Phineus' old age cf. e.g. 2.183, 197–201, 221 γῆρας ἀμήρυτον ἐς τέλος ἕλκω. The Kleophrades Painter, with characteristically innovative pathos, shows a blind and bald old man: Attic r.-f. hydria-kalpis Malibu 85.AE.316, *c.*480–70 BC (Kahil and Jacquemin (1988), 446–7 no. 9). For various aspects of the episode cf. Hunter (1993*b*), 90–5; Knight (1995), 169–76; Manakidou (1995), 203–8; Clare (2002), 74–83; Cuypers (2004), 60–1. The link across works with fr. 5.4–5 Powell is of interest (cf. Krevans (2000)).

[38] 2.236–9; Hom. *Il.* 24.543–6.

[39] Achilles' purports to make Lycaon's story unimportant by speaking of his own origin and death (Hom. *Il.* 21.108–112); but any simple adoption of Achilles' perspective is averted by 122–35. (126–35 are bracketed in M. L. West's edition (1998–2000), cf. M. L. West (2001), 258–9; but 122–5 are enough to arouse horror and pathos.) There is perhaps a metaliterary dimension to the episode too. The blind Phineus recalls not only the seer Teiresias but the poets Demodocus (cf. 2.257–8 with Hom. *Od.* 8.480–1, 488) and Homer (cf. M. L. West (1999), 371, and esp. Graziosi (2002), ch. 4). Phineus' avoidance of completeness compares and contrasts with the poet-narrator's own strategy; the theme of controlling speech, in Apollonius' version of the myth (cf. Σ 2.178–82b, Soph. frr. 704–5 Radt), relates to a concern of the narrator's that is prominent in the poem (cf. e.g. 1.919–21, handled as often with a near-Callimachean sense of play).

[40] 776, 803.

been fighting.[41] A sense of other lives and perspectives is thus built up, through first-person speech and the adumbration of a biographical narrative. The *Odyssey* is very much in point here, not least Book 4, where Menelaus both remembers Odysseus and reveals some of his own story.[42]

The sons of Phrixus are crucial to the plot and forcefully introduce us and the Argonauts to the central situation of Colchis. But they also forcefully bring in their own story, which is part of a longer story involving their father and their mother, Aeetes' elder daughter Chalciope. Their story now interlocks with that of the Argonauts, and there are numerous points of connection and contrast. They are trying to get back to Greece from Colchis, so as to recover their property; they are following their father's (not like Jason's their uncle's) ἐφετμάων, 'injunctions' (2.1152). Their own ship has just been wrecked (by the father of the Boreadae, 1098–1103); their despair strongly connects with Jason's in the poem.[43] Though their fates will now combine, they become a lever for opening up further divisions of understanding. Their mother has a very different attitude to their departure, based on her own sex and life-story (3.253–67). That scene is especially connected with Penelope's reaction to Telemachus' departure,[44] as is the related scene between Jason and his mother (1.268–305). Book 3 will develop further significant divergences between Chalciope's perspective and that of her sister Medea, despite their alliance. Aeetes too has an angle of his own.[45]

Diverging perspectives are plainly involved in the mourning of Alcimede and others for Jason before he leaves. The speech of Odysseus' mother at Hom. *Od.* 11.181–204, which is evoked in this scene, brings out the suffering Odysseus' absence has caused to different members of his family; but it does not mark the distinctness of the hero's own viewpoint with the force of this scene. (Jason,

[41] 135–41, 757–8, 796–8.
[42] On Lycus' reminiscences cf. Nelis (2001), 360–2.
[43] ἀμηχανέων κακότητι, (one son) 'in despair at their misfortune', 2.1140; the same phrase of Jason 2.410, 3.423.
[44] *Od.* 4.703–66, 17.36–56.
[45] 3.304–13, cf. 584–8, 594–605. For restraining parents cf. also e.g. Hom. *Il.* 22.33–92, Call. *Hec.* fr. 17 Hollis and *Diegesis*. Contrast AR 1.149–50. On the sons of Phrixus in the poem cf. Nyberg (1992), 62, 86–7; Clare (2002), 104–118.

though sad, is determined, and he has more confidence than Alcimede in the gods.) Particularly interesting is the elaborate connection of perspective and structure. The passage has strong associations
with both opening and closing. ὣς ὄφελεν (1.256, spoken by women),
'if only' Phrixus had perished on his ram, αἴθ᾽ ὄφελον (278, spoken by
Alcimede), 'if only' I had died, recall the opening of Euripides'
Medea: εἴθ᾽ ὤφελ᾽, 'if only' the Argo had never been made or sailed.
That very connection marks a different perspective again on the
Argonauts. ἄλγεα μυρία θείη (259), (so that Phrixus' ram might)
'cause' Alcimede 'innumerable woes', strongly recalls the opening of
the *Iliad*; however, it relates the woes to a figure subordinate in the
main story, but with her own viewpoint. The mourning of the
parents, and the attempt to restrain the son, recall the last part of
the *Iliad* (Books 22 and 24). Structurally, a striking inversion of the
Iliad's structure is implied: the family's mourning *begins* the poem.
But differences in characters' viewpoint are much involved too. The
idea of ending relates to Alcimede's perceived pattern of life, distinct
from her son's: now she is old, but after joy and prosperity have
come a peripeteia and a sad final period.[46] Such a fall in a life is a
highly Homeric theme for speeches, and is seen even on a child and a
dog.[47] In the *Iliad*, lament provides a supreme form for presenting
individual perspective and narrative. Apollonius pursues this Homeric inspiration, but at a greater distance from tragic finality.[48]

We have already touched on Glaucus' speech, delivered *ex mari*
rather than *ex machina*. It ends a quarrel within the expedition; the
contrast with the opening of the *Iliad* is made inescapable by μῆνιν
(1.1339), Telamon's 'wrath'. There is also a contrast between this
resolution of discord and Heracles' behaviour: he will later kill his
enemies (something Achilles only contemplated in the heat of the
moment, *Il.* 1.189–92). Heracles has his own plot, which this one has
been interrupting; his departure fulfils Διὸς ... βουλήν, as if he had

---

[46] 1.251–2, 284–9, cf. 253–5.

[47] *Il.* 22.484–507, *Od.* 17.312–23.

[48] Alcimede is not seen in Pindar; the old father is presented at *Pyth.* 4.120–3. In
Apollonius the parents appear as fortunate hitherto; Pelias' treatment of their property is not dwelt on (cf. Pind. *Pyth.* 4.110). The idea that Jason is Alcimede's only
child is presented in terms of her biography (1.287–9, cf. 97–100 and Helen in Hom.
Od. 4.12–14).

his own *Iliad*.[49] The *Argonautica* in fact includes a considerable number of Heracles' labours, and his paratactic plot is both separate from this one and fleetingly in contact with it. Hylas has already gained the end of marriage (and immortality); Jason will have to wait until 4.1121–69 for the former. Even Hylas' biography has been briefly conveyed, with conscious digression (1.1211–20). Other stories, then, appear, with their own timing and shape.[50]

These moments bring out how, even as Apollonius is marking the clarity and cohesion of his paratactic narrative, he is also, in pursuit of Homer, pointedly opening up a multiplicity of other stories and perspectives. Such opening up is not in the least confined to these moments (cf. e.g. the episodes of Hypsipyle or of the Doliones, or Hera's speech to Thetis, 4.783–832); but they bring out with special force how the poem is not confined to its central structure, characters, and ethos. The sense of other lives and viewpoints does not undermine the sense of structure and of selection; but it enormously enriches the vision and complexity of the poem. These passages of Books 1 and 2 also lead into the great fissure in the narrative of the poem.

As the poem moves into greater continuity and singleness with the central ἄεθλος, it also splits into two strands and two perspectives (cf. the *Hecale*). Not only different values and a different world but different styles and modes of narrative are seen in the writing on Jason and on Medea. It is characteristic that Jason has no long soliloquies.

Medea's life appears within and outside the borders of the poem. Within it, her active deeds and passive sufferings form a challenging mirror-image of the Argonauts' (and especially Jason's). Her deeds detract from his, her sufferings are his fault. Only a few points need be mentioned here. It is significant, as was mentioned, that she dreams of performing Jason's trial herself (3.623–7). The last line of Book 3

---

[49] 1.1315, 1345, cf. 2.154.

[50] Heracles in the poem is a complex mixture of lawlessness and lawfulness: shortly before, his motive with Theiodamas is raised to a concern with justice (1.1218–19); 2.147–50 more bluntly set ῥοπάλωι against Amycus' (deplorable) θεσμοῖσιν. Panyassis frr. 19–22 West (= 12–14 Matthews) may even seek to improve Heracles' image as a drinker; cf. M. L. West (2003a), 207 n. 21. Diverging treatments of Heracles in poetry were a topic of explicit discussion: cf. esp. Megaclides (early iii BC) F 9 Janko in Janko (2000), 142–3. Zeus' will is made to play a more prominent role in Heracles' story than in the Argonauts' (even after Apsyrtus' murder, note 4.576–9): cf. Feeney (1991), 58–69; DeForest (1994), 67–8, 108–9.

states the accomplishment of the ἄεθλος; the first of Book 4 speaks of Medea's κάματος, 'suffering' (joined with δήνεα, 'plans', for which cf. 4.193); the last sentence of Book 4 comes to the end of the Argonauts' καμάτων, 'labours' (1776). Her sufferings and their deeds thus join together. Passionate speeches by Medea emphasize her loss of her fatherland, parents, and home, which she has restored to the Argonauts.[51] Jason's, and the Argonauts', success in κάματοι, ἄεθλοι, and gaining of the Fleece, are due to Medea, and her suffering is due to those κάματοι and ἄεθλοι.[52] The symmetry, and its disquieting implications, are made clear.[53]

The Argonauts' plot and Medea's are just about kept together as stories, in that marriage is a climactic event for her (almost prevented by perjury from Jason, and brought within the poem's narrative by surprise). But her story, more than Jason's, is extended before and beyond the end of the poem; we can see how different a span it has from the Argonauts' journey. Her early childhood is recalled, like Achilles' in *Il.* 9.485–95, at 3.732–5. She there borrows language from Andromache (*Il.* 6.429–30), to show her closeness to her sister: she is figuratively Chalciope's daughter too (732–3). Significantly this language is later transferred to Jason, to whom she is daughter, wife, and sister (4.368–9): her circumstances have been drastically altered, as have Andromache's in very different fashion, and the change has disrupted all previous relationships. Her earlier life of witchcraft and power in Colchis is variously indicated.[54] Some of her future deeds and experiences are explicitly signalled: her destruction of Pelias,[55] her eventual marriage to the central figure of the *Iliad*

---

[51]   4.361–2, 1036–7; 1038–40, cf. 203 (Jason speaking).

[52]   360–5, 1031–5.

[53]   For a relatively recent discussion of the relation between Medea's and Jason's roles in the poem cf. Clauss (1997); see also the witty presentation in Calasso (1988), 372–4. Similes offer another important device for giving Medea's experience shape. Two suggest the radical changes in her life that confront Medea within the poem: 3.656–63, on a bride who has lost her husband before the wedding-night, and 4.1060–7, on a working widow with children, all mourning. As often with similes, there are also vital differences; the changes of life within the similes are in fact more tragic. (So too at 1.268–77.) The inset mini-narratives of the similes open up yet further lives. Such resonance is Homeric: especially pertinent is *Od.* 8.523–30, on a woman who has lost her husband at the fall of a city and is driven into slavery. (Cf. Macleod (1982), 4–5, 10–11; Garvie (1994), 339–40; de Jong (2001), 216–17.)

[54]   So 3.250–2, 528–33, 4.50–65.

[55]   3.1134–6, 4.241–3.

(4.811–16), now a child himself (cf. 1.557–8). Less explicitly, there are pointers to her desertion by Jason: so at 3.1105 Ἑλλάδι που τάδε καλά, cυνημοcύναc ἀλεγύνειν, 'I suppose in Greece it is thought good to care about agreements.' The irony relates to Jason's near-breaking of his oath in Book 4, but also, as Ἑλλάδι shows, to his actual breaking of that oath in Corinth. Heracles' purification from the killing of his own children, mentioned at 4.541, clearly connects with the purification of Jason and Medea for the killing of her brother Apsyrtus;[56] but it connects too with Medea's killing of her own children. The link with Heracles is interesting: just as his story runs alongside that of the poem, so Medea's, though in a way part of the poem, has also its own existence and validity.[57]

Like the Argonauts' story, and Heracles', Medea's is a paratactic narrative, of accumulated suffering but particularly of deeds, many of them in her case wicked. Later literature shows the celebrity of her series of crimes. The poem makes it clear that she, more than the Argonauts, is a figure of power. To her numerous achievements of witchcraft (above), the poem adds her decisive help for Jason with the trial and the Fleece, and her quasi-Iliadic conquest of the bronze Talos through witchcraft (4.1651–88). The murder of Apsyrtus brings her into particularly shocking territory. Her fatalistic parenthesis at 411–13 suggests the sequence of crimes that are bound to follow later, just like this one: χρειὼ γὰρ ἀεικελίοιcιν ἐπ᾽ ἔργοιc | καὶ τόδε μητίcαcθαι, ἐπεὶ τὸ πρῶτον ἀάcθην | ἀμπλακίηι, θεόθεν δὲ κακὰc ἤνυccα μενοινάc, 'it is necessary to bring this about too, to add to my shameful deeds, since I first acted in folly and error and, because of the gods, accomplished deplorable plans' (cf. 3.983). But this crime is also the responsibility of Jason himself, who weakly swings from possible oath-breaking to actual murder. It is not only by exposing passivity and showing pain that the figure of Medea raises questions about the Argonauts.[58]

---

[56] 4.541 νιψόμενοc παίδων ὀλοὸν φόνον, cf. 560, 587–8 . . . ὅτε μὴ φόνον Ἀψύρτοιο | νηλέα νίψειεν.

[57] On the marriage to Jason cf. P. Oxy. 3698; Spanoudakis (2002), 309–12. The marriage to Achilles creates a connection and contrast with the Λέcβου Κτίcιc (most likely by Apollonius) and the more disastrous life-story of Peisidice; cf. 4.815 with fr. 12.15 Powell, and Lightfoot (1999), 499. See also Korenjak (1997), 23–5.

[58] The idea of Medea's sequence of misdeeds is wittily exploited at Val. Fl. 8.106–8 (a catalogue which Medea hopes has ended with the putting to sleep of the snake; cf.

The story of Medea, then, presents a paratactic series, based on the life of one person; this disrupts and problematizes the main narrative of the poem, itself paratactic but not based on one person or one life. Far from disunifying the poem, Medea enhances its cohesion, and thickens its complexity. The same may be seen in many other enlargements of the poem beyond the Argonauts. In some ways, the poem might seem to share the unified perspective of the *Odyssey*: there the sympathetic characters, though all with their own viewpoints, are more united and allied than in the *Iliad*. But these complications pull the *Argonautica* towards the more tragic and terrible poem. The reader perceives the happy ending of the *Argonautica*, the natural conclusion of its tight formality, as in some respects a self-consciously artificial imposition.

Callimachus and Apollonius treat with the boldest experimentalism the fundamentals of design which Homer, in an important critical tradition, was thought to exemplify. These poets cannot be thought simply indifferent to current discussion of the chief epic writer; nor should their poems be considered either less thoughtful or less effective than Homer's in the deployment of structure. But they do not only diverge from Homer. The detailed texture of their poems also shows these poets drawing on the Homeric and especially Iliadic heritage to create narrative which challenges the reader's sympathies and values. The relation of these two strategies is evident: both the treatment of structure and the handling of perspectives surprise and stimulate the reader. Critically and ethically, the reader is engaged and provoked.

e.g. Man. 3.9–13, Sen. *Med.* 910–15). See further for Medea's life and image Moreau (1994); Clauss and Johnston (1997); Mastronarde (2002), 44–70. The image of the felled tree (4.1682–6) is an important one in the *Iliad* (Fränkel (1977), 35–7), here developed with a twist; it also recalls the Argonauts' conquest of Γηγενέες (1.1003–5). Contrast Dosiadas, *Ara* 5–8.

4

The New Posidippus and Latin Poetry

The purpose of this article is not in the least to provide a complete list of connections between this extraordinary discovery and Latin poetry. It is rather to illustrate how this big accession of new material enlarges our appreciation of the Hellenistic background to Latin literature, and our understanding of Latin elegy in particular. The article will concentrate principally on the poets of around the first century BC.[1]

The new text is magnificently published in Bastianini and Gallazzi (2001), with the collaboration of C. Austin. It occupies the first part of a papyrus roll dating from the third century BC. It consists of over 100 epigrams, arranged by subject, with subject-headings (οἰωνοσκοπικά, etc.). No author is indicated; two of the epigrams are known to be by Posidippus. It is a natural inference that all are by him; the internal evidence to my mind supports the idea of a single author. If they are all by one author, did he arrange the epigrams himself? Several sections

[1] The passages cited are merely, with one or two additions, those which occurred to me on reading through the text for the first time (without commentary); this reading was made possible by the kindness of Professor P. J. Parsons, to whom I am also grateful for valuable discussion. Mention of passages by the first editors is signalled explicitly. Poems are now also given the numbers of Austin and Bastianini (2002), but in this chapter the columns are kept to retain awareness of the papyrus and its structure. References to commentaries, other books, and articles on Latin poets are all but excluded: so many passages and areas are touched on that inclusion would greatly have enlarged and complicated the piece. It should be noted, however, that Nelis (2001) offers a detailed study of the interrelation of a Hellenistic and a Latin text which is of much interest for the wider concerns of what follows. For this papyrus and Latin poetry cf. now Magnelli (2002); R. F. Thomas (2004); Barchiesi (2005).

end with a reference to the Ptolemies (iv.5–6 = 20.5–6 AB, cf. xiii.35–xiv.1 = 88 AB), or to Alexander (vi.5–8 = 35 AB, xi.18–19 = 70.3–4 AB), which might be thought an authorial compliment. The ἰαματικά end with what might be considered an adaptation of the hymnic close on ἀρετή and ὄλβος (xv.19–22 = 101). The οἰωνοσκοπικά belong together as a series; so too, perhaps, the λιθικά. (The similar ending of consecutive poems i.28–9 = 6.5–6 and 34–5 = 7.5–6 suggests elegant variation rather than clumsy juxtaposition.) The collection seems to embrace a broad span of time (see especially the ἱππικά). This would presumably be a late arrangement by Posidippus of some of his epigrams, rather than simply his recent work. The design of the book is in any case of great interest.[2]

I. CONNECTIONS

We shall give particular attention, by way of example, to the first section, the λιθικά. We shall then look at some connections in the rest of the roll. The connections are not, for the most part, clear allusions by Latin writers to this specific text; but they show that these poems, and doubtless others like them, formed part of the context for their works. We should remember that epigrams were popular reading, not least with Latin poets, and that the particular popularity of Posidippus is indicated by a number of finds on papyrus (and wax tablets).[3]

We had some knowledge of poems about gems before this papyrus (Ascl. XLIV, also ascribed to Antipater of Thessalonica, and mentioned by the editors; Posid. XX = ii.39–iii.7 = 15; Adaeus IX, *al.*). This section, which handles many different stones, reminds us of Theophrastus, Sotacus, Pliny *NH* 37 (often mentioned by the editors), and the Orphic *Lithica*. From another angle, we may recall Ovid's poems on the ring (*Amores* 2.15) and on a portrait of Augustus and Tiberius set

---

[2] *SH* 705 suggests that Posidippus collected and arranged some works (note the ending on ὄλβος). The evidence on the Cωρός (*SH* 701) might seem to confirm Posidippus' arrangement of his own work at some point; but the matter is unclear. (For a fresh view on the Cωρός see Cameron (1993), App. V. We may observe that the word should denote quantity rather than variety or lack of arrangement; and Athenaeus' νῦν should be noted.)

[3] On some of the problems and possibilities involved in the questions of specific allusion and of intertextuality cf. Hinds (1998), esp. ch. 2.

in silver (*Ex Ponto* 2.8).[4] The section clearly focuses a reader's attention on the poetic treatment of gems and other stones.

There are two general points of special interest for Latin poets. First, the section stresses the exotic origin of some of the stones, often with details. Cf. esp. i.30–2 = 7.1–3, iii.8–10 = 16.1–3 τὸν πολιὸν κρύϲταλλον Ἄραψ ἐπὶ θῖνα κυλίει | πόντιον αἰεὶ ϲπῶν ἐξ ὀρέων ὀχετόϲ | πλήθεϊ πολλὴν βῶλον; ii.17–19 = 11.1–3 ου[. . . . . .]. ϲτίλβουϲ᾿ ἄγαν ἄργυρον, ἀλλὰ θαλάϲϲηϲ | Περϲικὸν αἰγιαλῶν ὄϲτρακον ἐνδέδεται.| οὔνομα μαργαρῖτιϲ.[5] The distant origin of the stones is an essential part of their luxurious appeal; such an origin is much used by Latin poets to stress, mostly with disapproval, the exertions expended on luxury. Cf. e.g. Prop. 2.16.17–18 *semper in Oceanum mittit me quaerere gemmas,* | *et iubet ex ipsa tollere dona Tyro,* and more widely 3.13, esp. 5–8 *Inda cauis aurum mittit formica metallis* (Call. fr. 202.57–64 Pfeiffer, Add. II; note already Soph. *Ant.* 1037–9), . . . *praebet . . . cinnamon . . . multi pistor odoris Arabs*; 4.5.21–8 (21, though corrupt, clearly refers to a precious object gathered on remote shores); Tib. 2.4.27–30 *o pereat quicumque legit uiridesque smaragdos . . .*; Ov. *Med.* 23 *induitis collo lapides Oriente petitos*, *AA* 3.129–32 *uos quoque nec caris aures onerate lapillis,* | *quos legit in uiridi decolor Indus aqua.* We now see more clearly a Hellenistic as well as a contemporary background.

Secondly, the jewels bear an especially intimate relation to women, whose bodies they adorn and whose attractiveness they enhance. Poems on women's jewellery are grouped together (most likely all the first eight in the book). The epigrams dwell sensuously on the interaction of women's beauty and the beauty of the gems, and relate gems to their place on the body: cf. esp. i.28–9 = 6.5–6, i.34–5 = 7.5–6 ὣ]ϲ ἐπὶ μαϲτῶι | ϲυλλάμπει λευκῶι χρωτὶ μελιχρὰ φάη (end of poem), 36–7 = 8.1–2 οὔτ᾿ αὐχὴν ἐφόρηϲε τὸ ϲάρδιον οὔτε γυναικῶν | δάκτυλοϲ. Again we see

---

[4] Cf. the ring gem Vienna Inv. IX B 806, 4–5 AD, with portraits of the Younger Drusus, Germanicus, and Livilla (see Zwierlein–Diehl (1973–91), i. 160–1). For extant Greek treatments of stones after Theophrastus see Halleux and Schamp (1985).

[5] If the text is sound here, ἄργυρον must be, not the object of ϲτίλβουϲ᾿, but the predicate (or predicative): the point is that the much-shining stone is not silver, as might be thought, but an oyster-shell; the similar shape of the two words adds to the neatness. (The editors translate 'non è una pietra con molti riflessi d'argento, ma una conchiglia persiana . . . , questa che è stata montata'.) It remains curious that ἐνδέδεται has no dative or the like to refer to. Lloyd-Jones (2005*b*) attractively suggests ϲτίλβουϲα πανάργυρον.

a literary background to such passages as: Prop. 2.22a.9–10 *siue uagi crines puris in frontibus errant,* | *Indica quos medio uertice gemma tenet*; 4.3.51–2 *nam mihi quo Poenis hic* (Hutchinson: *te* N, *tibi* Π) *purpura fulgeat ostris* | *crystallusque meas ornet aquosa manus?*; Ov. *Med.* 21–4 ... *conspicuam gemmis uultis habere manum;* | *induitis collo lapides* ... (above); *Met.*10.263–4 (Pygmalion) *dat digitis gemmas, dat longa monilia collo*; cf. also for φάη Prop. 2.16.44 *quasue dedit* (*sc.* a rival, to Cynthia) *flauo lumine chrysolithos*. The collection shows a particular interest in women; thus almost all the section of sepulchral poems is devoted to women, and encompasses a wide range of women's experience. The collection reminds us how significant Hellenistic poetry is, as well as Roman society, for the treatment of women by Latin poets.

One further general point on the section will be relevant later. It is tempting to see a metapoetic link between the small-scale artistry and craft of the gems and that of Posidippus' epigrams. The former is especially stressed at iii.6–7 = 15.7–8 ἣι καὶ θαῦμα πέλει μόχθου μέγα πῶς ὁ λιθουργός | τὰς͵ ἀτενιζούcας οὐκ ἐμόγηcε κόρας; one sees a similar idea at Sen. *Ep.* 53.12 *magni est artificis clusisse totum in exiguo* (the brevity of mortal life; perhaps Seneca suggests a secondary pointer to the 'short' genre of the epistle?). The approach is made attractive by the sudden length (14 lines) of the penultimate poem of the section, on a vast rock from the sea (iii.28–41 = 19). The position of the section at the start of the book makes the application easier. Connections between visual art and the poetry in which it occurs may be seen, for example, in Herodas 4, where the discussion of realism can be thought to extend to the author too. The section on sculpture, especially x.8–15 = 62, 16–25 = 63, makes the idea of connections between poetry and art the more attractive. For links between artefacts and poetry cf. e.g. Prop. 2.34.43 *incipe iam angusto uersus includere torno*, and the metaphor of polish, e.g. Lucr. 6.82–3 *multa tamen restant et sunt ornanda politis* | *uersibus* (individual lines); Ov. *Pont.* 1.5.61 *cur ego sollicita poliam mea carmina cura?*; Mart. 5.11.3 (of Stella's elegiac poetry) *multas in digitis, plures in carmine gemmas* | *inuenies*.[6] At all events, it seems not unnatural that a Latin poet should read Posidippus in this way.

---

[6] Because his literal hand is *culta*, his hand as a synonym for his writing is *culta* too. Shackleton Bailey in his Loeb seems not fully to take this point.

Now for particular passages.

i.2 = 1.1 | ’Ινδὸς ‘Υδάϲπηϲ [For once we have a fairly evident use of this passage, at Virg. *G.* 4.211 *Medus Hydaspes* |; this is confirmed by the length and sound of the adjectives. It is notable, first, that the passage comes at the very start of the book, a memorable position; second, that Virgil wilfully alters the geography to fit his argument. Cf. also Hor. *C.* 1.22.7–8 *fabulosus… Hydaspes*; Sen. *Med.* 725 *tepidis Hydaspes gemmifer currens aquis*; Stat. *Theb.* 8.237 *gemmiferum… Hydaspen* (in India); note Hor. *Sat.* 2.8.14 (slave) *fuscus Hydaspes*.

ii.35–8 = 14.3–6 Βελλε[ρ]οφόντηϲ μὲν γὰρ Ἀλήϊον εἰϲ Κιλίκων γῆν | ἤριφ’, ὁ δ’ εἰϲ κυανῆν ἠέρα πῶλοϲ ἔβη, | [ο]ὕνεκ’ ἀηνιόχητον, ἔτι τρομέοντα χαλινοῖϲ, | [.]..[....] αἰθερίωι τῶιδ’ ἐτύπωϲε λίθωι. This depiction comes especially close to Hor. *C.* 4.11.26–8 *ales* | *Pegasus terrenum equitem grauatus* | *Bellerophonten.* Manilius’ account has a related but different emphasis, 5.97–100 *Bellerophonten* | *imposuisse uiam mundo… cui caelum campus fuerat* (cf. Posid. iv.19 ἠερίων… πεδίων (cranes))… Cf. also Ov. *Ib.* 255 *quique ab equo praeceps in Aleia decidit arua.*[7]

iii.14–19 = 17 describes a stone which attracts iron μάγνηϲ οἷα λίθοϲ. This form of the adjective with noun for the magnet is very unusual, and not found elsewhere in poetry. It may then be significant that Lucr. 6.1047 calls it *lapis hic Magnes.* The poem fails to recognize that magnets can repel (the editors mention Lucr. 6.1044–57); but it still provides important background to Lucretius’ long account of the magnet, 6.906–1064.[8]

iii.34–5 = 19.7–8 (the rock) οὐκ ἄν μιν Πολύφημοϲ ἐβάϲταϲε, ϲὺν Γαλατείαι | πυκνὰ κολυμβήϲαϲ αἰπολικὸϲ δύϲερωϲ. Here the combination in a single couplet of enormous rock and the love of Galatea bring the story of Acis to mind: cf. Ov. *Met.* 13.882–4 *insequitur Cyclops partemque e monte reuulsam* | *mittit, et extremus quamuis peruenit ad illum* | *angulus e saxo* [*is motus* (*tus* in ras.) M], *totum*

---

[7] The fall of Bellerophon, not itself on the gem, is rare in art. Cf. the Cretan relief amphora Louvre CA 4532 (vii BC), etc., *LIMC* ‘Pegasos’, no. 241. On the treatment of the sky in the epigram see Gutzwiller (1995); cf. for the exploitation of colour e.g. the colour of the sardonyx used to represent the sea in the Augustan cameo Vienna Matthias-Inv. 2230 (see Oberleitner (1985), 35–6, with colour photograph).

[8] The Hellenistic background to Lucretius has been conspicuously enlarged by Hollis (1998*b*).

tamen obruit Acin. The person Acis is first encountered in Ovid; the story will not have been common.[9]

iii.38 = 19.11 ἴσχε, Ποσειδᾶον, μεγάλην χέρα (cf. Eur. *Erechth.* fr. 370.55–8 Kannicht). The whole poem, and the one that follows, bring out more clearly the unusually benign presentation of Neptune in *Aeneid* 1: he ends but does not begin the storm. Contrast *Aen.* 5.14 (Palinurus) *quidue, pater Neptune, paras?*; however, this points ironically to the end of the book, where Palinurus' own life is claimed by Neptune, but the other Trojans pass unharmed (863 *patris Neptuni*; cf. 779–815, 7.21–4).

iv.1–2 = 20.1–2 ὣς πάλαι ὑψηλὴν Ἑλίκην ἐνὶ κύματι παίσας | πᾶσαν ἄμα κρημνοῖς ἤγαγες (Poseidon) εἰς ἄμαθον, cf. *SH* 1134A (mentioned by the editors; note ὑψηλὴν Ἑλίκειαν). This poetic treatment makes it all the more conspicuous that Ovid does not refer to Neptune when mentioning Helice and Buris in Pythagoras' philosophical speech: *Met.* 15.293–5 *si quaeras Helicen et Burin . . . inuenies sub aquis*, etc. (mentioned by the editors). Contrast the importance of Neptune in the flood of Book 1. The significance of the presentation is made clear by 15.48.3–49.6 and Callisth. *FGrH* 124 F 19 (Sen. *NQ* 6.23.4), where we see the controversy on Poseidon's role in the disaster.

Now to links with the remaining poems.

iv.8–9 = 21.1–2 νηὶ καθελκομένηι πάντα πλέος ἰνὶ φανήτω | ἴρηξ, αἰθυίης οὐ καθαροπτέρυγος. From a formal point of view, the beginning and ending of the epigram with the same phrase (νηὶ καθελκομένηι) is interesting for Catullus: cf. e.g. Cat. 16. Perhaps the beginning of this poem and of Hor. *Epod.* 10 (*mala soluta nauis exit alite* | *ferens olentem Maeuium*) draw on the same original; the beginning of Hippon. fr. 115 West is not preserved. This and the following poem are relevant to Horace, *Odes* 3.27, the first part of which treats of omens for a voyage.

iv.16–19 = 22.3–6 ἡμῖν δ' Αἰγύπτου πέλαγος μέλλουσι διώκειν | Θρῆισσα κατὰ προτόνων ἠμεμονέοι γέρανος, | σῆμα κυβερνήτηι καταδέξιον, ἢ τὸ μέγ[| κῦμα, δι' ἠερίων σω[ιζο]μένη πεδίων. (Call. fr. 1.13 Massimilla presents the reverse journey.) Human safety is linked

---

[9] Merkel's *is molis* or *montis* misses the point; cf. Stat. *Theb.* 5.538–9 *occidis extremae destrictus uerbere caudae* | *ignaro serpente, puer.* For gigantic rocks thrown by Polyphemus cf., besides Homer, Demetr. *Eloc.* 115. On Acis, note the speculation in Hopkinson (2000), 40 n. 140.

with the safety of the journeying crane. The passage gives important literary context, and perhaps further edge, to Sen. *Oed.* 604–6 *nec tanta gelidi Strymonis fugiens minas | permutat hiemes ales et caelum secans | tepente Nilo pensat Ionium mare* (apparent link, then contrast (608–9), with the summoned ghosts);[10] Luc. 7.832–4 *uos, quae Nilo mutare soletis | Threicias hiemes, ad mollem serius Austrum | istis, aues* (attractions of corpses at Pharsalus: a ghoulish shift); Stat. *Theb.* 12.515–18...*tunc aethera latius implent...iuuat orbe sereno | contempsisse niues et frigora soluere Nilo* (simile linking the birds to the women arriving at the Altar of Mercy). See also above on ii.35–8.

iv.36–9 = 26: the heron is a good omen for purchasing an οἰκεύς. Herons seem to be good for households and property (cf. 39 οἴκων...κηδεμόνα), as they seem to be for cities (cf. Call. fr. 50.60–5 Massimilla). The combined evidence makes Ov. *Met.* 14.573–80 look like a pointed reversal: a heron (*ardea*) arises from the ash covering the houses of the sacked city of Ardea; the sound and appearance of the bird suit a captured city. The story comes only in Ovid.

v.30–1 = 32.5–6 τὸν βαρὺν ἥρῳ | ἐκ δῄων ὀλίγην ἦλθεν ἄγων cποδιήν (cf. Aesch. *Ag.* 438–44). ὀλίγην ... cποδιήν is made part of a more pointed contrast than in Erinna I.2, mentioned by the editors. On death and the hero's body, cf. Ov. *Met.* 12.610–11 *iam cinis est, et de tam magno corpore restat | nescioquid paruam quod non bene compleat urnam*, and, without the ash, Prop. 2.9.13–14 *tanti corpus Achilli | maximaque in parua sustulit ossa manu*. At Virg. *Aen.* 6.412–14 Aeneas in Hades remains the heavy hero: Charon *accipit alueo | ingentem Aenean. gemuit sub pondere cumba*, etc.

v.34–5 = 33.3–4 ὤιετ᾽ Ἀθήνης γαμβρὸς Ὀλυμπίου ἐν Διὸς οἴκωι | εὕδειν χρυσείωι πάννυχος ἐν θαλάμωι. The dreamer dies the next day. This poem provides interesting background to Prop. 2.3.29–32 (whatever the order of lines)...*Romana accumbes prima puella Ioui, | nec semper nobiscum humana cubilia uises*...; Cynthia will evidently sleep with Jupiter in heaven. It is still more interesting for Propertius 2.15, where sleeping with Cynthia will make the narrator immortal (39–40 *si dabit et multas* (sc. *noctes*), *fiam immortalis in illis: | nocte una quiuis uel deus esse potest*), but where death may come

---

[10] This passage is mentioned by D'A. W. Thompson (1936), 72, mentioned by the editors. Virg. *Aen.* 6.311–12 enhance the complexity here.

tomorrow for all their pride (53–4 *sic nobis, qui nunc magnum spiramus amantes,* | *forsitan includet crastina fata dies*). No such imaginative vistas are opened in the ἀθάνατος γέγονα of Dioscor. V.2, after the narrator's encounter with the vigorous Doris.[11]

vi.10–17 = 36: Arsinoe appears in a dream bearing arms, and having fought. The conception may be helped by that of Aphrodite bearing arms; but the presentation of the queen in so virile a guise throws light on Cat. 66.25–8 (Call. fr. 110 Pfeiffer), where Berenice's heroic action is treated. (Cf. perhaps Call. fr. 388 Pfeiffer.) xiii.39–xiv.1 = 88.5–6 again stress the woman's manly achievement: ἀλλ' ὅτι μάτηρ | εἷλε γυνὰ νίκαν ἅρματι, τοῦτο μέγα. This playing with gender makes a contrast with the poetic treatment of Livia, influenced as that must be by the poetic treatment of Hellenistic queens. She is entirely feminine; she welcomes the victors of her family as a woman, and is the *female* equivalent of her incomparable husband (cf. Hor. *C.* 3.14.5–6, Ov. *Fast.* 5.155–8, *Tr.* 2.161–4, 4.2.11–14, *Pont.* 2.8.43–50, 3.1.114–28, 4.95–112, etc.).[12]

vi.30–4 = 39.1–5 καὶ μέλλων ἅλα νηῒ περᾶν καὶ πεῖσμα καθάπτειν | χερσόθεν, Εὐπλοίαι 'χαῖρε' δὸς Ἀρcινόηι . . . ναυτίλε. It seems reasonable to see a specific trumping of this passage at Prop. 3.11.71–2 (end of poem; a result of Actium): *at tu, siue petes portus, seu, nauita, linques,* | *Caesaris in toto sis memor Ionio.*

ix.1–2 = 55.1–2 πρὸς ἑώιαν | κερκίδα Cαπφώιουc (cαμφωιουc Π) ἐξ ὀάρων ὀάρουc (cf. Austin's supplement at viii.23–4 = 51.5–6 δάκρυcι δ' ὑμέων | κολλάcθω Cα[πφῶι' ἄιcμ]ατα, θεῖα μέλη, cf. Demetr. *Eloc.* 127 Cαπφοῦc τῆc θείαc). If the restoration is right, ὀάρουc must denote songs, as sometimes in Pindar. Cαπφώιουc, as well as alluding to the setting of Sappho fr.102 Voigt (γλύκηα μᾶτερ, οὔτοι δύναμαι κρέκην τὸν ἴcτον κτλ.), will be the highest possible compliment for a woman singer, or poet. (Cf. Antip. Thess. (or Sid.) LXXIII.) This adds to the context for Cat. 35.16–17 *ignosco tibi, Sapphica puella* | *Musa doctior,* and Ov. *Tr.* 3.7.19–20 *ergo, si remanent ignes tibi pectoris*

[11] More development accompanies the exultant use of such a phrase at *Rig-Veda* 8.48.3.1 *amŕtā abhūma* 'we [the worshippers] have become immortal', thanks to the drink Soma.

[12] For the probable influence of portraits of 3rd-century Ptolemaic queens on portraits of Livia see Bartman (1999), 40–1. Purcell (1986) is arguing about Livia's image more broadly.

idem, | *sola tuum uates Lesbia uincet opus,* and for Catullus' choice of
Lesbia for his female protagonist, essentially a poet's name, which
matches and surpasses that of *Catullus.*

ix.15–22 = 57 tells of a snake which seeks to move over a mother's
body, from above her head, and attack her new baby. The action of the
snake on the woman's body, vividly described, has some connection
with the more disturbing assault of Allecto's snake on Amata's body
(Virg. *Aen.* 7.346–77). The lively description of the snake certainly adds
to our repertory of serpents: so 17 κ]υάνεον φολίδωμα· πυρὸς δ' ἀ ̣ ̣[,
cf. Sil. 2.585–6 … *caeruleus maculis auro squalentibus anguis;* | *ignea*
sanguinea radiabant lumina flamma, and also Virg. *Aen.* 2.210 *arden-*
tisque oculos suffecti sanguine et igne; Ov. *Met.* 3.33 *igne micant oculi,* etc.

ix.37–40 = 60.3–6: the dying father tells his children, μὴ κλαύσητέ
με, τέκνα; he is going to place of the pious. The scene recalls Xen. *Cyr.*
8.7.17–22, isolated and adapted by Cic. *Sen.* 79–81. Compare the noble
tones at Prop. 4.11.1 *desine, Paulle, meum lacrimis urgere sepulcrum;*
CIL vi.12652.c12–13 (i AD; dramatic intervention by the dead wife)
parce tuam, coniux, fletu quassare iuuentam; 21521.16 (Courtney
(1995), no. 183; the dead relative speaks in a vision) *desine flere deum;*
23551.13–16 (cf. 20370.9) *desine iam frustra, mea mater,* [|*te miseram*
totos exagitare die[*s.*

x.16–25 = 63: on a statue of Philetas. The fame of Philetas' statue
or statues (cf. Hermes. fr. 7.75–8 Powell, mentioned by the editors) is
relevant to his treatment in Propertius (cf. 3.1.1 *Coi sacra Philetae,*
9.43–6).[13]

x.31 = 65.2 (already known) of Lysippus πῦρ τοι ὁ χα ̣λκὸς ὁρ ̣ῆι;
cf. Prop. 3.9.9 *gloria Lysippo est animosa effingere signa.* The emphasis
on aesthetics in Posidippus' section on sculpture affects our reading
of Propertius' poem.

xii.20–1 = 78.1–2 ε]ἴπατε, πάντες ἀοιδοί, ἐμὸν [κ]λέος, ε[.].[| γνω
cτὰ λέγειν, ὅτι μοι δό ̣ξ[. The speaker, a royal Berenice victorious in
chariot-racing, will be Berenice II or Berenice the Syrian. This particularly
substantial epigram (14 lines), as well as Callimachus' *Victoria Berenices*

---

[13] Cf. Hollis (1996); that article becomes the more notable now, though Philetas is
here explicitly said not to be depicted like a hero (x.19 = 63.4). Note that Hertzberg is
wrong to claim, on Prop. 3.1.1, that a *Life* of Aratus (II in Martin's edition of the
scholia to Aratus) shows Philetas to have outlived Ptolemy II. Sbardella (2000), 71–5,
presents a very recent discussion of Philetas and Roman poetry; see now also
Spanoudakis (2002), 55–64, 66–7.

(*SH* 254–69), now looks to be used in the proem of *Georgics* 3.[14] The call to all poets in Posidippus to speak of things that are famous (cf. Hermes. fr. 7.20 Powell) contrasts interestingly with the individual poet's avoidance in Virgil of *uulgata* (cf. also Choeril. *SH* 317), through singing of Caesar as well as singing of the country. The Virgilian speaker is a poet celebrating the military victories of the *princeps*, and his ancestry (cf. xii.22– 31 = 78.3–12). But he also wishes to be a victor and to be celebrated himself (cf. *G.* 3.9 *uictorque uirum uolitare per ora*, echoing Ennius, with xii.20 = 78.1 above and 32–3 = 78.13–14 ἀείδετε ... ὦ Μακέτα[ι]); the language of *uictor... centum quadriiugos agitabo ad flumina currus* (17– 18) sets up a secondary suggestion of the speaker as a rider of four-horsed chariots (cf. xii.32 = 78.13 τεθρίππου). The passage essentially moves from the speaker's celebration of himself to the speaker's celebration of Caesar; the Posidippus gives a new interest to the movement.

xiv.4 = 89.2 θεοῖς μέμφεται οἳ᾽ ἔπαθεν (the empty tomb laments the death of Lysicles at sea); xiv.23–4 = 93.5–6 τὸν νέκυν, ὡς χρή, | πατρώιηι, πόντου δέςποτα, γῆι ἀπόδος. Both passages give relevant context for the speech of the drowning Paetus, Prop. 3.7.57–64; the whole poem is like a huge expansion of an epigram in the class ναυαγικά. The speech begins with complaint to *di maris Aegaei*, mentions Neptune (*caeruleo... deo*) in 62, and ends asking the gods (cf. *mandata* 55) *at saltem Italiae regionibus euehat aestus;* | *hoc de me sat erit, si modo matris erit.*

xiv.12 = 91.2 μὴ ταχὺς Εὐξείνου γίνεο ποντοπόρος. One part of the tradition behind Ov. *Tr.* 4.4.55–8: the Euxine is *Axenus, nam neque iactantur moderatis aequora uentis...*

xiv.30–1 = 95.1–2 (emaciated statue) ἐπ᾽ ὀστέα λεπτὸν ἀνέλκων | πνεῦμα μόγι[ς] ζωὴν ὄμματι (ἄσθματι Hutchinson) ςυλλέγεται. Related descriptions at Prop. 4.5.64 (Acanthis, in my view, at death's door) *per tenuem ossa <a me> sunt numerata cutem*; Ov. *Met.* 8.803– 4 (Fames) *dura cutis, per quam spectari uiscera possent;* | *ossa sub incuruis exstabant arida lumbis.*

xiv.38–9 = 96.1–2 πρὸς ςὲ μὲν Ἀντιχάρης, Ἀςκληπιέ, ςὺν δυςὶ βάκ- τροις | ἦλθε δι᾽ ἀτραπιτῶν ἴχνος ἐφελκόμενος. One could perhaps consider the possibility that Ovid's frequent metapoetic play on the

---

[14] On the *Victoria Berenices* and the proem to *Georgics* 3 see R. F. Thomas (1999), 68–92 (= R. F. Thomas (1983)), and (1988), i. 1–3, ii. 36–9, 42–3.

uneven elegiac metre was inspired by passages like this, whether or not such play was in Posidippus' mind. Cf. e.g. *Am.* 2.17.19–20, where *obliquo claudicet ille pede* (of Vulcan) helps lead into 21–2 *carminis hoc ipsum genus impar* (cf. McKeown on 19–20); 3.1.8 (Elegy) *et, puto, pes illi longior alter erat*; *Tr.* 3.1.11–12 *clauda quod alterno subsidunt carmina uersu,* | *uel pedis hoc ratio uel uia longa facit*; *Pont.* 4.5.3 *longa uia est, nec uos pedibus proceditis aequis*; perhaps *Ibis* 346 (Lycurgus, who had only one sandal because of injury to leg or foot) *in gemino dispar cui pede cultus erat.* For related play in Hellenistic verse, without explicit reference to poetry, cf. Hdas. 1.71 χωλὴν δ᾽ ἀείδειν χώλ᾽ ἂν ἐξεπαίδευϲα. Hipponax's stick in Hdas. 8.60 may possibly suit his lameness; there had been play on *feet* and *fingers* since Aristophanes.

xv.17–18 = 100.3–4 (a man long blind recovers sight) ἠέλιον δέ | δὶϲ μοῦ[..........]ν βαρὺν εἶδ᾽ Ἀΐδην: μοῦ[νον (μοῦ[νοϲ Hutchinson) βλέψαϲ τὸ]ν edd. pr.; βαθὺν ci. Parsons. The editors' restoration makes this an anomalous member of the ἰαματικά, which emphasizes the futility of the cure. If my view should be correct, there is a play between having, uniquely, two lives and having two separate periods of vision. (The spacing looks acceptable; for the emphasis on the sun cf. e.g. Call. *H.* 5.87–9, with Bulloch on 89; Tac. *Hist.* 4.82.3 *caeco reluxit dies.*) In that case, we would be made the more aware that Hellenistic poetry forms a bridge between Homer (*Od.* 12.22 διϲθανέεϲ, ὅτε τ᾽ ἄλλοι ἅπαξ θνῄιϲκουϲ᾽ ἄνθρωποι) and the use of *bis* in passages like Virg. *Aen.* 6.133–5 *si tanta cupido est* | *bis Stygios innare lacus, bis nigra uidere* | *Tartara*, Ov. *Met.* 8.504–5 *bisque datam, primum partu, mox stipite rapto* | *redde animam*, fr. 7 Courtney (ascribed by Heinsius to Lucan) Eurydice *bis rapitur uixitque semel*. Cf. also Dosiadas, *Ara* 16–17 (Odysseus) φὼρ | δίζωιοϲ.

xvi.19 = 110.1 (new poem and section) εἴαροϲ ἡ Ζεφ[υρ (edd. pr.). We may imagine Ζεφ[ύρου, or more likely Ζεφ[υρῖτιϲ (cf. Posid. XII.7 = 116.7, XIII.3 = 119.3 (Valckenaer), Call. fr. 110.57 Pfeiffer, Cat. 66.57, [Opp.] *Cyn.* 4.75 Ζεφυρίτιϲιν αὔραιϲ), with αὔρα, perhaps at the end of the line (cf. also e.g. Aesch. *Ag.* 692 Ζεφύρου γίγαντοϲ αὔραι). It then seems plausible to suppose a specific allusion at Cat. 46.1–3 *iam uer egelidos refert tepores,* | *iam caeli furor aequinoctialis* | *iucundis Zephyri silescit auris.* Compare and contrast the less closely similar openings Hor. *C.* 4.12.1–2 *iam ueris comites, quae mare temperant,* | *impellunt animae lintea Thraciae* and Ov. *Tr.* 3.12.1 *frigora iam Zephyri minuunt.*

These connections are a forceful reminder of how complex and how important the Hellenistic background to Latin poetry is. Some of the passages provide a probable original for Latin passages. Others add a further probable or possible model where we might have thought we knew the source, or sources, already; this is particularly striking with the proem to *Georgics* 3, where a major model in Callimachus had only recently been discovered. Others show the kind of tradition that lies behind the Latin poetry, without more specific imitation being provable. In other cases the existence of any connection is only an interesting (I hope, interesting) possibility. More widely, we can see particular areas of subject-matter presenting themselves to Latin writers already marked out and cultivated by Hellenistic writers. And we realize even more strongly that what seem especially contemporary concerns of Latin poetry also have a Hellenistic literary context.

Two conclusions follow. First, the Hellenistic background to Latin literature is richer and more extensive than we can realize from extant evidence, and even more pervasive. It must be recalled that these are only 600 lines; there must have been much more even of Posidippus' own work. Any similar discovery would in turn enlarge our under-standing. Second, the relation of the Hellenistic background to specific passages is complicated. We cannot know more than a fraction of the material that lies behind particular passages, and even where we think our picture of the background is clear, there may be much more that we do not know. The isolation of specific models seems ever more difficult. One reasonable step is to favour intertextuality, to consider relations between passages without too much anxiety about the historical pro-cedures of writers. Another reasonable step, which complements rather than contradicts the first, is to realize how intricate a process read-ing these works would have been at the time (for the reader who could get the most from them). Engagement with a specific original, with a series of originals, with traditions and forms, is to be perceived by the reader. These reworkings are not merely a decorative addition to the basic line of poetic argument: they sharpen the presentation of that argument. It is notable that even where a specific link with Posidippus is clearest, the Latin poets can be seen (when the Greek itself is sufficiently visible) not tamely to echo him but to outdo, reverse, or drastically alter him, in a way that calls for the reader's thought.

II. ELEGY AND EPIGRAM

We turn now to consider wider questions about a particular genre in the light of the papyrus. The scene may be set with general remarks, one of which will be modified afterwards, on the thesis that Latin love-elegy is derived from subjective Hellenistic love-epigram, not object-ive Hellenistic elegy. This thesis, aimed at allowing Latin poets the originality of combination, suffers from many weaknesses. (1) The negative generalization that there was no first-person Hellenistic elegy on love is precarious in the extreme. As this papyrus indicates, we are in no position to assert what Hellenistic literature did not contain, and in fact papyrus finds in recent years make this particular gener-alization seem ever more doubtful.[15] (2) In any case, the distinction between subjective and objective, equated with a difference between first person and third person, seems less clear in the light of modern theory: a first-person narrator can be as ironically treated as a third-person character. (3) The distinction between elegy and epigram might also appear less important than is implied. How far back can we trace the distinction? Some of the epigrams here have 14 lines; is the difference in length between epigram and elegy always going to be more important than the difference between an elegy of 32 lines (the average length in Propertius Book 1) and one of 82 lines (the average length in Tibullus Book 1)?[16] (4) Latin elegy is in fact by no means confined to love-poetry spoken by a narrator formally

---

[15] Cf. Parsons (1988); Morelli (1994); Butrica (1996). A poem which seems to produce a strange and distorted version of love-poetry is particularly interesting in implying there is something to distort: cf. P. Brux. inv. E. 8934 + P. Sorb. inv. 2254 (ii BC) col. i.3–4 μνήϲονται ἀοιδαί ... ὥϲ τε πυρὶ φλέγομαι. (Cf. on the lines Huys (1991), 38–9; Watson (1991), 262; Hutchinson (1992), 484.) See of course Jacoby (1961 [orig. 1905]), for the initiation of the theory discussed.

[16] The unpublished papyrus of epigram incipits P. Vindob. G 40611 includes a poem of 40 lines, though far the commonest number is 4 (Harrauer (1981), 51; Parsons (2002), 118–20). Professor Parsons suggests that the poem may have been unusual, say a prologue.

identified with the author. Should we simply segregate most of Propertius Book 4 and most of Ovid's elegiac poetry from what we accept as the essence of Latin elegy?

Better, then, than seeking for origins would be to see the extant successors to Gallus as creating, in some of their books, a rich and compelling picture of their own genre, with the love of the authorial narrator as its central concern. This concern affects aesthetics and ideology. From the image of the genre they have themselves created the poets individually diverge in interesting directions. So the *Heroides* are love-poetry, but from the time of myth, with first-person speakers not identifiable with the author; Ovid's exile-poetry is poetry about experience of the author presented as real, but not about love.

Yet while one should continue to doubt the thesis as a whole, (3) must be reconsidered, not as a point about the origins of love-elegy but as a point relevant to reading the Latin poems. This papyrus throws new light on the distinctness of epigram. It shows us more clearly and extensively than any hitherto what looks like an early author's own careful arrangement of his epigrams.[17] The reader is invited to consider the handling of related material in consecutive poems. The parameters of length, and the predominance of poems under ten lines, mean that brevity is a salient characteristic. The arrangement, together with the writing itself, focuses attention on the small-scale artistry of the poet, continually renewed. The meta-poetic aspect of the poems on gems, if accepted, reinforces this point. Even if the arrangement is not by the poet, it is made early, and is highly elaborate. For example, xv.3–6 = 97 and 7–10 = 98 give adjacent poems on six-year illnesses, 11–14 = 99 and 15–18 = 100 adjacent poems on deafness and blindness.

We should, then, be encouraged to think of epigram as from its early stages onward a distinctive type of elegy, at least: distinctive for its particular interest in concision and for its relation, in many cases, to material objects. Callimachus' thematized interest in brevity and concision makes the epigram for him a particularly significant sub-genre (cf. *Ep.* 8 Pfeiffer, 28, 35, 52, *al.*). In the *Aetia*, especially Books 3 and 4,

---

[17] See above (second paragraph of article). On other evidence, before Meleager, see Argentieri (1998); Cameron (1993), 3–4, 32, on Mnasalces and P. Köln 204; ch. 1 n. 7. P. Oxy. 3725 and 4501–2, probably all by Nicarchus II, are of interest later; the papyri are probably close in date to the poet.

we see much intriguing interplay between these elegiac poems and the more circumscribed category of epigram: cf. frr. 35–8 Massimilla (statue of Diana), 110 (statue of Athena); fr. 64 Pfeiffer (tomb of Simonides; Simonides speaking, but poem avoids indicating that it is inscribed), 101–2 (statues of Hera), 110 (Lock of Berenice; dedication, but object, which speaks, has vanished into heaven); fr. 64 Massimilla (statues of Apollo; dialogue with statue). *SH* 254–69 *Victoria Berenices* now looks among other things like an enormous expansion and elevation of a poem like the ἱππικά (cf. also fr. 384.48–52 Pfeiffer). The first part of the prologue to the *Aetia*, especially if we stress its connection with the genre of elegy, makes this aspect the more interesting. That first part itself could be associated with epigrams on material objects: the books of this poem. Cf. *Ep.* 6 (*Oechaliae Halosis*), 27 (Aratus' *Phaenomena*), perhaps fr. 398 (epigram on Antimachus' *Lyde*).[18]

In Latin, Cat. 95–95*b*, an *epigram* on a short epic opposed to a vast epic, well illustrates the significance of the form. Horace's poems in *Satires* Book 1 are to be seen both as chatty and as shorter and more highly wrought than Lucilius' poems; he exhibits not only connections with but differences from epigram, by explicitly weaving epigrams of Callimachus and Philodemus into the last part of a satire early in the book (*Sat.* 1.2.105–110, 120–2; now note also Philodemus (?) P. Oxy. 3724 fr. 1 v.29 τὴν ἀπὸ παλλιόλου). The great difference in scale between his treatment of desire and theirs is clearly felt.

The elegists are much concerned with epigram, both in its connection with their works and in its difference. This concern is displayed in all sorts of ways. Often elegies recast epigrams on a particular theme, but in greatly expanded form (e.g. Ovid, *Amores* 1.13 on the lover at dawn, with obvious play, as often in the *Amores*, on the poet-narrator's futile volubility). Propertius inserts a translation of a whole epigram (Leon. Tar. XXIX) into the middle of one of the longest and most wide-ranging poems of the wide-ranging Book 3 (13.43–6).

[18] The reconstruction of Parsons (1977), 44–50, still seems the most plausible to me. In that case, the first part of the prologue is added with Books 3 and 4; the issues of brevity are thus thematized by the four-book version of the poem much more than by the two-book version. The connections of the prologue to the *Aetia* with elegy are strongly emphasized by Cameron (1995). Play with epigrams on statues in the *Iambi* too does not alter the special significance of play with epigram in the *Aetia*. Cf. Kassel (1991*b*); Massimilla on his fr. 64; Kerkhecker (1999), 182–4, 206–7.

The contrast in scale and scope is evident. Parts of poems read like inset epigrams: so Prop. 4.1.89–98 (deaths in battle after Horus' prediction; cf. Posid. v.6–11 = 28), 99–102 (successful delivery because of vow to Juno—advised by Horus; cf. Posidippus' ἰαματικά, Call. *Ep.* 53–4 Pfeiffer, etc.). The range and size of 4.1 is thus brought out. (The whole poem, as I take it to be, begins like an epigram.) Similarly, the small entries in Ovid's *Fasti* can often recall independent epigrams: cf. e.g. 4.625–8 with Posid. v.20–5 = 31, vi.30–7 = 39. In evoking small but self-contained poems they bring out the massiveness of this whole work.

Propertius Book 4, which explores the genre with particular breadth, plays with the alleged materiality of epigram: 4.2.57 and 11.36 depict these two poems themselves as inscribed on objects. More commonly elegy presents imagined inscriptions on objects: cf. Prop. 2.13.35–6, 14.25–8 (note also 2.28.43–4), 4.3.72, 7.83–6, Tib.1.3.53–6, 4.81–4, [3].2.27–30, Ov. *Am.* 1.11.27–8, 2.6.59–61, 13.25, *Her.* 2.73–4, 145–8, 5.27–30, 7.193–6, *AA* 2.743–4, 3.811–12, *Fast.* 3.549–50, *Tr.* 3.3.71–6.[19] These inscriptions are often called *carmen* or *uersūs*. They are commonly plainer, and even briefer, than Greek epigrams; they obviously contrast in size and manner with the enclosing poem. At the same time, as Prop. 2.13.35–6 illustrate (his own epitaph, on a tiny tomb), the brevity can also make a statement about the poet's work.

There are, then, two sides to the use of epigram. Elegy can officially emphasize its brevity, by contrast with its supposed antithesis, epic (cf. e.g. Prop. 3.3.5, 17–18). Connections with the smallest version of the genre, the epigram, can be seen as supporting this self-presentation. Of interest here, besides size, is the idea of small-scale refinement in writing (see above on the λιθικά). Post-Catullan elegy as a rule is strongly divided into elaborately organized couplets; this is part of its ethos of seductive 'softness' (note Hor. *Sat.* 1.4.8 *durus componere uersus*). Posidippus' epigrams, though often running over the couplet, bring out well how the form of epigram throws the artistry of the individual couplet into particular relief. But there is another side too: we have seen how Latin elegy uses its differences from epigram to convey its own ambition and scope. Even in style, Latin elegy is marked out, not only by small-scale polish but by the abundant elaboration of

---

[19] Such inscriptions occur far more rarely in epic (cf. Virg. *Aen.* 3.288, Ov. *Met.* 2.327–8, Luc. 8.793), where they do not have the same generic point.

points in accumulated couplets. One part of this is Propertius' and Ovid's amassing of mythological exempla, a feature which would seem to have been important in what looks like Hellenistic love-elegy.

One might object that elegy must conform to its own picture of itself, and to the supposed commandments of Callimachus. But (1) in the *Aetia* itself, the difference from epigram is also to be felt. In fr. 1 Massimilla itself, and throughout the *Aetia*, Callimachus parades an inventive fluency in developing a theme or a story; this is connected, in the *Aetia*, with the traditions of archaic and classical elegy. In structure, as Cameron has emphasized, the *Aetia* is an ambitious poem as well as one made up of small pieces; our views should not be too limited by Callimachus' own overt self-depiction.[20] (2) Even if the elegists' reading of Callimachus were simple-minded, their own statements about their work are far from simple. These are full of play and irony, and modesty about the author is scarcely to be taken at face-value. (In any case, the usual interpretation is not to take it at face-value, but to translate such passages into earnest statements of a creed.) Thus when in Propertius 3.3 the poet-narrator is told to keep his little chariot within its prescribed track (*gyros* 21), the reader should remember the poet has already left it (3.2.1–2, note *orbem*), and will go far beyond the sphere of love in the book as a whole. This makes it hard to take the passage as a profession of belief. (3) Callimachus is the foremost Greek elegist, but hardly the Latin elegists' Lenin. It is especially implausible that Ovid, who sees limitations in Callimachus' poetry (*Am.* 1.15.13–14) and everywhere shuns unquestioning belief, should be in awe of Callimachus' declarations. In general, it is perhaps better to look for stimulus and provocation in the elegists than for firm and sincere credos.[21] (4) The elegists, if we look at the whole *œuvre* of each, are restlessly innovative, and clearly

---

[20] Cameron (1995), 336–7, 342, 354–9. There are theoretical complications in the whole idea of brevity and concision, and in Cameron's points about it, which cannot be gone into here. If concision is merely to include nothing that does not contribute to the work, all good literature must be concise and the term ceases to have much meaning. Ancient discussion suggests some reflection on the concepts involved (cf. e.g. Cic. *Inv.* 1.28, Quint. *Inst.* 4.2.40–3). For the importance of concision to some ancient literary criticism of poetry cf. Philod. *Poem.* 5 col. vii.2–6 Mangoni.

[21] Each book of the elegists should be viewed as a separate entity, which presents ideas in its own manner. Even in Book 2 (or 2*a*?) of Propertius, which is most

keen to enlarge the scope of their work as they go on. The *Fasti*, particularly close to the *Aetia*, plays much on its own size and subject-matter; it professes to transcend the author's small-scale and unelevated earlier work, and even the limits of the genre (cf. e.g. 2.2–18, 125–6). All these points make it legitimate to see elegy as using epigram, the little version of the genre, as one means to complicate the oppositions which elegy itself propounds, and to display its aspirations.

Posidippus' book in fact reveals another aspect here, in regard to (4). The book, in which little poems are grouped into small entities by subject-matter, bears a real kinship both to the *Aetia* and to Latin elegy, where the juxtaposition and relation of poems is of great importance.[22] However, even though themes and concerns link different sections in Posidippus' book, its structure appears altogether less dynamic and full of meaning than the structure of Latin books of elegies. The *Fasti* is still more interesting here. On the one hand, it contrasts with the epic *Metamorphoses* in its lack of continuity. On the other, its material is organized into a vast and sub-divided chronological edifice; this contrasts strongly with the small spans of Posidippus' design, and no doubt (as the papyri suggest) of many others like it.[23]

The new find of Posidippus is not itself a central intertext for Latin poetry like the prologue to the *Aetia*; it is none the less of great interest to Latinists. Besides its specific connections, it provides a forceful reminder of our ignorance, of the problems and rewards of reading the texts in their literary context, and of the enormous importance of Hellenistic poetry to Latin poetry. This importance is frequently asserted (though often on the basis of a limited range of Hellenistic poetry); but it now seems to extend into even more aspects than had been realized. The find also prompts us to reconsider

---

forthright in its presentation of political questioning, it is clear how playfully brevity is handled in poem 1: *longas... Iliadas* (14) on love-battles with Cynthia (cf. Aeschin. 3.100), etc. (I take 15–16 to be genuine; otherwise Butrica (1997), 199–200.)

[22] More light will be thrown on the organization of *Aetia* 3 with the publication of new fragments of the *Diegeses* (P. Mil. Vogl. inv. 28b and 1006; see now Gallazzi and Lehnus (2001)).

[23] The question of whether the *Fasti* is meant to end with Book 6 may be left on one side (see Barchiesi (1997)). At any rate, the large structure is one which the poem affects to have until a late point, and is therefore still of literary importance.

one of the best-represented genres of Augustan poetry, elegy. It leads us, if the suggestions here are not quite mistaken, to a new under-standing of the genre, both in large conception and in the very style of its writing. So anyone interested in Latin poetry should hasten to explore this remarkable papyrus.

5

The Catullan Corpus, Greek Epigram,
and the Poetry of Objects*

I

The foremost aim of this article is to throw some light on a particularly difficult part of Catullus' corpus, poems 69–116, by following a line of thought about the relationship between Catullus and Greek epigram. This line of thought is also of significance for other parts of his work. It is presented in section II below. For it to possess its full force, a particular view of the corpus as a whole is required. This is argued for in section I. The argument should be of interest in its own right, not least because it brings fresh material into the discussion.[1]

Greek papyri offer an abundance of material on epigrams and on books which ought to be considered in pondering Catullus. On the one hand, the papyri encourage the ever-increasing interest in looking beyond the individual poem to larger units, and supply it with important background. The pair or group of poems, whether by one or several hands, is confirmed as an established entity with authors and

* I am most grateful to the following for their help over various points, publications, and documents: Professor D. Feeney, Dr N. Gonis, Mrs J. Hammond, Dr S. J. Harrison, Dr S. J. Heyworth, Professor N. Holzberg, Dr B. C. A. Morison, Dr D. Obbink, Professor P. J. Parsons. A piece for a volume on Catullus edited by I. C. Du Quesnay and A. J. Woodman will dwell on further aspects of the books here called *a* and *c*, especially as regards desire.
[1] For bibliography on the Catullan corpus, see Scherf (1996), adding esp. Beck (1995); Heyworth (1995), 131–3, and (2001); Thomson (1997), 7–10; Jocelyn (1999); Holzberg (2002); see also p. 64 n. 1. In general the very selective references in the footnotes are to recent work. Many of the papyri mentioned, and O of Catullus, have been examined at first hand.

readers, even in contexts far from professional publication. The new
papyrus of Posidippus (iii BC) shows us much more fully than before a
published book of epigrams by one author (probably). In it selected
poems form blocks of 6–20, by subject; but the author (probably) takes
care not to conjoin blocks in the same underlying category, especially
dedicatory and sepulchral. These two principles of cohesion and
variety are seen too, for example, in a papyrus usually thought to be
a selection from Meleager's *Garland* (P. Berol. 10571, *BKT* v.1.75–6,
i AD). All the epigrams are love-poems; three are a homosexual group
also found in this sequence as *AP* 12.76–8; two are consecutive poems
by Meleager, addressed to a recurring female, and a recurring male,
love of his narrator's. The context of the papyri confirms that the many
connections, sustained themes, and signs of arrangement in Catullus
should continue to be vigorously explored.[2]

On the other hand, the papyri bring out two grounds for insecurity about the nature and structure of Catullus' corpus: much of it
consists of small poems, and the whole consists of disparate bodies of
material. The first aspect is less important for this article. The papyri
suggest that collections of epigrams were easily modified. In principle, authors, later editors, and readers could omit from or add to
an existing collection, or compile their own selection from one
(a process which could leave signs of the original planning while
not leaving anything like the original book). The informality of many
of the papyri of epigram need not make them the less revealing of
readers' attitudes and activities. Though there is an important distinction between the very common personal versions and generally
circulated texts, it seems doubtful that generally circulated editions of

---

[2] On the nature of the collection of Posidippus, see pp. 7, 90–1, 209, 253–4. The
currency of pairs, etc., in papyri raises some doubts about the origins of P. Berol. 10571.
Cf. for groupings P. Oxy. 662 (i AD), written on the verso of a text of Pindar and
eventually abandoned. It includes three poems on the same dead woman, two on the
same man's dedication, by three poets, one obscure. In Cameron (1993), a masterly
work, the papyrus is thought an excerpt from Meleager's *Garland*, in the mistaken belief
that all the poems are funerary (11–12, 27). Cf. also *SH* 977 (iii BC), two poems on the
same dead dog sent as a letter to the owner, and P. Firmin-Didot (ii BC), two connected
epigrams by Posidippus in a very mixed-up papyrus (Weil (1879); D. J. Thompson
(1987)). P. Oxy. 15 (iii AD) and 1795 (i AD; Powell (1925), 199–200) offer a different sort
of author's collection: the same poet and meiouric metre, and an alphabetic sequence.
On books of epigrams, see Gutzwiller (1998); Argentieri (1998); Parsons (2002).

single epigrammatists were always of complete works; the concept of modification, and particular modifications, might matter widely. The do-it-yourself element was not remote from Catullus' Rome, as poem 14 shows: Calvus has had a mock-anthology made, not of little epigrams but of 'low-lights' from monster poems.[3]

No large-scale scepticism need be considered here: the general argument in II would not be drastically affected even if 1–60 and 65–116 or 69–116 were reductions of substantially larger original books. It may simply be noted that specific past ideas now acquire further credibility, and that design and alteration can be more readily combined. The end of the apparent unit 1–60, a suspicious point for interference, displays two consecutive poems (59 and 60) in the same non-hendecasyllabic metre, contrary to the patterns of 1–60. They seem unlikely to be complete poems, as they lack a point. Poem 59 in its short span contains a resolution, unusually for the iambics of 1–60 (only 37.5), and does not well suit the manner of the collection. Since 59–60 make sense and are of the same length, we might suspect not scribal accident, but deliberate activity by someone other than the author (and jottings among the poet's papers are not the only possibility).[4] Poem 52, in a type of iambic elsewhere excluded from 1–60, works much better if it belongs, as looks obvious, in 47 BC. In the

[3] Authorial change: see *SH* 701, where Aristarchus was able to think that Posidippus had omitted a poem from his collected epigrams. Cf. n. 9; and note the change in P. Oxy. 4502.18, 26. The process of producing a personal anthology or selection seems widespread and elaborate. It is seen already in P. Vindob. G 40611 (iii BC; Harrauer (1981)) and most likely P. Mil. 309 (marginalia: cf. Bastianini and Gallazzi (2001), 16). P. Vindob. G 40611, *SH* 976 (ostracon, ii BC) and P. Oxy. 3724 (i AD) seem to show at least two people involved in the preliminary stages of production. P. Vindob. G 40611 lists from a series of numbered books, whether a pre-existing series or numbered *ad hoc*; P. Oxy. 3724 lists mostly from one poet (Philodemus). In the latter, two poems, presumably from a different volume, are written out in full; one is by Asclepiades. See Cameron (1993), 379–87; Sider (1997), 203–5, 220–1. Selections omit companion pieces: so P. Oxy. 3725 (i–ii AD: private copy?) has Nicarch. (II) *AP* 11.241 without 242; P. Berol. 10571 (very small) has Meleag. XXXIV = *AP* 5.152 without XXXIII = *AP* 5.151. XXXIII certainly did not precede XXXIV in P. Oxy. 3324 (i BC–i AD). This papyrus contains only Meleager, in what looks a professional hand; Cameron (1993), 27, thinks it 'undoubtedly' an excerpt from Meleager's *Garland*.

[4] On length cf. Holzberg (2002), 99. Even if 51 were two poems, the postulated lacuna would make it a poor counter-example for two consecutive poems in the same metre. See also Heyworth (2001), 119. For wider suspicion of the last part of 1–60, see Skinner (1981), 72–6.

light of our discussion, it is natural to suppose 52 a later addition to the main collection 1–60, which emphatically and purposefully proclaims itself as belonging in around 55 or 54 BC; less natural to force the poem into that period, and to assume from the careful self-dating of this collection and of 69–116 that Catullus wrote poems only *c*.56–54 BC.[5] The possibility of omissions from the collection does not depend on the existence of references to lost poems; but it does not, for example, seem likely that Porphyrio, a commentator not an essayist, would casually misremember 40.2 *agit praecipitem in meos iambos* as *at non effugies meos iambos* (fr. 3 Mynors). Nor does the line fit poem 54. It would well suit the generic self-presentation of the collection 1–60.[6]

The second ground for insecurity is more important. *Œuvres* made up of different types of works might be diversely arranged. Theocritus' poems after the bucolic are diversely placed in the papyri (and MSS).[7] Callimachus' may seem the model of an *œuvre* arranged by the author (fr. 112.9 is popularly held to pass from *Aetia* to *Iambi*). Yet in a papyrus codex which apparently contained all Callimachus' poems (P. Oxy. 2258, vii AD) the *Lock* is immediately followed, not by the Epilogue and the *Iambi*, as in P. Oxy. 1011 (iv AD), but by the *Victoria Sosibii*. Less probably 2258 included, from the *Aetia*, only highlights: the *Lock* and the *Victoria Sosibii* are both poems on public

---

[5] Cf. A. A. Barrett (1972). (Ryan (1995), prefers 56.) *per* 'throughout' is another joke on Vatinius' short consulship, in late 47, cf. Macrob. *Sat.* 2.3.5. The unepigrammatic 'he swears a false oath by his consulship' (he is sure of it, so it is inevitable) gives a less effective parallel to line 2 or reason for demise. The poem would have been put in this position to go with 53; without it, 51 (one poem) separates two on Calvus. On an argument suggested by Professor Feeney, 52 could probably be dated later than 1: *unus* (1.5) would be falsified by Atticus' *Liber Annalis* (published by early 46).

[6] If the text is sound at Charisius *GLK* i. 97 (the context suggests it is), *pugillaria* is said to appear *saepius...in hendecsyllabis*, not just in 42.5. Some brief points on the chronology of the poems: 61 may well be *c*.59 BC (n. 14). Veranius and Fabullus' return from Spain is presumably not in 57–55 BC (Piso returns summer 55); 54 BC is conceivable (9.6–8 make tourism a possibility). Rambaud (1980) dates 29 to 53 or 52 BC. 79 is probably before 52 BC (death of Clodius). Death at the age of 29–30 would perhaps remain possible if Catullus is writing *c*.59–47 BC (Asinius Pollio in 12 would not be the orator); Jerome's dates are wrong anyway (Helm (1984), 150, 154).

[7] It is particularly interesting that the Antinoe papyrus (v–vi AD) places 22 after the aeolic poems. Cf. Gow (1950), i. lxvi–lxix, 257; Parsons (1983), 100, 127–8 (see Ioannidou (1996), pl. 38 for photograph of P. Berol. 21182); Gutzwiller (1996). There seem to have been two different arrangements of the books of Lucilius (cf. e.g. Charpin (1978–91), i. 34–5).

figures, and might go together. Either view of 2258—complete works differently arranged or newly-arranged selection from complete works—should make us wonder about Catullus' corpus. To unsettle us further, a different 'public' poem precedes the *Victoria Sosibii* in P. Oxy. 1793 (i AD).[8]

Even if the corpus was published (generally circulated) by Catullus, it is still likely to have united earlier and separate publications. Poem 1 refers only to one *libellus*. It is probably a reasonable assumption that the corpus is much too long for one book, even at this period of Latin literature (cf. Lucretius' books). When Pliny writes, in his quasi-preface to his hendecasyllabic poems, *cogitare me has meas nugas ita inscribere, 'Hendecasyllabi' (Ep.* 4.14.8), he seems to envisage Catullus 1 as referring to a comparable volume, not all his works.[9] Poem 1 certainly need not imply there will be three books in all, to contrast with Nepos' three. Such an idea would actually spoil the contrast between the one *libellus* and Nepos' three, and the suggested contrast in their temporal range: *omne aeuum* against a forceful concentration on a very few years. The poem thus announces the publication of some part of the corpus as a distinct entity.[10]

The corpus consists of three different parts; traces of these divisions seem to appear in the MSS and other Renaissance material. 52 is quoted as *prope finem primi operis*; less decisively, in O 61 starts a new page, after a five-line gap at the bottom of the page before, and with

---

[8] *Iambi* follow *Aetia* in the *Diegeses* too. 2258 also contains: *Hymns* 2, 4, 6; hypothesis to *Hecale*; *Victoria Berenices* (B fr. 2 front from *SH* 259, not mentioned in *SH*; I suggest the back may come from scholia to the poem: note ἰπ[4; for 10–11 cf. Posid. 74.13–14 AB); *Acontius*. Cameron (1995), 105 n. 5, gives a misleading impression of the contents. 2258 treats the beginning of the *Hecale* differently; but the scribe clearly realizes the *Sosibius* is a new poem. A different, but no more comforting, theory on fr. 112 (moved from the end of *Aetia* 2 by an editor): Knox (1993); Cameron (1995), 143–73.

[9] Cf. also Auson. I.4, XV *praef.* 1–16 Green. If *passerem* at Mart. 4.14.14 denotes a book (cf. e.g. Gratwick (1991)), then the book is more likely to be a small one. Cf. however Mart. 1.7 (again playing on size), with 7.14.3–6, Stat. *Silv.* 1.2.102. Catullus' corpus contains 2287 lines (1–60 848, 61–4 795, 65–8 325, 69–116 319). Authors and publications: Ovid says he has reduced the *Amores* from 5 books to 3; in my opinion, Horace originally published *Odes* 1 and 2 separately (ch. 6).

[10] Poem 64, unlike 1–60, embraces a vast span of time: the heroic and the post-heroic age. The role of Nepos' work in 1 has been much discussed: cf. recently e.g. B. K. Gibson (1995); Rauk (1996–7).

65 the first words of poems are treated differently.[11] The fixed *ordering* of these parts is unlikely to precede codices: without book-numbers, internal pointers, or visible chronological succession, one does not see how an order of rolls would be imposed on the reader.[12] The parts themselves have very differing claims to represent, in some form, an earlier book produced by the author. The part with the weakest claim is 61–4 (or 61–8*b*, if they are taken together); this can be seen if they are compared with 1–60. 1–60 (or some part of them) appear to have a preface which groups them together. The citations of Catullus *in hendecasyllabis* suggest a body of poems, as early as Sen. Rh. *Contr.* 7.4.7; the specification, which ought to have been useful, could reasonably be applied to a group of poems where hendecasyllables predominated. The tradition of Greek epigram allows for metrical excursions within a collection (cf. P. Köln 204 (ii BC)). By contrast, the metrical differences of 61–4 would make for a generically heterogeneous collection. 61–4 also have a much stronger claim to have been published as individual items. The virtual confinement of the aeolic base of the hendecasyllable to one form in 2–26, but not 27–60, suggests consecutive composition.[13] By contrast, Torquatus cannot have had to wait for the publication of the corpus to receive 61. And if he is L. Manlius Torquatus, the poem is probably substantially earlier even than the original publication of the collection 1–60.[14] 62 is quoted *in epithalamio*; it later led an

---

[11] *primi operis*: copy of Terence, London, B. L. Harl. 2525 11ʳ (Billanovich (1988), 38–9). On O see Ullman (1973), 96–102. The gap before 61 could be related to the distinct status of 61 (see below). Illuminated initials are added from 65 on (that of 65 itself blue, like those of 80 (and 2) and the unique paragraphos of 31, the rest red; the whole first word is placed differently from before). The treatment may be connected with the irregular ink decoration of first and last initials of pages beginning two pages *before* 65. The initials themselves seem not to have been based on a good source: there are revealing errors and omissions with proper names in 89, 92, 100. One should be cautious, then, in making inferences about the tradition from these features in O. None the less, their location is striking.

[12] Catullus is never quoted by book-number in antiquity; this is hardly surprising with so disparate a corpus (cf. Vell. 2.36.2). Galen has to write a separate work on the order to read his books in (*Ord. Libr. Propr., Script. Min.* ii. 80–90 Müller).

[13] Cf. Skutsch (1969), 38–40. The poems after 26 with only spondaic base show that the arrangement is not due to an editor's principle.

[14] Torquatus was probably praetor in 50 or 49 (cf. Broughton and Patterson (1951–86), iii. 136; Shackleton Bailey (1996), 43); *c*.55 would be too late for his first marriage (cf. lines 119–41). On him see Berry (1996), 17–20.

independent life, anthologized as *Epithalamium Catulli*. At the end of 61 in O is written *explicit Epithalamium* (no other poems receive an *explicit* in OGR).[15] The epithalamia of Calvus and Ticida are referred to by grammarians and scholiasts as distinct poems. So are the small epics of Calvus, Cinna, Cornificius; Cat. 95 describes Cinna's *Smyrna* as a distinct book. It would be natural so to regard the dense and monumental 64. The eagerly awaited *Magna Mater* of Caecilius (35) sounds rather like the virtuoso 63.[16]

The theme of marriage connects 61, 62, and 64; but since the Neoterics were in any case keen on writing and toying with epithalamia, this is not a particularly strong argument for combining the poems into an authorial book. Nor is resemblance between parts of, say, 63 and 64: different plays of Sophocles or episodes in different works of Ovid may also have much in common. One can see why a collected or selected works might place the poems together, and, when the parts were given their present order, place them at this point. If, as will be argued, the long elegiac poems already belonged in front of 69–116, it would have been natural to place the other long poems next to them. As for the ordering of the other two parts of the corpus, 1 would have seemed an apt beginning, and the epigrams a natural coda. The present sequence of 61–4 could in fact be understood as simultaneous with the larger ordering: 61 next to the 'polymetrics', 62 after it to make a pair, 63 to complete the non-dactylic metres, 64 to make a pair of narratives, and precede the dactylic elegiacs.[17]

---

[15] It is written as if it were another line of verse, but with two lines to show the place for a paragraphos.

[16] Often seen as an exceptional poem in the corpus, cf. e.g. Braund (2002), 253. At Terent. Maur. 2899–900 *ipse* implies 63 is a *liber* (identified by first line); this may mean only *libellus*, as used by Statius of poems in the *Silvae*, but it shows 63 still thought of as a distinct work, not just one in a run of poems. As to small epics, the *Smyrna* received its own commentary (Suet. *GR* 18.2); Cato's *Lydia*, a single poem (Suet. *GR* 11.2), is described as a book by Tic. *FRP* 103. The *absence* of references to 64 as a separate poem would show only that it was not circulating alone in Nonius' or Macrobius' time; but possibly it was unclear how to refer to the poem. Cf. Scherf (1996), 39. On the date of 64: line 37 would suit but does not demand a date after Pharsalus. It was a novel locale for the wedding (Heslin (1997), 591), but a standard place for Peleus (Pherecyd. fr. 1 Fowler, etc.).

[17] On the placing of the long poems in the middle cf. Beck (1995), 289–90. Epigrams put last in lists of works: *Suda* μ 24 (Marianus' *Metaphrasis* of Callimachus); θ 166, and K of Theocritus (but his *Epigrams* are a complicated case). It is noteworthy that arguments on the theme of marriage have also been used to unite

The two parts 1–60 and 65 or 69–116 look much more like original books, as we have seen in regard to 1–60. The notion that they are simply or largely posthumous collections of privately circulated individual items or groups of items is excluded: by poem 1; by references to readers who sound like the general public (14*b*), and to the permanence of the writing (78*b*);[18] and by defences of the poems (104, 116, cf. 102). The groups of poems are often not straightforward groups which might be privately circulated, but arrangements in which connected poems are separated by another (cf. 2*b*?, 6, 17, 22, 38, 42, 70, 71, 108): this combination of connection and variety implies a book. The reason for the attacks on Rufus and Gellius (love) is kept for the last or penultimate poem on each in a way that implies consecutive reading.[19] Of course, previous limited circulation of particular items is compatible with later incorporation in a book by Catullus himself; but even this notion of two stages should not be too casually assumed. The metrical practice of 2–26 (above) makes against it; so too do the pseudonyms *Lesbia* and *Mentula*. They must mask or affect to mask the identity of individuals; the device should imply, at least in the case of Lesbia, readers unfamiliar with Catullus' life. Since Mentula is probably unmasked by the contemporary 1–60, the purpose will hardly be literal concealment within a social group, but rather play with concealment from the public.[20]

61–8*b* (see esp. Wiseman (1969), 20–5; Most (1981), 118–20, 124). For the Neoterics and epithalamia, cf. Lyne (2007*a*), 69–70, and the play in Cat. 6 (cf. 61.107–12, Tic. *FRP* 102; Prop. 2.15.1–2, Juv. 9.77–8). Relevant to the tradition behind 64 is Agamestor *SH* 14, an elegiac Θέτιδος Ἐπιθαλάμιος, with narrative. The inset epithalamium of 64 is marked out in G; cf. also 64.86–93. 1–61 would make a strange book by Catullus, esp. with 1 as prologue (Jocelyn (1999), 341, rather prefers an editor). And it would be too fortunate a coincidence that 61 should happen to be at the end of the book, where 62 could follow it.

[18] Cf. perhaps Suet. *Jul.* 73.
[19] Cf. Nappa (1999), 273–4.
[20] For a more positive approach to private circulation see Citroni (1995), chs. 3 and 4. Poem 79 seems to confirm that *Lesbia* is to be read as a pseudonym: cf. in 69–116 the brother–sister pairs Aufillenus, -a, Quintius, -a (Neudling (1955), 154), and *Rufa Rufulum* in 59. Otherwise, Holzberg (2000), 39–41. Ovid was presumably right that Ticida's Perilla was a pseudonym (*Tr.* 2.437–8). I have found no instance of the name Perillus in Latin inscriptions (not in <http://www.manfredclauss.de> accessed 30 Nov. 2007) or of the feminine anywhere; the pseudonym will be taken over by Ovid in *Tristia* 3.7.

Any idea that 1–60 and 65 or 69–116 were mingled in one original book seems excluded by their careful separations: no mention of Bithynian service in the latter or the brother's death in the former.[21] Each has its own recurring figures; the connecting ones are confined to: Catullus; Lesbia, Iuventius; Cinna, Calvus; Caelius; Pompey, Caesar (Mamurra/Mentula apart). The same points look like further grounds for seeing the collections as representing original books. If Catullus did not by accident use only the metres of 1–60 to write about Veranius and Fabullus or Bithynian service, then the poems about them scattered through 1–60 probably indicate that the original book is not represented only by the first few poems.

However, while the claim of 1–60 to represent an original book is particularly strong, the end of that book is much less clearly defined than for the elegiac poems. There 116, and other poems late in the series, affect to defend the poems themselves. The final poem, like the first elegiac poem (65), refers to giving a poem or poems by Callimachus (*mitto… carmina Battiadae* 65.16, *carmina uti possem mittere* (*uertere* Palmer) *Battiadae* 116.2). This forms a ring so palpable and significant as to indicate both that 116 is the end of the book and that 65 is the beginning. (69–116, unless a reduction, would be a short book of poems.) There is much point in opening and closing with allusion to the most celebrated author of elegy (Quint. *Inst.* 10.1.58, etc.). The epigrams proper virtually begin with an imitation of Callimachus (70); it would also be elegant that the book should *begin* from the *last* poem of the *Aetia*. Hellenistic books of epigrams can include longer poems, especially at beginning and end; this book seems to take the idea further. Its two parts lay claim to a full range, in this metre, of Callimachean talent.[22]

[21] See Holzberg (2002), 152. Lesbia's adultery is probably not mentioned in 1–60; for 11.17 cf. Hor. *C.* 1.25.9, with Nisbet–Hubbard.

[22] In the light of 70, the point in 116 would be that rendering Callimachus in Latin is natural to Catullus, not that the epigrams are un-Callimachean (and cf. e.g. 99 with Call. VIII = 42 Pfeiffer). The link does also mark a contrast within the book between 66 and the epigrams. Cf. Macleod (1983*a*). Callimachus' pre-eminence in elegy includes epigram: cf. Mart. 4.23.4, and note the implicit inclusion of epigram within elegy at 10.4.10. For all their allusions to Callimachus, Latin poets refer to him by name only in elegiacs or when elegy is referred to, save at Stat. *Silv.* 5.3.153–4 and Terent. Maur. 1886, 2941 (*GLK* vi. 381, 412). On 65 cf. Hunter (1993*a*). For longer poems in books of epigrams: Posidippus' sphragis *SH* 705 = 118 AB (wooden tablets, i AD); *SH* 976 (iii AD), elegy on marriage of Arsinoe (II?), 24 lines at least, part of a book of 'mixed epigrams' (title), by or including Posidippus; poem of 40 lines in the Vienna papyrus (poems of 14 lines Posid. 19, 74, 78 AB); Meleag. I.

It remains possible that 68*a* is a subsequent addition to the book. Lines in 68*a* pre-empt the powerful and unexpected passage of 68*b* on Catullus' brother, in a way that seems hard to parallel or, in my opinion, justify (68*a*.22–4 = 68*b*.94–6). 68*a* also has a notably different rate of elision—as an average, one in 52.5% of lines—from 65 (25%), 66 (37.2%, or less), 67 (29.2%), and 68*b* (35%). Since it seems addressed to a different person from 68*b*, it does not have an obvious connection with that poem. It could be thought not to suit the air of artistic display in 65–6, 67, 68*b*, nor their function of introducing, after a Callimachean opening, major aspects of the epigrams.[23]

The argument so far has contended that the Catullan corpus offers us, in at least somewhat distorted form, two books which we can have reasonable confidence were designed by the author: 1–60 and 65–116. In what follows, these books, or the extant versions of them, will be referred to as *a* (1–60) and *c* (65–116); the two halves of *c*, 65–68*b* and 69–116, will be referred to as *c*1 and *c*2. It follows from what has been said that we should be considering two sets of contrasts, one between *c*1 and *c*2, and one between *a* and *c*. Comparisons between any of Catullus' works are of course legitimate; but here they seem to be called for by the books themselves. Contrasts between *c*1 and *c*2 are invited by the very nature and structure of *c*. *a* and *c* present themselves as books to be confronted. They advertise that they concern the same narrow range of time (cf. 113!); key figures and themes connect them. The comparison will be particularly between *a* and *c*2: these are the two groups of short poems; it is here that we find the most obvious links (including the name of Lesbia).[24]

One basic aspect of these contrasts needs to be mentioned at once: that of metre. *c* appears to create a marked difference between its two halves in the rate of elision. In *c*1 there is one elision in 36.3% of lines (34.8% without 68*a*); in *c*2, one in 68.7%. If *c*1 and *c*2 are to be contemplated together, this difference is bound to strike the reader. The rate in *a*, 46.8%, comes in between (when allowance is made for the mostly shorter lines, *a* is probably closer to *c*2). This suggests that the general difference in rate has more to do with displaying a

[23] Cf. Hutchinson (1988), 314 n. 75. The repetition of 68*a*.22–4 is not akin to the repetition of a line or less between connected poems, cf. e.g. 23.1, 24.5, 10, Philod. XVII = 4.4 Sider, XVIII = 5.4.

[24] On contrasts between *a* and *c* cf. Solodow (1989).

difference in style, and stylistic level, than with emotion or uncouth epigrammatic tradition. *c2* likewise has notably fewer of the imposing *spondeiazontes* so common in 64 (29; *c1* has eight, in 65–6 and 68*b*): it has three, one expressive (76.15), two humorous (100.1 Veronese name, 116.3 parody of Ennius).[25]

It is important to realize, however, that *c2*, for all this paraded difference of manner, is not metrically less artistic than *c1*: it essentially follows the same norms as Catullus' other dactylic poetry. Though Hermann's Bridge is violated three times in *c2* and only once in *c1*, the more important point is that it is generally observed even in *c2*. *c2* like the rest of Catullus avoids ending hexameters with more than three syllables (save in *spondeiazontes* and Greek words); 97.5 *sesquipedalis* is a humorous exception, but there are actually more exceptions in 62 (8) and 64 (114, 152, 205 (archaic?)). Slight monosyllables at the end of the hexameter occur much more often in *c1* (66.63, 91, 67.43, 68*a*.33; 107.5). A weak caesura in the fourth foot is always accompanied in *c2* by a strong caesura in the second and fourth (13 times); in *c1* and 62 and 64 Catullus is less strict (*c1*: five out of 16 cases of weak caesura do not conform; 62: one out of ten; 64: eight out of 37).[26]

[25] Name: Syme (1991), 484. Figures for metrical features have been worked out afresh, with a text similar to Goold's. The prodelision of finite parts of *esse* is not counted as elision. It seems unlikely that Neoteric epigram was compelled to continue an unsophisticated Latin tradition (cf. Ross (1969), 160); nor do the exiguous remains of other Neoteric epigram accord. Emotion (cf. D. A. West (1957), 102) would not work as a general explanation. Further on informality: the huge sentence that comprises the first poem in *c1* among other things serves the role of stylistic differentiation. *atque* + consonant occurs once in *c1*, 3 times in *c2*; 8 in *a* (0.9% of lines, as in *c2*), never in 61–4. Probably informal too are, at the caesura of the pentameter, the commoner elisions (*c1* 4, *c2* 8), and the placing of a prepositive (76.18, 87.4, 111.2); the former feature Callimachus confines to his *Epigrams*, beyond τ' and the very common δ' (VIII.6 = 42.6 Pfeiffer, XII.6 = 30.6).

[26] Again, Catullus, like Virgil, prefers an elision before *et, ac*, etc., at the caesura of the hexameter (64.224, 67.35, 77.1, 90.3, 107.5, cf. 63.68); it is at 62.58, 64.229 that he foregoes this nicety. Hermann's Bridge breached (e.g. *aranea telam* |): 68*b*.49; 76.1, 101.1 (both prominent positions in prominent poems), 84.5 (a textually problematic passage: cf. Nisbet (1995), 97–8, 349; Harrison and Heyworth (1998), 106–7). 73.5 *nec acerbius urget* is not an instance. Different parts of authors behave differently here; thus Lucretius, often thought cavalier, has very few violations in Book 1. For this and other features, see Birt (1876), 25–6; Munro (1878), 152–3; Meyer (1884), 1040, 1076; D. A. West (1957); Zicàri (1964); Cupaiuolo (1965); Ross (1969), 115–31; Duhigg (1971); Scherf (1996), 86–90.

The fundamental division between *a* and *c* in metre is immediately visible. It is reinforced by the explicit references to Callimachus, the exemplar of elegy, in *c* (see above) and by frequent explicit references to metre in *a* (12.10, 36.5, 40.2, 42.1, 54.6). These latter commonly imply, by a convention internal to *a*, that *iambi* or *hendecasyllabi* (the terms overlap) are the medium generally expected from the poet of this book. The overlap confirms that *a* has its own metrical cohesion: the basic hendecasyllables probably connect both to the single-short (iambic) and to the aeolic metres. The metrical character of *a* serves to separate it firmly both from *c2* and from an ordinary book of Hellenistic epigrams. These metres were probably popular with other Neoteric poets; there is some sign of them in Hellenistic literature, and epigrams were sometimes composed in metres other than elegiacs. But it seems reasonable to suppose that a book with no elegiacs would not have struck a contemporary Greek reader as a normal book of epigrams, or probably as a book of epigrams at all. We thus seem to see in *a* and *c2* a different relationship with Greek epigrammatic tradition.[27]

A difference in stylistic tendency accompanies the metrical separation of the two series of short poems; it is much less relevant to *c1*. *c2* cultivates compression and the densely wrought couplet. *a* likes to accumulate exuberantly; its numerous repetitions, refrains and rings make part of a less constricted artistry. 39 (Egnatius' teeth) comes unusually close to *c2*'s territory (cf. 80, Gellius' lips); but the long delay of the revelation, the expressively recurring *renidet ille*, the piling up of ethnicities, give the poem a very different spirit. The relatively ample 99 comes close to *a* in subject (kisses) and especially form (beginning takes up end);[28] but the neat reversal of the opening (13–16), and the clogged mock-intensity of the narrative, result in a quite different impact.

---

[27] Even choliambics are found in the Neoterics (Cinna *FRP* 12); for Greek epigram cf. Aeschr. I (ἰαμβεῖα Athenaeus); Theocr. XIII (Hipponax). Relation of metres: one ancient analysis of the hendecasyllable sees the last seven syllables as iambic (Hephaest. 32, pp. 32–3 Consbruch, with scholia p. 143; Atil. Fort. *GLK* vi. 293). On the metres of *a*: Gow on Theocr. *Ep.* 17; Loomis (1972); J. K. Newman (1990), ch. 2; Kassel (1991*a*); Fuhrer (1994); Batinski and Clarke (1996); Jocelyn (1999), 336–41; Heyworth (2001); Holzberg (2002), 44–9.

[28] Cf. also Posid. 21.1, 6 AB.

II

It is apparent, then, that *a* and *c*2 both have a crucial, but different, relationship with Greek epigram. In some areas, their connection with Greek epigram is similar. Both have groups or series of poems to named lovers. These have links with Latin poetry too, but Hellenistic epigram is clearly an important model, both for the series themselves and for the combination of heterosexual and homosexual. Epigram is also one source for the abundant use of the poet's own name (seen also in *c*1, including 68*a*). It has a special force in *a* and *c*2, where the use of *Lesbia* (= Sappho) brings the narrator and his most unusual character almost on to a level—both characters, both 'poets'. But, in a particularly interesting and important area, *a* and *c*2 diverge in their use of Greek epigram. This area is the employment of physical objects or things. As the new Posidippus brings out vividly, objects have an especially prominent role in epigram, which often notionally concerns itself with something dedicated, or a tomb, or an object described. A brief survey may illustrate the treatment of objects in *a*; some particular Greek epigrams will be referred to, where not mentioned in commentaries and the like.[29]

Poem 1 plays on dedication (to a person, not a god); the physical book is conjured up.[30] In 2 and 3 the sparrow is described, in connection with love, and lamented; the parallels are well known, but the bird is made particularly bird-like, and the boundaries between thing and person explored.[31] 4 presents a crucial event for the book (Catullus'

---

[29] The later discussion of *c* will include material found in standard works. Several 3rd-cent. epigrammatists insert their own names (Cat. 13.7–8 surely evoke Leon. Tar. XXXVII.1–2); the usage is then conspicuous in Meleager, Philodemus, Crinagoras (Philod. VI.5 = 10.5 Sider, XXII.5 = 28.3, P. Oxy. 3724 col. ii.12, 15; one of Philodemus' loves is given the linked name Demo). Caesar's *Commentarii* may perhaps be relevant too. *Lesbia* chiefly shows cultural attainment, cf. 35.16–17, Prop. 2.3.21–2 (ἡ Λεσβία for Sappho e.g. Gal. *Protr.* 8.2 (*CMG* v.1.1 p. 126 Barigazzi)); a different approach: Holzberg (2000) and (2002), 33–9.

[30] The play on dedication is more marked in Catullus than in Meleag. I.1–4. (Gratwick (2002) like others expels the Muse.)

[31] Note also perhaps the birds in Posid. 21–35 AB. If there is an anatomical level too, that adds to the complication; but it would remain interesting that such obliqueness could hardly be imagined in *c*2.

return from Bithynia) through an object, a yacht.[32] The poem plays with epigrammatic categories (no dedication in the past (22–4); the yacht dedicates itself (26–7); it speaks, but through elaborate *oratio obliqua*). The yacht dwells on its own beginnings as a thing, evoking, like Call. XLV = 17.1 Pfeiffer, the beginning of tragedies on Medea.[33] 6, in developing epigrams where love is revealed, gives more weight than they to the evidence of things, in this case a bed and pillow, which are personified.[34] 12 concerns a gift, received rather than presented by the narrator; the thanks are conveyed obliquely by complaining of theft. Theft is a theme sometimes found in epigram (Theodorid. I, Antip. Sid. XIX, cf. Posid. 29 AB), and important in *a*. (In the commonest form of *furtum*, a *person* takes a *thing* from a *person*.) 13, an invitation, plays on the presence and absence of things, and the turning of a person into part of his body (the nose).

14 twists the sending of a present (Crinag. III, IV, V; books VII, XI) by repudiating a gift and threatening retaliation.[35] 17, a poem insulting a cuckold, begins unexpectedly from an old bridge, described graphically and with some personification; Antag. II celebrates a new bridge. 22 is not on a particular book, a common theme of epigram, but on the numerous books of a prolific and dreadful poet; the physicality of the books is prominent. 25 shows us a different thief, of objects including those which 12 treated. 31 presents the narrator's return from Bithynia; it concentrates on a place, not considering its past (cf. for example Antip. Sid. LIX) but portraying the elegant (12) beauty of this slender needle of land.[36] 36 presents a mock-dedication, addresses a collection of books, with abusive physicality, and presents a prayer to Venus (cf. Posid. VIII = 139 AB). 39 creates an insult from white teeth (effectively placed in the scazon); see above and below. 42, on a theft, turns poetry into things (writing-tablets) and people (the gang of hendecasyllables). Poems, like other objects, talk about themselves in epigrams

---

[32] Courtney (1996–7) favours a different view.

[33] Eur. *Med.* 1–6; Enn. *Trag.* 103 Jocelyn (the testimonia show the fame of the passage in Catullus' time).

[34] On the tradition of such poems see Cairns (1970).

[35] The idea of giving is at least less emphasized in Lucill. *AP* 11.135–6 (Syndikus (1984–90), i. 135).

[36] The property of the family (*ero* 12); cf. Wiseman (1987). For the final *salue*, cf. both Macedon. III (addressing the physical earth of places) and Virg. *G.* 2.173–6 (personifying and deifying).

(for example Call. LV = 6 Pfeiffer); but here the poetry of this book and of this poem is given words by the narrator to yell. 43 addresses a woman, with *salue*; but χαῖρε would not normally in epigram be addressed to a living individual. Both a god—in parody—and a thing are suggested. (See further below.)[37] 44, to a thing, the narrator's farm, parodies not just hymns but poems giving thanks for healing, as the new Posidippus makes clear (95–101 AB). The remaining poems have numerous connections with epigrams, but not so much in the areas that concern us.[38]

a, then, makes abundant use of epigrams on objects in poems which are not normal epigrams; the poems in *c*2 have the form of epigrams, but in general appear to make little use of this fundamental epigrammatic interest. Where *a* found fresh ways to emphasize objects, *c* excludes them. So 89, on signs of love like 6, omits the physical evidence. The second half of 76, using ἰαματικά metaphorically like 44, addresses the gods, not a thing. Theft is not of actual objects but of happiness, the beloved, kisses: 77, 82, and 99, which is all on punishment.[39]

The apparently slight use of Greek epigrams on objects in *c*2 is the more noteworthy because the long elegies of *c*1 use them extensively. 65 presents the gift of a poem (cf. Crinag. XI (Callimachus); Cinna *FRP* 13 (Aratus)). 66 translates a poem spoken by a dedicated object, now catasterized (Callimachus himself is extending epigram here). 67 consists of a dialogue with an object; one may compare for example Nicias I, Posid. XIX = 142 AB, Theodorid. V, Antip. Sid. XX, XXXI. The expansion of dialogue epigram is seen, for example, in the new inscription from Salmacis (*SGO* 01/12/02, ii BC).[40] 68*a* declines the

---

[37] Note Crat. 359 Kassel–Austin (scolion (?) to Pan), Hephaestion's example of hendecasyllables.

[38] So 46 presents the crucial return from Bithynia more directly than before, but in strongly epigrammatic form; add to the commentaries, etc., and Hezel (1932), 22–6, Philod. XIX = 34 Sider, Crinag. XXXII, Alph. I, Posid. 110.1 AB (cf. ch. 4, 100–1; Bernsdorff (2002)).

[39] Cf. with 76.17–26 esp. Posid. 101 AB. On sickness in 76: Booth (1997); Heyworth (1995), 133–6, argues powerfully that 76 is two poems. In my opinion, one should not lose the potent movement from the illogicality of desperation (16) to anguished prayer, or the expressive prolongation of a poem which, like the passion, refuses to close. The poem comes soon after *c*1, so the length has special point; but it separates itself from *c*1 by a particularly high number of elisions.

[40] Isager (1998); Isager and Pedersen (2004); Lloyd-Jones (2005*a*).

giving of a poem. In 68*b* sepulchral epigram is momentously exploited (87–100).[41] The foreign and inglorious tomb itself forms the culmination (97–100); the idea of burial has been broadened to include the destruction in the Trojan War and the ruin of Catullus' house (itself a theme of sepulchral epigram, cf. Call. XXXII = 20 Pfeiffer). Much less is contributed to *c*2 by such types of epigrams on objects; yet the instances in *c*1 remain important, as will be seen later, for the development of the whole book.

Poems on books—a special class—and on tombs have some place in *c*2 (especially 95, 101), and connect with *c*1. But the main debts of *c*2 to epigram appear to be debts to the epigram of love and the epigram of insult. The epigram of insult is significant for *a* too, but to a much more limited extent. It is less refined in register than ordinary epigrams (not therefore less artistic). In Greek it becomes clearly visible with Lucillius and Nicarchus II (AD i); but the earlier existence of the type is indicated by the close relation of Cat. 97 to Nicarch. *AP* 11.241 and 242 (241 also now found in P. Oxy. 3725, AD i–ii, close to the poet in time). The papyri indicate that whole books of such poems were circulating and popular.[42] Erotic and scoptic epigram come together in *c*2. Some of the main victims have injured the narrator in love—hence a dramatized sense of hatred behind the insults; and much of the behaviour assailed is sexual. The narrator's love-life contrasts with, but also shades into, the disgraceful world of the epigrams of scandal and abuse. 66, 67, and 68*b* prepare the way, with their sequence of loving and respectable—if notionally

---

[41] The lines follow on from the epigrammatic theme, shared with poem 66, of knowledge or ignorance about return or failure to return from war (85–6); cf. Posid. 32–3 AB.

[42] P. Oxy. 3725 and 4501–2 (i AD?) are in informal hands; they may have been private copies (Parsons (1999), 38–9). Scoptic poems do not attack classes (Cameron (1993), 15), but mock fictional individuals; the papyrus headings confirm: 'on an adulterer', haranguing the cuckold (with the opening πι]ϲτεύειϲ cf. Cat. 15.1); 'on an old man marrying a girl' (cf. Cat. 17). Cf. Hezel (1932), 39–48; Robert (1967); Burnikel (1980). Meleager and Philip probably eschewed such material. Antecedents include prose 'joke-books' of colourful insults (cf. P. Heid. 190 (iii BC)) and anecdotal joke-books, leading to the verse of Machon (iii BC). Note also the obscene mock-sepulchral epigram *SH* 975 (ostracon, ii BC). In Latin Lucilius' use of Granius may be relevant (11.15 Charpin, Cic. *Brut.* 172, etc.). Contemporary material includes: books of witticisms, some with narrative (cf. Kaster on Suet. *GR* 21.4); Calvus' epigrams against Caesar (Suet. *Jul.* 73; cf. the *spoken* mot of Curio, *Jul.* 52.3, with C. Edwards (1993), 91–2); Cic. *QF* 2.3.2.

incestuous!—marriage in Alexandria (66), shocking goings-on in Brixia (67), and something in between from the narrator (68*b*). The use of objects in *c2* is linked in, it will be seen, to the peculiar world and themes of its poems.

One special class of objects predominates in the scurrilous *c2*: parts of a person's body. The boundaries between people and things are transgressed and confounded in a particular and demeaning way: a part of someone's body becomes a distinct thing to contemplate, or even generates a creature, or becomes the whole to which a person is reduced. This has not happened to any great degree in *a*, though one could point to 39, and could perhaps argue that in 43 it is as if the woman were an assemblage of things, of parts of the body.[43] But the first main poem in *c* far more remarkably makes its speaker what has been a part of Berenice's body, and still longs to return there. This prepares strongly for the relation of people and parts of the body in *c2*, though without the degradation characteristic there. The close of *c* gives the central role to a person formally identified with his own penis (114, 115, resuming 94, 105). The man and his *mentula* (29.13) have appeared in *a*, but now he has been renamed and metamorphosed. The first poem on him, 94, plays on the apparent nonsense of the linguistic transformation ('*moechatur MENTVLA?*'). The last, 115, denies that he is a person at all (*non homo sed uero mentula magna minax*, 7). The basic, colloquial, form was a staple of the joke-book ('you have not a face *or* head, but ...', P. Heid. 190 cols. ii, iv, v). Catullus' version draws in Ennius and plays elaborately on reality and size.[44]

The first poem of *c2*, far from turning an animal into a person, like the first poem of *a* after the prologue, conjures up an animal from a person: the goat in Rufus' armpits, which reappears in 71. The basic connection probably appeared in abusive epigram; Lucill. *AP* 11.240 (cf. 239) goes near to implying that a foul-smelling woman is a goat. But Catullus has much more fun with the reality and independent existence of his goat.[45]

---

[43] This parodies the division of the body in unsophisticated desire (cf. Philod. XII = 12 Sider). Note also 13.14 (above); cf. *AP* 11.203, and Gogol's '*Nos*' ('The Nose'), where part of a body becomes a person.

[44] Enn. fr. 620 Skutsch (authorship not attested). Antip. Thess. XCIX treats the unusual size of a penis. Personification of the penis is common, notably in contexts of impotence, e.g. Strato *AP* 12.216 = 59 Floridi; Adams (1982), 29–30.

[45] 8 *nec quicum bella puella cubet* recalls Hom. *Od.* 4.441–3 (the husband of Helen on smelly seals). Nicholson (1996–7), 254, rightly stresses the goat's rusticity.

Fears of the brute cannot be overcome *perluciduli deliciis lapidis* (69.4); the phrase glances at, and puts aside, a type of object which now seems to have been conspicuous in the more normal epigram of things: the λιθικά begin the roll of Posidippus.

Poem 97 seems to show Catullus enlarging possibilities from Greek epigram in treating the body-part as object for description. Nicarch. *AP* 11.241 (cf. P. Oxy. 3725 fr. 1 col. ii.9–13), 242, 415 offer the basic confusion of ill-smelling mouth and bottom (which is which?). A similar confusion—red face and bottom—appears in a joke-book (P. Heid. 190.75). Rhianus I reports a conversation with a personified beautiful bottom. For Catullus the smell is merely the starting-point; he develops a grotesque and hyperbolic picture of Aemilius' mouth, deploying the huge (*dentis sesquipedalis*, 5, see above), the rustic (dialect *ploxeni*, 6, cf. 7–8), and the animal (*mulae cunnus*, 8: the confusion of body-parts thus returns on a different level). Poem 39 has nothing like this.[46]

The mouth and what it contains are much the most important area of the body in *c*2. The connections are twofold: with sexual activity and with speech. As for the first, at 88.7–8 the sexual use of the mouth forms a comic extreme in the poem on Gellius' depravity: the poem ends with an act of figurative self-devouring.[47] 97 (above) ends with another mouth and a humiliating obscenity: any woman who touched him (the verb contrasts with what follows) could *aegroti culum lingere carnificis*. 97–9 and 78*b*–80 in fact make trios of poems where mouths perform amorous or sexual actions. (78*b* may be one poem with 78.) 80 portrays Gellius' *fellatio* with violent language and graphic detail. 79 is for once less explicit, and adopts the allusiveness of scoptic epigrams on its theme (friends avoid

---

[46] Cf. for the comparison to part of an animal Hor. *Epod.* 8.6, again with country connections (Grassmann (1966), 54–5). On *os* and *culus* cf. also Richlin (1992), 27. Arist. *Gen. Anim.* 2.745ᵃ33–5 imagines vast teeth as a preposterous counter-factual.

[47] *uor-* is commonly so used in Catullus (cf. Adams (1982), 139–41, add 57.8); but this moment is like the climax of Erysichthon's eating at Ov. *Met.* 8.875–8, cf. Sen. Rh. *Contr.* 3.7. See also C. A. Williams (1999), 198; on the monstrosity of paradoxical sexual actions, H. N. Parker (1997). Syndikus (1984–90), iii. 67–8, understands the poem rightly in the main (following his daughter); but the interplay of mocking and grandiose condemnation in the poem does not disable its moral force. (On the text of line 6 cf. Harrison (1996), 581 n. 1.)

Lesbius' kiss); but the apparent restraint has a special point in the poem which actually reveals a crucial secret, the family of Lesbia.[48]

Connections with speech are obvious in 108. If Cominius were killed, the parts of his body would be severally devoured by birds and animals (the person is dissolved into constituent things).[49] First (*primum*), and so most important, his tongue, *inimica bonorum* | *lingua* (3–4), would be cut out and given to vultures. Readers would probably identify him with the orator P. Cominius.[50] The condemnation *populi arbitrio* (1) suggests that all Rome detests what his tongue has said to harm the *boni*. In 98 the addressee, who could use that tongue of his *culos et crepidas lingere carpatinas* (4), is probably himself one of the *uerbosis... et fatuis* (2). At any rate, the poem connects uncontrolled language, obscenity, and rusticity. The poem is itself a retaliatory, and curt, act of speaking (*dici* 1, *dicitur* 2). The close draws on a twist probably derived from scoptic epigram (cf. Lucill. *AP* 11.148): even opening his mouth, without speaking, would have a fatal effect. Through *culos... lingere*, the poem is clearly linked to 97; 99 on kisses is linked to 97 too (cf. especially 9–10). The trio 97–9 flaunts the range of the theme of mouths.[51]

Speech is significant in the other oral trio. In 78*b*, *purae pura puellae* | *suauia comminxit spurca saliua tua* (1–2: *comminxit* metaphorically connects another part of the body). This sexual misuse of the mouth will be punished by speech. Thanks to this poem, *qui sis fama loquetur anus* (4); the half-personifying *anus* neatly inverts *puellae*, also at the end of the line. In *c*1 a similar phrase plays rather on a thing (68*b*.46 *facite haec carta loquatur anus*).[52] The idea of

---

[48] Epigrams: Antip. Thess. XCVIII, Nicarch. *AP* 11.220, 252; cf. also the spoken wit at Suet. *GR* 23.7.

[49] The division is more detailed than in Hor. *Epod.* 5.99–100, Ov. *Ib.* 169–72.

[50] *ORF*⁴ nos. 143–4 (his oratorical brother is also possible). Cf. Neudling (1955), 48; Sumner (1973), 146.

[51] Interplay between different uses of mouth or tongue is familiar in Greek epigram: cf. e.g. Crates I, [Meleag.] *AP* 11.223, Adesp. *AP* 11.338. Cf. Cic. *Dom.* 25, and the very different interplay in L. Irigaray, 'Quand nos lèvres se parlent', *Ce sexe qui n'en est pas un* (Paris, 1977), 205–17, esp. 208–9. For Cat. 97–9 see Forsyth (1978–9). On the meaning of 98.1–2, see Syndikus (1984–90), iii. 97 (cf. 76.1–6, 96, 107.1–2; see also Fitzgerald (1995), 72–3). In line 4 presumably the rustic element at least is an importation into the proverbial phrase.

[52] The inversion in 78*b*.4 draws partly on the unattractiveness of old women, a theme prominent in scoptic epigram (it forms the first group in the scoptic part of *AP*

rumour appears again in 80, with a more colourful verb: *fama susurrat* (5) the sexual reason for Gellius' whitened lips. The play on speaking is heightened by the use of a metaphorical *clamant* (7, contrast *susurrat*); the subjects are body-parts: *ilia* and, with a further twist if sound, *labra* (*barba* Housman). The same play on *clamare* occurs with a non-human thing in 6.7, the bed (above). *c*1 has already prepared the relation of mouth and rumour, with its non-human door: the door has spoken (*diximus*), although its mistress thought it had no tongue (67.43–4).[53]

The emphasis on the mouth thus has links to the interests of the book in speech, as well as in sexual behaviour. Speech is a central concern of *c*2, not in form but in ideas. *c*1 has exploited the form of employing other speakers, derived from epigram on objects (66 and 67); *c*2 renounces this dramatizing possibility, but pursues the consideration of speech from a more generalized perspective.[54] One aspect of this, which we have seen, is rumour and revelation. 67 has already established this as a book of secrets disclosed and scandal dispersed (even in 66 cf. 13–25, 69–78). The very first poem in *c*2 invents a *mala fabula*. The second, 70, draws on the amatory Call. XI = 25 Pfeiffer to initiate a different aspect: the question of how words are related to thoughts. This is sustained particularly in regard to Lesbia (72.1–2; 83 (insults while husband is present); 87 (truth of poem's own statement); 92; 109 (her promise)). 109, the last poem on (the reader assumes) Lesbia, is ironically placed next to a poem about another woman's false promise (110), and a poem about a man who has misused his tongue in speech (108). 108 itself ironically comes in the middle of 107 and 109 (Lesbia's return).[55]

The last part of the book defends the narrator's utterance in *c*2: his own apparent betrayal of secrets, defamation of his beloved, and attacks on Gellius, probably with further ironies on speech (102,

11; Nicarch. 11.238 (surprise) comes in P. Oxy. 4502). Cf. also Posid. XVII = 122AB (contrast between the hetaera Doricha's death and Sappho's immortality).

[53] The Callimachean interest in impossible speakers (Hutchinson (1988), 71–2) is here made more physical.

[54] 65–6 present an elaborate *mise en abyme*: both the Lock and Callimachus are other speakers. On 66 and 67 see Macleod (1983*b*), 192.

[55] Other reasons for suspecting the 'happy ending' of 107 and 109: Holzberg (2002), 189–91.

104, 116).[56] The most comic and tragic poems in *c*2 relate to speech: 84 on Arrius, 101 on the brother's death. Both stand out from the book, though 101 had been much prepared in *c*1. In 101 sepulchral epigram, and the laments of *c*1, are powerfully reworked so that the emotional contact of address is combined with the futility of speaking to the dead. The dead person often speaks, and converses, in epitaphs (for example P. Oxy. 662.1–31); here the person has, from an objective viewpoint, become a thing, *mutam . . . cinerem* (4, cf. 96.1 *mutis . . . sepulcris*). So speech is vain.[57]

Catullus, then, exploits the connection of Greek epigram with objects very differently in *a*, *c*1, and *c*2. *a* is more distant in form from ordinary Greek epigram; but in using Greek epigram it pursues with avidity the importance of things. This suits the colourfulness and range of the book. *c*2, which follows the form of Greek epigram more than *a* or *c*1, gives a far smaller place to types of Greek epigram which relate intrinsically to material objects; for the most part, its interest in objects is slight. This suits the relative sombreness and restriction of its poetic world. But it greatly develops an interest, prepared by *c*1, in a particular sort of object, parts of the body. In doing so it is partly taking up leads from Greek scoptic and related epigram; but its use of objects seems much more remote from that of Greek epigram as a whole. The structure of *c*, the highlighting of Callimachus, the role of love epigram in *c*2, and the parallelism with *a*, all keep us aware of that larger epigrammatic tradition. So Catullus' version of Greek epigram, within his book of elegiac poetry, is perceived as highly distinctive. The treatment of objects is closely related to the particular thematic preoccupations of *c*2; these include larger and more generalized concerns than is usually supposed.

[56] 102 looks back particularly to 100, where the narrator tells of his friend Caelius' affair, and at least indirectly defends that poem; but at the same time it looks back to 67.35–6, which revealed the secrets of Cornelius (not a real friend in the narrator's eyes). For this approach to Cornelius, see M. W. Edwards (1990). 104 particularly looks back to, and conflicts with, 92 (*male dicere, amarem* 104.1, 3; *dicit . . . male, amat, amo* 92.1, 2, 4); but now the abuse is the abuse in the poems. The irony of 104 is more complex than that in 102, and intimates the lover's confusion or caprice; the deluded 107 ensues.

[57] Cf. Gelzer (1992), 29; Fitzgerald (1995), 187–9. The pentameter 101.4 subverts the hexameter. Of interest for the poem is Posid. 54 AB: Nicanor was in a different part of the world when Myrtis was buried by her brothers. There is a sense of story in the Catullus too, but the reader of the poem is kept without explanation: address absorbs the speaker.

If *c2* emerges with a more definite cohesion, so too does *c* as a whole. Effective connections and contrasts create a book which is both unified and strongly opposed in its two parts; this opposition itself displays Catullus' artistic range across a genre. Contrasts with *a* further hold up for view the inventiveness and diversity of the writer in these two substantial creations. The epigrams are not something of an anomaly in Catullus' work: *c2* is an integral part of bigger structures and oppositions, and itself exhibits the poet's characteristically extensive and arresting strategies.

6

The Publication and Individuality of Horace's *Odes* Books 1–3*

Horace's *Odes* Books 1–3, on the standard view of them as an entity, rather resemble Aristotle's animal ten thousand stades long (*Poet.* 1451ᵃ2–3): the resulting assemblage is so complicated that the mind can hardly take it in. Studies of the whole mostly tend to dissolve into studies of the individual books. And yet contemplation of the individual books is inhibited by the notion that 1–3 are the real entity, and, more specifically, by the idea that Horace first composed all the poems and then organized them into books. The opening section of this chapter will examine the chronology of composition and publication. It will particularly scrutinize the central thesis, which has long held the field, that the three books were published together for the first time in 23 BC. The second part of the article will sketch some critical consequences of looking at the books of the *Odes* in a different fashion.[1]

I

At first sight, *Epistles* 1.13 (discussed below) might seem to show that the three books were published simultaneously. But various types of

* This piece grew out of email correspondence with Professor D. Feeney; it owes its existence to his generous encouragement and aid. Thanks are due to other friends, especially Professors A. J. Woodman and O. Zwierlein, and to *CQ*'s referee and Professor R. Maltby.

[1] The decisive account of the chronology may have been Kiessling (1881), 48–75 (though many of the ideas are much older). Some views of Books 1–3 as a whole: e.g.

internal evidence should give us pause. First, aspects of language and metre indicate that the books were at least composed sequentially.

1. A notable feature is the use of *atque* with the second syllable unelided.[2] My figures for Horace are as follows:

Epodes: 9 instances in 625 lines = 1.4%
Odes 1: 9 instances in 876 lines = 1.0%[3]
Odes 2: 4 in 572 = 0.7%
Odes 3: 1 in 1004 (or 1000) = 0.1%[4]
Carmen: 0 in 76
Odes 4: 2 in 580 = 0.3%

Satires 1: 38 in 1030 = 3.7%
Satires 2: 22 in 1083 = 2.0%
Epistles 1: 11 in 1006 = 1.1%[5]
Epistles 2: 8 in 486 = 1.6%[6]
Ars: 5 in 476 = 1.1%

Three of the instances in *Odes* 2 occur close together, two of them in a single stanza (18.37, 40, 19.11). The change between *Odes* 1 and 3 is very striking, and made more so by the *Epodes*; probably the big division should be seen as falling between Books 2 and 3, with some reversion in 4. The picture is made even more striking by the context of changes over the period between Catullus and Ovid.[7] Lucretius has 94 instances (one by supplement; *simul atque* excluded) = 1.3%. Catullus has 8 in his polymetrics = 0.9%, 1 in 61–8*b* (68*b*.48) = 0.1%, 3 in

Mutschler (1974); Dettmer (1983); Santirocco (1986), a very helpful book; Porter (1987); Lefèvre (1995), 507–8.

[2] Cf. Axelson (1945), 82–5 (he goes astray on Horace by considering the wrong question, the proportion of *atque* before a vowel to *atque* before a consonant: once it is accepted that, as other evidence confirms, only unelided *atque* is a remarkable feature, its absolute frequency should be investigated); Platnauer (1948); Richmond (1965); Nisbet and Hubbard (1978), 4, 322; Zwierlein (1999), 435–8.

[3] 1.25.18 should perhaps be discounted, if *atque* there means *quam*; then: 8 instances, 0.9%.

[4] 3.11.18 is excluded as spurious or corrupt; with it the percentage becomes 0.2.

[5] 1.16.78 *simul atque* is excluded.

[6] 2.1.32 (doubtful) and 2.1.226 *simul atque* are excluded.

[7] On the date of Lucretius, see the argument in Hutchinson (2001*b*). As to the end of Catullus' poetic activity, poem 52 only works properly in 47 BC. See pp. 111–12 above.

his epigrams = 0.9%; perhaps the longer poems show a refinement here. Propertius and Tibullus certainly use the feature very little; whether they use it at all depends on one's view of the text (Tib. 2.2.8 is the most promising instance). The position is similar with Ovid's elegiacs: *Fast.* 3.363 looks the most plausible instance. There are five instances in the *Metamorphoses* (0.04%). (Grattius has no instances in 541 lines.) Plainly, then, some Augustan poets avoided this element. In Virgil there is a notable shift, scarcely explicable by genre, from the *Eclogues* (six, 0.7%) to the *Georgics* (nine, 0.4%) to *Aeneid* 1–6 (six, 0.1%, without Helen episode); a change in *Aeneid* 7–12 (twenty-seven, 0.5%) is due to a concentration of grandeur in Books 10 and 12 and in certain divine speeches. In Horace, there is an obvious difference in quantity of occurrence between the hexameter works and the lyric and epodic. It may be added that most of the instances in the lyric and epodic works can be described as appearing in grandiose, mock-gran-diose, or at least solemn contexts (the most obvious exceptions are in the *Epodes* and *Odes* 1); this is not the case with the hexameter works. But in both types we see a diminution. In the hexameter works, it coincides with differences in time of publication; in the case of the later hexameter poems, difference in genre may also be relevant. At all events, the change in the *Odes* cannot possibly be random, and clearly indicates sequential composition.

2. In the sapphic stanza the two main types of ending change in popularity: they are virtually equal in Book 1, but one is twice as common as the other in Books 3 and 4 and in the *Carmen Saeculare*. The significance of this change is confirmed by the high preponder-ance of the winner in Statius' sapphics, and also in Catullus' (though the figures for both are small).[8]

Odes 1: type *a* (*terruit urbem*) 23; type *b* (*rara iuuentus*) 20; sapphic
    stanzas 55
Odes 2: *a* 21; *b* 16; stanzas 40
Odes 3: *a* 29; *b* 15 (or 14, without 3.11.20); stanzas 56 (or 55)

---

[8] This finding suggests that the phenomena in the alcaic stanza discussed by Nisbet and Hubbard (1970), pp. xxviii–xxix, xl–xliii, should indeed be related to chronology, as they originally suggested (a change of view in Nisbet and Hubbard (1978), 4–5; but Nisbet and Rudd (2004), p. xxx, and Nisbet (2007), 13–14, now show some inclination to revert).

Carmen: *a* 10; *b* 4; stanzas 19
Odes 4: *a* 21; *b* 10; stanzas 35
Cat. 11 and 51: *a* 5; *b* 0; complete stanzas 9
Stat. *Silv.* 4.7: *a* 11; *b* 3; stanzas 14

3. What we may call prepositive monosyllables at the end of the line, words like *et* or *qui* which run on to what follows, show a notable pattern of distribution between metres in the *Odes*.[9]

Epodes: 0
Odes 1: alcaic 4; sapphic 0; other 4;[10] total 8 = 0.9% of lines in book
Odes 2: alcaic 3; sapphic 3; other 0; total 6 = 1.0%
Odes 3: alcaic 9; sapphic 6;[11] other 0; total 15 = 1.5%
Carmen (sapphic): 1 = 1.3%
Odes 4: alcaic 1; sapphic 2;[12] other 1; total 3 = 0.5%

Books 2 and 3 thus show a different approach to the feature from Book 1 in respect both of the sapphic metre (now allowed) and of metres other than sapphic and alcaic (now avoided, but the restriction will be lifted in Book 4). The significance of the difference is confirmed by the treatment of related disyllables (*neque, unde*, etc.): 3 instances in *Epodes*; 2 in Book 1, both in metres other than alcaic and sapphic; 1 in Book 2, in sapphics; 4 in Book 3, 3 in alcaics, 1 in sapphics; 3 in Book 4, 1 in alcaics, 0 in sapphics, 2 in other metres. Confirmation is suggested for sapphics by the appearance of synaloepha between lines 1–2 or 2–3 in Books 2 (twice) and 4 (once), but not in Book 1. The confinement to the two main metres is clearly significant in Book 3, where there are 78 stanzas not in sapphics or alcaics (excluding the unusual stanzas of poem 12). The failure to use the feature in sapphics is likely to be significant in Book 1, where there are 55 sapphic stanzas and 60 alcaic stanzas. The general frequency of the feature is probably not random, either; but it should be noted that seven of the instances in *Odes* 3 come in two long poems at the end, 27 and 29. The pattern of usage in particular metres not only confirms the composition of one book after another,

---

[9] Cf. Nisbet and Hubbard (1970), p. xliv, in relation to sapphics.
[10] One of these, 1.7.6, might be corrupt; if so, total 7 = 0.8% of lines in book.
[11] One of these at end of third line.
[12] One of these at end of third line.

but also shows a difference in practice between books. The partial reversion in Book 4, together with the reversion in frequency, supports further the notion of separate practice in distinct books; here it is not simply a linear development.

So far the argument has shown that the books must have been composed one after another: the poems were not all written and then arranged between books. It has also indicated marked differences between the books. It is tempting to see here a series of books published separately: one may compare the treatment of endings to the pentameter in Propertius. But even if the reality was only continuous composition and separate conception of the books, without separate publication, that would be enough for the critical argument that is to follow. However, some pointers suggest a different time of publication for the books.

1. The number of poems in each book forms a curious sequence if they are published together: the random-seeming 38, followed by 20 and 30. The numbers of poems look significant in *Satires* 1, *Epistles* 1, and no doubt *Odes* 4 (half 30). One can see that a collection of a large number of poems in different metres might not at first seem to call for precision, but that a tighter idea might appear with the smaller Book 2. Such a notion seems greatly preferable to the odd juxtaposition of random and elegant numbering.[13]

---

[13] The argument would fall if one should make any consecutive poems which share the same metre into a single poem. (Cf. Heyworth (1993), 96 n. 40, with reference to forthcoming work by A. Griffiths (now Griffiths (2002).) This thesis, though imaginative and exciting, has little positive point to recommend it (consecutive poems can have the same metre in the collection of Alcaeus, cf. frr. 68 and 69 Voigt (sapphics), P. Oxy. 1360). Presumably *Epodes* 1–10 and 14–15 should not be made into single poems (with 14–15 a weak but not impossible case could be made, as with the *Odes*). It is suspicious that instances occur only with alcaics, the commonest metre, or, in 3.24–5, 2 × (gl + ascl min), one of the commonest metres in that part of 3 (19, 24, 25, 28). Belief is strained by an ode of 336 lines (3.1–6), or of 88 (2.13–15) (and 56, 2.19–20) in a book where all the other poems are between 24 and 40 lines. The argument cannot be supported by links within these alleged poems, for these occur frequently between poems of different metres, and could be argued to be all the more noticeable when the metre is the same. On the other hand, some of the links would seem unsatisfactory if internal. So in 1.35 a request related to the poet would be needed sooner if the poem is to be fused with 1.34, cf. Catullus 36. The change of argumentative tack at 3.2.1 would not be marked by any adversative particle; it works excellently as a new but connected opening. 2.15 does not really form a convincing sequence of argument with 2.14 (it looks quite different). At 3.3 a continuation of

2. 2.4, the first poem in its book to deal with Horace, makes clear his age at the time of writing. One sees the same gesture, with different degrees of exactness, at the end of *Epistles* 1, and the beginning of *Odes* 4 (1.6). The placing has little point if the books are published simultaneously.[14]

3. 3.8 seems to mark the anniversary of an event made much of in 2.13, the falling of a tree which nearly killed the poet. It is presumably the first such anniversary, since Maecenas is surprised.[15] It is an anniversary because there is no cultic reason for the date, and it will recur year after year (9). 2.13 is written to give the air of immediacy, like reaction to the garlic in *Epode* 3. 2.17.32 looks like sacrifice not long after the event, to parallel Maecenas', not the annual offering of 3.8. One is not forced to assume that either 2.13 or 3.8 is to sound recent at the time of its reading. But an interval in time between the books seems more called for than if the poems were merely recreating the mood of particular historical moments (cf. 1.37). On the external chronology of 3.8, see below.

4. A related instance of pseudo-biographical cross-reference may be thought to occur at the start of 3.5, *caelo tonantem credidimus Iouem | regnare*. *credidimus* can certainly be taken as a perfect with present meaning, 'we have come to the belief'. But it seems hard not to make a more specific cross-reference, to 1.34, where Jupiter's thunder in a clear sky shakes the poet from the Epicurean beliefs espoused at the end of *Sat.* 1.5. The emphasis on Horace's biography in 3.4 encourages the link. A separation from Book 1 in time of publication makes the point more effective, and sharpens the play on the tense and the person of the verb.[16]

moralizing and return to the good man (3.2.17–24) would be dull and awkward. Conspicuous opening and closing gestures, not all of which can have caused a disjunction by scribes, would have to be bravely ignored: openings e.g. 1.27 (motto from Anacreon), 1.34, 2.14 (the opening name is otherwise left for 40 lines), 3.4, 3.6, 3.25 (cf. 2.19); closes e.g. 3.3.69–72 (cf. 2.1.37–40), 3.4.79–80 (cf. 4.7.27–8), 3.5.56.

[14] The phrasing *circa lustra decem* in *C.* 4.1.6 is vaguer than *octauum trepidauit aetas | claudere lustrum*; but the general link with 2.4.23–4 is hard to resist (Book 4 is particularly related to Book 2). The wish for a link may indeed explain the vagueness. Horace finished his fiftieth year in December 15; the dramatic date of *Odes* 4.2 and 5 is before summer 13, and 4.14 and 15 celebrate peace; early 13 BC is the most plausible date of publication. On *Epistles* 1, see below.

[15] Cf. e.g. Putnam (1996), 28. On the cross-referencing cf. Belling (1903), 147.

[16] This would be the only certain instance of this use of *credidi* in Horace: one could have an epistolary perfect in *Epist.* 1.2.5 (authorial perfect Livy 33.10.10). Subjunctives

5. The title *Augustus*, conferred in 27, appears in books 2 (9.19), 3 (3.11, 5.3), and 4 (2.43, 4.27, 14.3), and *Epistles* 1 (4 times) and 2 (2.48). It does not appear in Book 1, where six poems refer to him. One may not unreasonably postulate a change over time at least in Horace's poetic choice to use the name; Book 2 underlines the difference in the first of its two references to Caesar (9.19–20).[17]

6. Although one cannot always press identity and chronology for the names of mistresses, etc., the passage of time may plausibly be suggested for the reader when two names from previous books appear together: in 3.7.5 and 10 both Gyges (only a boy in 2.5.20–4) and Chloe (still afraid of love in 1.23); in 3.15 both Pholoe and Chloris (both of them again from 2.5 (17–20); in 3.15 Pholoe is less shy, Chloris too old).[18]

These are pointers only, some more notable than others; but together they lend colour to the idea of separate publication. We must now consider the absolute chronological indications in each book, or the places most likely to yield such indications. The object is partly negative, to see whether the chronological references exclude separate publication; it is also positive, to see whether they present a general picture which makes separate publication attractive. Different types of date can come into question: the dramatic date, the date of composition, the date of reading (i.e. of publication).[19]

are another matter. The idiom is first clearly seen in Silver Latin: so Sen. *Ep.* 78.14; Ov. *Fast.* 5.623 would be a questionable example. For the plural, and *regnare*, cf. Ov. *Met.* 13.842–4, Luc. 7.446–51. Also relevant may be the plans, realized in 22, to dedicate a temple to Juppiter Tonans after a miracle during Augustus' Cantabrian campaign.

[17] The name appears in Prop. 2 (or 2*a*).10.15; the poem probably precedes the campaign of Aelius Gallus in 26–5 or 25–4 (below).

[18] Some names of mistresses recur between books, not always as Horace's own mistress; but none appears more than once in more than one book. Note especially Chloe once in Book 1 (where she is very young), three times in Book 3; Glycera three times in Book 1, once in Book 3; Lydia three times in Book 1, once in Book 3 (3.9, which looks back). The general effect for the reader, though it cannot always be applied in detail, is to suggest both continuity and change in the scene of love.

[19] The fundamental discussion of the chronology is the masterly account of Nisbet and Hubbard (1970), pp. xxvii–xxxviii, with some developments in (1978), 4. See now too Nisbet (2007). It may be doubted (cf. Nisbet (2007), 14) whether the presentation of Augustus in 1.12 points to a later period of composition than 1.2: cf. 1.2.45–6, 50, 12.51–2; Virg. *G.* 2.167–72 (and Hor. *Epod.* 9.23–6). On Parthia and on Marcellus, see below.

Book 1

2 would suitably be referred to 27 for its dramatic date: the favourable interpretation of the flood by the soothsayers (Dio 53.20.1) only underlines the sense of hope in which the poem ends. There were floods on other occasions, and not all may be reported; but the poem evokes a time when things are uncertain. Mercury's guise is as a *iuuenis* (41–4); since the god is famed for imitating very young men, this does not suggest a forty-year-old Princeps (as Augustus was in 23). Cf. Hom. *Il.* 24.347–8 (with *Σ* 348*a*), *Od.* 10.277–9. The reader is also likely to think of the *iuuenis* in Virg. *G.* 1.500. 27 is thus a suitable time, later less suitable.[20]

4.14 *o beate Sesti.* The poem is held to be addressed to L. Sestius, who became suffect consul in 23, probably in July. This is supposed to date the publication of Book 1, and 2–3, to the second half of that year. It was a common practice (so it is averred) to dedicate works to consuls in their year of office, and 1.4 has a prominent position in the collection. The argument is far from compelling. The supposedly conventional practice does not seem to be supported by many examples: *Eclogue* 4; Velleius, presumably published in AD 30; Mart. 12.2 (a problematic book). Possibly too, if Lollius in *Epist.* 1.2 and 18 is the son of the consul of 21 BC, *Epistles* 1, published in 20 (note 1.18.56–7), celebrates a recent triumph of the family (1.20.27–8). But the strange thing in *Odes* 1.4 would be that the consulship is not mentioned, as it is in all these examples (with emphasis in *Eclogue* 4, and indefatigable reiteration in Velleius). *beate* in the context stresses simply Sestius' wealth; the advice not to begin long hopes does not seem especially apt to the actual time of his consulship. How will posterity be conscious of the honour done to Sestius? The year of publication would not be apparent to any subsequent reader (it is surely asking too much of the alleged convention to expect a later reader to divine the point from position alone). It would be highly exaggerated to assert that only a consulship could account for so prominent a position in the book, together with Augustus (2), Virgil (3), and Agrippa (6). Pyrrha did not hold a consulship (5); Plancus was not a consul at the time (7), and 1.6 and 1.7 are closely

[20] Note the change to a less youthful portrait type of Augustus around 27: Zanker (1988), 98–100.

related. The range of addressees in poems 1–9 may even suit the character of this book.[21]

12.45–8 *crescit occulto uelut arbor aeuo* | *fama Marcelli* (*Marcellis* Peerlkamp); *micat inter omnis* | *Iulium sidus uelut inter ignis* | *luna minores.*[22] Horace has been citing other memorable individuals from Roman history, and the reference to the Julian star either provides or includes a reference to one individual. The singular, then, may be accepted. Cf. Virg. *Aen.* 6.855–9, Prop. 4.10.39–44, Man. 1.787–8, where this Marcellus is named together with Fabricius, Curius, and others (cf. *C.* 1.12.40–2; for *crescit* note 3.30.8). The Princeps' nephew Marcellus will naturally be borne in mind; but we need not think such a reference first possible in 25, when he was married to Augustus' daughter. He was already a member of the family, and had had an extremely conspicuous role in the triumph of 29 (Dio 51.21.3, Suet. *Tib.* 6.4). At the other end, there is force in the point that this reference would seem rather unfeeling, without further qualification, after the young Marcellus' death in 23.

26.5–6 *quid Tiridaten terreat* | *unice securus* will be taken by readers from 27 on (see below on 1.29) to refer to the period of Tiridates' attempted kingship witnessed to by coins from January 28 to May 26. The phrasing, the perspective, and the parallel *rex* in line 4 suggest he is viewed as king. The worrying developments, for Tiridates and Rome, are the attempts of Phraates, whom Tiridates sought to displace, to displace Tiridates. The exact date can hardly be defined.

29 most likely refers to a specific expedition, Aelius Gallus' to Arabia Felix. The expedition may be dated 26–5, or 25–4.[23] The expedition

[21] See II below. 'Conventional practice': Nisbet and Hubbard (1970), pp. xxvi, referring to Syme (1958), ii. 672. On Velleius cf. Woodman (1975), 273–82. Mayer (1994), 8–9, argues that the Lollius of *Epist.* 1.2 and 18 is the son of *cos.* 21. Something of the strangeness of the address to Sestius, if consul, is felt by Lyne (1995), 75. (The reader of Ovid, *Ex Ponto* 4.1 is to suppose that the poet does not yet know of Pompeius' consulship (cf. 4.5).) If we still want to stress politics, the role of the Republican Cn. Piso as consul for 23 might suggest that even before July 23 Sestius, a quaestor of Brutus, might be a good choice for Horace, marking his own past and the indulgence of the regime (cf. *Odes* 2.7). Should the argument on Sestius not be accepted, it would remain the easiest of suppositions that Horace slightly rewrote the poem after the initial publication of Book 1 to include Sestius' name, if 1–2 were republished in 23 to form a set with 3.

[22] On the passage see R. Brown (1991).

[23] On this expedition see Dihle (1964), 80–5; Jameson (1968); Bowersock (1983), 46–8; Rich (1990), 164–5; Mayerson (1995); Dueck (2000), 87. The rhetorical

could be spoken of with pride at a later date (*RG* 26.5, cf. Plin. *NH* 6.160); but it was actually a failure. This is clear from Strabo's close and friendly account (16.4.22–4), and was publicly acknowledged much later at the trial of Syllaeus. Horace's bantering presentation would appear rather tactless and unpleasant if the result of the expedition were known at the time of publication. So an imagined date 27–5, and a date of publication perhaps earlier than 24.

31 is set at the time of Augustus' dedication of the temple of Apollo on the Palatine in 28. **33** will refer to Tibullus' elegies, but they need not have been published yet (his Book 1 after 25 Sept. 27). **35.29–32** are written as if Augustus were setting out for Britain: perhaps a dramatic date of 27 or 26,[24] though British expeditions continue later as an object of fantasy (cf. Prop. 4.3.9). **37**: the dramatic date is 30. The immediacy is a pose borrowed from Alcaeus (fr. 332 Voigt); and the poem forms a suspiciously neat link with the *Epodes*, which brought us to the victory of 31.[25] *Epode* 9 itself seems to offer us on a smaller scale an instance of difference between the notional time of the poem and the time of reading. Finally, 30 as a date of composition would bring us suspiciously close to the publication date of *Epodes* and *Satires* 2. It remains interesting that this is the earliest date in which the *Odes* affect to be set.

Thus Book 1 offers dramatic dates of 30, 28, and 27 or 26; 30 seems doubtful as a date of composition. 24 may be too late for publication.

Book 2

2.5–8 *Proculeius... notus in fratres* [note plural] *animi paterni...* is unlikely to allude to the conspiracy of 23 or 22 (cf. Dio 54.3.5), and presumably precedes it. **17** *redditum Cyri solio Phraaten.* There are likely to be at least two restorations of Phraates to rule. Phraates takes over from his father in *c.*38 (reportedly after murdering him). Tiridates appears to be active and coining at Seleucia from January 28 to May 26

purposes of Augustus and Dio, and Dio's errors on the overall length of the expedition, should be borne in mind in considering the support they appear to give to the later date (*RG* 26.5, Dio 53.29.3–8; cf. also Jos. *Ant.* 15.317).

[24] Cf. Nisbet and Hubbard on 35.30.
[25] Cf. Loupiac (1997), 130–2.

(coins minted at Seleucia are dated by month). He is *ΦΙΛΟΡΩΜΑΙΟΥ* on some coins; this suggests previous contact with Rome and fits well with Dio's report of Tiridates' defeat and flight to Octavian around 30 (51.18.2–3; cf. *reges* in *RG* 32.1, where *post*[*ea*] suits Dio's version better than Justin's, 42.5.6). A gap in Phraates' own coinage in 282 Sel. = 31/30 BC would suit a period of ascendancy by Tiridates. Phraates is certainly in charge again before 20.[26] The earlier return to rule (*c.*30) may well be in question here: the event need not just have happened. The apparent circumstances of Phraates' original ascent to the throne (cf. Just. 42.4.14–5.2) make the earlier restoration especially pointed for Horace's argument. On the other hand, there are some attractions in supposing recent news of Phraates' recovery of his rule; the ending of Tiridates' coinage may mark a significant stage. There would then be an advance in time for the reader on 1.26.5. However, internal considerations in 3.8 (below) would still prevent us from seeing here a confirmation of Justin's dating, whereby Tiridates actually flees to Augustus before 24 (42.5.6). If, then, Horace is alluding in 2.2 to a recent success by Phraates, this would be less final than the ending of all war (that would hardly surprise, and announcements of conquests of the irrepressible Cantabrians form a more than ample parallel).

4.21–4 offer a very clear date, shortly after Horace's fortieth birthday in December 25. This ought not to be far removed from the date of publication (especially if the argument on the passage above is accepted). **6.2** *Cantabrum indoctum iuga ferre nostra* sounds like the rebellion of 25 or 24, 'as soon as' (ὡc τάχιcτα) Augustus leaves (Dio 53.29.1).[27] **9.18–20** *noua | cantemus Augusti tropaea | Caesaris* is hard to date, but perhaps implies triumphs won since Actium (though it blurs these with his actions in the East, or perhaps rather projects forthcoming triumphs against Parthia, cf. 2.13.18–19, Prop. 2.10.13–14). **10**, as scholarly discussion has shown, is very unlikely to counsel the

---

[26] On the coinage see Simonetta (1976) (on overstamping and its possible significance cf. 27–8); Sellwood (1980), 159–81; Shore (1993), 30–3, 129–36. With regard to the argument from 'warts', note that some of the coins of Phraataces show warts, some not. 289 = 24/3 seems the latest datable year for Phraates' own coinage (Phraataces' begins in 3 or 2 BC). Isid. Char. *FGrH* 781 F 2.1 lines 3–4 implies at least two substantial attempts by Tiridates: φυγάc accords with Dio 51.18.2–3.

[27] The question of tact relates principally to the time of publication, and so cannot be used as an argument against applying the phrase in this way. Cf. Nisbet and Hubbard (1978), 93–4.

'conspirator' Murena in mid-downfall (and he should not be addressed as *Licini*). Since the conspirator and the consul are evidently different people, the balance falls in favour of 22 not 23 for the conspiracy, as in Dio 54.3 (preferably early 22, to help Vell. 2.93.1).²⁸ **11.1–2** *quid bellicosus Cantaber et Scythes…cogitet*: the dramatic date will be shortly before the end of 25 (if the Scythian expedition indeed comes in 25), or possibly in 24.

The dramatic dates for the book fall in 25 or 24, and publication of poem 4 soon after the end of 25 seems attractive.

Book 3

5.2–4 *praesens diuus habebitur | Augustus adiectis Britannis | imperio grauibusque Persis.* This need not be related to concrete plans for expeditions to Britain (the last we know of is in 26). Campaigns to Parthia and Britain are imagined as late as Propertius 4.3; cf. Prop. 2.27.5, etc. **6.1–4**: the Romans are urged to rebuild their temples. Augustus claimed to have done this in 28, to all the temples that needed it then (*RG* 20.4, cf. Livy 4.20.7 *templorum omnium*). And yet this group of poems in particular is addressed to an audience now. However, Prop. 2.6.35–6, probably published after 28, likewise refer to neglect of the temples now; Prop. 3.13.47–8, published in or after 23, also appear to do so. A similar point is implied by Hor. *C.* 2.15.18–20. We should either suppose a dramatic date for 3.6 before 28, or else a deliberate vagueness. The parallel material makes it clear that this is a special case.²⁹

8.17–24 appear to mark an advance on 2.11.1–2: Scythians and Cantabrians are a worry no longer. The Dacians are hard to date, save that the reference is probably later than the campaign of M. Crassus (*cos.* 30) in 29–28 BC.³⁰ The reference to Scythians would fit any time after 25, if that was indeed when the embassy came to Augustus. 21–2

²⁸ Cf. Swan (1966); Sumner (1978); Griffin (1980), 183; Woodman (1983), 270–1, 278; Syme (1986), 387–92; Rich (1990), 174–5; Arkenberg (1993).
²⁹ Kraggerud (1995) sees that the ode will have a date of composition after 28. Actual social legislation is not very relevant to the date of the poem: sexual morals are a concern throughout the period and before (e.g. Cic. *Marc.* 23), and social legislation in 28 is unlikely.
³⁰ See Nisbet and Hubbard (1970), pp. xxxiii–xxxiv.

seruit Hispanae uetus hostis orae | *Cantaber, sera domitus catena* suits a time after 25 (*sera* relates to *uetus*, not events in 26–24). *seruit* indicates that Augustus has completed his conquest.[31] This makes it difficult to harmonize 19–20 *Medus infestus sibi luctuosis* | *dissidet armis* with Justin's account of Parthian affairs. In Justin Tiridates flees from Parthia and comes to Augustus, who is still waging war in Spain (42.5.6). In Dio Tiridates comes to Rome in, or after, 23 (53.33.1). The coins from January 28 to May 26 are positive evidence for Tiridates' claiming to rule (they most clearly show Tiridates in 286 = 27/6); they cannot reveal when he abandoned his claim, when he actually left Parthia, and when civil strife ceased there. One would imagine Tiridates' arrival in Rome, his great source of hope, would have occurred fairly soon after his leaving Parthia. On Dio's chronology, there are few difficulties to this poem being imagined as a year later than 2.13, and later than the publication of *Odes* 2, if that comes soon after December 25. We could none the less accommodate Justin's chronology, should we really wish to, if war can be thought of as still in progress when Tiridates has left (after all, Tiridates' mere absence is not enough for Phraates' wishes), or if Horace is using events vaguely or loosely. 29.27–8 *quid Seres et regnata Cyro* | *Bactra parent Tanaisque discors* is unlikely to bear on the question: the three names suggest in *Tanais* a reference to Scythia.

14: a clear and important date, the return of Augustus to Rome from Spain in 24. This comes after the beginning of the year (Dio 53.28.1), perhaps after 13 June: the poem suggests a direct return from abroad rather than a long period in Italy, Augustus is evidently in Italy on 13 June (*Fast. Fer. Lat.* V.27, *II* xiii.1 p. 150), and on his glorious return to Rome he will not still be incapacitated by illness as he was both in January and on 13 June (cf. Dio 53.28.3). We appear to have the latest date in Books 1–3.[32]

---

[31] Even if it was only in 26 that Augustus fought the Cantabrians themselves (cf. Syme (1979)), it is improbable that Horace, who ignores the Asturians, would treat the conquest as settled before Augustus' departure from Spain and the closing of the gates of Janus at the end of 25. *sera* also bears relation to Spain in general (Livy 28.12.12, Vell. 2.90.1–4). Cf. Syme (1979), 848. Readers in 24 or 23 would naturally refer the phrase to after the crushing of the rebellion, Dio 53.29.1–2, and certainly not to 26. The new inscription throws light on Augustus' wider handling of Spain: Alföldy (2000).

[32] The *Fasti Feriarum Latinarum* mention Augustus' being in Spain as the reason for his absence from the festival in 26 and 25; that need not mean, as is often assumed,

Book 3, for all the Roman generalization of 1–6 and 24, is sparser than the other books in identifiable dates. One poem may have a dramatic date of 28, but if so it belongs in a particular category of material. The dramatic date of poem 8 seems to come after the end of 25; 14 proclaims a dramatic date of 24.

The discussion of dates within the poems has shown that the dramatic dates tend to be later from book to book. An earlier dramatic date need not be an argument against later publication; and in fact 3.6 appeared to be one of several poems which treated this subject after 28. The broad pattern seems to support the successive publication of the books. It remains possible that the semblance of chronological sequence is a literary construct. It is also possible that the books were written more or less as the pattern of dates suggests but were not published until later. But let us first consider the principal grounds for believing in simultaneous publication.

1. 3.30 takes up the metre of 1.1, used nowhere else in *Odes* 1–3, and shows that Horace has fulfilled the ambition expressed in that opening poem for canonization as a lyric poet.[33] As a point against the original separate publication of Books 1 and 2 this is no argument at all. As will be seen, the successive books build up an entity. No device is more common than a link between the beginning and end of a sequence of published books to establish cohesion, or (in weaker cases) connection. On the most plausible view of the *Aetia*, Books 3–4 are published later; fr. 112.5–6 Pfeiffer exactly repeat παρ' ἴχνιον ὀξέος ἵππου from fr. 2.1 Pfeiffer = fr. 4.1 Massimilla, second half of the prologue.[34] The last poem or pair of poems in Propertius 3 (24–5), the ending of the affair, clearly looks back to 1.1 in numerous ways. After the unifying gesture of *Odes* 3.30, *Odes* 4 presents itself as an unlooked-for resumption; but its

that he is actually at Rome in June 24 (so e.g. Kienast (1990), 63). Return to Rome in June is supposed by Syme (1986), 38. The illness is not of course certainly the same in January and in June. Suet. *Aug.* 26.3 (or the scribes) must in any case make an error in omitting this consulship from those not entered upon at Rome.

[33] On the relation of 1.1 and 3.30 see e.g. Putnam (1973), 13–17.

[34] Cf. Parsons (1977), 48–50. A different view of the chronology in Cameron (1995), esp. chs. 4, 6, and 7. The discussion here leaves aside the theoretical possibility that *Odes* 1.1 was first composed for a republication of Books 1 and 2 when 3 was published, so as to form a ring with 3.30.

exact quotation of *C.* 1.19.1 at 4.1.5 displays the same technique of recall. Similarly, it purposefully reuses the metre of 1.1 and 3.30 in 4.8.[35] The end of the *Georgics* looks back with exact citation to the start of the *Eclogues*. The last line of *Satires* 2 names Canidia, who links *Satires* 1, 2, and the *Epodes*, is the last speaker in the *Epodes*, and comes in the first poem of *Satires* 2 (48). It is not surprising that the metre of 1.1 is not repeated in Book 1 or 2: Book 2 only has four metres, Book 1 has two other unrepeated metres, and the first poem is marked off as a prologue (cf. Persius' choliambics) and is very different in structure from the other poems. It does, however, have some metrical connections within Book 1: the two brief poems of short-term hedonism in stanzas of major asclepiads (11, 18) contrast with the slow pace and long-term views of 1.1, in minor asclepiads.

2. Another internal point which is felt to be important is the placing of odes to Maecenas at the beginnings, ends, and middles of books (1.1, 20; 2.12, 17, 20; 3.8, 16, 29).[36] But this feature can equally well be seen as part of the entity accumulated in sequential publication. It is visible too in *Satires* 1 (1, 6) and *Epistles* 1 (1, 7, 19). There is a certain lack of absolute neatness: no poem to Maecenas at the end of 1 or the beginning of 2; 2.17 between the middle and end of 2; 3.8 not really at the beginning of 3. This actually suits the idea of books taking up and reworking each other's patterns better than that of a grand instantaneous architecture. In content, the differences between the three books in their poems to Maecenas fit at least as well the distinctness of each book which will be argued for below. To my mind, the most salient difference is the more intimate and affectionate language used to Maecenas in Book 2. Other internal points, it will be apparent, can be treated along similar lines: for example, the way 3.1 takes up 1.1 (which takes up *Satires* 1.1), and 3.30 takes up 2.20 (but not so much 1.38).

3. In *Epist.* 1.13 Vinnius is told to take *uolumina*, *libelli*, *libri* containing *carmina* to Augustus. Let us grant that these *carmina* are *Odes* Books 1–3.[37] Is it implied that the poems have not been previously published? In 16–18 *neu uulgo narres te sudauisse ferendo | carmina quae possint oculos aurisque morari | Caesaris* the occupation of Augustus'

[35] Ludwig (1961), 10; Harrison (1990*b*), 43.
[36] See Santirocco (1986), 153–68.
[37] Cf. Mayer (1994), 3–4. Another idea: Clarke (1972).

eyes and ears is likely to come after the presentation, not before; the present (not perfect) subjunctive and *posse* suggest the perspective of Horace now. The 'ears' may be because these are lyric poems, or could be read to him; a reference to previous recitations would be intrinsically awkward too, since the eyes are naturally referred to the books brought now.[38] The language thus suggests that the poems, or at any rate a large part of them, have not been read by Augustus before. Two main possibilities may be postulated: (i) Augustus has not read Book 1, 2, or 3; (ii) Augustus has read one or two of those books. Either possibility can be met by the supposition that Book 3 is now being published for the first time. For Augustus can be deemed, for Horace's purposes, not to have read Book 1 or even 2.

The *Epistle* seems to posit a journey within Italy (10), i.e. Horace is allegedly sending the works from the country to Rome. Now, Augustus has been absent from Rome from summer 27 until some point in 24 (summer?). It may be assumed, by a polite fiction, that he will not have had time for literature while ordering the affairs of the world. He may well have been absent for the first appearance of both Book 1 and Book 2. (The poem celebrating his return in Book 3 would be especially apt if it was the first book published after the return.) This would make still easier the fiction (or reality) of his not having read those books, and his request for the complete *Odes* (*si denique poscet* in *Epist.* 1.13.3 might seem to imply a previous request). If he returned before the publication of Book 2, we could at the least suppose a strong version of (ii), in which he has not read Books 1 or 3. But regardless of the time of publication, it is still a natural fiction that he has not read Books 1 or 2 (or of course 3). In *Epist.* 2.1.1–4, Horace affects to fear that Caesar may be kept from valuable public duties if Horace goes on too long. When Caesar is evidently in Rome, seemingly in the period 29–28, Vitruvius professes his initial anxiety *ne non apto tempore interpellans subirem tui animi offensionem*, when Caesar had so much to think of (1 *pr.*1). Horace is nervous within *Epistles* 1.13 that even now his emissary may choose an inopportune time.[39]

---

[38] If previous recitations were referred to here, that could be adopted into the argument. *Epist.* 1.19.43–4 in fact suggest, in context, the possibility of some *Odes* being recited to Augustus; if before publication, one might think especially of Book 3.

[39] Note that if Augustus did return before June 24, then he certainly had an illness, presumably of some significance, after returning (*II* xiii.1 p. 150). Date of the preface

So Book 3, we suppose, is being published for the first time when a set of *Odes* 1–3 is given to Augustus (cf. e.g. Crinag. VII for a set as a present). It would be a suitable moment too for the general republication of Books 1–3 as an entity. The request for, or the presentation of, such a set would seem apt gestures, and good publicity for Horace, subsequently further promoted by the *Epistle*. The hypothesis of general republication, though not essential, is unproblematic (Ovid's *Amores* are an example). Callimachus' *Aetia* (see above) probably provides a good model for a work of which some books were published earlier (1–2); most likely a complete edition, comprising all four books, is published later.[40]

So far, the argument has demonstrated that the books of poems were composed as a sequence, and that in some features of metre and language we see different approaches from Horace in different books. Enough has been said to make it plausible that Books 1 and 2 were published separately, and to show that the chronological indications present a picture broadly encouraging to this hypothesis. One possible pattern might be: Book 1 published 26, Book 2 published early 24, Book 3 published (and perhaps 1–2 republished) early 23.[41] One might, however, contend that the books were written successively and distinctly, but an imaginary chronology conferred, or publication simply avoided. The notion of imaginary chronology does not suit the statistics

to Vitruvius 1: *Augusti* in Vitr. 5.1.7, which also conflicts with Suet. *Aug.* 52, is commonly thought to be part of an interpolated passage. 1 *pr.*2 *publicaeque rei constitutione* suggests 28 or 27.

[40] By 'republication', 'edition', etc., no more is meant in the case of *Odes* 1–3 than the distributing of the three books in a set (with relatively little change, the statistics above suggest). Obviously sets of rolls could be distributed as belonging together (the *Georgics*, say, or the *De Finibus*). Containers were common; the absence of one in *Epist.* 1.13.12–13 is probably part of the humour.

[41] Conceivably Augustus' grave illness, his major changes in constitutional arrangements, and the grave illness and then death of Marcellus, make the months from, say, May rather less promising for a presentation. In *Epist.* 1.13.3 *si ualidus* does not in context suggest the major illness of 23, but slighter illnesses; cf. Suet. *Aug.* 81. 23 BC itself has advantages over the first part of 22; it would be, not essential but welcome, to have the book published before the arrival of Tiridates and the death of Marcellus (treated by Virgil and Propertius). The interval between *c.*30 and 26 would be readily explained by the need to work at evolving the new style and genre. If there is indeed a greater interval between 1 and the shorter 2 than between 2 and the longer 3, one may point to the considerable rethinking of the genre which Book 2 involves. But the productivity of poets cannot be plotted too minutely.

above. The mere avoidance of publication does not fit, in particular, the point above on the indication of age in 2.4. Neither notion meets the point on the number of poems. And neither seems so characteristic of contemporary collections of poems, where each book appears to be first published separately. (Propertius indeed offers evidence, unless it is more construction, for the separate publication of books, 2.24.1–2, etc.) Statius, *Silvae* 1–3, which probably were first published together, appear a genuine collection, re-edited, of poems composed and performed as separate entities; that is different from poems composed as part of a book.[42] Yet the sceptical position on separate publication, though it seems implausible, cannot ultimately be refuted. The difference between the two views (separate publication or not, but certainly sequential composition of distinct entities) is not of fundamental importance for the critical argument that is now to be developed. It is of some importance, for the idea of separate publication affects the original readers' conception of the books and of the combined edition. But the basic argument could still stand without that support.

II

The successive books of individual Augustan poets, in the same, separate, or related genres are characterized by innovation and exploration of new areas, as well as by continuity and the accumulation of a cohesive *œuvre*. An obvious example is Propertius' third book (much influenced by Horace's third), with its new programmatic mythology, its moves into indirectness, and its closing of the affair; his fourth book is a still more radical instance. Tibullus' incomplete second book switches mistress, by contrast with other elegists, drops the homosexual strand of the first book, creates a novel sort of elegy about the Roman past. The second book of Horace's *Satires* moves into indirectness, other speakers, philosophical investigations, in a way that is highly paradoxical for his genre (Propertius' fourth book likewise). The second book of *Epistles* is more difficult, and less epistolary, than the first,

---

[42] See K. M. Coleman (1988), pp. xvi–xvii. Ovid, *Ex Ponto* 1–3 seem to form another case of original simultaneous publication, in particular circumstances.

and markedly unlike it. Horace is the most daring of the Augustan poets in his cultivation of different genres, in two related groups; the *Epodes*, first book of *Odes*, and first book of *Epistles*, are themselves surprises. This makes the changes within these genres from book to book all the more characteristic.

The survey here is intended merely to signal some paths. Space compels concentration on the difference between the books of *Odes* rather than on their relation to Horace's other works. Particular areas are singled out, and considered with regard to all three books; detailed criticism is impossible here. Some of the points and aspects are by no means novel: for, despite the notional unity of the three books, the individual identity of the books has often in fact made itself felt to readers. Yet the three books will be seen to appear in an altered light.[43]

Book 1

1. It is well known that the book begins with nine poems all in different metres; and the sequence 9–18, or perhaps 9–23, presents a great stream of conspicuous imitations of different poets (9, 10 Alcaeus, 12 Pindar, 13 Sappho, 14 Alcaeus, 15 Bacchylides, 16 Stesichorus, 18 Alcaeus, 21 Catullus, 22 Alcaeus, 23 Anacreon).[44] All this display acquires a different appearance if we think of the book originally appearing on its own, rather than as simply the first act in a three-act play. The work embodies, rather than merely promising for the collection as a whole, its own virtuosity and generic range. (One may remember the contiguity of *Odes* 1.1–9 to the sudden explosion of different metres in *Epodes* 11–17; the metres of *Odes* 1.4, and 7 (same as *Epode* 12), recall the *Epodes*.) At the same time, the complexities of the book's use of lyric tradition are more visibly brought out.

Poem 1 has stressed Horace's place within the lyric tradition: the canon of poets, his debt to the Lesbian poets, but also the choral *tibia*. After displaying his metrical range in 1–9, Horace emphasizes his

---

[43] The footnotes to what follows necessarily present only a small selection of bibliographical material, mainly from recent years.

[44] Cf. Lowrie (1995). For 1.22 cf. Burzacchini (1976 and 1985).

special connection with Alcaeus (and Sappho) in 9 and 10, by marked imitations of Alcaeus (more marked than in 4), and the book's first alcaic stanza (9)—perhaps the first in Latin—followed by its second sapphic stanza (10). The eponymous alcaic and sapphic stanzas, little used so far, recall Sappho and Alcaeus with especial force: Alcaeus uses both, and Sappho uses the sapphic, very frequently; the other metres in Book 1, though mostly reminiscent of the Lesbians, do not evoke their freer creation of cola.[45] These stanzas are to become the foremost stanzas of the book (alcaic ten in all, sapphic eight, three other stanzas four times each). But shortly after the underlining of Lesbian tradition in 9–10, Horace embarks on a series of imitations that ranges widely among the poets. Particularly interesting is the late and striking appearance of imitations of Anacreon (23, 27; cf. 17.18): Anacreon is in fact a much more significant model than Alcaeus or Sappho for the Horatian narrator, and his age and tone. None the less, Alcaeus dominates among the imitations; the last large poem (37) begins from him. The sapphic and alcaic stanzas become more and more common as the book progresses: note the alcaic pairs 16–17, 26–7, 34–5, the alternating alcaics and sapphics at 29–32, 37–8, the alternations with sapphics at 9–12, 19–22. The relation of Horace to Alcaeus is dwelt on in 32. It is a relation of contrast as well as similarity; yet here the theme of love is not associated with Sappho, but, rather unrepresentatively, with Alcaeus. The book thus explores its own complicated relationship to a complicated tradition, which it both spreads out to view and draws into coherence. Books 2–3 are far less interested in imitations of lyric poets, particularly of the kind that trumpets a connection at the start of a poem.

1*a*. Other genres are highly important in this book, as in the others. One point may be singled out: Book 1, the first lyric book after the *Epodes*, explicitly confronts the change from the *Epodes* in poem 16 (note the connection with *Epod.* 17.42–4).[46]

---

[45] The point is independent of the names 'alcaic' and 'sapphic', but cf. Lyne (1995), 98–9. On the metres of 4 and 8 see Alc. fr. 455 Voigt; Page (1955), 326. Papyri suggest that Alcaeus and Sappho were the most read of the lyric poets, Pindar apart; indeed, there are two copies, or a copy and a related commentary, for each of Alcaeus' three best-preserved poems.

[46] Cf. G. Davis (1991), 74–6; Heyworth (1993), 93–4, and (1988), 80–2, for this and other links between *Epodes* and *Odes* 1.

2. There are speakers other than the narrator in 1.7.25–32 (Teucer), 15.5–36 (Nereus), 25.7–8 (Lydia's lovers), 28 (dead man—but there are other possibilities). Extended mythical narrative is seen in 15 (though speech dominates). In its penultimate poem the book goes beyond 15, and perhaps beyond lyric tradition, to an elaborate and tragic narrative of a recent event.[47]

3. The political poems are forcefully placed, and carry weight at the end and middle as well as the beginning of the book (contrast Book 2). As is well known, the sombre but finally hopeful poem 2 is answered by the politically triumphant 37.[48] But again this point looks different when the book is considered as an isolated entity. 37 further appears to reverse the grim implications of 35 on Fortune, which ends with politics: appears, for the generality of 35 remains (note *triumpho* at the end of the last stanza of 37 and the first of 35), and the dramatic date of 37 is earlier. 12 sets the present in a large context of Roman history. 15, we may add, presents the fall of the ancestral city; 7 recalls the foundation of a city, and may gesture towards Aeneas.[49]

4. The theological dimension of the book is important. 2 begins with Jupiter's anger against Rome; 3 ends with his anger against the human race; 12 presents a more encouraging image of his rule, though at the end of the poem he punishes the impure with thunderbolts (59–60). Jupiter's thunder supposedly converts the narrator to religious belief in 34. Jupiter has a far smaller and less conspicuous part to play in Book 2.[50] Venus is prominent, in a book where love is important, and her deity is apparent (19, 30, 33.10–12). 10, 21, 30, 35 are addressed to gods, though Fortune (35) is in various senses a most uncertain goddess.

---

[47] On the tradition behind 1.15, see Rutherford (2000), 233–9. On 1.37: Lowrie (1997), 144–64; Wyke (2002), ch. 6. Cleopatra breaks the rather fixed roles of men and women in the book hitherto; for other points on gender cf. on Book 3, points 2 and 6, and n. 60 below.

[48] For the connection cf. Mutschler (1974), 109–32, 111; Lefèvre (1995), 509.

[49] Allusion to the unpublished *Aeneid* 1 seems possible enough in, say, 26 BC. 1.14 is in my opinion best seen as a deliberately elusive allegory: cf. Santirocco (1986), 46–9.

[50] The theme of storms and sailing, important throughout the *Odes*, is particularly important and thematic in Book 1: so 2, 3, 7, 11, 14, 15, 28, 37. An especially charming twist is the movement after 2 and 3 to metaphorical storms of love in 5; the name Pyrrha is surely humorous (cf. 1.2.6).

5. Philosophically, despite the references to Jupiter, the most conspicuous strand is a stress on enjoying the present which recalls Epicureanism: e.g. 7.32, 11.6–8 (4.15 and 11.8 are the only occurrences of *spes longa* in the *Odes*).[51] There is little sign of Stoicism (*uirtus* does not appear). The 'conversion' from Epicureanism in 34, moving on from the *Satires*, is the more striking; 35 goes on to modify it.

6. The country, as the place where the narrator lives, is fairly inconspicuous. It had been made prominent in *Satires* 2.6, about the new estate (contrast *Epode* 2). It makes its first appearance as late as 17, then obliquely in 20, fleetingly in 22.9–12 (cf. Alc. fr. 130b Voigt), perhaps in 38.7–8. But it is hardly a major theme.

7. Death is significant throughout the *Odes*, but is treated differently in each book.[52] Here it accompanies hedonism at 4.13–14, 11.3–4, theology at 3.32–3, history at 12.35–6, mythology at 15.10–11. But it comes into its own as an aspect of the closure in the last part of the book. A series of actual deaths confronts us: 24, the death of Quintilius (contrast 3: Virgil is known to escape death there, but must lament here); 28, a death at sea (contrast 3 and 7), and the death of the philosopher Archytas; 37, the death of Cleopatra. 37 in particular expands the range of the book. The group of poems has much more power in a book which is a separated entity.[53]

8. Love receives different treatment in each book. A notable aspect of Book 1 is the use of *puer* to depict youths physically attractive to women (as the narrator is not), and in the heyday of love: cf. 5.1, 9.15–18, 13.11, 27.20. Otherwise in *Odes* 1–3 the word is so used only at 3.9.16, a retrospective poem. The narrator's own love, suggested in 11, first comes to the fore in 13, where he grotesquely dons the masks of Sappho and Catullus, and stresses his age through contrast with Telephus; similarly in 17. Contrasts of the narrator with specific younger male lovers are less sharply made in books 2 and 3 (3.9 again excepted). 16 shows how he has changed from the *Epodes*.

---

[51] Cf. e.g. Epic. 6.14 Arrighetti, and more widely 4 (*Men.*).122, 125, 128. Being 'present' is for Epicurus a matter of psychology and perception as well as time.

[52] Cf. Porter (1987), 222–3, and the excellent article Feeney (1995).

[53] 35 too brings an impressive expansion in scope. The closing throwaway gesture of 38 is much more telling if it is not merely the end of Part I. Cf. D. P. Fowler (2000*b*), 259–60.

Book 2

1. The book forms a considerable surprise; perhaps it is the book whose individual identity has been most appreciated.[54] The book is notably shorter than Book 1 (572 against 876 lines) and has virtually half the number of poems (20 against 38). The brevity of the book and its more forbidding content can be related: the severe concision of Book 2 contrasts with the genial abundance of Book 1.[55] In sharp contrast to the paraded metrical range of Book 1, the metres of Book 2 are almost entirely alcaic and sapphic, with only two exceptions (12; 18, a metre not seen in Book 1, cf. Alc. fr. 456 Voigt). The alcaics and sapphics alternate from 1 to 11; but after that the alcaics predominate: in 11–20 there are seven alcaic poems, and one sapphic, with blocks of three and two consecutive alcaic poems, 13–15 and 19–20. The book again explores tradition, but in markedly different ways from Book 1. A poem in the middle of the book (13) presents the Lesbian tradition, through a mock-κατάβαϲιϲ which gives the poet a surprising role. In this poem, unlike 1.32, Sappho and Alcaeus both appear as if models, and the political and the amorous are separated; Alcaeus, however, is given the preference (though by a crowd). There are, so far as we are aware, few flagrant 'imitations' of lyric poets of the kind displayed with such exuberant opulence in Book 1, and none of Alcaeus or Sappho. One, arrestingly, is of the crucial Anacreon (2.5). Another is of Bacchylides (18): the unusual metre, related to that of the original, marks out an unusual choice. 16 echoes Catullus' sapphics, again an unusual choice of poet from the possibilities of Book 1. However, poem 1 introduces one famous lyric poet not directly alluded to in Book 1 (only very indirectly in the lament of 1.24): Simonides.[56] His style of lamentation (*Ceae*) is marked out as generically unsuitable to the *ioci*, lightness, and love (*Dionaeo*) of Horace's poetry (1.37–40). But the book will then promptly prove its heaviness; and, despite this stanza, it will give a small place to love, and a large one to death. Thus a divergence from Book 1 on tradition marks a larger divergence.

[54] Characterizations of Book 2: Nisbet and Hubbard (1978), 1–6; D. A. West (1998), pp. xi–xviii. On 2.1–12: Ludwig (1957).

[55] A more necessary brevity of book is defended in the preface to Vitruvius 5.

[56] He looks increasingly important in Book 4; cf. Barchiesi (1996).

1*a*. Again an isolated point on other genres: explicit engagement with works in prose (history in poems 1 and 12) makes an interesting development.[57] And philosophy, a genre of prose, is vital to the book.

2. There are no mythical narratives (some exempla). There are no speakers in the book other than the narrator.

3. Politics, at least direct and intense confrontation of Roman politics, comes only in the opening poem, again on the borders of the book. Moral confrontation of the present, with history also in view, is seen in 15 and 18, and is more characteristic of the book. Wealth in general is much more of a concern in this book; in Book 1 it had appeared mostly in relation to the narrator.

4. The gods are of little importance in the book, until the hymn to Bacchus at the end (19). (Venus and her helpers have a little colour at 8.13–16.)

5. The metrical plainness of the book is matched by its relative intellectual austerity. The movement into greater severity and difficulty is very reminiscent of *Satires* 2 after *Satires* 1. Generalized moralizing comes much more to the foreground in Book 2 of the *Odes* than in Book 1. The moralizing itself makes a link back to the *Satires*. The language of Stoicism, in particular, is now deployed, and without the irony frequent in the *Satires*. Poem 2 sets the tone: the wise man is the true king; *uirtus* appears, personified (in the *Epodes* it comes only in the sense of 'courage'). Poem 3 begins with serious moralizing instruction unlike the beginning of any poem in Book 1 (nearest come 22, which turns out to be playful in application, and 18, which is on wine). 9 again opens in generalizing gravity unlike the openings of *Odes* 1; so does 10, which uses language of Peripatetic (5) and wider philosophical (14–15) resonance. 11.5 *poscentis aeui pauca* is much more blatantly philosophical than *frui paratis* (1.31.17). 16.9–12 move to metaphor and the mind in true Stoic style; the handling of the self in 19–20 recalls Stoics and others. *uiuitur paruo bene* in 16.13 has a strongly philosophical quality. 16.25 dwells on the present, in the Epicurean vein seen in Book 1.

6. The country is much more important in this book. The narrator includes *parua rura* as a defining feature in his lot (2.16.37); the

[57] On 1 see Henderson (1998), ch. 4; Woodman (2003).

well-known tree incident (2.13, 17) is emphatically a country event. Trees are most important in the book, not least to rest under (3.9–12, 7.19 *sub lauru mea*, 11.13–17 *hac* | *pinu*). Cf. also 2.10.9–10, now more significant thematically than 1.9.2–3 and 11–12; 2.14.22–4, 15.4–10 (both related to wealth).[58]

7. Death, as is obvious, is a still more important concern than in Book 1. There is now a much stronger interest in death as something universal, and hence as something which is coming to addressee and speaker (a theme foreshadowed at 1.4.13–20; cf. 1.28.15–16). Poem 1 depicts the carnage of the Civil Wars, far more drastically than 1.35.33–4. 2.3.4 starkly calls its addressee *moriture Delli*. The end of 2.6 movingly contemplates the narrator's own death (2.7 presents his escape from death, with some allusion to Alcaeus). Death comes forward especially in the later part of the book, 13–20, and so again is involved in aspects of closure. 13 presents the narrator's near death and near descent into Hades, not without humour; universal death is dwelt on even here (13–20). The poignant poem that follows confronts the death that must be faced by all, including the speaker (who laments), and the addressee.[59] The death of both speaker and addressee is touched on lightly in 16 (17–18, 29–32), and then elaborately and emotionally in 17. 18.17–19 bitingly remind the (nameless and generalized) wealthy addressee that he is forgetting his death. After all this, the final poem provides a spectacular reversal. The poet is exempted from universal death by poetic immortality; his becoming a swan is described with no less humour than his near destruction by the tree. It is a marvellous twist for this specific book. The final avoidance of lament looks back to the end of the first poem, and uses the same word *nenia*.

8. Love, as we have seen, is not of great moment in the book. In the second half, the poems on love (4, 5, 8) fade from view (12 is partly on

[58] On trees in Horace cf. Henderson (1999), ch. 5. The tree incident, like the poem on Horace in the Civil War (2.7), presents an occurrence in the narrator's biography; the humorous intellectual 'conversion' in 1.34 was less of a concrete event. The lyric poet is now, in Book 2, ironically giving his life a few incidents as if in weak imitation of the turbulent existence of Alcaeus (1.32, 2.13.27–32; ancient scholars toiled on it).

[59] On the name Postumus cf. Paschalis (1994–5), 181–2. The repetition at this point in the alcaic line is a device taken up in 2.17.10, 3.3.18, 4.4.70 (cf. in another metre 4.13.18); the alcaic examples are related to death. There is no instance in Book 1.

love); death then becomes even more prominent. A particularly interesting feature of the poems on love, if we see the book separately, is the ambiguous position of the narrator. In the first of these poems he explains, in an obviously unpersuasive fashion, that he is too old for love himself (4.21–4). 5 deliberately leaves it unclear whether the person in love he is addressing is himself.[60] In 8 he does not indicate whether he himself is in love with Barine. In 11.21–2 he summons Lyde, affecting contempt. In 12 he finally indicates that he loves Licymnia;[61] but the last two stanzas make it sound as if, for all her fidelity, she could readily be made over to Maecenas.

Book 3

1. This book, all the more appropriately if 1–2 are republished when it is published, joins the first and the second book together. It also makes many innovations. The first poem emphasizes novelty at the start; it also conspicuously draws together themes from Books 1 and 2: Jupiter, universal death, storms, trees, and so forth.[62] The length of the book (1,004 or 1,000 lines) outdoes Book 1; the number of poems (30) returns us nearly to that book. In metre as in content, Book 3 at first appears to outdo the austerity of Book 2, with a series of six poems in alcaics on weighty themes. Some of them (3, 4) are substantially longer than any in Book 1 or 2 (3, 72 lines, 4, 80 (5, 56); 1.2, 52 lines, 1.12, 60, no other in 1 or 2 over 40). For the repetition of metre, to be followed by change, we may compare *Epodes* 1–10. With an important shift in content, poems 7–16 return to a variety of metres reminiscent of Book 1 (five different metres, including one not seen in Books 1 or 2). There are three sapphic poems here but (understandably) no alcaics. Poems 17–29 produce something in between Books 1 and 2: only three metres occur, alcaic (five

---

[60] The name Lalage in 5.16, cf. 1.22.10, 23, provides a suggestion but not a proof that it is he; Pholoe in 5.17 teasingly cross-refers to a woman loved by others in 1.33.5–9; the boy Gyges in 5.20 plays on the confinement of the narrator's amorous interest in Book 1 to boys (but a boy indistinguishable from a girl: the poem ends stressing puzzlement).

[61] Cf. Lyne (1995), 104.

[62] On 3.1 see Cairns (1995*b*). For the whole book see now of course Nisbet and Rudd's great commentary (2004).

poems), sapphic (four poems) and 2 × (gl + ascl min) (four poems). In general, it is a notable difference from Book 1 that in Book 3 only three metres occur more than twice; it could be said that 2 × (gl + ascl min) grows at the expense of 2 ascl min + pher + gl and 3 ascl min + gl (all have four poems each in 1). The last poem makes the link with 1.1.

There are relatively few of the conspicuous lyric imitations of Book 1. We have one of Alcaeus (12), by contrast with Book 2; but, by contrast with Books 1 and 2, there is little direct discussion of the Lesbian poets: there is only the mention of *Aeolium carmen* at the end. A subtle imitation is the reworking of the supposed amorous dialogue between Sappho and Alcaeus (Sappho fr. 137 Voigt) into a dialogue with only one poet, the male Horace somewhat in the role of Alcaeus. 3.30 itself conspicuously imitates Pindar, as does, less conspicuously, 3.4. In this book, the poet claims priority in the transference of Aeolic song; the imitations of Catullan lyric in Books 1 and 2 are forgotten.

1*a*. The generic contrast at the end of 3.3 is not with history, as at the related end of 2.1, but with epic.[63] Narrative is of great concern to the book.

2. The book reverts to and exceeds Book 1 in using speakers other than the poet: 3.3.18–68 Juno, 5.18–40 Regulus, 9 Lydia (and Horace as a dramatic character), 11.37–52 Hypermestra, 27.34–66 Europa (57–66 imaginary speech of her father inset), 69–76 Venus, 29.43–8 speech for wise man. Extended narrative, especially mythological narrative, is much more important in this book than in Book 1: Juno poem 3, Gigantomachy 4, Regulus 5, Hypermestra 11, Europa 27. The importance of female figures is striking. (Regulus' state-centred heroism is to be contrasted with the family-centred heroism of Hypermestra (note 3.5.41–8), and also with the individualistic heroism of Cleopatra.)[64]

3. Politics has a much more dominating presence than in Book 2; but it gains most emphasis in the first part of the book. The opening

[63] For the connections with Ennius and *Aeneid* 12 cf. Feeney (1984). *Aeneid* 1 is likely to be relevant.
[64] Cf. Oliensis (1998), 140–2.

sequence 1–6, which ranges vastly, is concerned with present campaigns, past tradition, wealth, social mores, and Augustus. (The
relationship with Troy in 3 makes more explicit the connection
with Troy seen in Book 1.) Around the middle, Augustus' return is
celebrated (14); near the end, a poem deals with the need for social
legislation and the present obsession with wealth (24); the next
poem, as if taking off into another but imaginary genre, contemplates the future praise of Augustus.[65] For all the importance which
this structure gives to politics, the change after 1–6 marks, as we shall
see, a change of outlook; this creates a sense of clashing. Such clashes
in outlook are much more important in this book than in Books 1
and 2; they show the poet's interest in exploiting the complexities
which those books put together have presented.[66]

4. Jupiter, as we have seen, appears conspicuously as ruler of the
universe at the start of 1 (5–8); so he does in 4.42–8, at the beginning of
5, and, as god of weather and fortune, at 29.43–5. The rule of the gods is
important to Rome in 6.5–8. Here cult enters in; cult, both public and
private, urban and rustic, is particularly important in this book. (13
and 14 juxtapose these types of cult, just as 14 itself juxtaposes public
and personal.) There is also a hymn to Bacchus (25); Mercury is invoked
at the beginning of 11. The gods are particularly important for their part
in mythology: Juno in 3, all the gods in the Gigantomachy of 4, Mercury
and Amphion at the start of 11, Hercules at the start of 14, Jupiter and
Venus with Danae in 16, Jupiter and Venus with Europa in 27.

5. Philosophical language and generalized moralizing are particularly evident in the political poems mentioned; they form part of the
strenuous stance in those poems. 16 also deals with wealth and need.
3.2.17–24 present a personified Virtus; 3.3.1–8 are highly Stoic in
thought; the figure of Regulus in 3.5 has much Stoic resonance.[67] 24
too dwells on *uirtus* (21–2, 30–2). The narrator's stress on his own *uirtus*
at 3.29.54–5 is deliberately elusive in tone. The end of poem 1 presents

---

[65] Oliensis (1998), 129 describes the poem beginning as the reverse of a *recusatio*.
We should not be too definite about what Bacchus represents: the new type of poetry
is to be mysterious. Cf. Batinski (1990–1). On the poem, see Wimmel (1993).

[66] Propertius Book 3, which is slightly later, shows a similar interest in clashes: cf.
Propertius 3.4–5, 11–14.

[67] Lowrie (1997), 252; see also Harrison (1986); an interesting twist in Arieti
(1990).

a relaxed Epicureanism which purposefully clashes with the involvement in the state at the beginning of poem 2; acceptance of 'poverty' unites the narrator and the desired behaviour of young men, but the ethos is different. The abnegation of riches in 16.21–44 is much coloured by philosophical language, of a sort not particular to one school (*nil cupientium* 22 is not just Epicurean: cf. Sen. *Vit. Beat.* 4.3, 5.1). An Epicurean stress on the present is important in 3.29.29–48. The range and diversity of Horace's philosophizing is much more apparent in this book.

6. The country, as in Book 2, is a highly important motif. The narrator's own life in the country appears in the first poem (45–8), with philosophical point (cf. 17–32), and in the penultimate poem (1–12), again with point (cf. 49–64). The country is drawn into the argument on Roman history and morality in 6.33–44. Country ritual, as we have seen, plays an important part in the book, much more so than in Books 1 and 2: cf. 13, 18, 22, all to do with Horace's estate. In 23 he gives his ritual role to a woman; the use of the country there again has a wider point.[68]

7. Death and its universality appear by suggestion in the first poem (14–16), in a manner now particularly reminiscent of Book 2. The inescapability of death is grimly presented at 24.1–8 (the language recalls 1.35.17–20; but death is now introduced). Regulus' noble decision to die meets us in 5; his death recalls and contrasts with that of Cleopatra. (A mythical patriotic death (19.2) is not of great interest to the party-loving narrator: another dissonance of outlooks.) But already in 1–6 the idea of apotheosis for outstanding mortals is dwelt on (3.2.21–4, 3; more briefly and inexplicitly 1.12.25–32; in 1.2.41–52 we have disguise more than apotheosis). 8 reverts to the narrator's escape from death; 11 deals with an escape from death (but also with a memorial, 51–2); 14 touches on freedom from death. This theme gathers force in the last part of the book. 27 like 11 dwells on escape from death, but more genially: lurid possibilities are imagined, but the reality is safety, with suggestions of immortal fame (73–6).[69]

---

[68] The narrator's biography, as a series of events, is important in 4, which develops the idea considerably (playfully, of course; cf. e.g. G. Davis (1991), 102). Poem 8 returns to the tree; 14.25–8 allude to Horace's Republican past, and give him white hair.

[69] Lowrie (1997), 313–14. Zehnacker (1995), 78, sees 3.26–8 as all a farewell to love-poetry.

25 hints at apotheosis, and perpetual fame, for Caesar, both of these in or through poetry. 26 perhaps speaks as if the narrator's life had ended, but humorously; in 29 the same word, *uixi* (43), displays the unimportance of death to the wise man. Death is being reduced and evaded; the *merita... nenia* lamenting the end of the *festus dies* (28.16) should be seen in this light, as tinged with humour (contrast the word at 2.1.38). All this leads up to the final poem. This is not, as in 2.20, a bold undoing of universal death. The narrator proclaims, not that he will not die (2.20.5–8, 21–4), but that his death will only be partial (3.30.6–7). As he celebrates his immortality through praise, we feel not a reversal, as in 2.20, but a culmination: death has been persistently escaped and transcended.

8. The treatment of love particularly highlights the clashes of the book. The last in the sequence 1–6 harangues the deplorable sexual morals of the present in disgusted tones. 7, while at first it seems impeccably moral in tone, at the end treats the wife's hinted inclination to yield with a wry humour quite unlike the thunderings of 6.[70] Not much later, in poem 10, the narrator himself is depicted in the position of the would-be adulterer in poem 7, begging for the favour of a woman who is married (cf. 1–2, 15–16, esp. *paelice*). It is of course a humorous poem; but the humour highlights a radical difference of approach from 6, and the role of 'Horace' makes it cheekier.[71] This poem itself relates interestingly to 24, where Scythians are models not of barbarity (10.1–4) but of virtue (24.9–24). So it does to 16, the only poem of Book 3 in the same metre as 10. 16 begins from Jupiter's entering the tower as an *adulter* (*risissent* in 16.7 has generic implications too); but it turns to moralizing on wealth. Europa in 27 strikes very moral, and Roman, attitudes (*pater—o relictum | filiae nomen pietasque... | uicta furore!—*, 34–6); but Venus, like the reader, laughs at her (66–76). In this book, unlike Book 2, the narrator's own involvement with love is not in doubt. After the first poem about his own love (9), where he appears to favour Lydia more than Chloe, he professes love for Lyce and Lyde in 10 and 11. His behaviour as a lover sounds more youthful and active than hitherto, in the comedy of 10 and 26. But in 26 he professes at last to end his ever-ending career.

[70] For discussions of 3.7 see Mutschler (1978); Harrison (1988); Cairns (1995*a*).
[71] On 3.10 note Seager (1995), 28.

Book 4, though there is no space to consider it here, would reveal closely related techniques of adaptation and fresh invention. It comes after the sealing gesture of 3.30; but it follows Book 2 in size (580 lines).

Even this sketch should indicate that a different approach to the genesis and production of Books 1–3 leads to a more distinct perception of the individuality of each book. It also enables us to see more clearly how the books relate to each other, and how the cumulative entity of Books 1–3 is built up. The prodigious animal may even emerge as an elegant and satisfying creature.

7

Horace and Archaic Greek Poetry*

INTRODUCTION

Horace proclaims explicitly his use of Archilochus (vii BC) and
Hipponax (vii BC) in the *Epodes* and of Alcaeus (vi BC) in the *Odes*
(*Epodes* 6.13–14, *Odes* 1.32, *Epistles* 1.19.23–33). But the relationship
of these works to archaic Greek poetry is not easily grasped. They are
less closely and pervasively engaged with that poetry than the recently
published *Eclogues* with Greek bucolic; they discuss their relation to
their 'models' less explicitly than the *Satires*. Is broad difference from
the Greek poets significant divergence, or a sign of their relative
unimportance? Such questions are trickier because these poets
mostly survive in fragments.

  The primary aim here is not to compare archaic Greek poetry with
Horace, as we perceive both, but to see what function the Greek poetry
and ideas of it possess within the Horatian works.[1] Points should be
made on both source and target texts. The relevant Greek material is
not just naked fragments in neat modern editions. Papyri show abundant metatexts to archaic poetry in circulation: commentaries, lives,
treatises.[2] Such works would hardly be ignored, as Horace's evidence
confirms, by someone planning to conquer a Greek genre. Scholia—
with a marked interest in biography—frequently appear in the margins

---

* Professor A. Barchiesi and the greatly missed Professor R. O. A. M. Lyne
provided valuable discussion and encouragement.
  [1] There is not space here for close textual analyses, or the pursuit of wider
contexts.
  [2] So P. Oxy. 2306–7, 2733, 3711 (all Alcaeus), 2176, 2293, 3722, P. Köln 61; P. Oxy.
1800, 2438; P. Hibeh 173 (iii BC), P. Oxy. 2506.

of lyric texts.[3] Papyri and other material show us things no less essential than fragments: poets' lives, images, critical reputations, the placing of their poems in the Hellenistic editions.

Horace's own works are best approached as books of poems with a shape and a strategy, not just as individual poems collected together. Recent scholarship demonstrates the value of so viewing the *Epodes*.[4] But each book of the *Odes* too, even if 1–3 were first published simultaneously, needs to be considered as a distinct entity.[5] It will be shown how each of Horace's books uses archaic poets differently, how each deploys them to fashion an identity and create its own significant structure.

EPODES

Archilochus and Hipponax were the main archaic iambic authors; Archilochus supposedly invented the iambus (cf. *Ars* 79). Horace annexes the whole archaic literature, by pointing to both as models (*Epod.* 6.13–14), and marking a special connection with the founder (he avoids Hipponax's metrical hall-mark, choliambic lines, lines with 'dragged' end).[6] He goes beyond the Hellenistic poets, who had concentrated on reworking Hipponax. They, however, dramatize the idea of revival: Hipponax appears in a dream or as a ghost (Herodas 8, Call. fr. 191 Pfeiffer). Characteristically, the *Epodes* do not present their annexation so directly.

Horace later claims to have followed Archilochus' *numeros animosque*, 'metre and spirit' (*Epist.*1.19.24–5). The emphasis on metre is notable; and *animos* discourages us from finding in the *Epodes'* narrator a straight anti-Archilochus like Callimachus' peaceable new Hipponax. It will emerge, though, that these two aspects, *numeros* and *animos*, lead in divergent directions.

---

[3] So P. Oxy. 1234 + 1360 + 2166 (*c*) (Bod. MS. Gr. class. a. 16 (P); ii AD; wide margins left by writer of text; Alcaeus), 2387 (i BC/i AD; scholia various hands), P. Louvre E 3320/R56 (i AD; mostly same hand as text), P. Berol. 9569 (*BKT* v.2.3–6; i AD; same hand as text; Alcaeus).

[4] So Heyworth (1993); Barchiesi (2001*a*); Harrison (2001).

[5] Argument for successive publication: ch. 6.

[6] Usual in Hipponax's stichic iambic trimeters (contrast Horace, *Epode* 17) and trochaic tetrameters, but not in his epodes. Callimachus makes the first line of the couplet in *Iambus* 5 choliambic.

Archilochus and Hipponax were both famed for anger. Archilochus also seems to invite the listener's admiration or interest for his
toughness, bravado, and Achillean independence. Hipponax invites
amusement at himself. But anger is their crucial feature for Horace.

Their works were divided by metre. Archilochus (in more than one
book?): elegiacs, trimeters, tetrameters, epodes (couplets as written);
Hipponax: at least two books of iambi, perhaps at least one further
book, maybe including epodes.[7] All but the last of Horace's poems are
epodes. Even so there is division by metre: the same all-iambic combination for 1–10; an explosion of new metres, with dactylic elements, in
11–16; stichic iambi (not couplets) in 17. Callimachus' *Iambi* inspire the
plain close, and the movement to new metres after the earlier poems.[8]

P. Oxy. 2310 (Archilochus) seems to collocate unconnected iambi.
Related epodes appear together in P. Köln 58, but this need not be by
design: the epodes dwelt so much on Lycambes and his daughters
(one was promised to Archilochus in marriage). It remains notable
that the *Epodes* usually avoid placing the same subjects—including
politics—consecutively. This is part of their indirectness, in particular
as regards narrative.

Narrative had been very important in Hipponax and Archilochus,
particularly Archilochus' epodes.[9] Horace here differs strongly, on
various levels (including intensity of characterization for the
speaker). How pointed this difference is is shown by animal fables,
especially associated with Archilochus' epodes, and used in Callimachus' *Iambi*, and Horace, *Satires* 2.6. Their absence from the *Epodes* is
stressed by vestigial comparisons with animals (so *Epode* 6). No
Epode is straightforwardly narrative; 9 tells of Actium, allusively, 5
of a human sacrifice (it is more like a mime).

Archilochus' epodes included at least one erotic narrative on
Lycambes' daughters (fr. 196a West). The Lycambes story, recurrent
in his poetry, was expanded by biography into a further sensational
narrative, with the suicide of the daughters (cf. *Epist.* 1.19.31).[10] The
Epodes which deal with love and sex offer only fragments of multiple
and frivolous stories. The broken oath of 15 is merely a lover's oath;

---

[7] P. Oxy. 4708 now throws some light on the scale of Archilochus' elegiac poems.
[8] Marked in PSI 1216 by two long lines in the right margin.
[9] Cf. Bowie (2001); note also Archilochus P. Oxy. 4708 (myth in elegiacs).
[10] On the story and the poetry cf. Carey (1986); C. G. Brown (1997), 50–71.

the older woman of 8 and 12 is frustrated, not suicidal. Archilochus' corpus and tradition alike created a super-narrative of his life.[11] Horace's earlier *Satires* Book 1 had been full of biography, and dwelt on the narrator's status and circumstances; the *Epodes* touch on these very little.[12] They are post-Archilochean and oblique.

Instead of narrative and biography the book as a whole offers a more self-reflexive and metaliterary sequence; here poetry, and relation to the model, and the character of the narrator are combined. Poem 1, like many prologues, both introduces and misleads. We see possible links with Archilochus, but also a considerably modified narrator: not much of a fighter, though willing to accompany his friend to war, and friendly rather than (as in the stereotype of Archilochus) angry and abusive. The first third of the book seems to tease us on its relation to Archilochus; it works up to a trademark outburst of rage. Poem 2 sounds content—but turns out to be spoken by someone else (itself an Archilochean trick). 3 shows mock-anger, with Maecenas, on garlic. Much of 4, a brief attack on an unnamed person, is spoken by others. 5 culminates in a verbal attack on the witch Canidia by a character. 6 briefly threatens an attack, and finally mentions (periphrastically) Archilochus and Hipponax: the announcement of the model is delayed, as in the *Eclogues* and *Satires* Book 1, but also achieved.

7–10 offer Archilochean material (speech to citizens, insults to a woman, battle). In 7 the speaker is impressive; in 8 his impotence appears understandable, the affair sordid. 10 at last offers a full-scale attack, based on an epode probably by Hipponax (fr. 115 West). The moment is climactic; the enemy is even named. But the cursing discloses no misdeed or story; the reader of the *Eclogues* (3.90–1) takes Maevius' crime to be writing bad poetry. We are in a metaliterary world.

We should be struck by the poet's metrical achievement in 1–10. The couplets of iambic trimeters and dimeters in all ten poems create a special combination of craft and incisive vigour, new to Latin and remote from satiric hexameters. It is particularly potent when depicting anger. It produces a powerful, if elaborately polished, equivalent to Archilochean force; it gives an overwhelming sense of authorial control.

---

[11] The move from Paros to Thasos will have been crucial for readers of the book(s).

[12] Note poverty (11.11); birth-year (13.6, cf. P. Oxy. 2438).

11–16 explore aspects of Archilochus less apparent before: the narrator's sexual desire (11, 14–15); wisdom and drink (13). The ageing woman (12), the oath (15), the proposal to move city (16), have specific Archilochean associations (fr. 102, 188, etc.). In 11–15 and 17 the narrator now appears weaker and less acceptable. 11, in the metre of Archilochus' narrative of suave seduction (fr. 196a West), presents this narrator's passive amorous susceptibility—with self-conscious humour. 12 suggests, through a character's Archilochean direct speech, the narrator's heartlessness: even 'old hags' have a point of view. In 11 and 14 love stops the feeble narrator writing poems; it was a relative's death that made Archilochus claim he was not interested in poetry (fr. 215).[13] 16, with the narrator as prophet (*uate* 66), is deflated by 17. In 17, the narrator, afflicted by the witch Canidia, humiliatingly and vainly offers to retract his attacks.

Yet the mention of poetry points to contradictions in 11–17: the narrator *has* finished his book, the reader knows, nor can we swallow (in a poem) his lack of interest in poetry. This accentuates a drastic contrast: the good-for-nothing narrator is formally identified (note 15.12) with the poet so brilliantly handling in 11–16 a whole series of metres new in Latin. He mentions his distaste for poetry at the start (11.1–2), in a notably complex three-period metre. 12–16 all begin their 'couplets' with hexameters: Horace is displaying his metrical and poetic range, invading contemporary elegy and the recent *Eclogues*. Callimachus' epodes have no dactylic elements. 17, like 5 using Canidia from the *Satires*, emphasizes range beyond this book: stichic iambics besides stichic hexameters. The author's actual command of his creation is apparent in the whole fiction of 17 (including Canidia's closing speech, which ends with the word 'end').

The structure of the book in content and in metre diverges. The result is both humorous (on the level of content) and self-assertive (on the level of art).

---

[13] In my view Watson's somewhat different understanding of *Epod.* 11.1–2 (it is writing love-poetry that no longer appeals) suits rather less well the plausible connections with *Epode* 14 and with Archilochus fr. 215 West, and gives rather less point to the emphasis at the end on friends' advice and stopping love. This narrator does not need to be consistent with his behaviour two years ago. Cf. Watson (1983), (2003), 258–60, 363–4.

ODES I

Odes 1 advances beyond the *Epodes*. Horace takes on a more complex tradition. 'Archaic lyric' covers a multitude of dialects, metres, and subjects, and various modes of performance. Somewhat as in the *Epodes*, Horace wishes both to encompass the whole tradition, and to appropriate the genre through one paradigmatic author: Alcaeus. The Lesbian poets Alcaeus and Sappho (vi BC) appear from papyrus the most-read lyric poets, apart from Pindar (v BC), commonly regarded as supreme. When Horace refers to 'Lesbian' poetry in Book 1, he might seem to be modelling himself on both Alcaeus and Sappho. But in 1.32 he connects his tradition specifically with Alcaeus; Alcaeus there embodies amatory as well as symposiastic lyric. Seven poems are known to base themselves ostentatiously on Alcaeus (9, 10, 14, 18, 22, 32, 37), one on Sappho (13).[14] But Horace pushes his distance from his exemplar further than in the *Epodes*.

Alcaeus probably presented himself as Archilochus' successor in activities, ethos, and violent emotion (though without Archilochus' dashing charisma). Synesius, *Insomn.* 20 links them in the close relation of poetry and life.[15] Alcaeus' predominant subject-matter was political: he himself, with his brother, was a prime player in Mytilenean politics. In his papyri, some collocations of political poems could be chance; but sometimes at least editors have deliberately placed together poems on the same aspect or period of his life (so P. Oxy. 2165, or 2306 with 2734 fr. 6). Notes, commentaries, treatises show that reconstructing his life particularly interested scholars (e.g. *Σ* on fr. 114; P. Oxy. 2506 fr. 98).[16]

Odes 1.32 contrasts Alcaeus' turbulent life with the narrator's own inactive existence. This underlines both the slightness of implied nar-

---

[14] 31.17–20 (cf. *cithara carentem* 20) may more lightly allude to—and contrast with?—Sappho P. Köln Inv. 21351 + 21376.9–20 (P. Köln 429 col. i.12–col. ii. 8 + P. Oxy. 1787 frr. 1 + 2.11–22 (Gronewald and Daniel (2004*a*, *b*), M. L. West (2005)); but the Alcaean lyre emphatically takes over in 32.

[15] Cf. Susanetti (1992), 183–4.

[16] For ancient commentary on Alcaeus, see Porro (1994). Liberman (1999), i. xlviii–lx, effectively rebuts the firm division which Pardini (1991) posits in the standard edition between poems that touched on strife in Mytilene and those that did not. Probably the nature of Alcaeus' poems made some groupings natural but tight separations between types difficult.

rative about the narrator, and the positive role which this has in characterization. It suits the presentation of this relaxed, middle-aged, and supposedly unimportant person that he has nothing to do, and nothing happens to him. Horace is not continuing the anger of Archilochus, Alcaeus, and the *Epodes*, as 1.16, in the middle of the book, explains: he is older and gentler and renounces anger and *iambi*.[17] Even in the past, the main events were love-affairs somewhat more intense than his present ones: so 1.5, significantly presented as an allegorical shipwreck—Alcaeus experienced real storms.[18] The present love-affairs push a Sapphic world of shifting attachments towards a humour and a depiction of the aging male that evoke the self-irony of Anacreon (vi–v BC). Bereavements, warfare, illness happen to others. Changes of place were crucial to the events, and scholarly reconstruction, of many lyric poets' lives; this book is full of journeys, but they are other people's. The narrator stays put, in retreat but not in exile.[19] There is a philosophical aspect to this quietude, but it is lightly borne.

Let us return to the concerns of the book with its own literary procedures and status. Horace is not really a one-man band, playing all the instruments of lyric: he has transcribed pieces for different instruments on to one. Metrically all is turned into four-line aeolic stanzas. Horace is advancing beyond the couplets of the *Epodes*, and their range of metrical forms. He had important predecessors: Theocritus adapted aeolic metres (but not in stanzas), the Neoterics used aeolic stanzas (but simpler ones, the sapphic stanza apart). Sappho's Hellenistic books had been organized by metre—an indication of its perceived importance; mostly, this book juxtaposes different metres, as usually occurs (perhaps undesignedly) in papyri of Alcaeus.[20]

[17] This palinode neatly brings in the lyric Stesichorus (vi BC): fr. 192 Davies, recently discussed by Kelly (2007).

[18] Allegory itself is often remarked on in lyric papyri (Alc. fr. 306 i col. i Voigt, Pind. fr. 6a (g) Maehler *Σ*, P. Oxy. 3722 fr. 20.8). 1.14 uses Alcaean allegory to be inscrutable about the narrator's past.

[19] 1.22, beginning from Alc. fr. 130b.1 Voigt (Burzacchini (1976, 1985)), makes exile notional, irrelevant, and Sapphic.

[20] See P. Oxy. 1234 fr. 1 + 1360 for the same metre consecutively. Cf. Pardini (1991), 260–6. P. Köln Inv. 21351 + 21376 (early iii BC; n. 14 above) presents two poems of Sappho in the same metre; a different poem preceded the second in the standard Hellenistic edition (cf. P. Oxy. 1787 frr. 1 + 2.1–10). The new papyrus is not itself an edition of Sappho, the third poem suggests; but it may draw on a metrically arranged edition (even so, it could have excerpted poems that were not consecutive).

Horace's book is structured by various displays and links to archaic poetry. The end of 1.1 hopes he may join the lyric canon, but suggests, more ambitiously, that he is embracing it all. 1.1–9 are all in different metres: this display of range culminates in 1.9, with the first *alcaic* stanza (Alcaeus' favourite) and the first prominent imitation of Alcaeus.[21] We may compare the final arrival of the *Epodes* at Archilochus and Hipponax in poem 6, and the full imitation (if there are none earlier) in *Epode* 10.

Most of 1.9–23 begin from lines of, or otherwise conspicuously imitate, numerous poets: predominantly Alcaeus, but also Sappho, Pindar, Anacreon, and others.[22] Having shown metrical range, Horace is now showing the range of his generic re-creation. 12 starts from Pindar, the model of sublimity, and treats not one occasion but all Roman history; 15 presents myth and 'anterior' narrative, based on Bacchylides (v BC); 21 evokes choral poetry. 12 and 15 undermine Horace's overt limits of subject-matter: in 6 he eschewed epic and (despite Alcaeus) war.

Metrically, the last part of the book stresses Lesbian poetry: all but three of 25–38 are in the archetypal alcaic and sapphic stanzas (the latter popular with both Sappho and Alcaeus). Explicitly, too, Horace speaks of his Lesbian plectrum (1.26.11), and compares himself with Alcaeus (1.32): their life-styles contrast, but their works are alike to endure. This emphasis on Alcaeus *after* 1.9–23 shows that the specific allegiance is no artistic limitation: it sets the seal on Horace's unification of an unwieldy tradition. One final imitation of Alcaeus (1.37) shows Horace actually rising above his model: starting from Alcaeus' poem on the death of a Mytilenean tyrant (fr. 332 Voigt), he paints the war with Cleopatra, which involves vast spaces and world events. That rise is played with in the short final 1.38, which dismisses *Persicos . . . apparatus* (Persian armies as well as pompous parties).[23] 1.37 also takes up 1.2, an apocalyptic poem about recent history, on the margins of the book. Horace's scope again exceeds Alcaeus'.

As in the *Epodes*, depreciation of the narrator through the Greek model conflicts effectively with artistic self-assertion. Here, however,

---

[21] The name 'alcaic': Lyne (1995), 98–9. See now Lyne (2007*b*).

[22] Cf. Lowrie (1995). Note how Theocritus 28 begins with a phrase from Alc. fr. 129.26 Voigt.

[23] Choerilus of Samos wrote an epic on the Persian Wars (frr. 1–6, 8 Radici Colace, *SH* 314–23); cf. Man. 3.19–21. See further Cody (1976), ch. 1; D. P. Fowler (2000*b*), 259–60.

the combination possesses ironic charm, all the greater for the paraded achievement.

ODES II

Unlike the *Epodes* and *Odes* 1, *Odes* 2 displays the contrary of range—though its new approach to the genre on a larger view exhibits fresh invention.

Metrically, it restricts variety. 2.1–11 alternate sapphic and alcaic stanzas; 13–20 are all in alcaic stanzas, with two exceptions (one sapphic, one other). 18, like 12 not in sapphic or alcaic stanzas, begins from conspicuous imitation of a Greek poet (Bacchylides fr. 21 Maehler): this too is a rarity in Book 2, even for Alcaeus (2.5 is close to Anacreon fr. 417 Page).

Explicit statements on genre and models are few. 2.1, like 1.2, gives a sweeping vision of recent history, with author and events exceeding Alcaeus; but at the end this is supposed not to suit Horace's Muse, now directly defined as playful and light (*procax, leuiore*). Such dirges are said to be for Simonides (vi–v BC): a disjunction is made within the lyric tradition. In fact 2.2 and 3, and much of the book, are far from light. 2.13 imagines how Horace might have seen Sappho and Alcaeus in the underworld, had he died. One could suppose both are his models; but Alcaeus seems preferred. The book does not proceed to Alcaean political themes; but the predominance of alcaics begins here, and love-poetry disappears. The preoccupation with death recalls a symposiastic poem of Alcaeus (fr. 38a Voigt). This is a more sombre and moralizing version of lyric.

A little more narrative interest accumulates around the narrator. We learn more of his past: his poor parents (2.20.5–6), his fighting at Philippi against Octavian (2.7). His abandonment of his shield links him to Alcaeus (fr. 401B Voigt); mock-myth (rescue by Mercury) restores him to his present static repose. He has had a wearying life of travel and warfare (2.6.5–8): this recalls a poem by the ageing Alcaeus (fr. 50 Voigt). His present age is precisely marked (2.4.21–4), and adds biographical humour to the notional uncertainty in poems 4–12 as to whether he can still experience love; once this is resolved, the theme ceases.

Much more important is a topic connected with the biography of lyric poets: Horace's death. Many lyric poets were assigned spectacular deaths (Sappho: suicide for love; Pindar: death in his lover's arms; Anacreon: choking on a grape-pip).[24] We have 'almost-scenes' of death escaped, one at Philippi (above), one more akin to Anacreon's apt demise.[25] The country-dweller (a motif elaborated in this book) was nearly hit on the head by a falling tree (2.13). The deceased Sappho and Alcaeus (2.13.21–40) invite us to see here a parodic lyric death. There will be an unspoken contrast with Sappho's end. There is also a contrast, taking up 1.32, between Alcaeus' life and the narrator's present life: the narrator knows 'hard pains of war' no longer.

Contemplation of the poet's death also deepens the treatment of death in the whole book. He imagines himself dying in quiet retirement: Septimius will weep at this poet's death (*uatis* 2.6.24). He talks about his own death in consoling Maecenas (2.17). His preaching universal death includes himself—save that at the end, with a humorous twist, he escapes death precisely as a poet. His turning into a bird evokes the self-comparisons of lyric poets (Alcman, Pindar, Bacchylides).

The structure of the book moves it into greater severity, a movement connected with Alcaeus' success (in 2.13). Though the book is more distant from the archaic poets, they enter emphatically in the middle, and shape its concerns.

But 2.19, like 2.20, relaxes the austerity. It is a hymn, the first in Book 2; the narrator has seen Bacchus. Alcaeus' first book had begun with hymns (frr. 307–8, 343 Voigt, S264 Page); Sappho's began with her encountering Aphrodite (fr. 1 Voigt). 2.19 is a quirky poem, with the narrator as a ludicrous bacchant. But Horace, like Bacchus, is less limited to *ioci* (fun) than might be thought (2.19.21–8).

ODES III

Book 3 unlike 1 does not abound in obvious imitations, and unlike 1 or 2 does not talk about individual poets; but archaic poets and poetry produce another structure.

---

[24] E.g. Men. fr. 258 Körte, Val. Max. 9.12.*ext*.7–8.
[25] Almost-scenes: Nesselrath (1992).

The narrator's relation to Alcaeus and Sappho gains further twists, especially as regards audience. The narrator sings to boys and girls (3.1.4); this suggests primarily a development of the role of Sappho, as seen by scholars: a teacher of the noblest girls, approved by the city (S261A fr. 1 Page).[26] But distance from Sappho is marked by the revolted depiction of girls' education in dancing and love (3.6.21–4). The narrator's public importance rises: he sings for Augustus (3.4.37–40), and addresses the Roman people (*Romane* 3.6.2, *o plebs* 3.14.1; cf. also 3.24). Even Alcaeus addresses the Mytileneans (cf. *Σ* on fr. 74) more rarely than he does his comrades.[27]

Augustus has a more dominating presence in this book (thanks to his returning, and approving Horace).[28] In both 3.4 and 3.14 the praise of Augustus is linked with a reminder that Horace had fought against him; he had had parties *not* in celebration of him.[29] We could contrast the 'tyrant' Pittacus—once Alcaeus' ally, then his enemy and his target. Horace, no longer fighting, sings to relax the fighter, and celebrate his return. This is another reworking of the Alcaean role: relaxing his comrades, celebrating his brother's return from fighting in the East (frr. 48, 350).

3.9 shows a lighter side of Alcaeus and the narrator, after 1–6: Alcaeus in love with Sappho (cf. the spurious Sappho fr. 137 Voigt).[30] In 3.27 the narrator, like Sappho, bids a lover farewell. At 3.29.62–4 Horace depicts himself, like Alcaeus, as a sailor in a storm, to be rescued by the Dioscuri (cf. Alc. fr. 34 Voigt, S286 col. ii.1 Page); but the storm is purely notional. In 3.4 the poet actually sketches his biography, now including the tree-crisis (cf. 2.13). A fabled childhood incident links him especially to Pindar (Aelian *VH* 12.45). The rhetoric of the sketch stresses divine aid (cf. Simonides fr. 510 Page); but he appears as a small-scale figure, contrasting with the mighty Augustus.

---

[26] Singing 3.1 itself (and beyond) suggests more than just training a chorus. Contrast *Epist.* 2.1.132–8, etc. Of course Sappho is relevant to that conception too (notably so at *C.* 4.6.31–44). See P. Köln Inv. 21351 + 21376.13–14 (P. Köln 429 col. ii.13–14; n. 14 above); Battezzato (2003), 37–40. Cf. with *C.* 3.1.3 Sappho fr. 150 Voigt?

[27] Another audience in Book 3 are the addressees of hymns: cult, a vital theme of lyric, now bulks larger. These addressees stress the narrator as poet, drinker, and country-dweller.

[28] Cf. *Epistles* 1.13.

[29] 3.14.27–8, cf. 2.7.6–8.

[30] For the early origin of this notion, cf. Hutchinson (2001*a*), 188.

He has no warfare to finish, except warfare with girls; his farewell to such arms (3.26) unconvincingly closes a slender life-story.

In metre, the book begins, like Sappho's first three or four and *Epodes* 1–10, with poems all in the same stanza, alcaic (1–6): the opposite extreme from Book 1. It then opens into a range of metres, before settling (17–29) into alternations of *three* stanzas (alcaic, sapphic, and another); it ends with the same quasi-stichic metre as 1.1 (cf. the stichic *Epode* 17). The pattern marks the crucial shift in the book after 6. It also emphasizes Alcaeus.[31]

Book and narrator descend after 1–6 (he is nicely cynical in 7); the conspicuous imitation of Alcaeus on female passion in 12, like 9, marks the change. The structure resembles the *Epodes* as regards metre and the narrator: but here the point is neither metrical virtuosity nor deflation. One point is to show, in 1–6, how notional are the boundaries confining the world of the *Odes*. 3.3, after a long speech by Juno, is declared unsuitable to Horace's *iocosae . . . lyrae* and *modis . . . paruis* ('playful lyre' and 'little measures'). But 3.4 then uses those little Lesbian stanzas to rise to Pindar and the quintessentially sublime Gigantomachy. In 3.4 the cosmic range of poetry contrasts with the limited poet. 3.30 stresses Horace's achievement conquering *Lesbian* poetry; but the poem again proudly imitates Pindar, on his poetry as an imperishable monument (*Pyth.* 6.1–14). Horace himself becomes the Delphic victor for whom Pindar made that Delphic 'treasury'.

The book shows new ambition too in its prolonged mythological (historical) narratives (3, 5, 11, 27): actually a side of Alcaeus, as in his poem on Ajax's punishment (fr. 298 Voigt), but one little seen earlier in the *Odes* (1.15 Nereus, 1.37 Cleopatra).[32] Also notable are the long public poem 24, and the powerfully expanded symposiastic 29. Poems 1–6, and 11, 24, 27, 29, ten out of thirty, occupy two-thirds of the book.

The structure conveys the range and ambition of the book, and of the accumulated *Odes* 1–3. Yet the movement away from 1–6 also accentuates, by contrast with the structure of Book 2, Horatian charm, and the ironic modesty it depends on.

---

[31] 1–6 apart, alcaics open and close 17–29; 29 is particularly long.

[32] Cf. Lowrie (1997), chs. 7–8.

CARMEN SAECULARE

The *Carmen* presents a climax in Horace's career; but for readers it stands apart from the *Odes*. In what form it was circulated is obscure (an appendix to Book 4?); but even for readers it primarily records a performance. This creates a different relationship with Greek lyric: connection is chiefly with choral performances, not books.

The poem has an unparaded literariness. As a sort-of-paean, it has significant links with Pindar's (Simonides', Bacchylides') paeans, written, as in the papyrus titles, for particular cities.[33] *Paean* D4 Rutherford graphically depicts Ceos; *Paean* D2 presents the history of Abdera. This poem deals with a vaster city, which dominates the world; its beginning, present, and future are encompassed.

The poem is strikingly impersonal. Voiced by girls and boys, and destined for a religious occasion, it avoids subtlety and play, even on the performers (unlike archaic choral poetry). *Odes* 4.6 brings out the difference of the *Carmen* from the *Odes*. Yet the poem itself produces, especially but not only for readers, a sense of Horace's achievement. Implicit is the prestigious commission, recorded in the *Acta* (*ILS* 5050.149). Hellenistic and neoteric ceremonial poems make short stanzas expected, not Pindaric constructions; but the sapphic stanza surprises (no paeanic refrain), and makes a firm connection with the *Odes* (cf. 4.6.35 *Lesbium*). The dominant divinities are Apollo and Diana; this fits a paean (e.g. Simon. 519 fr. 35 Page), but creates a particular link with the fictive hymn 1.21.[34]

ODES IV

Book 4, though with fewer conspicuous imitations than 1, is absorbed by itself and its traditions. It retains its formal Lesbian identity (*Aeolio* 4.3.12, *Lesbium* 4.6.35). It begins, like Sappho's first

---

[33] Cf. Phlegon *FGrH* 257 F 37.V.3.18–20; Barchiesi (2000), 177–82, (2002), 112–18. The connection of *Odes* 4.6, on the *Carmen*, with Pindar, *Paean* D6 Rutherford is more ostentatious.

[34] On the gods and the ceremony, cf. Feeney (1998), 32–8; P. J. Davis (2001).

book, by addressing Venus/Aphrodite, now an enemy not a 'fellow-fighter' (Sappho fr. 1.28 Voigt). 4.1 alludes further to Alcaeus (fr. 296b Voigt) and Sappho (fr. 31 Voigt). But 4.9 implicitly draws attention to Horace's whole lyric tradition. *minaces* ('threatening', 9.7) of Alcaeus' Muses stresses how much Horace has departed from his model. *si quid . . . lusit Anacreon* (Anacreon's play, 9.9–10), point-ing back to 1.32.1–2 *si quid . . . lusimus* (Horace's play), suggests his special affinity with that poet.

The list begins with Pindar and Simonides (9.6–7): the book particularly aspires towards the lyrical summits.[35] This is partly because the poems praising the deeds of Augustus and his family gesture towards fifth-century poetry of praise. Thus poem 4 begins from a comparison with an eagle, a bird important in epinician; opening with a simile is an epinician idea.[36] Families and heredity concern epinician.[37] But no less important is epinician's concern with itself, and its gift of immortality. The fame of the actual poetry, not least this book, is more prominent than in Pindar (cf. 4.8 and 9). 4.6, which draws on Pindar, dwells explicitly on Horace's fame. 4.3 sets Horace's fame alongside that of athletes (compare epinician) and generals (compare 4.4, etc.).

4.2, a second prologue, alleges the folly for Horace of imitating Pindar; but the language used of both belies the claim.[38] A simile likens Pindar to a river; the device itself acquires sublime, and poetological, associations. The eagle (4.4.1–12) is usually a compari-son for the epinician *poet*; Tiberius too is compared to a river (4.14.25–32)—the river by which Horace was born (cf. 4.9.2).

The narrator's birth is one of the few biographical elements in the book (cf. also 4.3.1–2). His homosexual passion in 4.1, anomalous for *Odes* 1–3, connects especially with Alcaeus (cf. 1.32.11–12 and Σ Alc. fr. 71 Voigt). His loves are ending, again (4.11.31–4). But the crucial biographical element is fame, and the actual works. A com-mentary on Sappho, for example, stresses contemporary glory (S261A fr. 1 Page); works are given in many biographies. Horace's

---

[35] Cf. Barchiesi (1996).
[36] Cf. esp. Pind. *Ol.* 7.1–7; Bacch. 5.16–30 restarts with the eagle.
[37] Cf. 4.4.30–2 with Pind. *Ol.* 11.19–20 and P. Oxy. 2438.43–8.
[38] Cf. Harrison (1995*a*) on the poem.

own name appears (4.6.44), uniquely in the *Odes*. Someone else speaks it, as in Sappho (fr. 1.20, etc.); but here the point is renown.

After 4.1, the narrator's life of love and drinking, so characteristic in *Odes* 1–3, seems to disappear. 4.7, of symposiastic type, elides the symposium. 10–13 finally bring these elements back, before more poetry on Augustus in 14–15. Earlier subjects are roughly: 4.1 love, 2–3 poetry, 4–5 *princeps* and family, 6 poetry, 7 near-symposiastic, 8–9 poetry. Partly the reader is being teased: Venus' 'long-suspended wars' (4.1.1–2) have been suspended again (for real wars); love returns in the very short 10. But 10–13 especially emphasize range. In this book, Horace has unexpectedly developed the grandest side of lyric tradition; but his once standard world is not abandoned. Juxtaposition with the immortality of poetry gives themes like ageing a new poignancy; but the series 10–13 ends with laughter (13.27).

The metrical structure also stresses range. It presents eight different stanzas, only seven sapphic or alcaic poems, and, until the last two poems, none in the same stanza consecutively. Variety increases in 7–13. One may particularly contrast the similarly short Book 2.

The emphasis on range is part of the self-glorification. The book celebrates itself, and the whole series of Books 1–4, to which it forms not a coda but a finale.

Each book builds from archaic poetry its own structure, based on the relation, and conflict, between art and the narrator. Each structure is dynamic, and metaliterary. These books are greatly preoccupied with themselves.[39]

---

[39] Further reading. Standard editions: Archilochus, Hipponax: M. L. West (1989); Alcaeus, Sappho: Voigt (1971), and Page (1974); Alcman, Stesichorus, Ibycus: Davies (1991); Bacchylides: Maehler (1982–97); Pindar: Maehler (1987–9), with Rutherford (2000) for *Paeans*; other poets: Page (1962). Tarditi (1968) and Degani (1991) give fuller testimonia for Archilochus and Hipponax. Gerber (1999) and D. A. Campbell (1982–93) include translations. The introductions in Hutchinson (2001*a*) set each poet in context. Lives: Lefkowitz (1981), chs. 3, 5, 6. Commentaries of course give a great deal of material: Cavarzere and Bandini (1992), Mankin (1995), and Watson (2003) on the *Epodes*; Nisbet and Hubbard (1970 and 1978) and Nisbet and Rudd (2004) on the *Odes*; Hill's and R. F. Thomas's commentaries on *Odes* 4 are eagerly awaited. Recent thinking on the *Epodes* and archaic poetry: see Barchiesi (2001*a*); Harrison (2001); Lyne (2007*c*). *Odes*: G. Davis (1991); Feeney (1995); Barchiesi (1996, 2000); Paschalis (2002); Woodman (2002); Lyne (2007*b*); *Carmen*: Barchiesi (2002).

8

Ovid, *Amores* 3: The Book

The sophistication and force of *Amores* Book 3 as an entity have yet to be fully recognized. Recent discussion has made a welcome start; but attention has been too exclusively focused on the three-book structure which Book 3 ends, and on the larger *œuvre* which follows it. The present chapter seeks to enter more deeply into the book itself. Awareness of this structured book as an artistic achievement may be hindered by the five-book version and possibly by a lingering perception of the *Amores* as artistically lightweight. But the three books are clearly marked as finished artefacts for the reader (cf. 1.1, 15, 2.1, 3.1, 15); and 'light' and 'lightweight' are not synonymous.[1]

I. FRAME AND INSET

The frame of the book, poems 1 and 15, turns the rest into a kind of narrative 'middle', in an Aristotelian sense. The outcome of Elegy and

---

[1] On the five-book version cf. Cameron (1968); but one should not suppose that incoherences visible to us would be acceptable to Ovid. Scepticism: Barchiesi (2001*b*), 159–61. Consistency on the stage reached in Ovid's production need not be expected across books: contrast 2.18.13–34 with 3.1 and 3.15. Indeed the *Amores* could be seen as playing against external chronology a structural movement from remaining with an expanded love-elegy in Book 2 to renouncing love-elegy in Book 3; this thought arises from discussion with Professor J. Booth. Obvious links within *Amores* 3: e.g. 1.1–2 and 13.7–8 (grove); 4.39–40 and 6.45–82 ((next poem); Ilia; cf. also 7.21–2); 6.13–18, 7.31, 10. 11, 29–36 (Ceres). Some important recent work on *Amores* 3: Boyd (1997); Holzberg (1998*b*), 68–74, (2001), esp. 130–40; Weinlich (1999), 181–271, 272–80; Bretzigheimer (2001), esp. 177–82; Fantham (2001), 199–205; Harrison (2002), 80–2. Less recent: Lörcher (1975), 74–98; Wille (1984); Rambaux (1985), 141–76. Professor J. C. McKeown's commentary is eagerly awaited.

Tragedy's battle for Ovid is a limited temporal space: a brief time in which the poet can write elegy before he turns to tragedy, and the lover can continue with love before the *finis amandi* (1.15, cf. 2.19.52). The idea of a short space for action is a fundamental generic characteristic of known tragedy (Arist. *Poet.* 1449^{b}9–16); Tragedy herself is asked to permit this to a poet: *exiguum uati concede, Tragoedia, tempus* (67). A particularly striking example of this short space is the story of Medea, where the character herself is allowed a short time, and within in it must accomplish her terrible deeds (cf. e.g. Eur. *Med.* 339–75, Sen. *Med.* 288–95, 420–4). Since the reader of the three-book version is aware of Ovid's *Medea* (2.18.13–14), his only tragedy, it seems natural to bring Medea in here. Tragedy may present herself as *facta uirorum* (25), not a description apt to the *Medea*; but the *Medea* serves precisely to underline Tragedy's rhetorical distortion. That distortion is underlined too by the debate in the *Frogs* which this poem recalls: tragedy includes not only the grave Aeschylus but the erotic Euripides.[2]

Within the short span of a tragedy, momentous and decisive events occur. This contrasts with the world of love as seen in the inset, a world—as Tragedy already complains—of repetition and failure to change. Medea, pre-eminently a figure of dilemma, eventually reaches firm decisions; so too does the narrator in the frame of Book 3. His eventual decision in poem 1 is realized, despite the suspicious

[2] Cf. *Frogs* 939–49 for Euripides' changes to the personified art of tragedy. *Romana tragoedia* at *Am.* 3.1.29 does not indicate *praetexta* any more than *Romanus* at Prop. 4.1.64, 6.3. For a different view cf. Holzberg (1998*b*), 43–4, (2001), 110–11. Figures of Tragedy and Comedy: marble statue, Berlin AvP VII 47, from Pergamum, ii BC (*LIMC* 'Tragodia' 4); mosaic, Princeton 40. 435, from Antioch, iii AD (*LIMC* 'Komodia' 9; Kondoleon (2000), 156). In the latter (Menander), mistress and genre appear together; comedy and Glycera are connected in the poet's dilemma of Alciphr. 4.19; cf. *Am.* 3.1.7–10, 49–60. For the motif of the single day see Schwindt (1994), esp. 89–99. There were of course many dramas on Medea; but even in Carcinus, where she did not kill the children, she killed Glauce (P. Louvre E 10534.7–8: Bélis (2004), 1308). Cf. e.g. Apulian r.-f. volute crater Munich 3296 (J 810), attributed to the Underworld Painter, *c*.330 BC, *RVAp.* ii. 533.283, *LIMC* 'Kreousa' 17 ('Creonteia' killed, one child escapes). Ov. *Med.* fr. 1 Ribbeck suggests the temporal framework; cf. also *Am.* 2.14.29–32, *Her.* 6.127–8, 12.181–2, 207–12, etc., for her actions. On the figure of Medea see Clauss and Johnston (1997); Mastronarde (2002), 57 n. 94, 64–70. On *Amores* 3.1 see Schrijvers (1976); J. T. Davis (1989), 108–13; Döpp (1992), 43–7; Boyd (1997), 195–200; Bretzigheimer (2001), 76–84; Wyke (2002), ch. 4; Hunter (2006), 28–40; R. K. Gibson (2007), 72–92.

procrastination, in poem 15. The contrast between frame and inset includes genre: the inset is (supposedly) to consist of love-elegy. But matters are more complicated; even within the frame, the narrator's role as Medea, no less than his role as Hercules, is a kind of parody.[3]

II. LOVE

If we concentrated on the relation between this book and what precedes and follows it, we might see two simple parallel movements: the lover gradually abandons love and the poet gradually breaks free of love-elegy. But such a view would not do full justice to the structure of the book and its complexity. Let us take love first.[4]

The inset often teases the reader with feints towards an ending of the love-poetry, but then immediately thwarts them. Love, in the elegiac world of the inset, cannot be escaped; there can be no decisive change, nothing perfective. An important instance is poem 11*a*. This suddenly announces the end of the narrator's affair with a woman. The angry rupture that closes Book 3 of Propertius is strongly evoked. Even that ending turned out in the next book not to be final; this decision is revoked in the very next poem, one of an antithetical pair. The form itself repeats that of the antithetical pair 2.9*a* and 9*b* (wish to leave love, wish to love): both repetition and reversal are strong forces against closure in love-poetry. The very opening *multa diuque tuli* is itself a repetition, of the last poem of

---

[3] Medea is probably shown in agitated indecision at Ov. *Med.* fr. 2 Ribbeck *feror huc illuc ut plena deo* (*ut* Gertz: *ue* codd.; *uae* goes with adjectives in Ovid; Håkanson's doubts on Sen. Rh. *Suas.* 3.7 are needless): cf. Sen. *Med.* 382–6; AR 3.650–4. Further for her dilemmas in Ovid cf. *Her.* 12.60, *Met.* 7.7–72; for her decision on her children, cf. Eur. *Med.* 1012–80, 1236–50, Gal. *Plac. Hipp. Plat.* 4.6.19–27 (*CMG* v.4.1.2 p. 275), cf. Chrysipp. *SVF* iii. 473; Neophron *TrGF* 15 F 2; Antip. Thess. XXIX, Plin. *NH* 35.136, paintings, Pompeii VI 9.6, 7 (Casa dei Dioscuri) and IX 5.18 (Casa di Giasone), Naples inv. 8977, 114321, i AD, Pugliese Carratelli and Baldassarre (1990–2003), iv. 975, ix. 678–7. Cf. Ov. *Am.* 2.18.15–16 for Ovid the tragedian as a tragic character (cf. Cic. *Fam.* 7.6.2). The connection with Prodicus, *Horae* B1–2 Diels–Kranz (2 = Xen. *Mem.* 2.1.21–34) is evident; cf. also Ar. *Clouds* 889–1111, Cic. *Cael.* 33–6. The connection with the *Frogs* makes Ovid into Dionysus (cf. *Am.* 3.15.17), with a different kind of parody.

[4] For conceptions of the whole book see esp. Holzberg and Fantham as in n. 1. Holzberg (2001), 113, stresses the limited role of chronological sequence.

Book 2 (2.19.49); there the poet comically threatens to abandon the affair because of the husband's lack of effort. The poem also gestures to a Catullan poem of attempted closure (*perfer et obdura* 3.11*a*. 7, cf. Cat. 8.11, 12, 19); in that poem the repeated *obdura* (*obdurat*) highlights a lack of perfective decision.[5]

The change in 11*b* is not an abrupt move, as in 2.9*b*, to a contrary position; it slides to the contrary through a depiction of indecision, itself antithetical. The concise epigram (85) in which Catullus sets extreme poetic order against emotional chaos is here expanded into a prolonged series. While displaying the author's declamatory fertility, the series also expresses the narrator's endless oscillation. The pair of poems drastically exhibits the state of mind which ensures the continuation of love, and robs attempted closes of finality.[6]

Poem 13 introduces a remarkable surprise: the narrator, a subordinate clause reveals, is married (*Cum mihi pomiferis coniunx foret orta Faliscis*, 1). The reader does not even know whether this is to be accommodated within the fiction of the rest—after all, a man's own marital status did not even legally affect his love-life—or whether we have moved outside it altogether. In either case, so drastic a change seems to indicate an end to love or love-poetry. But another surprise promptly follows.[7]

Poem 14 reverts to 11*b*, and by contrast with 13 gives no reason to suppose the love presented will ever end. The narrator begs his beloved to keep her infidelities from his knowledge. One should not say that so unsatisfactory a situation could hardly be imagined to persist:

[5] Cf. Barthes, *Fragments d'un discours amoureux* (*Œuvres complètes*, ed. E. Marty, 3 vols., Paris (1993–5), iii. 591), 'la répétition (comique ?) du geste par lequel je me signifie que j'ai décidé—courageusement !—de mettre fin à la répétition'. For poem (poems) 11 see L. Müller (1856), 89–91; Gross (1975–6), (1985), 159–68; Cairns (1979); Pallotto (1982); Keul (1989), esp. 6–166; Damon (1990); Döpp (1992), 51–60.

[6] The absence of adversative or direct contrast makes against seeing 11*a* and *b* as one poem. Asyndeton within monologues is justified by a violent revulsion or an exclamation (7.38, 8.509). Dense oscillations are required within 11*b*.35–6, if genuine (for the forceful *habet* 'has got now' cf. Tac. *Ann.* 1.7.6). It has been woven into a new entity with Propertius in *CIL* iv.1520, originally from the atrium of VI 14.43 (cf. Pugliese Carratelli and Baldassarre (1990–2003), v.2.426–67); this suggests an author of classic status.

[7] On a biographical level, the wife is presumably Ovid's second: cf. *Tr.* 4.10. 69. For continuing affairs while married, cf. *Rem.* 565–6, deleted by Goold (1965), 49–50, probably wrongly.

irrationality is the abiding condition of the Ovidian lover, and the mental stance goes back all the way to 1.4.69–70. Clamorous echoes return us to 11*b* and the state of mind it depicts: love prevailing over hatred and desiring union coextensive with life (14.39–40 *tunc amo, tunc odi frustra quod amare necesse est*; | *tunc ego, sed tecum, mortuus esse uelim*). The Catullan connections here underline the potential of dissatisfaction as a permanent state, and source of love-poetry. The narrator actually wishes to go beyond dissatisfaction: into a state of wilful ignorance. *liceat stulta credulitate frui* (30) pointedly reverses 11*a*.32 (close) *non ego sum stultus ut ante fui.*[8]

The narrator's failure to end his love-affairs is here given the most drastic emphasis. On other levels closure may be found in the poem, the last of the inset; but on the level of amorous story its salient feature is that closure is not achieved. The apparent movements in that direction, especially in 11*a*, have been firmly reversed. The imperfective nature of love-elegy has again reasserted itself.

A less direct instance of apparent ending is poem 7, where the narrator has been impotent. This suggests the end to love-making which poem 1 has implied (*finis amandi* 1.15: the narrator's love and the poet's love-poetry go together). Not that 7 indicates a fading out of love on the level of literal narrative: the impotence is presented as a sudden surprise, and contrasted with recent prowess (23–6); it is not a sign of age (19–20). But the impotence has a symbolic aptness to the end of love; this is connected metapoetically with an end to generating love-poetry (see below). However, within the sequence, this appearance of closing love down is abruptly annulled by poem 8 (the sudden *Et* of 8.1 matches the *At* of 7.1). Poem 8 brings us back to an archetypal elegiac situation: the lover has been displaced by a soldier. Such displacement is of course generically normal rather than closural: the narrator's frustrated desire is the prime motive force of elegiac books. Love-affairs, and love-poetry, are back in familiar mode. The theme is merely given a contemporary twist, one suited to the book: the soldier embodies the type of *eques* who

---

[8] On poem 14 cf. Gross (1985), 168–75; Keul (1989), 213–47; Bretzigheimer (2001), 38–41. Weinlich (1999), 270–1, acknowledges that the poem does not show the end of an affair.

has risen through the army, in accordance with Augustan patterns of mobility.[9]

Continuity and contradiction go together in the world of the inset: the narrator's irrational oscillation keeps the pendulum of love and love-poetry endlessly swinging. Poem 4 presents a memorable instance early in the book; notably, it is the last poem of the preceding book with which it stands in contradictory continuity. The elegant argumentative opposition may best be explored with the aid of formal logic, a powerful tool which critics of poetry should exploit. Here it oversimplifies the argument, but brings out the structure of ideas: a kind of coarse geometry.

In 2.19 the underlying thought can be presented thus:

> p: I will want your wife more.
> q: your wife will be guarded.
> $[q \rightarrow p]$ (i.e. q entails p).
> So : q! (i.e. bring it about that q is the case)
> so that p.

Here $[q \rightarrow p]$ shows the irrational (Callimachean) mentality of the lover. The likely feelings of the husband make it comic and cheeky that $[q \rightarrow p]$ should be urged on the husband as a reason for q!.

In 3.4 the underlying thought of the first part (1–32) can be presented thus:

> r: your wife will want lovers more.
> s: lovers will want her more.
> q: your wife will be guarded.
> A. $[q \rightarrow r]$.
> So : $\neg q$! (i.e. bring it about that q is not the case)
> (because otherwise, r because q).

---

[9] Cf. Demougin (1998), 361–5, and on Augustan reforms 13, 18, ch. 3. Cf. Devijver (1976–93), iii. 1121, and ii. 621 (O26; *CIL* ix.3082) for a member of Ovid's family. In *Am.* 3.7.23–4 the girls, with their real but expressive names (*CIL* xiv.1542; *IG* ii–iii/2.1034*d.* 20; e.g. *CIL* vi.33744), are clearly on a different level from *mea...puella* at 73; the impotence is not part of a temporary rift with Corinna, as in Tib. 1.5.39–46, cf. *memini* 26 against *nuper* 23. If the poem offered any literal suggestion of lasting impotence, it would soon be cancelled by poem 10, which implies a context of sexual activity, only temporarily suspended. On 3.7 see Baezo Angulo (1989); Tränkle (1990), 345–8; Holzberg (1998*b*), 25–7; P. R. Hardie (2002*a*), 241–2.

B. $[q \rightarrow s]$.

   So : $\neg q!$

         (because otherwise, s because q).

$[q \rightarrow r]$ and $[q \rightarrow s]$ (and implicitly $[q \rightarrow p]$) are all seen to follow from the general principle t: $\forall x \forall y[x$ is difficult to obtain for $y \rightarrow y$ wants $x]$ (i.e. for all instances of x and y it is the case that . . .).

Here $[q \rightarrow r]$ and $[q \rightarrow s]$ show the irrational mentality of the wife and of lovers, part indeed of a wider irrationality. The contradiction with 2.19 on the desirability of q suggests further the irrationality of the narrator-lover; the contradiction is highlighted by the affinity of the arguments for $\neg q!$ and $q!$ in the two poems (cf. t). The likely feelings of the narrator make it comically implausible that he should urge $[q \rightarrow r]$ and $[q \rightarrow s]$ on the husband as reasons for $\neg q!$: his own aim in seeking $\neg q$ must be to continue as a lover himself. In 37–48, contradicting himself within the poem, he indicates the practical advantages to the husband of a wife with lovers (suggesting $\neg[q \rightarrow r]$). The risk of closure at the end of 2.19 has now receded. The paraded irrationality, and the games with argument, show love and its poetry running on with unstoppable momentum.[10]

   The world of the inset is affected by the treatment of Corinna and other mistresses. The analogy of Propertius 3.21 might prompt us to see new mistresses in this book, and the rare naming of Corinna, as signs that the grand passion of the love-elegist is ending, that the diminishing passion is climbing downwards through more transitory contacts. But whereas Propertius 3.21 forms part of the closing sequence, in *Amores* 3 we see a new mistress in the first poem of the inset (2.57 *nouae . . . dominae*, cf. 4); this beginning takes up the beginning and end of the previous book. There the first poem after the prologue and the last poem had seen the narrator's fancy caught by a new woman (2.2.3–8, 2.19.19, contrast *uiderat . . . Corinna* 2.19.9). The first two poems in that book to name Corinna (2.6, 11) are immediately followed (7 and 8) or preceded (10) by poetry which shows the lover unconfined by fidelity to one woman. Indeed,

---

[10] For *custodes* see McKeown (1987–), ii. 27–8; McGinn (1998), 333–4 (*comites*); R. K. Gibson (2003), 334. Note *AA* 3.613–14. On 3.4 (and 2.19), see Lyne (1980), 274–80. I am very grateful to Dr B. C. A. Morison for discussion of the logic.

his roving eye in Book 2 makes us look back differently at Book 1, where as in Book 3 Corinna had rarely been named: should we have assumed that unnamed mistresses were Corinna? If then in Book 3 the narrator is sometimes explicitly ennamoured of other women (poem 2, poem 7, cf. 7.25–6), and is mostly ennamoured of women unnamed, this is not a clear closural signal. The amorous impulse continues unabated, producing problems and poems.

Tibullus' switch of mistresses between books is emphasized in 3.9 (29–32, 53–8; Marathus is kept unmentioned). Ovid follows a different tack. The frame (3.1.49–52) marks Corinna implicitly as the formal subject of his love-poetry. The reader recalls the more explicit 2.17.28–34 (besides Corinna, no woman *nostris cantabitur... libellis*), abruptly falsified by 2.19. The formal fiction, however, is at least maintained. But the appearance of a new woman in the next poem, the disappearance of Corinna into a memory in 3.7.25–6 (*exigere... Corinnam... memini...*), and the scarcity of Corinna's name by comparison with Book 2, make the reader uncertain whether we have despite the frame moved to a world where Corinna is absent, or the narrator is wholly promiscuous, or the identity of the mistress is irrelevant. But near the end of the book a new surprise restores Corinna's formal position. In poem 12, *ingenium mouit **sola** Corinna meum* (16). This further implies that the woman unfortunately lauded to others by the narrator's poetry is Corinna. And it must be she, if *nostris innotuit illa libellis* (7): no other love-object has been named in the *Amores* save the maid Cypassis and the three women accumulated in 3.7.23–4. Of course, the logic does not really work: the name Corinna is a pseudonym. *sola* in this book raises questions, as does the poet's requirement that we should believe in Corinna and the assertions of the poem while disbelieving the assertions of poets in general and himself in particular. The games with belief and self-subversion are highly Ovidian; but the poem is more a reaffirmation of the original status quo than a closural revocation of *laudes.*[11]

---

[11] The reader is to contrast Prop. 3.24.1–8. That poem is motivated by the disappearance of love, this by the wish to continue it. Here it is the allegation of fiction which is (within the fiction) false. On poem 12 see Bretzigheimer (2001), ch. 4; P. R. Hardie (2002a), 6–7, 41, 240. *Amores* 2.4 (promiscuity) and 2.10 (love for two women at once) are both inspired by Propertius 2.22a; but Ovid's work implicitly opposes Tibullus' two mistresses to Propertius' one: cf. *AA* 3.536 (538 sides Ovid with Propertius), *Rem.* 763–4. For the dispute in *Am.* 3.9.55–8 cf. Luc. 3.20–3.

The inset has a contemporary force which intensifies the interest of abandoning love-poetry outside its borders. The inset goes further than Books 1 and 2 in its ostentatious impudence towards the *Lex Iulia de adulteriis coercendis*. Although adultery is often suggested as the situation in Books 1 and 2 (e.g. 1.13.41, 2.2.51), explicit words like *maritus, coniunx, adulter(a)* are rarely used in regard to the narrator's affairs in earlier poems. Poem 2.19, where *marito* twice occurs near the end (51, 57), in various respects prepares for Book 3. Book 3 does more than make adultery explicit: it directly entangles itself with the stipulations of the *lex*. Poem 4 closes by presenting as the final attraction of not guarding a wife gifts from her friendly lovers (*et quae non dederis multa uidere domi*, 48): receipt of such gifts is specifically punished by the *Lex Iulia*. For all the sly phrasing, this trumps in outrageousness the ending of 2.19, where the narrator calls the husband *lenone*: another allusion to the law. The end of 3.8 goes further again: the narrator indicates that husbands will permit adultery within their houses if and only if lovers make gifts (57–64).[12]

So far the narrator has appeared in the literal role of (would-be) adulterer. But in the last part of the book, he arrestingly moves into the figurative role of compliant husband. In 11*a*, where he even declares himself metaphorically the woman's *uir* (17), he comically and allusively tells of finding her in bed with a rival (25–6). It is a distorted version, in the woman's house not his, of the scene which the *Lex Iulia* makes so important in Ovid's work: the husband catches wife and adulterer in the act. The *lex* obliged the husband to take action against the adulterer and divorce the wife; so when the narrator finally continues the relationship at the end of 11*b*, this characteristic reversion is coloured by behaviour which the *lex* condemns. With an extra touch of impertinence, the narrator's attitude to the woman in 11*b* is supported (38–9) by allusion to a speech on marriage delivered by (probably) Q. Metellus Macedonicus (*cos.* 143) as censor in 131; when Augustus *de maritandis ordinibus ageret*

---

[12] Cf. *Dig.* 48.5.2.1 *lenocinii quidem crimen Lege Iulia de adulteris (-iis?) praescriptum est, cum sit in eum maritum poena statuta qui de adulteris uxoris suae quid ceperit* (add to McKeown on 2.19.57–8). Cf. also P. J. Davis (1999), 446–7, (2006), 81–3. Further on the *Leges Iuliae* see M. H. Crawford (1996), ii. 781–6; Treggiari (1991), 277–98; Mette-Dittmann (1991); McGinn (1998).

(Livy *Per.* 59), he read this speech out to a no doubt fascinated Senate.[13]

In 12, the narrator appears as a quasi-conjugal *leno*: *me lenone placet, duce me perductus amator* (not *riualis*), 12.11. After 13, where he is a real husband in a respectable marriage, 14 makes the play with Augustan legislation more extensive and elaborate. Provided she denied it, he could disbelieve his own eyes *si... in media deprensa tenebere culpa* (43). The quasi-marital toleration is as in 11*a*–11*b*, but the language directly evokes the law (note *deprensa*), and the stance is more extreme. Lines 8–12 allude to prostitutes as beneath the law on adultery: so the legislation decreed. The talk of *indicium* (12, normally the activity of an *index*) and the implication of a reward (42) point to the practical workings of the *lex*. Words like *censura* (3), *pudicam/as* (3, 13), *crimina* (20), *inquiram* (41), *probra* (44), *causa* (50), *iudice* (50), add to the legal and Augustan resonance. Entrenchment in love is vividly tinted by the law on marriage. The weakness of the lover is in counterpoint with the audacity of the author.[14]

The decision to abandon love-poetry in the frame might itself have larger implications. The poet could in theory be thought to turn at the end of the book in an Augustan direction, away from dangerous material and from immoral behaviour. In 3.1.44 Elegy had appeared as a *lena*. But the discussion of genre will show this question in a different light.[15]

---

[13] *ORF*[4] 18 F 4–7 (including Suet. *Aug.* 89.3). Livy *Per.* 59 suggests a striking forward reference in the narrative of 131. For 3.11 and Metellus see Barchiesi (2001*b*), 155–9. The comedy of 11*b*. 25–6 is enhanced by *cucurri*; cf. Plin. *Ep.* 1.12.9; see also *AA* 2.315–26, 3.641–2. For adulterer (and wife) *in domo deprehensum* (direct quote) see *Dig.* 48.5.30 pr., and also 48.5.2.2, 26 pr., *RS* 60. Adultery may be suggested in 3.10: the mystery cult might seem to have been predominantly for *matronae* (Livy 22.56.4, Fest. p. 86 Lindsay; παῖδας and ἀλόχων Phlegon *FGrH* 257 F 36 10 A 16, 19 for offerings, cf. Val. Max. 1.1.15). In Athens at least, the corresponding festival probably involved predominantly married women only, cf. Austin and Olson (2004), pp. xlvii–xlviii; R. C. T. Parker (2005), 270–1.

[14] *in media... culpa* intensifies the law, cf. *Dig.* 48.5.30 pr. (Ulpian has to add *in ipsa turpitudine*, cf. 24 pr.). Lines 31–2 provocatively suggest that the addressee is the narrator's wife (cf. Hor. *Epist.* 1.1.87–8, Prop. 4.11.85), all the more strikingly after 13.1–2; 33–4 undo the suggestion (cf. Propertius 2.29*b*). For the exemption of prostitutes see McGinn (1998), 197–8, 202–3. *indicium* (not surprising with the *quaestio perpetua*) appears likely to be topical from *AA* 2.573–6; cf. Stroh (1979), 350; Holzberg (1990), 137–52; Hutchinson (forthcoming). Suet. *Aug.* 34.1 seems to designate the law itself as *de adulteriis et de pudicitia*, cf. *Dig.* 48.5.14.5.

[15] For *lenae* in Augustan legislation, see *Dig.* 23.2.43.7–9; Flemming (1999), 51–3.

We do not, then, see in the inset a gradual withdrawal from love. Appearances of ending are followed by resumptions in a way that toys with the reader but also displays the endless to-and-fro of the amorous universe. The perfectivity of the frame contrasts. The reader is also teased on who the mistress of each poem is, and whether alterations are opening up in the amorous world. Such alterations, even if realized, would not clearly indicate closure; and the conventions of the earlier books are formally reasserted near the end (and then contravened by a married narrator, a contravention dropped in its turn). The momentousness of the inset and the frame is heightened by the increased and increasingly provocative involvement of recent legislation. In general the overarching structure of the book is both reinforced and played with.

III. GENRE

The notion that the poet gradually escapes from love-elegy would reduce and simplify the generic adventures of the book. An initial point to be made is that the most obviously excursive poems are ordered in a sequence that moves downwards generically, and in some ways moves back closer to elegy. Poem 6 includes a narrative on Ilia (45–82) within the narrator's monologue to the river: love-elegy encloses the epic and tragic (a sort of reversal of Book 3's frame and inset). The story comes from Ennius (*Ann.* 44–5, 60, I.xxxix, 63 Skutsch), and features a lamenting female character (*Am.* 3.6.47–8 *ungue notata comas, ungue notata genas*: tragic anadiplosis turned into elegiac elegance). Ilia is a highly unelegiac woman: not interested in love and an appalled ex-Vestal, now *horrida cultu* (47). Metapoetically, rivers of course have epic connotations. In poem 10, an amatory situation encloses a narrative of Ceres' love for Iasius. The poem has connections with Hom. *Od.* 5.125–8, but primarily evokes, not like 6 the vast epic of Ennius, but the small epic genre of the hymn (cf. esp. 5–14). Callimachus' hymns to Zeus and to Demeter are much in mind. The love-lorn goddess comes closer to love-elegy than Ilia did. Poem 13 turns to the aetiological elegy of Callimachus, and explains the ritual of Juno's festival at Falerii Veteres. The Greek character of the poem matches the Greek character of the ritual (27–34). Elegy, then, rather than epic, and not even a version of elegy completely separated from love.[16]

A second point to be made is that the book also includes poems which go as it were beneath rather than above the norms of love-elegy. This is most conspicuously the case in the poem that immediately follows 6, poem 7 on impotence. Its impropriety is much more drastic than is usual in elegy, which keeps something of a distance from the genitalia. The poem expands an obscene type of epigram. The contrast in elevation with poem 6, and especially its inset narrative, could not be more obvious; it is especially marked at the end, which focuses on the woman and gives her like Ilia a speech (77–80). For this un-Vestal woman, the disgrace is to be *intactam* (83–4, the final couplet).[17]

The first poem of the inset transgresses norms in a different fashion. Like 7, it is in a way hyperelegiac. The urban location of elegy is intensified by the setting of the poem in a specific contemporary place, the Circus Maximus. The notion that elegy deals with the narrator's life is pushed to minute detail on quotidian physical events as they occur. A mime-like action monologue presents in detail a modern Roman event: a chariot-race as seen by the jostling and excited audience (and the unsporty narrator). The experimentalism of the book is not confined to generic ascent.[18]

---

[16] See below. The unusual depiction of Ilia on a 3rd-cent. AD Vatican sarcophagus (*ASR* iii. 2.188a–b; Sichtermann and Koch (1975), 66–7; Klementa (1993), 64) depicts her as a Vestal, led to her doom through the country to a river (probably the Anio, *pace* Sichtermann and Koch). It is likely to derive from Ennius. See Klementa (1993), 126 for a marble statuette of the Anio as a god (Tivoli, private collection).

[17] The address to the personified penis in 7.69–72 highlights the link with epigram: cf. Petr. 132.9–14 (with self-conscious discussion), Strato *AP* 12.216 = 59 Floridi, Scythinus 12.232. Address to the river becomes less elevated in the last part of 6. Some other epigrams related to poem 7: Philod. XXVII = 19 Sider, Automedon II, Strato *AP* 12.240 = 81 Floridi, Rufinus *AP* 5.47 = 18 Page; cf. also *Priapea* 83.

[18] Prop. 2.22*a*.1–10 on the theatre, perhaps a starting-point for this poem, point up Ovid's originality of technique. For the Circus Maximus see esp. Humphrey (1986); for the races themselves *CIL* vi.10044–82. Contemporary as the place is, Ovid declines to mention Augustus' contribution to the Circus (Ciancio Rossetto (1993), 273), and his presence (cf. Aug. *Epist.* 1 Malcovati, Suet. *Aug.* 45.1, Tac. *Ann.*

The range of the writer is conspicuously displayed by the book, and relates to his final escape; but any simple affirmation of generic hierarchy would not well suit the inset, or Ovid. Generic relationships within the poems are complicated, and Ovidian love-elegy retains its power to drag down. We may look first at the most excursive poems. The relationship of the narrative on Ilia to love-elegy is only suggested lightly. The argumentative point is to show that river-gods, like the narrator, are affected by love, an experience which somewhat demeans divine power (cf. 23–42). The Anio's speech of amatory persuasion (55–66) is a more dignified version of a love-poem (within a narrative within a love-poem); but with the closing *ne me sperne, precor, tantum* (65) the actual loss of dignity shows through, and the mention of *munera* (66) has elegiac resonance. The crudity and cunning of desire shows through his action: *supposuisse manus ad pectora lubricus amnis | dicitur* (81–2). Much more parodic is the relation of the outer narrative to epic. The narrator impeded by the river recalls Achilles in *Iliad* 21. Although Achilles' own epic dignity is infringed in that book, divine aid enables him to pass the obstacle and achieve the greatest martial deed of the poem. The narrator of the *Amores*, in a typical pattern, gets nowhere, for all his flood of eloquence (cf. 1.6, 1.13, etc.). He also refuses (86–106) to allow his river the status that would get it into his Hesiod-like catalogue of amorous rivers; the river was not even a fit audience for it (101–4). The poem as a whole shows an elaborate and often comic interaction between genres.[19]

1.54.2). On the poem see E. Thomas (1969); Hollis (1977), 58–60; Tracy (1977), 498–9; Lyne (1980), 255–6, 280–2; Gauly (1990), ch. 2; Henderson (2002); Opsomer (2003).

[19] With 65 cf. *Met.* 1.597. Achilles and the river: note Hom. *Il.* 21.192–5, with P. Oxy. 221 col. ix.1–25 (Erbse (1969–88), v. 93–4; cf. D'Alessio (2004)); on dignity, 21.279–83. For Ovid as Agamemnon, cf. *Rem.* 781–2. Line 91 *nomen habes nullum* plays on the poet's power, and on 1.29 *nunc habeam per te Romana Tragoedia nomen* (cf. 2.17.28, *AA* 3.536, *Rem.* 366, etc.); Horace, *Odes* 3.13 is relevant. The catalogue involves various rare myths, and may draw on a prose source, to judge from the catalogues in *Her.* 19.129–40 and Philod. *Piet.* pt. 2 P. Herc. 1602 fr. 6 + 243 fr. 3 col. i (see Obbink (2004), 181–201). Presumably it is not based solely on Hesiod here (cf. 30 with fr. 10*a*.20–4 Merkelbach–West); but it suggests the epic form of the catalogue (cf. 45 *nec te praetereo*). It is probably related too to Callimachus, as in fr. 66 Pfeiffer and *H.* 1.18–27 (it is not clear whether περὶ ποταμῶν included myths, frr. 457–9 Pfeiffer). *certus . . . amor* seems hard to explain in 30: *caecus*? On poem 6 see Courtney (1988); Suter (1989–90); Ramírez de Verger (1992); Boyd (1997), 211–19; Barchiesi (2001*b*), 54.

The narrator of hymns should in theory laud the god, and defend the deity's fame. The narrator of poem 10 handles the deity infelicitously. Callimachus' narrator in the *Hymn to Demeter* (7–23) anxiously breaks off from the subject-matter of the *Homeric Hymn to Demeter* itself, and from Demeter's tears (gods should not weep). The narrator of poem 10 has no sympathy for her sorrow: now Proserpina has been found she should, he implies, get a grip (45–6). He tells rather the more ignominious story of her passion. This is supposed to be to her credit; but he sounds more like a prosecutor, adducing *testes* to her *crimina*, which she will confess (19–24, reworking Callimachus' praise of Zeus). The epic deity is made like the narrator of the book, in the fluctuations of her indecision; cf. 10.28–9 *hinc pudor, ex illa parte trahebat amor. | uictus amore pudor* with the opening of the next poem but one, 11*b*.1–2 *luctantur pectusque leue in contraria tendunt | hac amor, hac odium; sed, puto, uincit amor.* Love-elegy pulls down divinity and epic.[20]

The imperfectivity of the narrative suits the inset and love-elegy rather than epic. The devastating consequences of Ceres' passion for the world's agriculture (29–36) recall the consequences of her grief for Proserpina; but the narrator, as indifferent to such matters as the enamoured Ceres, leaves the story unfinished. Even union with Iasius is only implied (43).[21]

In poem 13 the matronly Juno's festival is *casta* (3) and celebrated by youths and *timidae...puellae* (23–4, cf. 25). But even Juno seems to have a past. The myth, told briefly and allusively, presents the *aition* of goading and sacrificing a she-goat (18–22). The she-goat, however, is an informer betraying a wife's flight to her husband

---

[20] Ceres' amorous role is especially striking in view of the Augustan values associated with her: cf. Spaeth (1990); Livia is often depicted as Ceres: cf. Spaeth (1990), 119–23, 169–73; Bartman (1999), 93–4. *Homeric Hymn* 5 actually complicates the genre (contrast Isocr. *Hel.* 60); but *Amores* 3.10 is pointedly post-Callimachean. On it see Lenz (1932–3); on the genre cf. M. L. West (2007), 312–16. Cf. also Philic. *SH* 678–80. For more audacity to gods cf. e.g. *Amores* 3.3; in 35 *Iuppiter igne suo lucos iaculatur et arces, lucos* seems too vague, and we should surely read *suos*: cf. Ar. *Clouds* 401 τὸν αὑτοῦ γε νεὼν βάλλει, Lucr. 2.1101–2 *aedes...suas,* 6.417–18 *suas...sedes,* Cic. fr. 10.36–8 Courtney (note *ignis*), *AA* 2.540 *Arce Iouis.* On poem 10 see Lenz (1932–3); Le Bonniec (1958), 407–8; Boyd (1997), 67–79.

[21] Iasius killed by Zeus: Hom. *Od.* 5.125–8; grows old: Ov. *Met.* 9.422–3; mystical union and rites: Theocr. 3.50–1, cf. Clinton (2003), 67, 69.

(19 *indicio*, 21 *index*); the informer is not rewarded but becomes a reward (22). Disrupted marriage and legal language bring in the provoking contemporary elements seen elsewhere in the inset. The generic mix is complicated by light hints of tragedy in the festival, for the reader of *Amores* 3.1: the role of the goat, the long *palla*.[22]

Generic intricacies appear too in the poems which take elegy lower. In poem 7, the narrator parodies Achilles, the supreme exemplar of masculinity. *sed iacui pigro crimen onusque toro* and *truncus iners iacui, species et inutile pondus* (4, 15) clearly point to Achilles' self-reproach ἀλλ' ἧμαι παρὰ νηυσὶν ἐτώσιον ἄχθος ἀρούρης (Hom. *Il.* 18.104). A figure from hymn is suggested too. In 44–8 the narrator wonders in bewilderment what new type of prayer he can utter, since all his prayers were granted; it is evident to the reader that he omitted to ask explicitly for the natural accompaniment to what he asked, namely an erection. The pattern points towards the story of Tithonus, who is actually mentioned at 42.[23]

Poem 2, first in the inset, makes abundant connections with other types of elegy, the Hellenistic celebration of royal chariot-victories in epigram and *Aetia* (at the *beginning* of Book *3*); it connects too with other genres of literature, particularly the epinician (15–16 allude to the *first* of Pindar's epinicians, in the order of the Hellenistic edition). We may see hints of poetic ambition, especially when we come to the chariots of 3.15.2, 18. But the upward links mostly drag higher things downwards: the chariot-racing bores the narrator, Pindar's heroic Pelops is assimilated to love-elegy and the narrator (15–18). The

---

[22] Lines 19–20 look unlikely to indicate a flight from Jupiter as wooer (*indicio, siluis inuenta sub altis, inceptam destituisse fugam*). Comella (1986), 186, though retaining this view, notes that a ἱερὸς γάμος is not well supported by the votive finds at the probable site (Celle). The most plausible context seems a story like that of Hera's hiding herself from her husband after a disagreement (Plut. fr. 157.6 Sandbach, cf. Paus. 9.3.1–2). Goats are of course important in the cult of Juno (e.g. at Lanuvium, *RRC* i. 439–40 no. 412). On the poem, see Lenz (1932–3), 312–13; Le Bonniec (1980); Cahoon (1983).

[23] Cf. *Hom. Hym.* 5.218–38; Sappho P. Köln Inv. 21351 + 21376.9–20 (P. Köln 429 col. i. 12–col. 2.8) + P. Oxy. 1787 frr. 1 + 2.11–22, Call. fr. 1.29–36 Pfeiffer = 1 Massimilla (Tithonus not named), Ov. *Am.* 1.13.1, 35–42. 7.47–8 were famous, to judge from the unnoticed adaptation in *AE* 1928 no. 37 (ii AD). Hom. *Il.* 18.104 is seized on by Racine as an Achillean phrase, *Iph.* 252 *de la Terre inutile fardeau*. Achilles' male heroism is extended analogically to sex in Petr. 129.1 *illa pars corporis qua quondam Achilles eram*, cf. Prop. 2.22a.29–34.

religious *pompa* (43–60) does join with religious elements later in the book (10, 13); but the narrator's viewpoint is resolutely amatory, and he tells the woman that if she promises her love she will be a greater goddess than Venus (60).[24]

The lament for Tibullus, poem 9, draws on the notion of elegy as lament; it also raises the status of love-elegy—somewhat at the expense of epic. Tibullus is made a kind of parallel to Achilles and Memnon, explicitly mentioned at the start. He like them is to be mourned by a goddess. The end of the *Odyssey* (24.35–94) and the whole of the *Aethiopis* are evoked; Elegy's lament recalls the lamentation of the Muses (Hom. *Od.* 24.60–2; M. L. West (2003*a*), 112). The elegiac poet is put on a level with epic heroes: an anti-hierarchical move. The point emerges more directly at 25–32. The two books of love-poems by Tibullus are daringly matched with the two monumental epics of Homer. Allusion to elegiac books is especially pointed in the last book of the *Amores.*[25]

A highly significant absence in the poem is that of Virgil. He had died at around the same time; the synchronism is the subject of Marsus *FRP* 180, clearly used in this poem and possibly to be seen as the epigram which the whole poem expands. Here Tibullus is the *comitem* (*FRP* 180.1) not of Virgil, but of Calvus, Catullus, and Gallus, who all died early (3.9.61–6). To stress the absence, *Elysia ualle* (60) and *tu quoque* (63) pointedly underline the connection with Marsus, and *his comes umbra tua est* (65) pointedly echoes Virg. *Aen.* 6.447–8, as *auxisti numeros* recalls *Aen.* 6.545. This is a club for Latin love-poets. Tibullus' death is no less distressing to Cupid than that of his brother Aeneas (13–14): another anti-hierarchical point.[26]

Both poem 9 and poem 7 are metaphorically apt to the end of the series: elegy dies, elegy cannot be generated. But interpretation should not be too exclusively negative. In poem 7 a reading of

---

[24] The close takes up her divine promise (83); her laughter has, for the narrator, divine suggestions, cf. 1.6.11, *Fast.* 4.5–6, Sappho fr. 1.13–14 Voigt. Epigrams on royal and other equestrian victories: see esp. Posid. 71–88 AB. For the *pompa* see Bernstein (1998), 35–48, 254–68, 341–4.

[25] For the *Aethiopis* cf. M. L. West (2003*b*), 1–2. There Memnon is immortalized, unlike here. Cf. Ov. *Met.* 13.621–2, Papaioannou (2003). On the poem see McGann (1970); Taylor (1970); Privitera (1989); Boyd (1997), 179–89; F. Williams (2003).

[26] For 3.9 and Marsus cf. Courtney (2003), 303–4 (add lines 37–8?), and Hollis (2007), 311. Much other epigram is relevant, e.g. *SH* 980; Courtney (1993), 47. Cf. also [Mosch.] 3, and for *Am.* 3.9.25–8 the epic Lucr. 3.1036–8.

exhaustion is balanced by the poem's own brilliant generation of a large structure from the content of mere epigrams. That expansion ironically combines expression of the self-reproachful lover's futility with display of the author's fertility. The death of Tibullus points to the continuing life of his successor. The mention at the end of Calvus, Catullus, and Gallus, now joined by Tibullus (61–6), inevitably gestures to the end of Propertius Book 2 (or 2*b*) (2.34.89–94), where Propertius hopes to continue the line; we are bound here to think of the successor who has composed the poem. This poem is not at the end but in the middle of its book; the next poem prefers sex and song to mourning (10.45–8).

The repeated engagement with Augustan legislation in the inset raises an important question about the significance of the narrator's abandonment of love-elegy. Is he moving not only towards a higher genre but also towards pro-Augustan and patriotic poetry? These two movements are frequently associated in literature of the period, as superficially Ovid's own later works will exemplify. But *Amores* 3 declines to follow this path. The progression from 6 to 10 to 13 takes us not only away from epic but away from Roman mythology. Poem 6 presents a central Roman myth, from an unusual perspective. Poem 10 leaves a Roman festival for the country, a Greek island, and the subject-matter of Greek elegy. Especially relevant is Philetas' poem on Demeter (probably set on Cos). The Roman rites in question were actually called *Graeca sacra*; but in any case the narrator detests them.[27]

Poem 13 is aetiological; but it treats the cult of a city which had been conquered by Rome (*moenia . . . uicta, Camille, tibi*, 2), and later supposedly destroyed. Livy (5.26–28.1) and others present the original conquest of Falerii Veteres in a benign light; Valerius (6.5.1) stresses the moderation of the Romans at the final conquest. (The inhabitants were dislocated, most of the cults not.) Although Roman actions are not criticized here, it is notable that the poem presents traditions parallel to Rome's, and no less ancient.[28]

---

[27] *Graeca sacra*: cf. Cic. *Balb.* 55, *Leg.* 2.21.12, Festus p. 86 Lindsay. See Wissowa (1912), 300–2; Le Bonniec (1958), 400–46; *II* xiii.2 p. 493; Spaeth (1990), 103–13; Scheid (1995), 23–4; Beard, North, and Price (1998), i. 70–1. For Philetas' poem, see Sbardella (2000), 44–9, 112–27; Spanoudakis (2002), 142–308.

[28] *Fast.* 4.63–78 stress the late arrival of Aeneas, and the Greekness of Italy. Cf. Leigh (1998). For Falerii see Comella (1986); Corretti (1987); Moscati (1990); De Lucia Brolli (1991), 72–4.

Halaesus, the Greek founder of Falerii and the cult, is presented in
language strongly reminiscent of Aeneas: *iamque pererratis profugus
terraque fretoque | moenia felici condidit alta manu* (33–4). The
beginning of the Roman epic is thus radically reapplied near the
end of this poem and book; connected is the beginning of this poem,
where the walls are conquered by Rome (*felici* is not without longer-
term irony). In the *Aeneid*, the goddess here celebrated is the enemy
of the Trojan band. In *Fast.* 6.49–50 she will indicate that she would
(if not acknowledged as the origin of June) regret allowing her old
favourites the *Iunonicolas... Faliscos... Romanis succubuisse.* Her
former feelings are not dwelled on here; it remains striking that the
final *Iunonia sacra... sint mihi, sint populo semper amica suo* should
not refer to Rome.[29]

The Italian emphasis is not relinquished when we revert to the
frame: it is sharpened. The poet emphasizes his Paelignian origins (cf.
2.16, and his wife's Italian origins in 3.13.1). The anti-Roman actions
of the Paeligni in the Social War are admired; the Romans are seen as
intimidated (*Paelignae... gentis..., quam sua libertas ad honesta
coegerat arma, | cum timuit socias anxia Roma manus,* 8–10). Roman
confiscation of her land may be intimated in *campi iugera pauca* at 12.
The poet's proud standing as part of a family long equestrian is now
explicitly contrasted with that of those who ascended through military service (6, cf. poem 8; the triumviral period may be suggested).
The poet does not, like Propertius in 4.1.55–70, integrate the glory he
brings to his native region with fervent dedication to Rome: only
Sulmo's walls appear, small but made great by the poet (cf. Halaesus at
13.32; contrast Prop. 4.1.55–7). In the context of 7–10, the north
Italian origins of Virgil and Catullus (*Mantua Vergilio gaudet, Verona
Catullo*) intimate the dependency of Rome on foreign talent more
than its appeal. *Paelignae dicar gloria gentis ego* (8) pointedly reworks
Troianae gloria gentis of an Alban king in Virgil (*Aen.* 6.767).[30]

---

[29] *sit... sit* (*V*_b, cf. *H*) is of interest. Boyd (1997), 51–3, rightly stresses the
subversiveness of the Virgilian echoes in 31–4.

[30] Sulmo was completely destroyed by Sulla (Flor. 2.9.28): the walls (11–14) must
have been rebuilt; its fate was like that of Falerii, but much worse. The smallness of its
territory may have been the result of Sullan confiscations: see Mouritsen (1998), 147
n. 1. See further on Sulmo and its territory van Wonterghem (1984), 223–303. On
poem 15 cf. Schmitzer (1994); Bretzigheimer (2001), 38, 44–6.

The generic stance and implications of the final poem are not straightforward. The opening *quaere nouum uatem, tenerorum mater Amorum* parodies and reverses Agave's abandonment of the Bacchic cult at the end of Euripides' tragedy (*Ba.* 1387 βάκχαις δ᾽ ἄλλαισι μέλοιεν; cf. 17 *corniger increpuit thyrso grauiore Lyaeus*). *quaere nouum uatem* also continues the sequence of 2.19.59 (last couplet of the book) *quin alium...quaeris?* and 3.11a. 28 *quaere alium pro me qui uelit ista pati.* The repetition there had underlined the suspiciousness of lovers' renunciations; should we now see more suspiciousness, or a contrast? The same question arises with *tenerorum mater Amorum:* it recalls Hor. *C.* 4.1.5 *mater saeua Cupidinum,* which echoes *C.* 1.19.1 and so displays the renewed onslaught of love once meant to be at an end (1.19.4). The penultimate poem of Book 2 already shows us, as if from a different perspective, the subsequent relapse from tragedy.[31]

The actual smallness of Sulmo's walls and land (11–14) could be thought to match the generic smallness of the *Amores,* as against the *area maior* of tragedy (18, cf. 3.1.24, 64); the poem itself is pointedly short. But the transformation of the walls through Ovid suggests the poems could also be seen as *magnus.*[32]

The poem carries out the promise of poem 1, and leaves behind Venus and elegy. But although the poet is obeying Tragedy, poem 15 does not simply share Tragedy's attitude to elegy. (The narrator's attitude to the permanent value of elegy had been a little more ambiguous in 1.65–8.) 15.17–18 *corniger increpuit thyrso grauiore Lyaeus;* | *pulsanda est magnis area maior equis* patently takes up 1.23–4 *tempus erat thyrso pulsum grauiore moueri.* | *cessatum satis est; incipe maius opus.* But this poem shows the present *opus* (20) as lasting, and mostly celebrates the achievement of the *Amores;* the future mostly envisaged is not the composition of tragedy, but the fame of the *Amores* (8, 11–14, 20). The final pentameter does not, as so often, undercut the hexameter, but rises to a higher level; even the hexameter winningly implies a fondness that defies the hierarchy of

[31] A tragedy has been written (2.18.13–14). In 19–20, *quod licet* (cf. e.g. Virg. *Aen.* 3.254) and the parallel with tragedy and the *Heroides* indicate a permitted excursion beyond the *Amores* themselves, so the *Ars Amatoria.*

[32] The imagined speech of praise from the future is itself a device of epic, and tragedy (cf. e.g. Hom. *Il.* 7.87–91, Soph. *El.* 975–85; Wilson (1979)).

genres: *imbelles elegi, genialis Musa, ualete,* | *post mea mansurum fata superstes opus* (19–20). *opus* ended the first poem too, but referred to tragedy.[33]

The book thus parades immense generic scope and invention. This broadening of the *Amores* is related to the decisive poetic movement in the frame; the movement remains a crucial event in the book, even if infringed by suggestions in the last poem. The excitement of new possibilities is forcefully and tantalizingly conveyed. But the inset does not chart a straightforward generic rise, or a straightforward endorsement of generic hierarchy. The play and interplay between Ovid's version of love-elegy and other generic possibilities is many-faceted; overall within the inset love-elegy dominates and pollutes its rivals. (Even 13 is stained, and followed by 14.) The move to tragedy in the frame has aspects of an imposing ascent; but the poetic value and attractiveness of elegy are strongly felt by the reader of the inset, and are affirmed in the final elegy.

The inset resists an overall plot for the lover; it also resists a plot for the poet. No Augustan or Roman motivation is seen to drive the generic expansion of the inset, or the final move to tragedy. Even the cultural pride of *habeam per te Romana tragoedia nomen* (1.29) is voiced by grave Tragedy, with whose views the narrator's are not altogether identical. The emphasis on Italian rather than Roman tradition near the end of the inset continues into the frame, and creates a distinctive stance. This combines with the book's marked increase in pointed and audacious reference to Augustus' legislation on adultery. In consequence, that increase is not seen as part of a larger plot in which immorality is finally repented of—much as Tragedy would wish this (1.15–30); rather it becomes part of an outlook maintained to the end of the book, one of lively independence.

[33] Poem 12 levels the genres in a different fashion: it formally obliterates the formal claim of love-elegy to reality, and treats elegy, tragedy, and epic with equal frivolity. For the *Aeneid* cf. 38 and *Aen.* 9.101–2; tragedy ends (39–40), and may be suggested at the start (21–2, cf. *Tr.* 2.393–4). For *historica ... fide* 42 cf. the play at Sen. *NQ* 7.16.1. The overt lament of generic choice (15–16) implicitly celebrates Ovid's love-elegy, cf. 2.17.27–32, *AA* 3.535–8, *Tr.* 4.10. 59–60 (note *uestra* 44 to the readership).

IV. INTERTEXTUALITY

These ideas of Book 3 gain enhanced definition from the literary context of, say, 23–7 BC. Some points have already been made on Propertius 3 in particular; a few brief points may be added here. The interest of the book as a coherent structure is highlighted by various other recent 'last' books: books which are, or present themselves as, last in a series. *Odes* 3 and especially 4 are of relevance here; but particularly important are 'last' elegiac books.

Propertius' third book begins by elaborately announcing fidelity to love-poetry, but in its last part moves gradually towards a renunciation of love and love-poetry; this is explosively achieved at the end. Within the book, the limits of love-poetry are expanded; there is one full-blown narrative (poem 15: 15 and 16 together lie behind *Amores* 3.6). Propertius' fourth book begins with an announcement of aetiological poetry, followed by a summons back to love-poetry. The ensuing book occupies a varied distance from love-elegy as seen in earlier books; after its first half (poems 1–6) love-poetry on Cynthia is dramatically reopened, closed, reopened (7–8), then left (9–11). Against this background, the strategy of *Amores* 3 becomes the more notable: a firm structure, itself playing on genre, sets most of the book within a promise made at the beginning and realized (it seems) at the end. The firm, though more serious, designs of intellectual prose are related; see ch. 10. The contrast of frame and inset is strong. Instead of a gradual shift in the later part of the book, as in Prop. 3.20–5, surprises appear in the inset and are surprisingly reversed; this plays on and confirms the central conception. The generic ventures of the inset, more considerable than those of Propertius 3, are more mastered than in Propertius 4 by the concerns and self-assertion of love-elegy. The whole book unites, and sets in conflict, exuberant invention and a constraining form: a form which illuminates both love and genre.

To read *Amores* 3 against Propertius 4 throws many aspects of the former into sharper relief. We notice how *Amores* 3 gives more significance than *Amores* 1 and 2 to female viewpoints, and to deities; we notice that here, by contrast with Propertius 4, heroic males appear only in parody, or polemic (the soldier of 3.8). The heavy emphasis of Propertius 4 on Rome and Roman *aitia* gives more weight to the un-Roman aetiology and outlook of the last poems in *Amores* 3. Particularly important are the elaborate contrasts between the last poem in the inset and the last poem of Propertius 4. That poem presents the defence of her *fama* which an austere wife gives, or might give, to the judges of the underworld; she implicitly justifies Augustan law, though she needs no public laws or *iudex* (4.11.47–8). The narrator urges the woman in *Amores* 3.14 to win her case with her partial *iudex* by two words of denial (47–50); she insists on proclaiming her own ill fame. He tries, figuratively, to avoid a *quaestio* and the demands of Augustan law.[34]

Tibullus 2 is palpably relevant to *Amores* 3, which brings Tibullus into a near-central position in poem 9. Indeed the death of Tibullus, a purely poetic event, replaces the death of Cynthia at a similar point in the structure of Propertius 4. The two books of Tibullus are indicated (31–2); his last book is implicitly contrasted with the last book of the *Amores* but not of Ovid. Tibullus 2 shows an excursive impulse, but without the contemplation of a new genre; ritual and narrative gain a new significance in that book. The lover-gods Anio and especially Ceres in *Amores* 3 are connected with Apollo in Tibullus 2.3 (11–32); Ilia and Ceres appear in Tibullus 2.5 (51–4, 58). Tibullus 2.5 like *Amores* 3.13 goes back to Troy's refugees; to Halaesus corresponds Tibullus' Aeneas, brother of Amor (2.5.39, echoed at *Am.* 3.9.13). Tibullus 2.5 and *Amores* 3.13 are in similar positions in their books. But Tibullus' poem, while not naming Augustus, devotes its energies to Rome. The individuality of Ovid's stance is brought out all the more.[35]

---

[34] The chronological relation of the two books is not certain; but the connection of *Am.* 1.14.45–6 *nunc tibi captiuos mittet Germania crines*; | *tuta triumphatae munere gentis eris* with *Fast.* 1.645–8 *passos Germania crines* | *porrigit auspiciis, dux uenerande* (Tiberius), *tuis.* | *inde triumphatae libasti munera gentis* strongly suggests that the former passage too refers to the actual triumph of Tiberius on 1 January 7 BC (Dio 55.8.1–2), and is meant as a marker of date. It could have been inserted after the first publication of the three-book version; but problems over triumphs in 12–7 BC would lend an extra point to 2.12 (note 2.12.13). *Amores* 1.8 probably follows Propertius 4.5 (cf. Hutchinson (2006*b*), 139).

[35] *pererratis* ‖ *profugus* at *Am.* 3.13.33 conjoins *profugis* ‖ and *errantes* ‖ Tib. 2.5.40, 42, as well as echoing Virg. *Aen.* 1.2 *profugus*. The penultimate couplet of Tib. 2 (6.51–2 *tunc morior curis, tunc mens mihi perdita fingit*, etc.) is taken up in the last poem of the inset, 3.14.37–40 *mens abit et morior quotiens peccasse fateris... tunc amo...*; cf. also 24 with Tib. 2.6.52. Ovid turns the dead poet's ill-omened *morior* into paradoxical routine; his paradox is transformed in Petrarch, *Canz.* 164.12–13 'e perché 'l mio martir non giunga a riva, | mille volte il dì moro e mille nasco'.

Such comparisons show the intensity with which the structure of *Amores* 3 should be studied. It repays consideration no less than books often regarded as more monumental achievements. The point of focusing attention on this book of the *Amores* has not been to minimize the significance of the series or of the *œuvre* as artistic entities; fuller appreciation of this book will lead in turn to richer appreciation of what the larger entities involve. But it is hoped that this attempt at exploring the book itself shows how impressive a work Ovid has here created.

9

The Metamorphosis of Metamorphosis: P. Oxy. 4711 and Ovid*

Knowledge of the Greek models for Ovid's poem of metamorphosis rests on very slight foundations. Our most substantial verbal quotation (Nicander fr. 62 GS) lasts only four lines; it is actually far from certain that it comes from the *Heteroeumena*, and need not be typical of that work. A newly published papyrus, P. Oxy. 4711 (vi AD), presents something much more sizeable, and a surprise: a series of metamorphoses in elegiacs.[1]

The papyrus codex is often very difficult to read. Dr W. B. Henry has edited it with his exceptional skills and acumen. The text below is very similar to that in the *editio princeps*. I have examined the original; I have also used CDs of multispectral images taken of → on 15 April 2005 by Dr G. A. Ware (Brigham Young University). For this ink they unfortunately offer little improvement over the microscope (the images taken

---

* Professor A. Barchiesi encouraged the writing of this piece. I am grateful to Dr N. Gonis, Dr W. B. Henry, Professor R. Kassel, and Dr D. Obbink for much valuable assistance.

[1] Nic. fr. 62 has no attribution of work. ἔνθ’ in 1 certainly could mean 'where', and the particulars of the ὅτε clause make 'then' and a preceding elaborate narrative somewhat less likely; Ἑκάβη Κισσηΐς suggests the character has not appeared before. 'Where' would make possible a short mythological excursus of a kind common in Nicander (if we assume this is the poet of the didactic works); see Jacques (2002), pp. lxxix–lxxxi and cf. *Ther.* 607–9, metamorphosis with ἔνθα, *Alex.* 300–4 'where' with Marsyas and lament of tree, 445–51 'where' with genesis of bees. Cf. also fr. 108 (Troy). Otherwise: Schneider (1856), 67. The date and identity of the Nicanders is discussed by Cameron (1995), 194–208; Jacques will support a different view (cf. (2002), pp. ix, xiii n. 1). For Nicander's and Boios' metamorphosis poems, see O. Schneider (1856), 42–6; Forbes Irving (1990), ch. 1.

with the filter centred on 600 and 650 nm are the most helpful). All supplements below are by the first editor.[2]

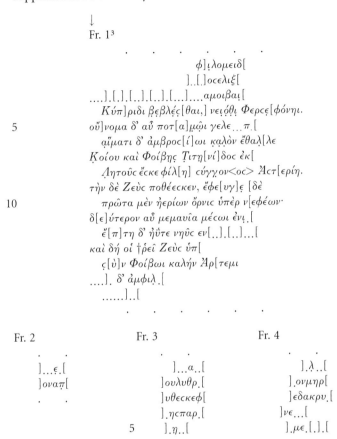

↓

Fr. 1[3]

. . . . . .

$\phi]\iota\lambda o\mu\epsilon\iota\delta[$

$].[.]o\sigma\epsilon\lambda\iota\xi[$

$....].[.].[..].[..].[...]...\alpha\mu o\iota\beta\alpha\iota[$

$K\acute{\upsilon}\pi]\rho\iota\delta\iota\ \beta\epsilon\beta\lambda\acute{\epsilon}\varsigma[\theta\alpha\iota,]\ \nu\epsilon\iota\acute{o}\theta\iota\ \Phi\epsilon\rho\sigma\epsilon[\phi\acute{o}\nu\eta\iota.$

5      $o\ddot{\upsilon}]\nu o\mu\alpha\ \delta'\ a\ddot{\upsilon}\ \pi o\tau[\alpha]\mu\hat{\omega}\iota\ \gamma\epsilon\lambda\epsilon...\pi.[$

$\alpha\ddot{\iota}\mu\alpha\tau\iota\ \delta'\ \dot{\alpha}\mu\beta\rho o\sigma[\acute{\iota}]\omega\iota\ \kappa\alpha\lambda\grave{o}\nu\ \ddot{\epsilon}\theta\alpha\lambda[\lambda\epsilon$

$K o\acute{\iota}o\upsilon\ \kappa\alpha\grave{\iota}\ \Phi o\acute{\iota}\beta\eta\varsigma\ T\iota\tau\eta[\nu\acute{\iota}]\delta o\varsigma\ \acute{\epsilon}\kappa[$

$\Lambda\eta\tauo\hat{\upsilon}\varsigma\ \acute{\epsilon}\sigma\kappa\epsilon\ \phi\acute{\iota}\lambda[\eta]\ \sigma\acute{\upsilon}\gamma\gamma o\nu<o\varsigma>\ \acute{A}\sigma\tau[\epsilon\rho\acute{\iota}\eta.$

$\tau\grave{\eta}\nu\ \delta\grave{\epsilon}\ Z\epsilon\grave{\upsilon}\varsigma\ \pi o\theta\acute{\epsilon}\epsilon\sigma\kappa\epsilon\nu,\ \acute{\epsilon}\phi\epsilon[\upsilon\gamma]\epsilon\ [\delta\grave{\epsilon}$

10      $\pi\rho\hat{\omega}\tau\alpha\ \mu\grave{\epsilon}\nu\ \acute{\eta}\epsilon\rho\acute{\iota}\omega\nu\ \acute{o}\rho\nu\iota\varsigma\ \acute{\upsilon}\pi\grave{\epsilon}\rho\ \nu[\epsilon\phi\acute{\epsilon}\omega\nu\cdot$

$\delta[\epsilon]\acute{\upsilon}\tau\epsilon\rho o\nu\ a\ddot{\upsilon}\ \mu\epsilon\mu\alpha\upsilon\hat{\iota}\alpha\ \mu\acute{\epsilon}\sigma\omega\iota\ \acute{\epsilon}\nu\iota.[$

$\acute{\epsilon}[\pi]\tau\eta\ \delta'\ \acute{\eta}\ddot{\upsilon}\tau\epsilon\ \nu\eta\hat{\upsilon}\varsigma\ \epsilon\nu[..].[..]...[$

$\kappa\alpha\grave{\iota}\ \delta\acute{\eta}\ o\acute{\iota}\ \dagger\rho\epsilon\hat{\iota}\ Z\epsilon\grave{\upsilon}\varsigma\ \acute{\upsilon}\pi[$

$\varsigma[\grave{\upsilon}]\nu\ \Phi o\acute{\iota}\beta\omega\iota\ \kappa\alpha\lambda\acute{\eta}\nu\ \acute{A}\rho[\tau\epsilon\mu\iota$

$....].\ \delta'\ \dot{\alpha}\mu\phi\iota\lambda.[$

$......].[.[$

. . . . . .

Fr. 2   Fr. 3   Fr. 4

. .   . .   . .

$]...\epsilon.[$ $]...\alpha..[$ $].\lambda..[$

$]o\nu\alpha\pi[$ $]o\upsilon\lambda\upsilon\theta\rho.[$ $].o\nu\mu\eta\rho[$

. . $]\upsilon\theta\epsilon\sigma\kappa\epsilon\phi[$ $]\epsilon\delta\alpha\kappa\rho\upsilon.[$

$].\eta\sigma\pi\alpha\rho.[$ $]\nu\epsilon...[$

5      $].\eta..[$ $].\mu\epsilon.[.].[$

---

[2] Extensive supplements are suggested by Luppe (2006*a*, *b*, 2007). Further letters could well be identified in the more damaged lines; but the attempt is hazardous, and minimalism is more suited to present purposes.

[3] Reed (2006) would prefer in 4 $\kappa\alpha\grave{\iota}\ \beta\lambda..[$ ($\beta\lambda o\varsigma[\upsilon\rho\hat{\eta}\iota$ Reed), in 5 τ for γ (so too Luppe (2007), 311), in 6 perhaps $\acute{\epsilon}o\iota\kappa[\epsilon$. Bernsdorff (2007) approves in the first two places. These suggestions look understandable from the on-line photograph; but the original under a microscope shows ink between the two feet of the putative κ (4) and inside the putative o (6), and a cross-stroke touching the second β in 4. (For the spacing of $\epsilon\beta$ cf. e.g. 8 $\epsilon\phi\iota\lambda$, 10 $\mu\epsilon\nu$, 12 $\epsilon\nu\eta\upsilon\varsigma$.) In 5 the tear may mislead, but there is not space for τ (for γ cf. e.g. → fr. 1.12); in 4 $\beta\lambda o\varsigma[\upsilon\rho\hat{\eta}$ (no adscript) would be too short, and in 6 $\iota\kappa[$ could not be read.

.　　.　　]κ.[
.　.

→
Fr. 1

.　.　.　.　.
].[
].ο.φ...[
].......[
]...κεραιη..[
5　　　]..........[...].δ....[
]......[..... ἄ]μβροτό[ϲ ἐ]ϲτιν.[
].....ν...[...]...δ..[..]...[
]......[.......]..εικελον ε.[
]....[......].[.]....[
10　　]ον εἶχεν ἀπεχθαίρεϲκε δ᾽ ἅπανταϲ
μ]ορφῆϲ ἠράϲατο ϲφετέρηϲ
]ρ πηγῆϲ [ὁ]λοφύρατο τέρψιν ὀνείρου
κλα]ύϲατο δ᾽ ἀγλαΐην
].. δῶκε δὲ γαίηι
15　　　]...φέρειν
].....[
.　.　.　.　.

Fr. 3　　　　　　Fr. 4
.　.　　　　　　.　.
]..ον..[　　　　].ε..[
.　.　　　　　　].[
.

The date and the authorship of the piece are unknown, and have led to valuable discussion since the original version of this piece. The unusual phrase which Gregory of Nazianzus twice uses of Narcissus μορφῆϲ τιϲ ἑῆϲ ποτ᾽ ἐράϲϲατο (1.2.29.155 (in Knecht's edn); 2.2.3.52 (*PG* 37.1484)) seems likely to be related genetically to → fr. 1.11 μ]ορφῆϲ ἠράϲατο ϲφετέρηϲ, used of Narcissus. Gregory is probably not the father of the phrase: in the following four lines in 1.2.29 he borrows his account of another metamorphosis, with strong verbal and other links, from Parthenius (or, less probably, from a source deriving from Parthenius). It could always be that both this poet and Gregory have appropriated the same phrase from an earlier treatment (say, Parthenius'?); in that case, the papyrus may reflect other aspects of earlier poetry. But with such a close and contextual echo, the initial hypothesis should perhaps be that Gregory is borrowing directly from this poet; it is an obvious possibility that 1.2.29 borrows from Parthenius' *Metamorphoses* in both cases.[4]

If Gregory is borrowing from the poet of the papyrus, the poet is at least two centuries earlier than the papyrus itself. The limited range of texts found in papyri of this period makes it more likely that we have a reasonably well-known Hellenistic poet than an obscure but not recent imperial writer. This dating is supported by the use of elegiacs. The use of elegiacs for a substantial poem points away from a later imperial poet, and towards the Hellenistic period. The suggestion that this is a series of epigrams does not suit well with the language, which has a much more heavily epic quality than epigrams. Poems on the heroism of Ajax which evoke the *Iliad* (Ascl. XXIX, Archias XVI) do not form a good analogy, or show the same degree of epicism.[5]

---

[4] Henry (2005), 47, cautiously suggested Parthenius; Hutchinson (2006*a*), 71, cautiously welcomed the suggestion. Luppe (2006*a*), 55, and Magnelli (2006), 10–11, think the case for Parthenius strong. Reed (2006), 76, and Bernsdorff (2007) disagree; Reed accepts a Hellenistic dating, Bernsdorff argues for a date close to the papyrus. Professor Bernsdorff kindly showed me his fine article before publication. The combination μ]ορφῆς ἠράσατο σφετέρης makes a decidedly distinctive phrase; even μορφῆς ἐρᾶν is found only at Xen. *Symp.* 8.29 (see also Bernsdorff; Greg. Naz. 1.2.2.665 (*PG* 37.630) could derive from our passage too). Knecht (1972), 93–4, following others, seems unduly confident in positing another source for Greg. Naz. 1.2.29.157–60 rather than direct imitation of Parthenius fr. 28 Lightfoot (contrast Lightfoot (1999), 95–6, 178–9). The story is demythologized by Gregory, just like that of Pan and Echo in 153–4. It is not clear whether one could argue that Gregory would only refer to a relatively well-known poet like Parthenius (cf. Wyß (1983), 849–53; and does e.g. Antimachus in *Epistle* 54 come from Callimachus?). I am grateful to Chr. Simelidis for discussing this point with me.

[5] For texts on papyri see <http://www.trismegistos.org/ldab/> accessed 30 Nov. 2007. The most unusual Hellenistic poet found in the fifth to seventh centuries is Euphorion, who appears in a probably 5th-cent. parchment codex (*BKT* v.1 no. 273). Also of interest is the appearance of Eupolis in a 4th–5th-cent. papyrus codex (Cairo 43227; Koenen (1978), pll. XLIX–LIV). For the general fading out of elegiacs see M. L. West (1983), 181; cf. also Anubion (ii AD or earlier), P. Schubart 15, P. Oxy. 4503–7. For epicizing diction, including some ordinary words, cf. ↓ fr. 1.1 φ]ιλομειδ[; 4 νειόθι (in epigram (to the end of ii AD) only Erucius IX.3 νειόθεν; νειο- comes in Apollonius, Aratus, Nicander, not Callimachus or Theocritus); 11 μεμανῖα (in epigram only German. I.2 (*FGE*); cf. also *AP* 7.148.3 (Adesp.)); 12 ἠΰτε (in epigram only Dioscor. V.5; in Theocritus only the epic 22.49 and [25].130, 245; Apollonius, Aratus, Nicander, Euphorion, not Callimachus). Even ἀγλαΐη (→ fr. 1.13) is uncommon in epigram (Euphor. I.2 (= fr. 1.2 van Groningen), Strato 36.2 Floridi). Further points are added by Bernsdorff (2007), 3 n. 13.

A Hellenistic dating, then, seems promising but not certain; the dating is the most important question for our purposes. Consideration of the author may throw light on date and quality. Parthenius has some appeal, both because of the sequence in Greg. Naz. 1.29.155–60 and because of the papyrus' date (a well-known poet is more likely than a lesser-known). The weightiest argument against Parthenius is the metre. Parthenius' fragments keep Callimachus' rules; but this papyrus uses (1) a feature found only once in Callimachus (ἔϲκε φίλ[η] || at ↓ fr. 1.8 (pent.); cf. Call. *Ep.* 25.2 μήτε φίλον), and (2) a feature not found in Callimachus (ἠΰτε νηῦϲ || at ↓ fr. 1.12). However, only eight complete pentameters and twelve complete hexameters of Parthenius are extant. Especially after the third century, most Hellenistic writers of elegiacs follow 'Callimachean' practices most of the time, but deviate intermittently and are notably inclined to (1). (2) diverges mildly from standard practice with its trisyllabic prepositive (cf. Call. fr. 89.28 Massimilla ἢ περὶ ϲήν ||); it does so in order to create an epic phrase which stresses the monosyllable (cf. Hom. *Il.* 2.480 | ἠΰτε βοῦϲ—Tryphon's first example of an εἰκών, *Rhet. Gr.* iii. 200 Spengel—*Il.* 17.737 ἄγριος ἠΰτε πῦρ ||, *Hom. Hym. Dem.* 386 ἤϊξ' ἠΰτε μαινάϲ ||; for stress Philod. 16.4 Sider καὶ πῦρ ||, 17.2 Sider καὶ μνοῦ ||, etc.; effective divergence e.g. Posid. 16.2 AB αἰεὶ ϲπῶν ||). Parthenius' allusions to Callimachus, and his supposed role as a conduit for Romans, perhaps lead to misplaced expectations. His style is not particularly Callimachean; like most writers of elegiacs, he does not keep to the practices and norms specific to Callimachean elegiacs (outside the fifth hymn, which is assimilated to its epic fellows). Thus in fr. 28.2 Lightfoot a masculine caesura is not followed by bucolic diaeresis; in fr. 2.4–7 there are three correptions close together, at least one in a pentameter.[6]

---

[6] For the former, and *Hymn* 5, cf. Clarke (1955); Maas (1973). There are only 15 correptions in Callimachus' *Aetia* (excluding fragments of uncertain work) and *Epigrams* (including fragments), none in pentameters; PSI inv. 1923.11 (Ozbek (2005), 11) | ἐκλεγχω[(hex. or pent.) seems a dubious example, in meaning and tense, and in the vowel (very rarely correpted in Callimachus). In *Hymn* 5 there are 11 correptions, two in pentameters; in the rest of Callimachus I count 225 correptions. Parth. fr. 27 (*b*).8 πουλὺ πνέουϲαν clashes with Callimachean practice; an epic justification (Bernsdorff (2007)) would fit the view of ἠΰτε νηῦϲ above. Callimachus' own μήτε φίλον || . . . μήτε φίλην | diverges for effect. For disyllable without preceding monosyllable cf. e.g. Ascl. I.2, XXV.10, Posid. 50.2 AB, 78.6, 125.2, 4, 130.4, Simias fr.

The writing of the papyrus poet has been thought too plain for Parthenius, or unhappily manneristic. → fr. 1.12 [ὁ]λοφύρατο τέρψιν ὀνείρου creates difficulties for the first objection, as does ↓ fr. 1.4 βεβλέϲ[θαι]. In any case, the vocabulary of Parthenius' fragments would not especially support description of his style as ornate and recherché. Sometimes indeed his syntax and expression seem very simple (syntax fr. 28.2 ἀγχίγαμος δ' ἔπελεν, καθαρῶι δ' ἐπεμαίνετο Κύδνωι; expression fr. 28.4 εἰϲόκε μιν Κύπρις πήγην θέτο, fr. 33.5 δείρην ἐνεθήκατο); this may be pertinent to the initial ↓ fr. 1.9 τὴν δὲ Ζεὺς ποθέεϲκεν, ἔφε[υγ]ε [δὲ... As for ambition, [ὁ]λοφύρατο τέρψιν ὀνείρου could be thought comparable to fr. 28.4–5 μῖξε δ' ἔρωτι | ... ὑδατόεντα γάμον (cf. ↓ fr. 1.6 for the dative, one causal, one instrumental?). Disappointment with papyri of famous authors has not been unknown. On the other hand, it would not be unnatural to judge ↓ fr. 1.9–12—for all the hyperbole and impacted imagery of 10 and 12 and the contrast of high and low—too straightforward in structure for the celebrated poet.[7]

If a Hellenistic dating looks promising and Parthenian authorship not without attractions, it will be reasonable to explore circumspectly and hypothetically how the piece, or pieces, might affect the reading of Ovid's poem. In most cases the papyrus draws our attention to aspects which retain significance if in fact the poem or its models are post-Ovidian; if pre-Ovidian, these aspects would have been made the more striking for contemporary readers.

For these purposes, the first question to investigate is the length of the stories. The length of one of these can in my view be demonstrated, whichever page came first, ↓ or →. Suppose (i) that ↓ came first. Then a new story (Asterie) begins in ↓ fr. 1.7; but by → fr. 1.10 we are on another story (Narcissus). Hence Asterie will last at most just over a page; a page would probably have not more than 45 lines. Or suppose (ii) that → came first. Then the story of Narcissus has

---

20.2, 21.2 Powell, Meleag. X.2, XXIX.6, XXXIII.8, XXXIV.4, XL.2, Philod. 20.4 Sider; Magnelli (1995) (under 'pentametri'). ↓ fr. 1.13 should be supposed corrupt: apart from the sense, a historic present or an imperfect (cf. Hom. *Il.* 17.86, Theocr. 13.16) would be unsatisfactory.

[7] For the epicizing πρῶτα ... δ[ε]ύτερον αὖ (Bernsdorff) cf. e.g. Hom. *Il.* 6.179–86; AR 4.771–5; and also Call. *H.* 2.72–3, 3.120–2. 'Ornate, recherché': Reed (2006), 76. Otherwise on the dative of Parth. fr. 28.4: Lightfoot *ad loc.*

ended by ↓ fr. 1; the second story (Adonis) has ended by ↓ fr. 1.7. Hence Adonis will last at most 36 lines, if we postulate a page of not more than 45 lines: if 45 lines, there must be 30 lines between → fr. 1.15 and ↓ fr. 1.1.

A page of more than 45 lines would be surprising: very few non-biblical sixth-century codices exceed 45 lines. Conversely, on account of its evident breadth, the page is unlikely to have had much fewer than 29 lines: 29 lines would give a maximum of 20 for the story of Adonis on hypothesis (ii). As to that breadth: the written area alone might have had a maximum of 21.3 cm—the result of combining the longest extant first four feet in the hexameter on ↓ with the longest extant last two feet on →. The left-hand margin was at least 1 cm. This breadth makes against supposing a height of less than 27 cm, including upper and lower margins; if the written area was 21 cm high, there would be about 29 lines to the page.[8]

The argument can be taken further. The story of Narcissus seems to move in five to six lines from his rejection of lovers to his transformation. The probable present tense in → fr. 1.6 would suggest the end (or beginning) of a story there, rather than a narrative: a historic present is unlikely in Hellenistic or post-Hellenistic poetic narrative. The story of Asterie might seem to be nearing its end by ↓ fr. 1.16, if the emphasis is on metamorphosis; but the textual problem in 13 leaves it unclear whether Delos has by that point already achieved stability. At all events, if the work were by Parthenius, this account of Delos should be set intertextually as a miniature against the larger account of his *Delos*, which is unlikely to be a section of this poem. The story of Adonis moves with similar rapidity, if ↓ fr. 1.2 deals with the boar; certainly aetiology and metamorphosis occupy only a couplet (5–6). (There is no space here for Parth.

---

[8] For lines to the page see Turner (1977), table 16, pp. 101–85; cf. also pp. 95–7: no example of 6th-cent. codex with more than 50 lines per page—except P. Oxy. 1614 (v–vi; Pindar; Cantab. Add. 6366), which has double columns probably of *c*.26 short lines each (it is missing from Turner's table 3, p. 36). Of codices published later than 1977, particularly interesting is P. Oxy. 4094 (vi; Menander; original breadth *c*.18.5–19 cm, actual and probably original height 31.5 cm, with large upper and lower margins; 29 and 33 lines to the page). The height of the written area in our papyrus, if 45 lines, would be about 32 cm, excluding upper and lower margins. This would be a 'very tall' page, particularly possible in vi (cf. Turner (1977), 14–15); the breadth would be perfectly compatible with that supposition.

fr. 29; it could conceivably come at the beginning.) Narcissus, then, and perhaps Asterie suggest that there may have been more than one story within 36–45 lines. If so, the two flower stories might not have been consecutive, even on supposition (ii).[9]

Nic. fr. 62, if it is from the *Heteroeumena*, looks like a short account; the narratives in Antoninus Liberalis would suggest something more extended if they do not expand on Nicander and Boios. Nic. fr. 50 suggests a more detailed narrative than in this poem. This papyrus certainly offers evidence of relatively short narratives. They could in theory be exceptions within their poem. Ovid tells some metamorphoses briefly or in passing (so with Asterie, see below). But such variation has more of a rationale within a continuous narrative like Ovid's than in a series of detached entries like this poem. The stories of Narcissus and Adonis assuredly give scope for more extended narrative; even Conon 24 indicates this in the case of Narcissus.

The poem seems, then, to present a series of fairly short accounts, especially if there was more than one to a page. They are also formally unjoined. Asterie begins without connecting particle or obvious link. ἔνθ᾽ in Nic. fr. 62.1 could suggest connections in the *Heteroeumena*— but the fragment may not come from that poem. In any case, a series of unjoined hexameter items from Nicander is not an immediately inviting possibility. The elegiac metre of this poem might well make a difference.[10]

Are the sections linked in theme, if not in syntax? As we have seen, we cannot say that the two flower stories must come together: even if → precedes ↓, another story may very well separate Narcissus and Adonis. What we are certain of is that Adonis is followed directly by Asterie. These two stories seem to be connected only by the general

---

[9] It is doubtful whether we can determine the structure of the stories from the use of tenses (cf. → fr. 1.10–15). In ↓ fr. 1.6 the imperfect is used for the metamorphosis itself. Cf. for variation between tenses e.g. Call. *H.* 2.60–3; AR 3.1317–18, 1354–8, 1363–73, 1405.

[10] Cf. *Aetia* 3 and 4. Anubion's elegiacs include, as presented in P. Oxy. 4505, separate horoscopes with headings. The many detached sections in 'Manetho' Book 1 (Köchly) are not wholly comparable. A collection e.g. of hexameter headache recipes (*SH* 900) forms an obviously different category from a poem like this. If ἔνθ᾽ in Nic. fr. 62.1 did mean 'then', it would suggest an at least partial chronological sequence, with large implications for Ovid; but against any type of systematic order in the *Heteroeumena* cf. O. Schneider (1856), 42–6.

themes of desire and perhaps different parts of the cosmos (underworld (and heavens?) 3–4, air and sea 10–11). Names (5, by implication 8, 10) might make a very general link. Desire or its absence
might indeed form a general connection between all the stories (cf. ↓
fr. 1.9, → fr. 1.10–11, also -ϵϲκϵ). More specifically, however, the
flower-transformations of Adonis and Narcissus would be at most 48
lines apart. It seems inevitable that the reader would see a link in
these metamorphoses. → fr. 1.14–15 may well have mentioned
blood, like ↓ fr. 1.6. Types of metamorphosis can clearly be perceived
as thematic: so Boios' *Ornithogonia* shows. And of course the notion
of metamorphosis itself implies a thematic link between all the
sections. We see, then, a series of formally separated entities which
nevertheless connect, individually and as parts of a whole.[11]

At this point, we should consider some aspects of Hellenistic and
post-Hellenistic poetry more broadly. The thoughts which the papyrus invites on Hellenistic poetry are arguably even more important
than those it invites on Ovid. Much Hellenistic poetry can be seen as
presenting a set of parallel entities; these are either (a) formally
continuous or (b) formally discontinuous. Type (a) is the older: it
has its origins in Hesiodic poetry. It includes Books 1 and 2 of the
Aetia, where a frame provides continuity to what would otherwise be
a series of type (b) accounts. Aratus' *Phaenomena* is particularly
relevant to our poem in the first part of its section on the stars
(19–453); there separate paragraphs on each constellation are joined
in syntax and in spatial continuity. So too, without the spatial
sequence, the paragraphs on snakes, say, in Nicander's *Theriaca*
(principally 157–492). The voyaging parts of the *Argonautica* are
also relevant for type (a). Their distinct sections are syntactically,
temporally, and spatially continuous; they often culminate in an
aetiological point. Most pertinent to ↓ fr. 1.5–6 are episodes or
short sections which end, or almost end, with a name: the name
of the spring in 1.1067–9, or the river-name and place-name in
2.904–10, with the place-name at 2.909–10 closing the larger section.
Phanocles' *Erotes* fr. 1 Powell, with its Hesiodic ἢ ὡϲ formula, its

---

[11] In Nicander it is notable that, for example, all the metamorphoses into stones
come from Book 1 (frr. 38, 40, 42 Schneider). Cf. Forbes Irving (1990), 31–2.

relatively short narrative, and its aetiological close, shows the link between type (a) and our poem, though our poem is itself of type (b).[12]

Type (b) particularly interacts with the idea of a book: a book which collects smaller and separated entities. The new roll of (at least mostly?) Posidippus provides a conspicuous and elaborate example of (b). Separate epigrams are grouped thematically into larger units; whether and how these units are themselves related has not yet been sufficiently explored. If the sections of the present poem are really short, an affinity with series of epigrams would be evident; at the same time, its epicizing diction distinguishes it from that genre. The Posidippus papyrus also illustrates, by the marking out of some poems, a further development: the making up of new books through selecting from others. Thematic anthologies flout even unity of author in the distinctness of their related entities. *Aetia* Books 3 and 4 move their poem into type (b); despite the formal breaks between sections, the pair of books is ringed in its opening and close, and forms a larger ring with Book 1. The two books provide a strong example of numerous unannounced connections between discrete parts, even when those parts are not placed next to each other. The *Aetia* also provide an example, much strained in the later books, of a structural and thematic feature (aetiological closes) which like metamorphosis furnishes the work with its formal coherence. These aspects of design, and the move from type (a) to type (b), are important to the prologue of the *Aetia*. Herodas' *Mimiamboi* are a further instance of type (b) on a large scale in a book. These are separate poems, not the scenes of a single connected mime (though 6 and 7 play with such connection). Adjacent poems can be connected in theme (so 1 and 2 *lena* and *leno*); the total poetic and aesthetic plan and ideology create a larger cohesion (cf. poems 4 and 8).[13]

Prose must be brought into the discussion. It illustrates types (a) and (b), but it is also involved with poetry in a two-way process

---

[12] On the Hesiodic *Catalogue* and Hellenistic poetry see the important new volume Hunter (2005*b*), esp. Hunter (2005*a*) and Asquith (2005). For the meanings of Apollonius' parallel series, cf. ch. 3 above.

[13] For radical doubts on the Posidippus papyrus see Schröder (2004), esp. 52–4; even if the collection is largely by one author, as looks likely, the possibility of insertions could not be excluded (cf. P. Oxy. 3724). On the *Aetia*, cf. ch. 2. Theocritus is the main Hellenistic poet not discussed above; this is precisely because it remains doubtful whether and how he gathered his poems into books.

of appropriation and rearrangement. It adds to the connotations of
these structures in poetry, by comparison and by contrast. Parthenius' own Ἐρωτικὰ Παθήματα offer a series of narratives, separate
but syntactically joined (so type (a)), and united in general theme.
(Indications of source, which interrupt the syntax, must be later.)
The preface formally envisages the excerption of the items to make
part of different poetic structures, hexameter and elegiac. The *Aetia*
selects from local historians, that is from formally *more* connected
originals (as fr. 75.51–77 Pfeiffer brings out), to produce its own
thematic construction. The *Phaenomena*, like other didactic poetry,
'translates' prose originals into verse (in this case two prose works
joined together). The imperial Antoninus Liberalis exemplifies a
reverse selection to Callimachus'; he selects from books of poetry
to create a work on metamorphoses in prose. The sections are
unjoined and so type (b) (the indications of source are perhaps
later). A papyrus alphabetical list of metamorphoses (P. Mich. inv.
1447 verso; ii–iii AD) gives unjoined and very brief narratives; the
sections are ended by indications of source (pre-Hellenistic poets),
and separated by forked paragraphoi. The hand has non-literary
features; there is a document on the other side. Systematic and
functional, the work none the less exhibits a kind of prose structure
which our poem could be seen as transforming and liberating; in
this area, however, the causal relationships of prose and verse are
complex.[14]

Ovid in the *Fasti* and *Metamorphoses* presents two immense versions of Hellenistic types of poem relatively unfrequented by Roman
writers. The *Fasti*, like the *Aetia*, deals with rituals. A firm chronological structure, 'translating' that of inscribed calendars into a poetic
form, gives continuity to the distinct sections. Sometimes this is
reflected in the syntax, e.g. 4.625 *luce secutura*, sometimes not, e.g.
4.621–2 *occupat Apriles Idus cognomine Victor | Iuppiter.* One may
see formally a mixture of type (a) and type (b). The frame which
provided an (a)-type structure for *Aetia* Books 1 and 2 is not
embraced for the *Fasti* as a whole; but vestiges remain. They do not

[14] On P. Mich. inv. 1447 (michigan.apis.2937), cf. Renner (1978); Lloyd-Jones
(1979). For the Ἐρωτικὰ Παθήματα see Lightfoot (1999), 215–302. For the tradition
of prose on metamorphosis cf. Cameron (2004).

offer an overall formal continuity; rather they underline thematic unity in individual books.[15]

The *Metamorphoses* again present a chronological structure, but one of a different kind: historical, not calendrical (so not endlessly repeated in an exact cycle). The chronological structure is most ostentatiously present, and most similar to that of the *Fasti*, in Book 14's canter through Alban history and the beginnings of Roman history (609–851). This papyrus suggests the possibility that there were (b)-type versions in Ovid's tradition; probably there were (a)-type versions too (cf. Nicander). Ovid aims ostentatiously for (a), and achieves continuity in a multitude of ways; none the less, the artifice, and the difference from more straightforward narrative poems, are to be perceived vividly. This point would be accentuated by the poem's relationship with works like the present, which would serve as intertexts in structure, stories, and detail. The length of most of Ovid's narratives will create, in comparison to the present work, a new order of interconnections not officially advertised. One might liken, say, Bernhard Schlink's recent *Liebesfluchten* (Zurich, 2000): stories linked only in theme and shape which have abundant and uncircumscribed connections and differentiations.[16]

A further factor is presented by the many books of Ovid's design. Antigonus perhaps had only one book; Didymarchus had at least three (*SH* 50); Nicander had four or five, Boios perhaps two. But Ovid's poem clearly invites comparison with the structures of Homer—as divided into rhapsodies—and of Virgil. The single-book epic like *Smyrna*, *Ciris*, or, in my view, Catullus 64 also enters in as a foil. The individual book of the *Metamorphoses* draws entities

---

[15] So the section of conversation with Mars in 3.167–258; note the shift to a different addressee in 259–62. Books 5 and 6 make the pattern more complicated. The calendrical signs in modern editions do not appear in the MSS; but this does not mean that either *Fasti* or *Metamorphoses* need have lacked markers of sections or paragraphs. Cf. P. Herc. 817 (Scott (1885)), pll. F and H): paragraphs in epic. Such division is made a particularly plausible proposition in the *Fasti* by the visual presentation seen in papyri of the *Aetia* (coronides and paragraphoi between sections). On Aemilius Macer's *Ornithogonia* see Courtney (2003), 292, and Hollis (2007), 103–7; Ovid's reference (*Tr.* 4.10.43–4) and Macer's poems could suggest the link felt in this period between Nicander's didactic poetry and his work on metamorphosis. (He was probably taken to be one writer.)

[16] Connections and transitions in the *Metamorphoses*: cf. e.g. Solodow (1988), 15–17, 41–6; Tronchet (1998), 282–329, 584–8.

together, like the papyrus poem; but it is itself an entity which forms part of a larger entity. The individual books of Nicander, or of the papyrus poem if it had several books, may possibly have done the same; but certainly with the papyrus poem there could not have been the same generic and narrative resonance as in Ovid. The book-structure enables the *Metamorphoses* to achieve a fruitful tension: it visibly and simultaneously transgresses the limits both of 'Aristotelian' epics and of metamorphosis-poems. Though Ovid deliberately blurs the transitions between books through overlaps, the book remains a significant unit, both in its actual form (e.g. Book 10) and in its distorted form (e.g. the 'long' Book 10, i.e. 10.1–11.84). The importance of books in the *Metamorphoses* is beginning to be recognized, but the papyrus throws the question of what those books are into greater relief.[17]

Consideration of the specific stories that appear in the papyrus will show how Ovid's overt structuring and implicit interconnections would have been more striking for readers of Ovid who had read this poem. This will also be shown by some further features of the papyrus' narratives.

First, we may look at ↓ fr. 1.1–6 on Adonis. The metamorphosis itself presents two features, the name of the river and the existence of the flower (5–6); the couplet form is neatly exploited. The dense union of aetiology and metamorphosis at the close of so short a narrative is not matched in Ovid's far longer account (3–4 imply aetiology too). The close in 5 of itself belongs to a kind seen in Ovid, e.g. 6.399–400 *aequor | Marsya nomen habet, Phrygiae liquidissimus amnis*, 7.380–1 *flendo | deliciut stagnumque suo de nomine fecit*, 9.664–5 *fontem qui nunc quoque...nomen habet dominae*, 10.297 (just before Myrrha) *illa Paphon genuit, de qua tenet insula nomen*. In the present story Ovid incorporates ritual aetiology (10.724–7); he merely alludes, indirectly, to the division neatly encapsulated in the Greek between Aphrodite and Persephone (names at either end of pentameter, with asyndeton): cf. 724 *at non tamen omnia uestri | iuris erunt*, 728–30 (Persephone's metamorphosis of Mintha), *punica*

---

[17] Importance of books: cf. Holzberg (1998*a*); von Albrecht (2000), 209. On the relation to Virgilian epic, Marino's letter of 1624 to Girolamo Preti (*Lettere*, ed. M. Guglielminetti (Turin, 1966), 394–7, esp. 395–6) remains of interest.

736–7 (cf. 5.536, 10.28–9). All the allusion makes a link to the other end of the story, where *Venus* changes her part of the cosmos to be with Adonis (532 *caelo praefertur Adonis*); it also connects with the appearance of Persephone at the other end of the book (15, 28–9).[18]

αἵματι … ἀμβροc[ί]ωι could have helped to suggest Ovid's narrative, through a connection with ἀμβροcία (cf. Bion fr. 1.3–4 Reed): 731 *sic fata cruorem | nectare odorato sparsit*. In the Greek, blood and flower are opposed by their placing at either end of the pentameter, an opposition softened by the intervening epithets. The opposition is made starker by Ovid (728 *at cruor in florem mutabitur*), or else rendered paradoxical through physical detail (735 *flos de sanguine* [note placing] *concolor ortus*).[19]

The name of the river (οὔ]νομα ↓ fr. 1.5), which directly perpetuates Adonis' glory, is in Ovid replaced with the name of the anemone, which does not: 738–9 *namque male haerentem et nimia leuitate caducum | excutiunt idem qui praestant nomina uenti*. Ovid would not be merely thinning out and reducing the aetiological and scholarly density of the papyrus poem; there is a pointed contrast within his structures. Adonis' story grows out of Myrrha's, as Adonis grew out of Myrrha. At the end of the Myrrha story, Myrrha is excluded from both earth and underworld—unlike the future Adonis with his two realms; and yet she receives *honor* (501) for her grief through a name: *murra | nomen erile tenet nulloque tacebitur aeuo* (501–2). The glorification within the song itself is a kind of redemption from the secondary narrator's guilty and condemnatory prelude (300–15). On the other hand, in 737 (*flos… ortus…*) *breuis est tamen usus in illo*, the *tamen* diminishes the perpetuation. The short life of the flower could have been made to enhance the perpetuation by commemorating the early loss (cf. Nonn. *Dion.* 11.235–7, 15.355–6). The flower shares rather in the mortal's transience. Since this passage comes at the end of Orpheus' song, his, the secondary poet's, ability to

[18] ῥόδον is conceivable as a supplement in ↓ fr. 1.6: the plant would not then be unnamed. For Adonis and Myrrha, and esp. Ovid's telling, see, along with many of the works on Orpheus in n. 20 below: Atallah (1966); Simon (1972); Nagle (1982–3); Capomacchia (1984); K. Newman (1984); Tuzet (1987), 92–4; Lowrie (1993); Detienne (1994); Reed (1997), 18–26, (2006); Santini (1999); Putnam (2001). On Mintha, Detienne (1994), ch. 4; on names in Ovid, P. R. Hardie (2002*a*), 239–57.

[19] Cf. the placing at 9.344–5 *uidi guttas e flore cruentas | decidere*.

celebrate also seems to be infringed; the placing at the end of the book invites contemplation of the primary poet.[20]

This ending contrasts with the secondary poet's power at the beginning of the book, and especially with Orpheus' first main story, that of Hyacinthus. There too *cruor* is transformed by the loving god, but it is a *honor* (214); the god's grief is most explicitly written on to the flower (198–216). The ritual of the Hyacinthia (217–18) forms the climactic close of the section, whereas diminution follows mention of the Adonia (725–7). The *honor... durat in hoc aeui* (217–18; Ovid's time as well as Orpheus'); Hyacinthus' name, the actual name of the flower, resounds in the repetition (217, 219; cf. the secondary poet's address in 185). The pessimism at the end of the book leads in forcefully to the sudden breaking of Orpheus' spell by the violent maenads (*uentos* 11.43 at the close marks the link, cf. also *leues... auras* in 11.6).[21]

The large bridge to Hyacinthus across the book and Orpheus' narrative involves an implicit connection by type of metamorphosis. Explicit connections by metamorphosis are evident, as we have seen, in the plan of Boios' *Ornithogonia*, imitated by Ovid's older contemporary Macer (*FRP* 49–53); implicit connections by metamorphosis are visible in this papyrus. The ring of flowers in Ovid (Hyacinthus, Adonis) is enclosed by a ring of trees. Orpheus' narrative is preceded by an account of all the trees that were listening to him (86–142). The last of these, Cyparissus, forms a very close parallel to Hyacinthus. At the beginning of Book 11, which undoes the scene of Book 10, Orpheus is killed, and mourned by the trees that had listened to

[20] For a pessimistic reading of the flower as monument see Janan (1988), 131–3. The common connection of name and metamorphosis is forcefully broken in Giuseppe Conte, 'Metamorfosi d'amore' 1–2 'Giuseppe era il mio nome di | cristiano, ora non ho più nome' (*L'Oceano e il Ragazzo* (Milan, 2002), 62). On Orpheus in Ovid, see also Leach (1974), 105–7, 118–27; W. B. Anderson (1982), esp. 36–50, and (1989); Knox (1986), ch. 4; Barchiesi (1989), esp. 64–73; Segal (1989), 54–72, 81–94; Hill (1992); Mack (1994–5); J. Heath (1995–6); M. Thomas (1998); Fantham (2004), 76–82; Cahoon (2005); Henneböhl (2005). For art see, besides Garezou (1994), Huber (2001).

[21] Segal (1989), 89, suggests a possible link to 10.59 *cedentes... auras* at the beginning of the book. There is a connection and contrast too with the passage on Achilles' death at the end of the (clearly ringed) Book 12 (612–19). Tuzet (1987), 92, 94, sees the difference between the treatments of Hyacinthus' and Adonis' death, but takes it as a difference in poetic quality. For the Hyacinthia in Roman Sparta, see Cartledge and Spawforth (2002), 193–4.

him (45–7, cf. 29). The near humanity of the trees is reversed when his human killers are turned into trees (67–84). The list of trees in 10 further connects with Myrrha, a new tree to add to the series (10.310 *tanti noua non fuit arbor*, cf. 14.390–1). The opposition of Adonis' and Myrrha's metamorphoses, just discussed, includes an opposition between tree and flower. Even the inset story of Hippomenes and Atalanta highlights the tree from which the apples grew (647–8). The possibilities of the structures and connections in the Greek poems generate ever-ramifying intricacies in Ovid.

Intricate too is the narratological structure which accommodates the story of Adonis: not a formally random unjoined sequence as in the papyrus, but a mixture of chronological and thematic connection. This story flows from another story (Myrrha's), which follows the preceding story genealogically and chronologically but also fits the teller's thematic pattern (152–4). Such thematic patterns in the mouths of secondary narrators reproduce on a different level the thematic patterns seen in the primary narrative of Greek poems (implicitly in our papyrus, where there are no formal connections). The relationship between Latin secondary narrative and Greek primary narrative is particularly interesting in Venus' inset story of Hippomenes and Atalanta. She is making a link between animals (Adonis is endangered by the lions into which Hippomenes and Atalanta are transformed). Such a thematic link resembles e.g. the link between Boios' birds, and is more purely illustrated by a hetero-diegetic secondary narrator at 11.749–95 (an anonymous old man of uncertain date). The present link, however, has for the narrating character a more practical and a more ominous point. Structurally, the inset within an inset shows Ovid not only expanding the story of Adonis but reaching a climax of involution near the end of his book. He outdoes in complexity the inset narration of Achaemenides near the end of Aeneas' narrative and the *Aeneid*'s third book.[22]

It emerges as the more important that *mise en abyme* in the *Metamorphoses* is not primarily the reflection of the outer plot on a

---

[22] Tarrant's excellent new text (2004) sadly denies us the delight of triple quotation marks for speech inside the Hippomenes story. Venus' swift change from narrator to suffering character will be repeated by Orpheus. For narratology and the *Metamorphoses* cf. e.g. Myers (1994), ch. 2; Wheeler (1999), ch. 3 and Appendix A; Rosati (2002); Nikolopoulos (2004).

smaller scale but the reflection of the narratological situation in which the poet tells us stories of metamorphosis. The Greek material enhances the interrelation of tellings. The case of Myrrha complicates the antithesis between involved and uninvolved narrators (homodiegetic and heterodiegetic), and brings in a further twist on the theme of names. The revelation of Myrrha's incest by characters, by heterodiegetic secondary narrator, and implicitly by the primary narrator, is *alike* fraught with dangers. Hence her actual name, now perpetuated in *murra*, was concealed from her father (cf. *nomine mentito*, 439). Ovid further plays on the application of *nomen* both to proper names and to words denoting family roles. They 'perhaps' called each other, the narrator unnecessarily lets us know, *filia* and *pater, sceleri ne nomina desint* (467–8, cf. 8.522). Cf. also 346–7 (*nec quot confundas et iura et nomina sentis? | tune eris et matris paelex et adultera patris?*), 358 (names of eligible young men), 366 (*pietatis nomine dicto*), 401–3 (where *pater* has the same revealing power as the proper name in Eur. *Hipp.* 310), 429–30 (*parente* suppressed). This all advances on the matching story of Byblis in the preceding book: the story of Myrrha goes still further in horror. Cf. 9.466–7 (*nomina sanguinis*), 487–9, 528–34, 558, 569–70 (*fratri* only at first suppressed), 664–5 (Byblis' name perpetuated in a spring, see above). If the papyrus poem is used by Ovid, we can see how he weaves details from his intertext into far-reaching structures and meanings.[23]

The story of Asterie (↓ fr. 1.7–15), by contrast with that of Adonis, receives extremely short and dislocated mentions in Ovid. All are cloaked in narratological complications. The first mention is at 6.108, as part of Arachne's artefact: *fecit et Asterien aquila luctante teneri*. It sounds as if Jupiter was immediately successful, and as if Jupiter rather than Asterie became the bird. This mention occurs in a catalogue of Jupiter's metamorphic amours, followed by other gods'. The catalogue form goes beyond the brevity of the papyrus poem: the virtuoso variation in pace is marked out by the repetition of Europa (103–7) from Books 2–3. But the mention of Asterie here prepares her later role as Delos shortly afterwards, inset in Niobe's derogatory speech (188–91), and inset in a speech inset within the

---

[23] For types of *mise en abyme* that reproduce the plot and reproduce the telling, cf. Dällenbach (1977) (note 100). The story of Byblis is more concerned with writing than that of Myrrha. The name is also crucial in the following story of Iphis, 9.708–10.

speech of a Lycian (331–6); cf. also the speech of Pythagoras 15.336–7 (with *Ortygie*). An island story elaborately told in Parthenius' own *Delos* and Callimachus' fourth hymn (cf. Virg. *G.* 3.6 *cui non dictus Hylas puer et Latonia Delos...*?) is here only teasingly glimpsed.[24]

The thread of these mentions of Asterie, and their brevity, is made more noticeable by possible allusion to the papyrus poem. ↓ fr. 1.7–8 give an elaborate statement of family, denser indeed than one would expect in Ovid. *Κοίου*, *Τιτη[νί]δος*, and *Λητοῦς* appear together in *Met.* 6.185–6, just before the mention of Delos, with play on the obscurity of the genealogy: *nescioquoque audete satam Titanida Coeo | Latonam praeferre mihi.* In significant contrast, at 366 *filia Coei* marks out Leto's divine status.[25]

Ovid's treatment of Asterie could be read against the unobtrusive density and organization of the account in the papyrus. The two metamorphoses there, each starting a line (10, 11), superficially resemble, say, *Met.* 11.243–5 (Thetis) *sed modo tu uolucris...,* | *nunc grauis arbor eras...,* | *tertia forma fuit maculosae tigridis.* However, in the papyrus the learning and mythology is tightly packed. The first metamorphosis, with its unspecific *ὄρνις*, alludes to Asterie's acquisition of the name Ortygia (cf. also *Σ* AR 1.419). *ἠερίων...* *ὑπὲρ ν[* extravagantly emphasizes place, a concern of the poet's, and contrasts with the sea; but there is some play too on the low flying of ordinary quails (contrast Himer. 54.3 on eagles). In the second metamorphosis, the graphic *ἔ[π]τη δ' ἠΰτε νηῦς* underlines the sea, like *μέσωι*; the comparison also contributes to a renunciation of the Callimachean version. Asterie, in Callimachus a random Cinderella not Leto's sister, was so called because (*H.* 4.37–8; apostrophe) *βαθὺν ἥλαο τάφρον | οὐρανόθεν φεύγουσα Διὸς γάμον ἀστέρι ἴση.* The disparate history of Delos is now deftly joined into two attempts to escape

---

[24] The earliness of the events makes against a full narration in Ovid's poem. Bömer (on 6.108) thinks Asterie cannot have been a quail in Ovid; *luctante*, indeed, would be hard to reconcile with eagle and quail. Murgatroyd's analysis of Ovid's rape narratives ((2005), ch. 3) brings out how different from Ovid the account in ↓ fr. 1.9–14 is. One is perhaps bound to wonder if ↓ fr. 4 might have presented the fortunes of Bacchus, cf. 2]͈ονμηρ[and *Met.* 3.310–17).

[25] Cf. AR 2.710. Ovid in the *Metamorphoses* does not usually give both father and mother, unless plot or point demands: cf. 3.341–50, 4.288–91, 5.302–11, 11.754–63. For the opening 'there was' cf. *Met.* 7.694–5 *Procris erat...raptae soror Orithyiae*, with immediate exploitation (696–7) of the link to the end of Book 6.

from Zeus; Delos' floating state is not usually so explained. Zeus has a further role, it seems, in 13 (perhaps corrupt). The final glory of hosting the birth of Leto's children (14) is neatly prepared in 8 *Λητοῦς ἔςκε φίλ[η] cύγγ ον<ος> Ἀcτ[ερίη.* (15 might have celebrated her final name.) All this cohesion would actually be split up in Ovid. He would exhibit his ability to be surprisingly brief as well as surprisingly long.[26]

The account of Narcissus in the papyrus poem again shows elegant handling of the couplet and probably a firm design. In → fr. 1.10–11 the couplet neatly opposes *ἀπεχθαίρεcκε δ' ἅπαντας* to *ἠράcατο cφετέρης.* In 12–13 *[ὀ]λοφύρατο* matches *κλα]ύcατο,* both after the caesura. *ἀγλαΐην* (13) takes up *μ]ορφῆς* from 11; it was doubtless modified by a pointed adjective in 15 (cf. 12), and so underlined how Narcissus' beauty brought him no benefit but rather grief. *τέρψιν ὀνείρου* (12) makes the same point in a memorable phrase. Narcissus may in a more radical sense too lose his own *μορφή,* through desiring it, in a poem which quite probably had *Μεταμορφώcεις* for its title: Ovidian play on *forma* may be more quietly suggested here.[27]

The argument on beauty means that *μ]ορφῆς ἠράcατο cφετέρης,* though pointed, does not accentuate the paradox of self-love as strongly as the story itself suggests (cf. Conon (epitomized by Photius) 24.9–10 Brown *καὶ μόνος καὶ πρῶτος ἑαυτοῦ γίνεται ἄτοπος ἐραcτής*). Ovid develops the paradoxes of identity with zest; the simple and forceful *se cupit* (425) comes near the start of Narcissus' captivation. However, *μ]ορφῆς ἠράcατο cφετέρης* (which appealed to Gregory) could be variously exploited. So especially at *Met.* 3.455–6 *certe nec forma nec aetas | est mea quam fugias*: encouraged by Echo's wilful misreadings, we may until the half-sentence is finished hear an ironic falsehood in *nec forma... est mea* (*est* is conspicuously positioned, and

---

[26] On Call. *H.* 4.37–8 cf. Mineur; the placing of *οὐρανόθεν* stresses the parts of the universe. Hyginus' account (*Fab.* 53), well adduced by Bernsdorff (2007), connects the elements of the story in a less satisfying fashion.

[27] Cf. for play on *forma* as beauty and as species e.g. 4.783, 794 (beauty lost in metamorphosis), 12.393–4. For Echo and Narcissus, esp. in Ovid, cf., among other works, Zanker (1966); Segal (1969), 45–9; Manuwald (1975); Loewenstein (1984), ch. 2; Elsner (1996); Hinds (1998), 5–8; Gildenhard and Zissos (2000); Wheeler (2000), 20–3; Parise Bandoni (2001); Bonadeo (2002); M. K. Brown (2002), 172–8; P. R. Hardie (2002*a*), ch. 5; Keith (2002), 253–7; Macho (2002), esp. 20–3; Vogt-Spira (2002); Fantham (2004), 44–6; Rudd (2005); Barchiesi, Rosati, Koch (2007), 175–207.

in this distorted reading 463 takes it up: *iste ego sum, nec me mea fallit imago*). Ovid's play is much more ingenious and lively than the papyrus', and in the first person. Further play on the phrase could occur at 416, 418 *uisae correptus imagine formae,* | *adstupet ipse sibi,* 439–40 *spectat inexpleto mendacem lumine formam* | *perque oculos perit ipse suos.* The beauty must be described more amply in Ovid; if θ]ϵοϵίκϵλον ϵἶ[δοϲ is correct and is used of Narcissus, cf. 421 *dignos Baccho, dignos et Apolline crines.* Movement from beauty to its loss is conveyed by an epic run of similes in 483–90; there follows *nec corpus remanet quondam quod amauerat Echo* (493).[28]

A chief way in which Ovid expands and elaborates his account, as against the papyrus' version, is through the numerous figures other than Narcissus. The papyrus isolates him; ἀπϵχθαίρϵϲκϵ δ' ἅπανταϲ, with its strong verb, may remind the reader of the male, here omitted, who answers Narcissus' rejection with a curse. This figure, who occurs in Ovid (404–6), comes in Conon too. As for Echo, it would be rash to think it likely she was not associated with Narcissus before Ovid. The evidence is quite inadequate to support a negative generalization; and it would be implausible to posit a Roman origin for the name *HXΩ* on the Narcissus mosaic of the House of the Buffet Supper in Antioch (Daphne; Ankaya, Arch. Mus. 938; iii AD). The papyrus may engage in perceptible subtraction by isolating Narcissus; Ovid, if read against the papyrus, would be seen to add, from whatever sources. He can also be seen to pursue, through his additional figures, the large themes and structures of his book.[29]

The river Cephisus near the start of the book (3.19) prepares us to meet Cephisus' son Narcissus later (341–6, 351 *Cephisius*). Tiresias, who prophesies his fate, brings him into the Theban cycle of Books 3–4 (Book 3 appears at its end to have completed a structure centred on Bacchus). Plotting is taken beyond the needs of narrative to thematic elaboration. Tiresias and the male admirer (Ameinias in Conon) seem to provide a double verbal determination: a prophecy and a curse. The admirer himself seems to duplicate Echo's exemplification of those

---

[28] The phrase draws the plot together, cf. e.g. 2.480–1 (*Fast.* 2.181–2), 14.149–51. Ovid finally goes beyond the earth with its flowers (→ fr. 1.15–16?) to the underworld, where Narcissus is with indomitable wit made to continue his self-contemplation (3.504–5). Death is essential to the argument of the episode (346–50).

[29] For the mosaic (*LIMC* 'Echo' 13) see Levi (1947), i. 60–6, 136–7, ii. pl. XXIII c.

Narcissus rejected (353–5 neatly bring in both sexes, with allusion to flowers and *forma*). Through these figures, and Narcissus himself, Ovid explores the themes of speech and communication. In Ovid's version these themes are no less important than visual elements. If his version were read against the papyrus, they could be seen as, whether or not original, his decisive addition. They also exhibit Ovid's elaborate structuring of his book, and will tie up in another way with the papyrus poem.[30]

The utterances of Tiresias and the spurned male are concise utterances which are related to the future. Tiresias' *si se non nouerit* of course inverts the compressed Delphic γνῶθι ϲεαυτόν. The prophecy is connected to the prophecy which Cadmus receives at the end of the book's first story (96–8), and which will ring the Theban narrative of 3–4 (4.569–603: Perseus provides the overlap into Book 5). Related to both Tiresias' and the male's utterances is Diana's brief (193) announcement of Actaeon's doom, *cladis praenuntia uerba futurae* (191); Juno's declaration to Echo is further connected (366–7, cf. *minas* 369 with *minata* 193). Brevity will prove important.[31]

Echo and Narcissus both have problems in communicating with the one they love. Echo is severely restricted (375–8), though verbally she turns out to enjoy remarkable luck. Narcissus cannot hear his reflection's words (461–2); his last brief words (*uox* 499, cf. 359, 369, 398–9) bring no response, but a meaningful repetition from Echo (499–501). It might seem needless to connect their difficulties with Actaeon and his struggles for human sound (201–3, 237–9: failed speech, half-human groans), or with Pentheus' failure to make his mother and aunt understand his words (719–20, 723–9; note the explicit pointer back to Actaeon in 720). Such things might be thought merely part of the work as a whole. But the episode of Echo draws direct attention to questions of communication and speech, and especially to the matter of brevity.

Echo, though in a sense *garrula* (360, cf. Soph. *Phil.* 188–9), has been punished for deliberate long-windedness by *uocis . . . breuissimus usus*

---

[30] For Book 3 as an entity, cf. Feldherr (1997) and von Albrecht (2000), 220–3. For Books 3–4 cf. P. R. Hardie (1990).

[31] At 4.790 *ante expectatum tacuit tamen* Ovid plays on the prolongation of Book 4 and the overlap.

(367). The brevity of her 'speeches' to win Narcissus' love contrasts with his substantial monologue, an Ovidian amatory declamation, which includes an address to his reflection (454–62; cf. 382 *ueni* with 454 *huc exi*, 383–4 *quid... me fugis?* with 454 *quid me... fallis* and 456 *fugias*, 392 *sit tibi copia nostri* with 466 *inopem me copia fecit*). The uneven distribution of power and initiative between the sexes is played on by the contrast; cf. in the monologue 465 *roger anne rogem?*. The shorter speech of Narcissus that follows lessens the contrast, as his speech diminishes (477 *quo refugis?* also links to 383–4 *quid... me fugis?*). Now that length has been thematized, Pentheus' *praebuimus longis... ambagibus aures* (692) gains further point. His own brief utterance in 692–5 attempts to assert power by contrast with Bacchus' narrative (Diana's masterful brevity to Actaeon may be compared, 192–3). It in fact leads, however, to his own brief and futile pleas in 719–20 and 725 (cf. 717 *iam uerba minus uiolenta loquentem*); there *he* is the one tortured and killed (cf. 694–5).[32]

The book thus provides a special focus for concerns that run through the poem. Brevity and length of utterance have more aspects in Latin poetry than is often realized; in the *Metamorphoses*, as we have seen, they can relate to issues of power, and brevity can present both assurance and helplessness. But the question of brevity and length is likely to have a metaliterary dimension too. Ovid's copiousness and fertility were themes of discussion from his own lifetime on; so probably was his epigrammatic concision. (Cf. Sen. Rh. *Contr.* 2.2.12, 7.1.27 (Ovid on brevity); 3.7 (read *non amatoriis artibus?*), 9.5.17). The *Amores* already show the poet-narrator having fun with his own unavailing abundance of words. Callimachus' pronouncements are central to Augustan and to Ovidian poetry, and had made an oblique appearance at the very start of the poem; they are a prominent object of play in the work.[33]

The brevity of Echo's utterances is particularly striking within an epic tradition. In the *Aeneid* only a few speeches last under a line; they are made in effect to fill the line: 5.166 (*iterum* in the middle), 7.116 (*inquit Iulus* at the end; note *nec plura, adludens* 117, cf. Ov.

---

[32] For the norm of male initiative in love (contrast 3.375–6) cf. e.g. *Am.* 1.8.43–4, *AA* 1.277–8.

[33] It would be misguided to suppose that Ovid, who can be disrespectful of everything, must always treat Callimachus with unquestioning reverence.

Met. 3.193), 12.425 (*Iapyx* at end; cf. also 6.45–6; 3.523–4 avoids
direct speech). Hitherto in the *Metamorphoses*, if we exclude instances where the indication of speech and/or speaker fills out the
line (1.710, 2.464, 818), and also 1.481–2, which virtually fit this
pattern (*saepe pater dixit* twice), only 1.498 *quid si comantur?*, Apollo's remark to himself, has lasted less than a line. The short utterances
in Book 3 thus stand out: 3.201 *me miserum!* (this first not a speech
actually made; it exceeds Diana's potent brevity), 348 *si se non
nouerit*, 380 *ecquis adest?*, *adest* (two utterances in one line; one of
one word), 382 *ueni* (one word) (383–4 *quid...* | *me fugis?* runs over
line-end), 386 *huc coeamus*, 387 *coeamus* (one word), 392 *sit tibi
copia nostri*, 495 *eheu*, 496 *eheu* (both one-word exclamations), 500
heu frustra dilecte puer!, 501 *uale, uale* (both one word, two utterances in one line), 605 *adsumus en*, 614 *pro nobis mitte precari*, 644
capiat... aliquis moderamina (674–5 *in quae miracula...* | *ueteris?*,
689–90 *excute...* | *corde metum Dianque tene*), 725 *aspice, mater*.
   Later books do not match this quantity. In Book 3 there are
17 such utterances, not counting those that run over a line (383–4,
674–5, 689–90); in the dialogue of Echo and Narcissus there is a high
concentration of them; there are six in the book even apart from Echo or
Narcissus. If we omit virtually full lines (with 'and' and/or with indication of speech and/or speaker) and speeches which run over a line-end
(e.g. 1.607–8), the other books present: 4.251, 356, 523, 524; 5.625
(really just indication of speaker); 6.227 (*ei mihi*: exclamation), 327,
328 (one word), 640, 652, 655; 7.377, 487, 755 (839 continuation of
837), 843 (*ei mihi*: exclamation); 8.767; 9.131, 379 (within a speech);
10.62 (one word: *uale*), 364, 422, 429, 441, 467 (one word: *filia*), 468
(one word: *pater*; the numerous instances of short speeches in the
Myrrha episode, 298–502, play on the problems of utterance and of
explicitness in such a situation, cf. 429), 673; 11.7, 263, 323, 725 (*ille est!*:
arguably almost one word); 12.241, 259; 13.420, 534, 669, 942; 14.657
(but perhaps a lacuna), 751; 15.607, 609. Instances per book from Book
1 are thus: 3 (including 481–2), 0, 17, 4, 1, 6 (3 in the tale of Tereus,
where utterance has special point), 4, 1, 2, 8 (6 in the story of Myrrha), 4,
2, 4, 2, 2. Rarely do we have only one word, never two utterances in one
line (5.625 *et bis 'io Arethusa, io Arethusa' uocauit* hardly qualifies).[34]

---

[34] On 10.440–1 cf. Schiesaro (2002), 68–9; this is not here a purely amatory
ambiguity. For the importance of Actaeon's inability to speak see Theodorakopoulos
(1999), 153–6. Alfieri's *Mirra* takes the problem of speech into powerful dramatic

The present papyrus might give the issue of brevity and length
new point. Ovid's work would set itself against poems at least
one of which was extremely compact. The expansion of this
episode through Echo and through Narcissus' love-poem to himself
would form a striking illustration. The episode would demonstrate
Ovid's inventiveness and his massive scale, but also his ability
to compress meaning into the pithiest of language. Later in this
book, Pentheus, as we have seen, pronounces on the length of
Bacchus' narrative, by which Ovid expands the *Bacchae* through a
Homeric Hymn; we are invited to ask questions about the literary
strategy too.[35]

The papyrus poem has emerged, even from these difficult fragments, as a tightly written and densely learned treatment. It gives
intense attention to scholarly concerns, but also shows elegance and
imagination, in a style more restrained than Ovid's. It probably
stands further in form from Ovid than Nicander did; it may well
show, like Ovid, an individual approach to the tradition. It could still
illuminate the poetic tradition, of which our knowledge is very faint;
it may be a well-known text, and one with which Ovid's interacts.
The very starkness of its concision and discontinuity would make it
a particularly telling point of contrast. It would give new force to the
range and richness of Ovid's structural ideas and connections; it
would lend new importance to continuity, length, and the book in
the impact of Ovid's poem. Ovid's most primary Hellenistic models
had not aroused great enthusiasm in critics. Yet if Ovid spectacularly
transforms the type of poem, it may have undergone transformations
before, and its incarnation in the papyrus may show, not dull raw

form. 11.725 *ille est* as virtually one word might be defended by pentameter endings
and 14.801, 15.694; but cf. 1.500, 6.175, etc. Compare with it the deliberately un-
Virgilian '*Anna est!*' at *Fast.* 3.607.

[35] The short speeches inset in Bacchus' narrative add to the complications. At the
end of Book 5, after a full re-run of Calliope's elaborate song to Minerva, *nunc quoque
in alitibus facundia prisca remansit | raucaque garrulitas studiumque immane loquendi*
(677–8, cf. 294–9) raises humorous questions, and makes telling contrasts, in regard
to both the secondary and the primary narrator. Cf. Hinds (1987), 130, for aesthetic
reference here. The extreme brevity of most of the narratives in *Eclogue* 6, and the
speech and inset example in 45–60, might also gain force from reading with this
papyrus.

material, but a striking text for Ovid's to engage with. The papyrus may help to underline the central and manifold importance of Hellenistic metamorphosis-poems for educated first readers of Ovid's poem; this importance can easily be obscured for modern critics by more accessible intertexts. The papyrus also brings out the relation of Ovid's procedures to large aspects of Hellenistic poetry which it helps to makes newly visible. Recent finds show Hellenistic poetry as ever more important for Latin poetry; they also reveal how little we know about it.

APPENDIX:

Metamorphoses 9

The value of considering the books within the *Metamorphoses* as significant structures may be further illustrated from a single book. Book 9 participates in larger patterns, as is seen from the palpable relation between Byblis' story and Myrrha's; but this does not preclude an internal structure. Nor does the typically blurred transition from Book 8 (8.884–9.2 *gemitus sunt uerba secuti.* ||| *quae gemitus…Neptunius heros | causa rogat…*): Ovid strongly evokes the transition between Books 1 and 2 of the *Aeneid* (cf. *Met.* 9.4–7 with *Aen.* 2.3–13). Gender, which dominates the structure of Book 9, is the basic organizing principle of the *Ars Amatoria* and the double *Heroides*; it also creates a vital opposition between the single *Heroides* and the *Amores*.[1]

The first third of the book (1–275), unlike the rest, is emphatically masculine. By contrast with the primary source, Sophocles' *Trachiniae*, Ovid drastically reduces the prominence and perspective of Deianira. The book's structure as a whole reverses the equally challenging structure of the *Trachiniae*: most of the play is primarily feminine in its concerns and point of view, until Heracles characteristically irrupts and dominates the final quarter. Within the *Metamorphoses* as a whole, lines 1–275 strike the reader through the interaction of bodies in wrestling not love, and through the heroic elevation (some think, mock-elevation) of Hercules' long speech and agony. At all events, the impact of Hercules' torments, and the celebrity of the Sophoclean scene, make those torments a natural point of reference for the comparable sufferings of women that follow.[2]

---

[1] A summary of the book: 1–97 Achelous tells of his fight with Hercules; 98–275 Hercules dies and becomes a god; 275–325 Galanthis becomes a weasel; 325–97 Dryope becomes a tree; 396–446 Iolaus is rejuvenated; 444–665 Byblis desires her brother and becomes a spring; 667–797 Iphis desires Ianthe and becomes a man. On Book 9 as an entity, cf. Janan (1991), 242–4; von Albrecht (2000), 242–4.

[2] Heracles' speech at Soph. *Trach.* 1046–1111 is imitated *TrGF* Adesp. 653 (P. Oxy. 2454; cf. Adesp. 126; [Sen.] *HO*, esp. 1131–418), translated Cic. *Tusc.* 2.20–2. Ovid removes the female and amorous elements of the narratives at *Trach.* 6–20, 497–530. For wrestling cf. *Met.* 6.239–44 (in art e.g. Decker and Thuillier (2004), 98–9, 117–18, 223, 239); for love and wrestling esp. 4.356–67, Prop. 2.1.13–14, 15.5–6 (note stripping), Apul. *Met.* 9.5.2. For Ov. *Met.* 9.1–275 see Otis (1969), 194–201; Galinsky (1972*a*), (1972*b*), 156–60; Feeney (1991), 206–7; W. J. Schneider (1998); Wheeler (1999), 136; Segal (2001–2), 86–7; Fantham (2004), 94–9; Rimell (2006), 32–3. On suffering and gender in the *Trachiniae*, cf. Hutchinson (1999), 48–51.

The first such woman is his mother. Her bodily agonies at Hercules' birth are clearly compared with Hercules' own agonies at his death, or rebirth. The experiences are joined by groans, arms lifted in prayer, and especially the agency of Juno (163, 175, 176–82; 284, 293–4, 295–6, 297); more widely cf. 264–5: Hercules loses likeness to mother; 180: his *animam natam... laboribus*; 273, 289: Hercules' *pondus* felt by Atlas and Alcmene; 285–6 *laboriferi... Herculis*, 289–90: Alcmene could not *tolerare labores | ulterius*; 199 *indefessus agendo*, 293 *fessa malis*.[3]

Next comes Dryope. Her speech as she turns into a tree (371–91) is unexpectedly made into a death-speech (391 *morientia lumina*, 392). While Hercules' skin is peeled off, hers is covered in a layer of bark (*detegit* 169, *contegat* 391); devouring fire moves over his body, soft (*mollis*) bark moves over hers (201–2, 388–9). Her speech like his dwells on injustice, but to protect her good name; the woman tenderly speaks to and of her family, while Hercules addresses and mentions only his stepmother.[4]

Just before Byblis, the episode on Iolaus recalls Hercules again (explictly at 401). But the exposition will be clearer if we turn now to the end of Book 9. In a neat conclusion to a book where the masculine is succeeded by and contrasted with the feminine, Iphis suffers pains which ought to be suffered by a man (cf. 726–44), and finally turns into one. Hercules' death is connected to tragedy; Iphis' story, despite homosexuality and metamorphosis, evokes the plots of New Comedy. The malevolent Juno and kindly Isis contrast (181 begs Juno for the *munus* of death; Iphis' preservation at birth was Isis' *munus*, 779–80). The transformation of Iphis into a man resembles that of Hercules into a god. Both unusually move the human upward in hierarchical status, and are visually subtle: Hercules *parte sui meliore uiget maiorque uideri | coepit* (269–70), Iphis walks *maiore gradu. . . . uires augentur . . . plusque uigoris adest habuit quam femina* (786–90). *uires* are denoted by the names of both: 110 . . . *Alcide; tu uiribus utere nando* (cf. ἀλκή); 715 *Iphi*, 745 *quin animum firmas . . . , Iphi* (cf. ἲφι).[5]

---

[3] The story of Galanthis/Galinthias (Nic. fr. 60 Schneider) is enhanced with Roman deities of childbirth, 293; for *Nixūs*, cf. Petersmann (1990), *AE* 1934 no. 238, 1975 no. 671, 1999 no. 1203. For *Met.* 9.275–325 see Dietze (1905), 29–30; Schachter (1981–94), ii. 25, 27; Segal (1998), 27–8; Forbes Irving (1990), 205–7; Fantham (2004), 67–8; Salzman-Mitchell (2005), 193–7.

[4] His instructions to Hyllus (278–80) are left out of the speech. Dryope becomes a nymph in Nic. fr. 41 Schneider (Ant. Lib. 32.4–5). For *Met.* 9.325–97 see Dietze (1905), 33–4; Forbes Irving (1990), 130, 263–4; Segal (1998), 28–9; P. R. Hardie (2002*a*), 252; Fantham (2004), 68–9; Salzman-Mitchell (2005), 197–201.

[5] βίη and ἲς in periphrases for Heracles e.g. *Il.* 2.658, Hes. *Theog.* 332, 951. Ovid would not have seen the link between *uis* and *ἲς*; for *Alcides* and for *uir, uis, uigor* cf. Maltby (1991), 22, 645, 647. *Met.* 9.723 *quamque uirum putat esse uirum fore credit Ianthe* alludes to Soph. *Trach.* 550–1 ταῦτ᾽ οὖν φοβοῦμαι, μὴ πόσις μὲν Ἡρακλῆς | ἐμὸς

We may return now to Byblis. She and Hercules have the two extended narratives of the book; it is natural to compare these narratives. The man's suffering is physical. The woman's is mental and amorous; such suffering has become particularly characteristic of women by this stage in the poem. (Iphis' paradoxical desire will bridge the male and female.) Male and female suffering are similarly contrasted in the *Trachiniae*. Byblis tears her clothes from her body through mental causes (635–7); through physical causes Hercules seeks to do so (166–9, 209). Both fight *flammae*, of poison or love (172, 509), and Hercules conquers literal *flammae* (249–51): common imagery gains new force. Cold amid heat is used in an image for Hercules' torture, and literally for Byblis (170–1; 581–3, cf. 516, 541, 562, etc.). Both are at first ignorant (157, 456 *nullos intellegit ignes*). Byblis claims she has endured (*tuli*) more than would be thought possible for a girl (544–5, cf. 4.149–50, 13.451); her virile imagery runs into anticlimax (543–4 *pugnauique diu uiolenta Cupidinis arma | effugere*). Hercules conquers fire; the weeping Byblis dissolves into water (659–65). Female tears abound in the book from after Hercules' death, though at the last they turn into joy (792).[6]

Whereas in Ovid's explicitly amatory poetry the sexes are inwardly the same, this book presents us with a colossal opposition of the extreme masculine and the feminine. But the final episode elegantly questions the firmness of the division. The structure contributes to the larger exploration of gender in the poem.[7]

καλῆται, τῆϲ νεωτέραϲ δ' ἀνήρ. The ambiguous name Iphis is imported by Ovid into both this myth (cf. Nic. fr. 45 Schneider) and the connected episode at 14.698–761; cf. Bömer (1969–), iv. 470, 489, vii. 214. For 9.667–797 see Dietze (1905), 34–7; Otis (1970), 417–18; Nicaise (1980); Rosati (1983), 124–6; Forbes Irving (1990), 152–5; Hallett (1997); S. R. West (1998); Hershkowitz (1999), 190–3; P. R. Hardie (2002a), 250, 258; Pintabone (2002); Fantham (2004), 61–2.

    6 The spring is called Δάκρυον Βυβλίδοϲ: Nic. fr. 46 (Ant. Lib. 30.4); cf. Parth. ΕΠ 11.4, Nonn. *Dion.* 13.561. In the first part of the book even Deianira renounces tears (142–4, cf. 149–51); Hercules does not weep (contrast 163–4 with Soph. *Trach.* 1070–5, cf. Σ Soph. *Aj.* 318). Hercules' *ardor* (140) for Iole is not elaborated (contrast *Her.* 9.5–6, 11–12, 25–6), and is made factually dubious (37–41). For 444–665 see Dietze (1905), 37–9; Rohde (1914), 101 n. 1; Heinze (1960), 393–4; Tränkle (1963), 460–5; Otis (1970), 217–26, 415–17; Hollis (1976), 143–5, 149; Ranucci (1976); Nagle (1983); Forbes Irving (1990), 24, 31, 300; Janan (1991); Holzberg (1998b), 141–2; Farrell (1998), 317–23; Auhagen (1999), 144–52; Lightfoot (1999), 187–91, 433–43; Jenkins (2000); P. R. Hardie (2002a), 107; Spentzou (2003), 157–9; Salzman-Mitchell (2005), 113–15.

    7 On Hercules and the feminine see Jourdain-Annequin and Bonnet (1996).

10

Structuring Instruction: Didactic Poetry
and Didactic Prose*

Most Latin didactic poems of the first century BC, unlike most
pre-Imperial Greek didactic poems, are designed in several books.
This structure radically alters the ambition and character of the
poems; it also displays a relationship with the structure of prose
treatises. The general relationship of didactic poetry with prose is
more intricate than is commonly realized; in exploiting structures
characteristic of prose, poetry is annexing and twisting the properties
of a different literary genre. Didactic poetry does not merely transfer
content from an aesthetically worthless form into literature. Notions
of didactic poetry as virtuoso or metaphorical transformation of base
and unliterary matter, though they contain elements of truth, fail to
capture the complexity of generic interaction.[1]

Plurality of books separates Lucretius, the *Georgics*, the *Ars Ama-*
toria, Manilius from Hesiod's *Works and Days*, Aratus' *Phaenomena*,
and Nicander's didactic poems. Aratus imitates Hesiod in his

---

* A version of this chapter was heard by the ICS seminar in London; thanks
especially to Professor J. G. F. Powell and Dr N. J. Lowe.
[1] A future article will discuss further the relations of didactic poetry and prose.
Horster and Reitz (2003) and (2005) together provide a valuable way in to the
relationship; cf. Reitz (2003). Investigation remains at an early stage. For general
discussion of didactic poetry see Kroll (1925); Pöhlmann (1973); Effe (1977); Schiesaro, Mitsis, Strauss Clay (1993); Dalzell (1996); Toohey (1996); Atherton (1998);
Wöhrle (1998); D. P. Fowler (2000a); Volk (2002, 2005); Gale (2004); Glei (2004);
Kruschwitz and Schumacher (2005); Feeney (2007a). On didactic prose see Fuhrmann (1960); Kullmann, Althoff, and Asper (1998); Langslow (2000, 2007); Goldhill
(2002), ch. 4; Fögen (2005); Mayer (2005); Diederich 2007; and e.g. Schulze (2003).
Too many large poems are discussed below for bibliographical indications to be more
than slight.

combination into a single book of two different subjects (and two different prose sources). One could imagine Nicander, had he written later, conjoining *Theriaca* and *Alexipharmaca* into a work of more than one book, or covering *Georgica* in more than one book like Virgil.[2]

The divergence of all the Latin poems mentioned from earlier norms is hardly to be explained by an evocation of narrative epic. The similar divergence of Anubion, Oppian, and [Oppian] will not be a coincidence. Sostratus' *Cynegetica*, in at least two books, is likely to be earlier than Lucretius and unlikely to be influenced by him; it is considerably earlier than 45 BC (*SH* 735). The Latin poems, then, may well be influenced by late Hellenistic poems. But relevant too to Lucretius is Empedocles. His Περὶ Φύϲεωϲ had at least three books, his Καθαρμοί at least two (some think they are one work); they totalled *c*.5,000 lines.[3]

Yet despite the impulse of Greek poetry, prose too is bound to be suggested by the move from a supposedly Hesiodic drift to an explicitly demarcated design. It could have been suggested too in late Hellenistic poetry; but in the Latin poems we can look at the detail. The prose sources which the poems actually or notionally 'translate' into poetry make this an obvious point of comparison. The resonance of prose is enhanced by the rapid growth in this period of didactic prose in Latin: we should look beyond the

---

[2] Aratus' approach may suggest the title *Works and Days* (first attested ii AD; *Works* e.g. *Σ* Pind. *Pyth.* 4.507, Argent. XV.4), with the *Days* referring to the section *WD* 765–828; or he may imitate the general heterogeneity seen in Hesiod. (Hesiod's poem should actually be seen, not as discourse meandering without an initial plan, but as an elaborate expansion of a traditional form, the framed list of instructions (cf. the material of M. L. West (1978), 3–25, (1997), 306–9; the expansions in the *Theogony* support).) Aratus' is a subtle transition; the coronis at 732 in *BKT* v.1.47–54 (P. Berol. 7503 + 7804, i AD) should not be seen as dividing the two halves of the poem (cf. Kidd (1997), 425), as there is another at 776.

[3] Cf. Trépanier (2004), 1–30, with literature. In my view, Diog. Laert. 8.77 clearly indicates two poems, by what are found elsewhere as titles (cf. 1.61, 112, 5.27 for the joint total); although Diogenes is not thoroughly reliable, the grounds for demanding a single poem seem insufficient. Sufficient grounds are not provided by the just claim that the two poems were not radically opposed in outlook. Gale (2005), 182–3, sees Lucretius' six books as evoking narrative epic (cf. Mayer (1990)). On Sostratus, see Lightfoot (1999), 412 n. 103, 428–9; the similarity of the myth at *SH* 735 to that at Ov. *AA* 3.685–746 is of interest.

relation of each poem and its particular sources to an intricate literary scene.[4]

The explicit articulation of works into books is a notable development of prose after the fifth century. It grows out of rhetorical and philosophical structuring; intellectual organization is now applied to the physical form of the work. The firm and overt divisions suit the subject and help the reader; they fulfil initial undertakings, in a kind of contract with the reader, and display the completeness with which the author has covered his topic. Statements or promises of what is to be treated commonly indicate the division into books; books very often end and begin with summary of the book about to close or lately closed and with prospective of the book begun or about to begin. Summaries and prospectives can also take in several books, explicitly divided. Elaborately excursive proems can underline and exploit the divisions. The significance of all this apparently obvious detail tends to escape scrutiny because we inherit the tradition.[5]

Some examples: already in the third century BC, Apollonius of Perga, *Conica*, begins with a letter stating the contents of his eight books, divided neatly into two parts of four books each. He now sends the first, revised, to the addressee, and will send and revise the rest (1 *pr*. p. 2 Heiberg). At 4 *pr*. p. 2 Heiberg there is a change of addressee, now Eudemus has died: such changes often mark an alteration in plan. In the first century BC, Apollonius of Citium begins the second book of his commentary on Hippocrates 'On Limbs' (CMG xi.1.1 p. 38.3–7) ἐν μὲν τῶι πρὸ τούτου βιβλίωι, βασιλεῦ Πτολεμαῖε, περὶ ὤμου καθ᾽ Ἱπποκράτην ἐμβολῆς δεδηλώκα μεν, ἐν δὲ τούτωι περί τε ἀγκῶνος καὶ ... διασαφήcω. After showing the structure of this book he adds that he is not unaware (οὐκ ἀγνοῶ) that the matter is difficult to grasp in words; blame the nature of the subject, not him, he urges (μὴ ἡμᾶς ἀλλὰ τὴν τοῦ πράγματος αἰτιῶ φύcιν, p. 38.13). He will make it as clear as is possible—with the help of drawings. Philodemus justifies ending a book where he does by the needs of cυμμετρία, due measure (*Ad Contub.* 1 col.

---

[4] The detailed connections confirm that there is a relation between the division into *books* in both genres; they are not accidental products of a general concern with rhetorical *partitio*.

[5] Genette (1987), on preliminary matter in modern books, offers effective defamiliarization.

xviii.6–12). Other books end announcing what is to come (*Rhet.* 4 col. xliv.5–11, *Vit.* 10 col. xxiv.21–7).[6]

Historiography, more copiously represented, shows the same patterns as other prose. Diodorus desires self-contained books in history (5.1.4, 16.1.1). He announces his design in terms of books, not yet published (1.4.6–7), and at the end of Book 2 refers back to his ἐπαγγελίαν at the start of it (2.60.4). The start of Book 2 elaborately summarizes the first book, and announces the subject of the present book; Book 3 does the same, summarizing the first two books. The fourth book begins with self-justification: he is not unaware (οὐκ ἀγνοῶ) of the difficulties of mythography. He then proceeds (4.1.5) to retrospect and announcement. The thirteenth book explains he has no time to spend on the usual discursive prologues (13.1.2 τὸν πολὺν λόγον τῶν προοιμίων), and proceeds to retrospect of the previous six books and to announcement. It is pleasing that the fourteenth book has a moralizing prologue.[7]

Polybius strongly emphasizes his design and his undertaking, commonly in terms of books. The fourth book, for example, summarizes the previous book, and proceeds 'now I shall tell of...' (4.1.1–2); the proem to the non-narrative sixth book, which was announced at the end of the third, included a justification of his procedure, beginning 'I am not unaware' (οὐκ ἀγνοῶ, 6.2.1). In the proem to Book 11 he discussed his move from a list of contents at the start of each book to a summary before each Olympiad; the relation of Olympiads and books is carefully explained (14.1*a*.1–5).

These procedures are conspicuously taken over in Latin prose: Varro, Cicero, Vitruvius are full of examples. In Vitruvius, who well illustrates convention, beginnings and endings of books typically display summaries and prospectives (e.g. 2 *pr.*5 (with involved justification); 4 *pr.*; 7.14.3); the beginnings of the exposition proper are commonly preceded by an excursive proem, or followed by a short digression. Completeness of the work as a whole, and the cohesion of

---

[6] οὐκ ἀγνοῶ ὅτι (διότι), in introducing a possible criticism or objection, is a phrase highly characteristic of Greek intellectual prose; the device perhaps enters it particularly from the combative milieu of oratory. Cf. e.g. Xen. *Hell.* 6.3.7 (beginning of speech), Isocr. *Pac.* 114, Dem. 23.6, Aeschin. 1.67.

[7] On elaborate historiographical prologues, cf. Lucian, *Conscr. Hist.* 23, with Jacobson (2007). Cf. Marincola (1997), ch. 3.

individual books, are significant concerns (1 *pr.*3; 7.14.3 *omnes aedificationum perfectiones*; 9.8.15; 10.16.12 *uti totum corpus omnia architecturae membra in decem uolumnibus haberet explicata*). Varro announces the total plan of his *De Rebus Rusticis* at the beginning of the first book (1.1.11), though the books are published separately, to different addressees. The organization into books rests on his own original conception of the divisions of the subject (3.1.8–9). The internal organization of the first book will follow *naturales diuisiones* (1.1.11). The work's excursive proems or dedicatory epistles are notable. *De Lingua Latina* 5 begins with a summary of Books 2–4, and introduces the next three books, with their new addressee. Book 9 ends because it has fulfilled the promise at the start of it; a prospective of the next follows. The initial summary in the first book is referred to in the prospective of Book 6 at the end of 5; the book is also said to allow of no more (*neque si amplius uelimus uolumen patietur*, 5.184).[8]

Excursive proems are popular with Cicero, and often end with self-conscious breaking off (*De Orat.* 3.9 *non uagabitur oratio mea longius*, *Off.* 2.8, 3.6). The *non eram nescius* reply to (potential) criticism at the beginning of *De Finibus* is eminently Hellenistic. Summary and prospective are seen, for example, at the start of *De Officiis* 2; *De Orat.* 2.13 puts the summary into the dialogue form. The anonymous *Ad Herennium* likewise summarizes and announces at the beginning of Book 2 (*in primo libro, Herenni, breuiter exposuimus*...). The emphasis on brevity, past or future, is very characteristic of Latin writers in particular: the reader's valuable time must not be wasted.[9]

All this strong division and structuring transfers into Latin the intellectual ambition with which Greek prose masters the world. The

---

[8] On Latin prefaces, see Janson (1964); more generally on organization in prose of this period, see Rawson (1991). On Vitruvius and structuring cf. Gros (2006), 418–22; on Vitruvius' prose, see Callebat (1982). Varro's structuring within books is treated by Skydsgaard (1968); Diederich (2007), 410–19. On Varro's writing and the image it creates cf. Diederich (2005), 277–81, (2007), 172–9. Cic. *Fam.* 5.12.3 suggests proems to separate books in Lucceius' history.

[9] Cicero follows the quasi-contractual suggestions of Hellenistic structures in faulting Panaetius' failure to carry out his original division, and his prospective at the end of a book: *de tertio pollicetur se deinceps scripturum sed nihil scripsit* (*Att.* 16.11.4, cf. *Off.* 3.9); perhaps the subject of τὸ καθῆκον adds irony. On Cicero and Panaetius see Dyck (1996), 17–29.

relevance of this material to Lucretius is easily seen. Thus *nec me animi fallit Graiorum obscura reperta | difficile inlustrare Latinis uersibus esse* (1.136–7) immediately recalls the standard Greek and Latin 'I am not unaware' (cf. 5.97, also in self-justification, at the very beginning of the exposition; 1.922, taking up the prologue). The self-defence is reminiscent of Apollonius of Citium, and still more, with relation to translated terminology, *Ad Her.* 4.10 *ergo haec asperiora primo uideantur necesse est, id quod fiet rei, non nostra difficultate* (retrospective justification, near end of proem to last book).[10]

Book 3, after the proem standard in Lucretius, moves to a summary of the previous two books; an announcement of the subject of this one ensues. *et quoniam docui* (31) performs the same function as δεδηλώκαμεν or ἐδηλώσαμεν. The sequence of subjects is seen as necessary: *hasce secundum res animi natura uidetur | atque animae claranda meis iam uersibus esse* (35–6). *uersibus* stresses that Lucretius is writing poetry; books are not mentioned—that would bring him too close to prose. The sentence sweeps on to evoke unprosaically the more emotional aim of expelling the fear of death; description of that fear pollutes the rest of the sentence.[11]

The fourth book, after its problematic proem, begins in the authentic or final text with *quoniam docui*, a summary of the third book, and *nunc agere incipiam* (cf. Polyb. 4.1.1–3); it stresses the relevance of the new subject to the preceding argument (*quod uementer ad has res | attinet*, 29–30). 5.55–81 also summarize what has come and what will come. It is not so explicitly indicated that the summary of Books 1–4 is a summary of what has already been said; but *quod superest, nunc huc rationis detulit ordo, ut…* makes this clear, and emphasizes the philosophical justification of the plan. At 6.43–6 the summary is only of Book 5; the image of the chariot (47) poeticizes the exposition of the order. Metapoetic images in didactic

---

[10] Cf. further on didactic prose Cic. *Att.* 2.6.1 *et hercule sunt res difficiles ad explicandum* (with further stylistic comment), *Fam.* 7. 9.1 (introducing the *Topica*) *sin tibi quaedam uidebuntur obscuriora*, etc. (the difficulty of learning any art from *litteris*). For *egestatem linguae* (Lucr. 1.139, cf. 832, 3.260) see Fögen (2000), and note the personal modesty of *paupertate* (Ser. Sulpicius quoted) at *Fam.* 4. 4. 1.

[11] For *et quoniam docui* cf. P. G. Fowler (1983), 106. *uidetur…claranda…iam* is striking in the light of the argument that Lucretius at this point inverts Epicurus' order (and his own original order): see Sedley (1998), 110–19, 135–8.

proems mark a distance from the prose that the proems evoke. The prospective of the coming book is interrupted and deferred by drama with the addressee; conflict with religion is delayed by warnings to the addressee on religion. Verse is emphasized at the beginning and end of the prospective proper (80–95), with *sunt ornanda politis | uersibus* (82–3), a Muse, and more sporting imagery.[12]

Lucretius' development and defamiliarization of these prose forms is already apparent. One notable feature is the formulaic series of lines on dispelling fear with intellectual light which forms a bridge between proem and exposition in 1 and 3 (1.146–8, 3.91–3) but between proem and announcement in 2 (*nunc age... expediam* 62–6) and between proem and summary in 6 (*et quoniam docui* 43). This seems like poetic and epic formularity rather than the standard formulae of prose; the lines connect emotive proems with scientific exposition, and give the latter an emotional justification.[13]

Elaborately poetic means are used to segregate book from book— an aim important to Hellenistic prose. The end of Book 1 drastically contemplates, though in a negative purpose clause, the end of the cosmos (1102–10; cf. the counter-factual close which ends the whole of Manilius' poem, *totus et accenso mundus flagraret Olympo*). This book itself will enable the reader to see *ultima naturai* (spatial). Book 2 ends with the idea of everything getting worn out, *spatio aetatis defessa uetusto* (1174, cf. 1105–74); the infinity of death ends Book 3. Book 5 ends *ad summum donec uenere cacumen* (1457), on civilized arts; but this is not the end of the work. By strong contrast, Book 6, the last of the work, begins *primae... primae*, and starts with the beginnings of civilized life, and then the beginnings of philosophy's consolation. The prologue of the book ends looking at the total structure of the work, and the *supremae... calcis* (92).[14]

---

[12] On the proem to 4, see the diverging approaches of Deufert (1996), 81–96, and Kyriakidis (2006); for 45–53, see Deufert (1996), 155–64; Sedley (1998), 39–42. For the metapoetic chariot in 6, see P. G. Fowler (1983), 115–17. For Calliope, cf. Emped. fr. 10 Inwood.

[13] Such repeated lines and phrases could go back to Empedocles, cf. frr. 4.1, 6.2 Inwood; 8.2, 16.7; 16.8, 25.29; 25.1, 15–16; 25.6, 12, 28.11; 25.7, 37, 28.5, 38.2; 26.10–12, 27.6–8; 34.1–2, 110.2–3. Cf. also Schiesaro (1994), 98–100.

[14] 5.1456 *alid ex alio clarescere corde uidebant* (1456) looks back to the end of 1 (1115); 1.1114–17 can retrospectively be seen as suggesting the interrelation of the separated books.

In his stress on structuring by books—never so called—Lucretius is appropriating the intellectualism of prose, to which division is so important (division in general, and division by books in particular). The lucidity of prose is to be annexed, excelled, and enriched.

The *Georgics* notably begin, not with Lucretius' Aratus-like invocation, but with a summary of contents, addressed to Maecenas. Some sort of prospective is common in epic, narrative and didactic; but the strong if inexplicit division by books indicates the affinity to treatises. The summary actually highlights in retrospect the unexpected proportions of the design: it syntactically joins the first two books (*quo sidere terram* | *uertere, Maecenas, ulmisque adiungere uitis* | *conueniat*); it mirrors the split in the third book, and the limited subject-matter of the fourth: *quae cura boum, qui cultus habendo* | *sit pecori, apibus quanta experientia parcis.* The poetic verb of singing comes after the announcement of subjects (*hinc canere incipiam*, 5). The prayer emphasizes the world of poetry (*cano* in the early parenthesis at 12; note *ferte ... pedem* 11, at least suggesting dance); it also conjures up the proem of Varro's first book (*RR* 1.1.4–7).[15]

2 begins with summary (*hactenus*) and prospective (*nunc*). *canam* comes again, not a verb Lucretius uses of the poet. The subsequent invocation of Bacchus takes us into the energetic world of poetry; *tuis hic omnia plena* | *muneribus* (4–5) presents a more modest version of Aratus' opening. The end of 2 emphasizes the distance covered and the need to stop: common themes in prose (Philodemus above, cf. also e.g. *Ad Her.* 1.27, Varr. *LL* 10.84). The image of the horse poeticizes; *immensum spatiis ... aequor* poeticizes, and plays with, the professions of prose (the book has been short).[16]

At 3.284–94 the division of the book is marked, exactly half-way: both halves have 283 lines. The prose-like *hoc satis armentis: superat pars altera curae* (286) is surrounded by much more ornate language; but the theme of time (284–5) is also treated, and more lengthily, by Athenaeus Mechanicus (see below). The formal division of Diodorus 1 into two parts, because of size and measure, may be compared.

---

[15] Cf. on the prayer Nappa (2005), 25–8.
[16] With Lucretius' avoidance of *cano* for the poet, contrast *canor* at Lucr. 4.181–2, 910–11, where the poetry is the target domain; *carmine* 1.143, 946, etc. With Virg. *G.* 2.542 *et iam tempus ... soluere* cf. e.g. *Ad Her.* 4.10 *nunc tempus postulat ut ... transeamus.*

Diodorus refers back explicitly to the plan announced at the beginning; Virgil takes up implicitly the opening invocation to Pales (294, cf. 1), with emphasis on poetry: *magno nunc ore sonandum*. This is itself made problematic by the nature of the subject-matter (290), and its relation to technical prose. *nec sum animi dubius uerbis ea uincere magnum | quam sit et angustis hunc addere rebus honorem* (289–90) presents in its first part a problem familiar in prose (and cf. for *uerbis* Apoll. Cit. *Hipp. Art.* 2 p. 38.11–12 Kollesch–Kudlien οὐκ ἀγνοῶ δὲ διότι τὰ διὰ χειρουργίας ἐνεργούμενα δυϲκόλωϲ διὰ λόγου καταλαμβάνεϲθαι δύναται); but as the second part shows, the reference is now specifically to poetic decorum, and Callimachean aesthetics are toyed with.[17]

Book 4, like 2 without an elaborate proem, announces the new subject, and implies the new book following the earlier books: *hanc etiam, Maecenas, aspice partem* (not *hunc... librum*). 116–48 show the writer allegedly near the end of his work and strapped for space: the passage uses, and plays with, actual endings of books allegedly compelled by a shortage of space or invited by length (e.g. Varr. *LL* 5.184, Cic. *Inv.* 2.178). The end of Book 4 briefly summarizes Books 1–3 (559–60), with *canebam*.

The close of Book 1, while magnificent, ends by being unended. A close is sought to civil discord; *satis* (501) gives a reason for ending not the book but the wars. Yet this pessimism suits the distinctness of the individual books; so does the related close of Book 3, which replays the end of Lucretius' whole work. Its emphasis on cattle also revokes the descent in size for the book's second half. The book ends, however, not with the firm closure of actual death but with ongoing disease, evoking funeral pyres (*artus sacer ignis edebat*, note tense). The bees immediately follow. The opposition of whole books in the *Georgics* will be seen below to have its links with prose.[18]

---

[17] For the division of *Georgics* 3, see Holzberg (2006), 109, 112–13. The general gesture at 3.286 is common; cf. e.g. Cic. *Top.* 32 *quod ad definitiones attinet hactenus; reliqua uideamus*. For *satis* cf. e.g. Diod. 1.98 ἀρκεῖ τὰ ῥηθέντα, Varr. *LL* 5.184 *satis* (both end of book); Cic. *Leg.* 3.32 (end of excursus).

[18] The chariot at the end of 1 links with the chariots at the end of 2 (note *satis*) and the beginning of 3 (17–18). The motif connects with the subject-matter of Book 3, and is thus returned to the primary didactic material. The end of 4 is also connected to the end of 1, and the beginning of 3. Cf. Schindler (2000), 209–11; Cadili (2001), 189.

The gestures towards prose order and organization have a less straightforward rationale in Virgil than in Lucretius. For structuring *within* the books commonly confounds obvious order, as intertextuality with Varro highlights. So the sequence of the year, which makes a structure in Hes. *WD* 383–617, Varr. *RR* 1.26.1–36.1, Man. 3.616–68, is only gestured towards in *G.* 1.43–6, 291–315. The very division of Book 3 into two halves brings out how each half defies the prose tradition by blending the exposition of two species; the aesthetic and poetic emphasis at the point of division (3.284–94) adds to the generic complexity. The poem continually withdraws from philosophical firmness into poetic fictions, and the interaction with prose intensifies the opacity.[19]

The book-divisions of prose enable us to make much fuller sense of Ovid's didactic poetry on love. Summaries and prospectives subserve not order but a game of deferral and surprise. The first book of the *Ars Amatoria* all but ends with a very unclosural close, a postscript (755–70) which evokes the beginning of exposition in *Georgics* 1 (1.50–70, cf. 2.109–35). The final couplet looks backward and forwards: 771–2 *pars superat coepti, pars est exhausta, laboris:* | *hic teneat nostras ancora iacta rates.* (The pentameter poeticizes the closure with a standard image.) The couplet creates the appearance of a two-book work. The opening of Book 2 is like a proper close to Book 1, a celebration of victory achieved. But the *palma* awarded the teacher here (3) cannot actually be awarded until the end of this book (733 *palmam date*); the ship (cf. 1.722) of addressee and teacher cannot yet reach port (9–10): it is in the middle. The idea of summary and prospective is turned into an animated dispute with the male reader (9–14; 11–12 *non satis est uenisse tibi me uate puellam;* | *arte mea capta est, arte tenenda mea est*). Dispute on the content of a book appears for example in the proem of Polybius 6; especially germane is 3.4–5, justifying the prolongation of his work beyond his plan. Here the addressee's haste (*quid properas, iuuenis?,* 9) and lack of interest after conquest is made to sound youthful and male. The poet glamorizes the new closure aimed at, and makes it

---

[19] The recent alignment of year and calendar (cf. Varr. *RR* 1.28.1–2; Feeney (2007*b*), 200–1) makes the poem's divergence from Varro particularly striking.

sound impossible: the purpose is *imposuisse modum* on the wings of love (20).[20]

2.733 brings the close at last, *finis adest operi*. But a final couplet again points to the next book. Here, by contrast with the end of Book 1, there is no sense of planned order: there is an interruption from outside, and new addressees enter the poem. *ecce, rogant tenerae sibi dem praecepta puellae*: | *uos eritis chartae proxima cura meae* (745–6). Changes of addressee and a new book or series of books go together in the prose tradition (cf. e.g. Varr. *LL* 5.1); an explicit change of plan within a series of books sounds more like prose than verse. The connections of 2.733–46 with the end of 1 and the beginning of 2 remain striking despite the change; these connections are strengthened by the beginning of Book 3. The standard summary and prospective is made mock-epic and warlike (1–2 *Arma dedi Danais in Amazonas; arma supersunt* | *quae tibi dem et turmae, Penthesilea, tuae*); it again turns into a lively self-justification and dispute. This time it is not the same addressee who is forced to continue the lessons, but the old addressee who resents help to the new: *dixerit e multis aliquis* (7). The air of polemic and controversy at the start of a new book rather calls prose to mind; the ensuing epiphany and speech of Venus (43–56) import a distinctively poetic element. The poet is beginning a new voyage (99–100), not in the middle of one voyage (2.9–10); but the continuation of the image highlights how Ovid is going one stage further in the surprise of sequence.[21]

Book 2 had ended with the supreme closure of love-making (closure, though, more on the principles of Book 1). It had almost ended with the specific closure of orgasm (727 *ad metam properate simul*); but awkward circumstance had prevented ending on the *plena uoluptas*. Book 3 deliberately returns to love-making for its

---

[20] For the relation of 2.9–10 *mediis tua pinus in undis* | *nauigat*, etc., to the structure of the work, see P. R. Hardie (2004), 152; see also 153–4. For much rewarding discussion of the *Ars Amatoria* and *Remedia Amoris*, with further bibliography, see R. K. Gibson, Green, and Sharrock (2006), adding Armstrong (2005); P. J. Davis (2006), chs. 6 and 7; Rimell (2006), ch. 2; R. K. Gibson (2007). R. K. Gibson (2003) offers an excellent commentary on Book 3.

[21] Horace, *Satires* 2 begins with controversy; but that fits the pugnacious character of the genre, and even so is turned into dialogue. The changes of plan in *Odes* 4 and Propertius 4 are still more obliquely presented. The changes in *Aetia* 3 and 4 are not made explicit, though they are reflected in the new prologue (frr. 1–2 Massimilla).

end, as it returns to the end of 2; there is, however, less sense of climax, narrative and sexual (note 2.703–4). The work has again to reach port (3.748 *ut tangat portus fessa carina suos*); the end is again proclaimed (809). The girls are to inscribe the same words as the boys once did. Those words, *Naso magister erat*, were a deception in 2.744, when a couplet suddenly introduced Book 3. But now they really close the book and poem. The very parallel, however, and the nature of love, make the reader suspicious. And in fact another book will eventually appear, in antithesis to this one; the relation is like that of antithetical books in prose.[22]

This book is a new poem, the *Remedia Amoris*; the opening explicitly, and unusually for didactic, presents the *libellus*, its *titulum* and physical *nomen* (1). And yet it is simply taking the idea of subversion to a new stage: Book 3 counterbalanced Books 1 and 2, the new book counterbalances Books 1, 2, and 3. So at the close of the new book the beginning of *Ars* 2 and the ends of 2 and 3 are encompassed, in a final allusive summary: *reddetis sacro pia uota poetae,* | *carmine sanati femina uirque meo* (*Rem.* 813–14). In 41–52 girls as well as men are included in the audience: the conflicting books of the *Ars* are combined. The opening dramatizes summary and prospective still more than the opening of *Ars* 3; the narrator's awkward meeting with Amor turns the encounter with Venus (3.43–56) into self-defence. He achieves a reconciliation: his accomplishment of the *propositum…opus*, a characteristic prose goal, is sanctioned by Love (*Rem.* 39–40). At the close of the poem the author reaches his goal (*quo mihi cursus erat*, 812). He has gained port at last (811–12); the connections with closing in *Ars* 2 and 3 are manifest (811 *hoc opus exegi: fessae date serta carinae*, cf. *AA* 3.748 *ut tangat portus fessa carina suos*, starting the final part; 2.735–6 *finis adest operi:… serta… ferte*). The port of the lover is pointed to as well, through a link with 609–10 (*inque suae portu paene salutis erat*, with metapoetic overtones); the contrast with the port sought by the lover in *AA* 2.9–10 is palpable.[23]

[22] On these see below.

[23] *Rem.* 9 *quin etiam docui* evokes the *et quoniam docui* at the start of exposition in Lucretian books (3.31, 4.26 (45), 6.43); here it refers to the whole *AA*, but allusively places that work in a sequence after the *Amores* (cf. *Rem.* 7–8, 10).

The series thus forms a brilliant sequence, whatever the author's original plan. What has been said does not determine the chronology: the *Remedia* seems to be later than the earliest version of the *Ars*, in that *Rem.* 361–98 imply attack which it is most natural to associate with that poem. If *Ars* 2 were later reworked to add on *Ars* 3, one could see humour for readers of the original edition. Yet the positive arguments for that addition seem slight when the point of Book 3 is surprise. This point is ignored in the objection that there is so little forward reference to Book 3.[24]

The sequence of these amatory books exploits the conventions of prose in order to play with a seeming absence of plan, and an appearance of felicitously improvised extension. To do even this it draws on the strategies of prose. Awareness of the prose greatly sharpens perception of Ovid's playful and pointed sequence, which opposes perfective and imperfective views of love, male and female, the satisfaction and the abandonment of desire.

Manilius shows little of conjoined summary and prospective to link books. That may at least serve to illustrate that such turns are not automatic or inevitable in any exposition. The feature could in fact relate to the particular distinctness of his individual books. Even if we disregard the controversies about dating Book 4, 1.114–17 might seem to suggest serial publication: he there prays that Fortune will let him reach old age and so finish his work (*faueat magno Fortuna labori,* | *annosa et molli contingat uita senecta*). It would be less natural for the prologue to be notionally written at the literal beginning of a work published all together than for this book to be published before others. One evident prose parallel is Polybius' hope that he will have the fortune to live long enough and complete his plan (3.5.7–8 ... προϲδεῖ δ' ἔτι τῆϲ τύχηϲ, ἵνα ϲυνδράμηι τὰ τοῦ βίου πρὸϲ τὸ τὴν πρόθεϲιν ἐπὶ τέλοϲ ἀγαγεῖν ...). A paucity of summary and prospective would suit books separated in time, though they do not demand it.[25]

---

[24] Cf. Sharrock (1994), 18–20, and Holzberg (1998*b*), 111–12, on Book 3 as purposeful surprise; otherwise R. K. Gibson (2003), 37–9 and on 1–6, and also (2000). For a different line of argument in defence of Book 3 as part of a structure, see Henderson (2006).

[25] 4.119–21 do not link books as they stand, and are probably spurious. An Augustan dating is maintained e.g. by Bowersock (1990), 385–7, but 4.763–6 suggest the reign of Tiberius, cf. Kellum (1990), 292–5. Goold thinks that Manilius is already middle-aged at 1.114–17 (n. ad loc.), but it is not apparent how the reader would perceive this.

In accord with this deliberate distinctness and with serial publication, the only forward references beyond books are to subjects Manilius never treats. The concern of prose with promises is used and defied. The end of Book 2 and the beginning of Book 5 both notionally promise a treatment of the planets (cf. 3.156–8). Book 2 contrasts that subject with a summary of the book (*nunc satis est* 966, taking up 747–51, cf. Cic. *Leg.* 3.32, *Mil.* 92, and above for *satis*). Book 5 marks itself as the last (*non ultra struxisset opus* 4), while suggesting the planets as in theory a subject to come. 5.9 *semel aetherios ausus conscendere currus* points to the proem of Lucretius' last book (6.47). The planets had famously been eschewed by Aratus as a subject, but treated in another work (454–61, *SH* 90 (Achill. 15 p. 42 Maass), cf. *Σ* 460, esp. p. 291.8–12 Martin). Subsequently 'Germanicus'' uncertainty at 443–5 on whether he will treat them, and his *patiantur fata* (cf. on fortune above), make it probable that his actual treatment (frr. ii–v Gain) forms a separate and chronologically later book (this is confirmed by the length a single book would have needed). Manilius artfully uses the Aratean tradition, and Lucretius' deliberate false promise on the gods (5.155), to evade a subject central to astrology but incompatible with his structure.[26]

His last book effectively deploys the rhetoric of addition and abundance. *hic alius finisset iter* uses the tradition seen in Polybius, when he talks of the extension of his plan that will come later: 3.4.1 ἐνθάδε που λέγειν ἂν ἡμᾶς ἔδει. The end of Vitruvius 7 (14.3) tells how he will in the next book continue beyond *omnes aedificationum perfectiones*; Manilius too will offer us further riches. The book seems not so much a tidying-up addition, or the treatment of a more advanced topic (cf. Apoll. Perg. 1 *pr.* p. 4.22 Heiberg); in literary terms it forms the climax of the poem, with its magnificent satirical gallery of humans, and its human mythological excursus.[27]

---

[26] Man. 5.26–31 also falsely promise treatment of another subject; this is probably part of the same strategy. On the structure of Manilius, see Romano (1979); Hübner (1984), 227–68. For Eudoxus' elaborate views on the planets, and ensuing discussion, cf. Eudox. D 6 (add Arist. *Metaph. Λ* 1073^{b}35–1074^{a}14) and F 121–6 Lasserre.

[27] See below on *Georgics* 4 for the placing of the humans and the mythological excursus; but the movement to humans in Book 5 and some of Book 4 is not a simple ascent as in the *Georgics*. Housman produces a complicated and puzzling sentence in 5.8–11: *me properare etiam* (Housman: *uiam* codd.: *tamen* Gain) *mundus iubet* (*b*: *libet* codd.), etc. More suitable would be, say, *me properare uetat mundus; iubet*, etc.

The books are segregated by elaborate proems; especially elaborate are those to Books 2, 3, and 4. Those to 2 and 3 dwell on poetry. Book 1 ends with the desired pragmatic close of peace (914 *necdum finis erat*); its wish for peace after Triumviral war *sed satis hoc fuerit* (922) recalls the end of *Georgics* 1 (*satis G.* 1.501), but comes nearer to achieving political closure. Book 3, although ending in a technical fashion, has just taken us through the course of the year. The last lines of Book 4 refer to the deification of Augustus (whether future or past), and thus link with the last lines of Book 1, which desire the postponement of that deification. A circle is closed, before the move on to Book 5.[28]

Manilius exploits the structural conventions of prose in a different way from earlier didactic. He pushes the idea of the self-contained book to a new extreme. Extensions and prospectives are reworked to purposes forcefully different from those of prose instruction.

We can now mention a few further aspects of the relations between prose and verse didactic book-structure. It has already been apparent that the beginning of poetic books show the interplay with prose at its most complex. In different ways and degrees, proems of exalted poetry mix in with lucid and intellectual demarcation of structure. But even apparent exaltation can draw on prose; the prayer at the start of *Georgics* 1 has been mentioned (it is answered by the prayer to the gods of the City at the end of the book). The immediate model Varr. *RR* 1.1.4–7 is not itself anomalous: in the capacious category of prose prayers can often serve to close and open. When the subject of the proems is the poem (or book) itself, such self-reflection both recalls prose and necessarily marks the difference. The last part of the *Georgics* does these things in a more surprising fashion.[29]

3.218 *nec me uulgatae rationis praeterit ordo* illustrates adaptation of prose phrasing (οὐκ ἀγνοῶ; Cic. *Caec.* 101, Col. *RR* 1 *pr.*28, etc., Quint. *Inst.* 10.1.12; οὐ . . . με λανθάνει, sim., Plat. *Ap.* 19a5, Xen. *Cyr.* 6.1.12), at a point where prose treatises are implicitly referred to. For Manilius 5 cf. e.g. Hübner (1984), 139–44, 174–213, 254–68, (1993); Baldini Moscadi (1993); Santini (1993). Against the view that there were once eight books (Gain (1970)), see Goold (1977), pp. cviii–cix, (1998), pp. v–vi.

[28] Both moments relate to the lightning tours of Roman history in 1.777–802 and 4.23–62. The second passage, in taking up the first, shows despite Rome's rise the immutability of fate, which should still human restlessness. On fate and history in Manilius, cf. Salemme (2000), ch. 3.

[29] For opening and closing invocations and prayers in prose cf. e.g. Plat. *Tim.* 27c1–d1, Cic. *Ver.* 5.184–9, *Dom.* 144–5.

The single substantial mythical narrative is a standard feature
of didactic poems: those in Aratus (96–136) and Nicander (*Ther.*
342–58) set a pattern clearly evidenced in Manilius (5.538–618). But
the narrative in *Georgics* 4 is remarkably placed at the very end of the
poem (4.315–558), so that the work does not return to its technical
matter after the digression, but proceeds immediately to the short
epilogue (559–66). Various reasons can be supposed: that a future
move to narrative epic is here anticipated, or that humans end a
poem which has treated first inanimate then animate nature. But
once prose is considered, it is evident that the placing also marks a
connection with another genre, and one work in particular. In Plato's
philosophical dialogues, 'myths' are commonly placed at the close, in
the *Republic* at the close of the last book; this pattern is imitated in
Cicero's *De Re Publica* (6.9–29).[30]

There the Younger Scipio meets the Elder Scipio and his own
father, and sees with wonder the heavens to which his own deeds
will bring him. In Virgil Aristaeus, born from gods, is a future god,
promised heaven (325 *quid me caelum sperare iubebas?*; cf. Cic. *Rep.*
6.24 and 26). He meets his mother, and sees with wonder a divine
world of water, to which he descends (358–9 *fas illi limina diuum
tangere*). This part of the cosmos may reasonably be seen as contrasting with the heavens; the unexpected application of *limina diuum*
implies this (cf. *Ecl.* 5.56–7 *miratur limen Olympi…Daphnis*, who
reaches heaven like Scipio). The opening of the poem has contemplated different locales for the future god Octavian, including the sea
(1.29–31; the mention of the underworld and Proserpina is also
significant for Book 4). The heavens will be Aristaeus' destination,
and Octavian just after the myth is making his way to the skies
(*uiamque adfectat Olympo*, 4.562). Orpheus' visit to the underworld
forms a further contrast. He and Eurydice cannot escape death.[31]

[30] For the movement from inanimate to animate, see e.g. Farrell (1991), 327–8.
The *Aeneid* follows (cf. Nelis (2004)).

[31] The parts of the cosmos in the myth of course contrast too with the earth as
subject of the poem. Sky in *Georgics* 4: 1 *aerii mellis caelestia dona*, 58 *ad sidera caeli |
nare* (60 *nubem*, cf. 557), 79 *aethere in alto* (contrast dust 87), 103 *caelo…ludunt*,
(152 *caeli regem*), 311 *aera carpunt* (just before myth). Parts of the cosmos are also
significant in the myth of Manilius, probably influenced by Virgil in his placing: the
poem itself is set in the heavens; the sea contrasts, and the sky too is important, cf.

244 — *Talking Books*

The heavens have appeared too as the destination of living souls at 4.219–27: ... *nec morti esse locum, sed uiua uolare | sideris in numerum atque alto succedere caelo,* cf. Cic. *Rep.* 6.14 *hi uiuunt qui e corporum uinclis ... euolauerunt; uestra uero quae dicitur uita mors est.* (*uolare* in Virgil also suits bees, who embody renewed life at the end of the myth, and it echoes 3.9–10 *qua me quoque possim | tollere humo uictorque uirum uolitare per ora.*) By contrast with that passage and the Dream of Scipio, the myth immerses itself in a world of poetic mythology, not philosophical vision. But the philosophical model strengthens the suggestion of deeper significance to the myth.

A less specific point may be made about the organization of poems into books. Latin prose works often show a strong interest in antithetical books. Varro's *De Lingua Latina* in Book 8 presents arguments against analogy in grammar, Book 9 for; Book 10 offers a more nuanced position. Books 2–4 had a similar structure (5.1). In Cicero the device is helped by the dialogue form: in *De Finibus*, 2 refutes 1 (cf. 3.1), 4 refutes 3; in *De Divinatione*, 2 refutes 1; in *De Natura Deorum*, 3 supposedly refutes 2 (but cf. 3.95, *Div.* 1.8–9). In *De Finibus* and *De Natura Deorum* the individual antitheses form part of a more complicated structure.[32]

The role of antithesis is evident in the *Remedia Amoris*; *Ars* 3 is at least a mirror image, for the opposition. The idea may also be relevant, in modified form, to the *Georgics*. The work renounces philosophy, and philosophical singleness of argument. The divergent images of the human lot in Books 1 and 2, and perhaps 3 and 4, have something of an antithetical quality, as has often been felt. So 1.121–2 *pater ipse colendi | haud facilem esse uiam uoluit,* 127–8 *ipsaque tellus | omnia* [cf. πάντα Arat. 113] *liberius nullo poscente ferebat,* as against

---

5.616–18 *dedit Andromedae caelum*; 539, 541–3, 514, 549, 561–4, 565–6, 575–7, 579–85, 591–2, 593, 597–9, 601–2, 603 *ecflat et in caelum pelagus ... pontumque exstillat in astra,* 609–10. Parts of the cosmos are fundamental to Aratus' myth, 96–136 (discussed by Schiesaro (1996)): 101 ἐπιχθονίη πάρος ἦεν, 110–12 (no sea, but ploughing, Dike for Earth), 114 (Earth); 118 (mountains), 127 (mountains), 134 ἔπταθ' ὑπουρανίη. Cf. *G.* 2.473–4 *Iustitia excedens terris.* On subterranean waters, cf. esp. Seneca, *Naturales Quaestiones* 3. For the connections between Aristaeus and Octavian, cf. Morgan (1999), 93–4.

[32] In the case of the *De Natura Deorum* traces of earlier plans and P. Herc. 1428 enable us to see something of Cicero's working processes. Cf. Obbink (1996), 96–8, (2001); Dyck (2003), 2–4.

2.460 *fundit humo facilem uictum iustissima tellus*. The theme in the first case is theological, and so connects with both philosophy and poetry; in the second it alludes to the Stoic Aratus' myth on Dike (Arat. 112–14; note *iustissima*, cf. 473–4 at the end of the paragraph). At 2.536–40 the Golden Age subsists, contrast 1.125–30; Aratus is again in view, and denied. The position in 2 is one of conscious hyperbole; the positions in both 1 and 2 are mythologized. The 'pessimism' of the first book is much less extreme on the gods than is Epicureanism. While these passages look towards philosophical views and prose, the *Georgics* has gone further than Lucretius in adopting a specifically poetic world and discourse. In the matter of antithetical books, the relationship of poetry and prose cannot be proved inescapably, but looks perceptible and plausible.[33]

The idea that didactic poetry might exploit and evoke structural and intellectual aspects of didactic prose leads to further conclusions and requires wider support. The prose is commonly misconceived by readers of the poetry as a flat and unliterary basis upon which the elaborate constructions of poetry can be raised. This misconception makes a more complex interaction seem unlikely. But much more is involved in didactic prose than this view perceives. Furthermore, the prose works, like didactic poems, vary widely in their aspirations; Cicero and Varro had brought especially ambitious and organized writing into Latin technical prose. The individual parts of didactic prose works, like those of didactic poems, vary strikingly in stylistic level; these differences in level are related to the structure. Nor are the stylistic and intellectual goals of poetry and prose so completely separate as may be thought.[34]

These issues are well illustrated by Athenaeus Mechanicus, who was writing for a Roman (a Marcellus, perhaps Augustus' intended

---

[33] The antithetical *Remedia* need not of course be thought to impose closure on its addressees' amorous experience; cf. Fulkerson (2004). The language of *G.* 1.121–2, 127–8, 2.460 joins them with stances adopted in recent discussion: cf. e.g. Cic. *Tusc.* 5.99 *quam multa ex terra arboribusque gignuntur cum copia facili…!*, *ND* 2.131–2…*artes* [cf. Posidon. fr. 284 Edelstein–Kidd] *denique innumerabiles ad uictum et ad uitam necessariae*; 156 *terra…feta frugibus*; *quae cum maxima largitate fundit*; (animals have no) *colendi…scientia*; see also Lucr. 5.206–17, 925–6 (cf. *G.* 1.63 *durum genus*). Oppositions in Lucretius, as between spring and plague, are part of a firm and univocal argument on an unplanned universe.

[34] See piece mentioned in n. 17. Vitr. 9 *pr.*17 and Col. 9.2.1 join poetry and prose in an interesting way.

heir). This treatise on siege-machines is very short, nine pages in the
latest edition; but over a page is taken up with an introduction. The
treatise itself, though quoted authorities and an anecdote complicate
its texture, contains much precise and unvarnished detail on dimen-
sions and constructions. But the introduction is a highly elaborate
piece, possibly rhythmic; it parades acquaintance with a wide range
of literature, and offers an opinion on poetry (Homer is the only poet
justly so called). It argues that the prolonged writing and numerous
digressions of other technical writers sin against the need to save the
reader's time. The author's own need for timeliness helps to excuse
the writing of such a work, which needs not rhetorical injunctions
but conciseness and clarity (cυντομίαc καὶ caφηνείαc, p. 7 Wescher).
The author is fully conscious of the irony, in a long prologue, and
plays with the point (6). In general the prologue aims to show that he
is not without literary skill, and well illustrates self-conscious difference between parts of a work.[35]

Noteworthy too is the defence through the nature of the work:
Athenaeus (7) quotes Callisthenes *FGrH* 124 F 44: δεῖ τὸν γράφειν τι
πειρώμενον μὴ ἀcτοχεῖν τοῦ προcώπου ['role', e.g. as historian], ἀλλ'
οἰκείωc αὐτῶι [i.e. προcώπωι] τε καὶ τοῖc πράγμαcι τοὺc λόγουc
θεῖναι. Differences are supposed between prose works, and perhaps between technical works, in stylistic demands (cf. ὁ δέ
γε περὶ τοιαύτηc τέχνηc γινόμενοc πᾶc λόγοc); these differences relate
to subject-matter. However, even if we take his words at face-value, at
least some of the writers whom he has mentioned (5) did not share his
opinion on this particular subject. And the fear of stylistic criticism, of
'those accustomed to judge πικρῶc τὰc cυνθέcειc τῶν λέξεων' (6),
shows that such interests could be and were applied to technical writing
like his own. Differences in ambition and aim may be indicated even
within this narrow region of technical prose; but stylistic criteria are
clearly not an irrelevance.[36]

The criteria Athenaeus approves, of cυντομίαc καὶ caφηνείαc, are
striking. (Cf. Vitr. 5 *pr.*2 *paucis et perlucidis sententiis.*) They immediately recall one view on *poetry* criticized by Philodemus: concision and

---

[35] Athenaeus can now be read in the valuable edition of Whitehead and Blyth
(2004). On the date, see also Cichorius (1922), 271–9.

[36] Whitehead and Blyth (2004), 45, 73, misunderstand Athen. Mech. 7.1–6, not
least through translating ἀcτοχεῖν τοῦ προcώπου as 'fail on character'; similarly Jacoby
on Callisthenes *ad loc.*, but apt speeches are not relevant to Athenaeus or suitable to

vividness (ἐνάργεια) are fundamental qualities for poets (*Poem.* 5 col. vi.12–vii.25). Philodemus objects that these are not peculiar to poets, but produced by prose-writers too. ἐνάργεια, used in Philodemus of the clear witness of the senses (*De Signis* col. xv.25–8), stands in some relation to cαφήνεια, commonly declared as an aim by prose writers.[37]

Brevity, an aim with vital Callimachean connections, is significant in Lucretius as a tactic: 1.401–2, 499, 2.143, 4.115, 723 (cf. Man. 2.738; 3.447; 3.276–7 *animo cognosce sagaci,* | *ne magna in breuibus lateant compendia dictis*), 6.1081–3. Clarity is of great importance in Lucretius. The prose writer Heraclitus fails through his *obscuram linguam* (admired by a philosophically, and aesthetically, misguided taste), 1.638–43; his own poetry, *tam lucida carmina*, makes *obscura* clear (921–34). His own poetry offers the illumination of both imagery and truth, and in Book 1 brings the unseen atoms into the visible world.[38]

The prose work of Epicurus has a double position: its discoveries and its subject-matter are *obscura reperta, res... occultas*, which Lucretius' *uersibus* can *illustrare* (136–45); it also brings light itself (147, 3.1–2 *o tenebris tantis tam clarum extollere lumen* | *qui primus potuisti inlustrans commoda uitae*), to mankind and to Lucretius as he reads these *aurea dicta* (3.9–30; *lumine*, 22; *natura tua ui* | *tam manifesta patens ex omni parte retecta est*, 29–30). Lucretius' illumination of Memmius has accordingly a double role too. His poetry as poetry gives light to truth, as it fills Epicurus' abstraction with the vividness of perceived phenomena, enhanced by Lucretius' expression. Lucretius also transmits the intrinsic light of Epicurus' doctrines. But even the poetic aspect shares an aim of expository prose, or presents a more powerful version of that aim. (The doctrines are not only made clear, as those of Anaxagoras are made clear at 1.830–44, but shown to be true (cf. *Ad Her.* 4.5 for this opposition); and vividness as well as

---

τὸν γράφειν τι πειρώμενον. Callisthenes is one of τοῖc ὀρθῶc παραινοῦcι. παρ' ἄλληλα (6.2: Schwartz), ἀκριβέcτατα (5.11), and probably καὶ αὐτοί (6.2) suggest divergences within writers on sieges. The discussion at the start of *Ad Herennium* 4 shows another divergence within one area of prose: to give one's own rhetorical examples is said by others to be *ostentare se, non ostendere artem* (4.1).

[37] At Apoll. Cit. 2 p. 38.14–17 Kollesch–Kudlien ἐναργῆ and cαφῆ are linked (ἐναργῆ of perception produced by the actual circumstances).

[38] For brevity cf. D. P. Fowler on 2.143. On Lucretius' treatment of Heraclitus, see Piazzi (2005), 24–42.

clarity is attained.) Both concision and clarity are connected with the firm and lucid division of books.[39]

One final element in prose may be mentioned, an element which illustrates the concern of prose with structure, vividness, and literary impact. The use of the dialogue to enhance the presentation of technical subject-matter has connections with the drama of instruction in didactic poetry; it also affects to introduce ordinary speech into a literary work. It helps in the presentation of opposed points of view, and produces a complex relationship of work and writer.

The form is discussed in P. Oxy. 3219 (as a marvellous invention envied Plato by Aristotle). The expansion of its use beyond philosophy is seen already in Xenophon's *Oeconomicus*. The continued existence of the form is illustrated by *CPF* 56 Heracl. Pont. 1 (P. Oxy. 664 + 3544, iii AD, dialogue set in the time of Pisistratus, with first-person narrator); the papyrus indicates issues about the period and personnel of setting which are taken up by Cicero. In Cicero's hesitations and rewritings we see literary questions, which are primarily formal (and personal) rather than a matter of content. In *CPF* Plato 139T (P. Ryl. 63, iii AD), we see the Platonic dialogue extended, with Plato (not Socrates) as a character, in conversation with Egyptian holy men (cf. *Tim.* 21c1–25d6, *Crit.* 113a1–b5). The work ends with baldly informative exchanges on astrology: the use of the form extends even into writing of obvious technicality. But the form plainly carried significance, as the title indicates: Πλάτωνος τοῦ Ἀθηναίων φιλοσ[ό]φου [π]ρὸς τ[ο]ὺς προφήτας...[ἁ]πάντηςις ςύνοδ[ο]ς [..] διαλύςεως.[40]

Especially relevant here is Varro's dialogue *De Rebus Rusticis*; it is evident that this work provides literary as well as technical inspiration

---

[39] Vitr. 5 *pr.* explains that he has made his books short for ease of understanding; he mentions comedy's division into acts with intervals—an aesthetic and poetic connection. For Lucretius, and Epicurus, cf. Fögen (2000), 61–76. Apoll. Cit. 3 p. 112.7–11 Kollesch–Kudlien claims at the end of his work to have made *Hippocrates'* utterances clear (ἐμφανῆ cf. 1 p. 14.8–11), despite their obscurities of language; Hippocrates himself also makes things clear, or aims to (e.g. 3 p. 96.6–11, 98.4–6). Cf. Erot. pp. 3–4 Nachmanson.

[40] On the Egyptian priests in Plato, and interest in them see Nesselrath (2006), 113, 363–4. On the dialogue as a communicative form cf. Föllinger (2005) (and Kalverkämper (2005), 322–4. For the dialogue in Cicero see among other works Gorman (2005); Arweiler (2003), 23–38; for the rewriting of the *Academica*, Lévy (1992), 129–40. For the history of the form see Hirzel (1895).

for the *Georgics*, though this literary inspiration has been viewed in condescending terms. The element of dialogue is much connected with structure, as in Cicero: each book reports a separate conversation. Books 1 and 3 delimit their conversation by a wait for an individual; in Book 1 this provides a startling end (and at 3.5.18 a striking interruption). The term *actus* that is often used of parts of the conversation and so of the book plays with the author's artifice and sometimes with the speakers, through genres of poetic dialogue. The fear at 1.26 *ne ante aeditumus ueniat huc quam hic ad quartum actum* alludes to comedy (cf. Vitr. 5 *pr.* above); *actum* is used internally of Scrofa's single structured speech, and externally the *aeditumus* looks to comedy (cf. Plaut. *Curc.* 203–4: *aeditumus* interrupts action). In fact the entry of the *aeditumus* will be replaced by a tragic messenger to conclude the book. Cf. 2.5.2 *nos interea secundum actum de maioribus adtexamus.* 'in quo quidem' inquit Vaccius 'meae partes, quoniam boues ibi.'; 2.10.1 *hoc silentium, inquam, uocat alium ad partes. relicum enim in hoc actu quot . . .* The play relates both to artifice and to the use of dialogue.[41]

Endless humour and linguistic sport is extracted from the interaction of dialogue with subject-matter: so at 2.3.1 *quoniam satis balasti, inquit, o Faustule noster* (Atticus on sheep), *accipe a me cum Homerico Melanthio cordo de capellis, et quem ad modum breuiter oporteat dicere disce* (Ennius and Homer, epic and brevity, are probably opposed in the elaborate game here). The comic *balasti* is far too lively and unelevated to be used of people in didactic poetry; but 2.7.1 *ego quoque adueniens aperiam carceres, inquit, et equos emittere incipiam* brings us close to Virgilian play like *G.* 3.286–7 *superat pars altera curae, | lanigeros agitare greges hirtasque capellas* (both come at points of transition).[42]

---

[41] For *actus* see also *TLL* i. 450.78–451.18; Diederich (2007), 206–8. See Diederich (2007), 172–209 for dialogue in Varro. For the *aeditumus*, Pomponius' Atellana *Aeditumus* (2–3 Ribbeck) is also of interest. On Varro and Virgil cf. e.g. Wilkinson (1969), 65–8. R. F. Thomas (1987) looks at Virgil's adaptations of Varro, but with the emphasis only on Virgilian transformation; more engaged with Varro is Leach (1981).

[42] For the comic transference of *bal(it)o*, cf. Plaut. *Bacch.* 1123, 1138a. *cum* makes little sense at 2.3.1: the speaker is the late-born Melanthius. *con* has equal support; perhaps adverbial *contra*? *cum* and *contra* can be similarly abbreviated. Homer and Ennius: cf. 1.1.4, *Men.* 396 Cèbe. Homer is involved in the play between Greek and Roman at 2.5.1. Lucretius and Manilius make a very limited use of dialogue with the addressee, reader (cf. Man. 3.158–9), or a philosophical ('diatribe'-like) interlocutor. Cf. Lucr. 1.803–8, Man. 4.387–9, 869–72; Hutchinson (1993), 44 n. 12.

Detailed comparison of Varro and Virgil would show not only their difference but the concern of both to enrich and animate their exposition. The elaborate sub-divisions and micro-structures of Varro stand at an opposite extreme from Virgil; his blurring and blending of sequences on a smaller scale is very unlike Lucretius or Manilius. But if we conceive of didactic prose not as a dull source of material but as a genre with scope, outlook, and much to offer poetry on a formal and an intellectual level, we can make sense of the poets' multitudinous appropriation and diversion of prose book-structure. Prose contributes fundamentally to the ambition and enterprise of didactic poetry in the first century BC.

11

Books and Scales

This work has concerned itself with division as well as connection. It has often emerged that individual books need to be looked at more closely as internally organized entities, not just as part of a series. This final chapter will draw together some elements from the detailed discussion in earlier chapters; it will also briefly survey once more the works discussed, from a rather different angle (a somewhat Kantian move!). Various scales of structure can now be seen to interact, within great chains of design; various authors can now be seen in immediate juxtaposition. Series and groups of books will be of particular interest. We shall also give some consideration to the idea of the *œuvre*: like many more directly connected series, the *œuvre* is built up in chronological succession, and need not have been planned from the first. But one may legitimately consider the *œuvre* which authors accumulate and display; in this light, earlier works may acquire new or more pointed meaning in the context of later ones, like earlier books within a single work. The *œuvre* itself is a literary entity, with shape and point.[1]

The scales of division and connection which emerge as significant for poetic books are related to each other. They are also contrasted, in significant ways; generic conflict and play with size are concerned. The different scales, types of entity, and relations may be conceived as

---

[1] In later literature, an especially striking example of the ostensibly planned and structured *œuvre* is of course Balzac. In the preface to the first part of *Illusions perdues* he notably extends the conception of the individual work to a larger 'édifice' (*Études de mœurs au xixe siècle*): 'En effet, ici chaque roman n'est qu'un chapitre du grand roman de la société'. But he is leading into the point that this very novel has expanded beyond his original plan, 'malgré l'auteur'. For 'career criticism' see now Cheney and de Armas (2002), including Farrell (2002).

follows: (a) very small poems, less small poems, and blocks of very small poems (Posidippus), in relation with each other and their book; (b) (i) books that form part of a single argument or narrative, in relation with the whole work, whether these books are published simultaneously (like the *Georgics*) or sequentially (like Manilius?); (ii) books that explicitly take up an earlier book or work, though with a distinct title (*Remedia Amoris*), in relation to that book or work; (iii) books that within a genre or sub-genre form part of a series, in relation to that series (Propertius 1–3, Ovid, *Amores* 1–3, Horace, *Odes* 1–3, *Satires* 1–2, etc.), whether or not published over time; (iv) books that mark a new departure in an author's *œuvre* (e.g. Horace, *Epistles* 1), in relation to earlier works; (c) the *œuvre*, in relation to the constituent works and books. Intertextual structures between different authors' works take us on to another level of complexity; they will only be touched on incidentally here.

Relations inside single books and beyond single books may obviously have affinities. Thus the internal breaking out of the generic world in the last poems of Propertius 1 has connections to the more drastic breaking out of the genre at the end of Propertius 3, which ends a series (so far). Tibullus' switching to Nemesis in Book 2 after Delia in Book 1 relates not only to Propertius' rupture with Cynthia at the end of Book 3 but to Tibullus' moving between love-objects within Book 1. Tibullus' pair of books contrasts with Gallus' four: *FRP* 139 (*a*) (Serv. *Ecl.* 10.1) *amorum suorum de Cytheride scripsit libros quattuor*. Again, it is movement beyond the single book which is more momentous. Antithesis or opposition between poems (e.g. Propertius 3.4 and 5; 3.12, 13, 14) matches that between books of continuous poems (so Apollonius 1 and 2, Virgil, *Georgics* 1 and 2).

Some principles and aspects of relationship have already been mentioned; 'principle' denotes a basic mode of relating (antithesis, connection, parataxis, variety), not a rule which cannot be broken. Argument and narrative are both cohesive forces (cf. (b) (i) above). Narrative can involve contrasts of perspective, or a single, uniting perspective. Antithesis is an element related to argument of a more complicated kind (different views competing, a single complex view), but can also occur within narrative. Against antithesis, the opposition of two contrasting entities, can be set connection, a link between two entities, and especially what we may call by extension parataxis, the accumulation of more than two parallel entities in a sequence (cf. ch. 3). Variety, or regular and striking change between consecutive entities, is only visible over a substantial body of text (e.g. a book). The pattern of a book, or a series of books, can be seen as dynamic—changing decisively—or as static or fluctuating. Further relevant aspects include time, length, genre.[2]

We may look first, and more briefly, at Hellenistic poetry. The principle of parataxis we saw to run through much Hellenistic poetry (ch. 9). In P. Oxy. 4711, if Hellenistic, we appear to see a relatively simple structure of short sections parallel in basic theme and narrative shape, without narrative connection between them, and with inexplicit thematic links. Posidippus shows us something similar, but here the paratactic and very short poems form part of blocks. The headings conspicuously incorporate the formal structuring into the written text. (They do not necessarily add an element of hypotaxis, for all paratactic sequences are unified by a concept ('deeds of Heracles', etc.).) Within the blocks, antithesis can occur: men suddenly opposed to women (in 'ἐπιτύμβια'), large opposed to small (in 'λιθικά'); the latter opposition clearly relates to genre and the small scale of the structure. The blocks themselves sometimes relate: so the ἰαματικά come between two sepulchral blocks, with antithesis and deliberate interplay (95.1–2, 12 AB (first piece in ἰαματικά): statue as if dying or dead, but the sufferers cured). The overt 'rule', however, seems to be change between consecutive sections. Poems can connect to or contrast with different blocks (e.g. chariots in 'λιθικά'—8.3–4, with elaborate play on size, 15.3–8, with play on size (cf. 14 the horse Pegasus)—and in ἀνδριαντοποιϊκά, the

---

[2] The accumulation of books as well as poems, and its significance, is seen strongly in Propertius and Ovid: Prop. 2.1.1 *Quaeritis unde mihi totiens scribantur amores* (significantly at the start of the book), 3.3–4 (*another* book, after a short interval, shaming the lover), 24.1–2 (cf. *iam*); Ov. *Am.* 2.1–4 | *hoc quoque...ille ego nequitiae Naso poeta meae*; | *hoc quoque iussit Amor*, 18 (near end of book; escape to a different genre prevented), 3.1.15–16 *'ecquis erit' dixit 'tibi finis amandi,* | *o argumenti lente poeta tui?'*, *Tr.* 5.1.1–3 | *hunc quoque...libellum...* | *hic quoque talis erit qualis fortuna poetae*, 35–6 *'quis tibi, Naso, modus lacrimosi carminis?' inquis.* | *idem fortunae qui modus huius erit*; *Pont.* 3.9.1–2 (end of series 1–3) *quod sit in his eadem sententia...libellis,* | *carmina nescio quem carpere nostra refers*, 39 *cum totiens eadem dicam.* Hor. *Sat.* 2.1.24–60 are making a point about quantity too, more subtly; 2.3.1–4 are ironic for the reader; *Epist.* 1.1.1 *prima dicta mihi, summa dicenda Camena* exploits the quantity of Horace's books.

section before ἱππικά—67, with play on size). Politics can form a climactic and structuring device (35, ending section; 36–9, beginning section; 70, end of section; cf. 87–8, ending section). Other themes appear to run through the book (e.g. women, representation). Among them are the large and the small (e.g. 67 (with sculptural *mise en abyme*), 68); this theme extends to the size of individual poems, like the expressively long poems about the huge rock (19), and Berenice's victory (78). The book itself will have related paratactically to Posidippus' other books of epigrams.

Callimachus' *Aetia* presents paratactic entities: the individual sections. These are linked, especially in the first two books, by their structure and their theme as wholes (aetiology). A narrative framework joins them explicitly together in the first two books, not in the third and fourth. There are elaborate specific links between *aitia* in Books 1 and 2: stories of bad words and of Heracles (frr. 9.19–27 Massimilla, note Σ Flor.); *Icus* and *Sicily* (probably: frr. 89, 50.1–83 Massimilla). Links occur between *aitia* in Books 3 and 4 too, on the most cautious view: so in 4 human sacrifice (frr. 91–2, 93 Pfeiffer: consecutive); in 3 *Thesmophoria* and *Fontes Argivi* (frr. 63, 65–6: probably separated by only one short *aition*), *Acontius* and *Elean rites* (frr. 67–75, 77, 77a, with *Dieg.* I 3–9: separated by two or three), *Acontius* and *Phrygius* (the latter frr. 80–3 with addenda).

Books 3 and 4 present an instance of something common in Roman poetry too: a later addition creating a new total structure. The books now become themselves a paratactic series (1–4); the work also becomes conspicuously organized into two halves, with a dynamic change in internal structure. (Politics again provide significant structural shaping, at the beginning and end of the second half.) The separation between the halves in time makes possible a narrative for the whole work, based on the life of the narrator. This enhances the sense of dynamic movement in the whole, and also enhances its static quality: despite the biological changes, the narrator's passions remain the same—especially the passion for knowledge. The narrative on the narrator in turn adds to the thematic range of the work; it enables the work, as has been seen, to encompass the whole range of human life (men, women, young, old), and it creates an opposition between poet's world and characters' world. The narrator's perspective forms a dominating element, which joins the series together; but other perspectives and speakers, besides the Muses, now offer a more forceful contrast, and add to the range of the whole sequence. The Lock's feminine experience, the dead Simonides', the poor Molorcus', the young Acontius' (he has a monologue): different perspectives are presented by the different sections. In the four-book version the issue of length and brevity is explicitly brought to the fore; that issue has a complex application to a large and hugely ambitious work in relatively small sections.

Apollonius' epic presents a structure notably similar to the elegiac *Aetia*: a work in four books, strongly divided in the middle. For an epic, it looks strikingly neat, and brief: the Homeric epics, though turned into an elegant number of rhapsodies, present in many ways a massive continuum. In the *Argonautica* there are strong antitheses between halves and between and inside books, within a sustained narrative. The antitheses are related in particular to a dialectical opposition between male and female, which in turn relates to the multiplicity of perspectives in the poem; the narrator's own perspective is less dominant than in the *Aetia*. That feature, like the multiplicity of perspectives, accords with the epic genre—the Iliadic narrator's philosophical vision is actually more dominating than the Apollonian narrator's. The conflict of male and female perspectives helps to question the epic genre; from a different angle, the reader is struck by so large a scale for the poetic treatment of love.

Despite its antitheses, and its narrative continuity, much of the work is framed as a paratactic sequence of smaller entities; this is full of meaning, as we saw, for the experience and achievement presented in the work. The form also makes more conspicuous the scholar-poet's activity. The books themselves can be seen as paratactic entities which, on a simple level, magnify the series of ἄεθλοι. However, the narrative heightens and is heightened by the sense of dynamic movement and change within the poem. At the same time, the poem's rigorous selectivity and structure bring the whole narrative back to the place it started from. But this neat return will not mean that nothing has changed.[3]

---

[3] It would be interesting to know if the notable series of Apollonius' κτίcιc poems was formed of one-book works, with which the *Argonautica* contrasted in scale and scope. (Frr. 4–12 Powell; the Καύνου κτίcιc is referred to in the manchette of

The *Hecale* pushes the play on length and genre still further, with an epic in a single book. Again Homeric narrative encourages a plurality of perspectives, with less sense of the narrator's perspective than in the *Aetia*. The plurality is above all a duality; the antithesis between young man and old woman has affinities with the *Aetia*, but less scope. In fact, it links with the central antithesis of male and female perspectives in the *Argonautica*—though that is more extreme, and though there is in the *Argonautica* a wider range of additional perspectives. The poem moves to a decisive end for its foremost character Hecale. The aetiology of Zeus Hekaleios provides a link with the *Aetia*, and a contrast of oneness in story here with multiplicity there.

The inventiveness, self-reflexivity, and elegance of the third-century poets' designs would be displayed more extensively if we had more books; this point is borne out by the discovery of the Posidippus, but also by Herodas and the *Iambi*. The Roman poets of the first century BC continue the exploration, and in some respects seem to go further.

Catullus' corpus, if rightly reconstructed in ch. 5, offers the striking conception of parallel books, set (and presumably published) at much the same time, in different metres. They are connected, but also contrast. Each builds up a world of its own: while centred on the same narrator and the contemporary present, each, as we saw, has differing concerns and generic procedures. In both, there is much clear connection between adjacent poems, and poems separated by one other poem or a few others (adjacent: 12–13; 15–16; 95–96; 110–11; 114–15; separated by one: p. 116; by a few: 23, 26; 55, 58*b*; 72, 75). Antithesis is sometimes apparent: cf. e.g. 7, 8; 100, 101; with 100–1 variety or change also seems relevant. That principle is clearly significant in the metres of *a*, where outside hendecasyllables

Parthenius *EΠ* 1 as *Καῦνος*; the author of the *Λέσβου κτίσις* is not named by Parthenius (*EΠ* 11.3), who may express doubts on the authorship.) Apollonius' *œuvre* looks of interest; the total *œuvre* includes scholarly prose, which affects perception of the poetry. Rhianus' *œuvre* evidently included works on a larger scale than the *Argonautica* (the *Messeniaca* had at least six and the *Thessalica* at least sixteen books). Demosthenes of Bithynia might be an intriguing figure if we knew more: *Bithyniaca* at least ten books; *Κτίσεις* fr. 12 Powell, *FGrH* 699 F 10, whether in prose or verse; date uncertain.

consecutive poems in the same metre are avoided. The principle of parataxis can be forcefully deployed, as in 88–91 on Gellius.

c is an elaborate structure; it is divided into two halves distinguished by length of poem. The two halves, with a dynamic structural movement between them, have some links with the far larger *Aetia* (from the end of which *c* begins). *c* is an unusual adaptation of Hellenistic books, and makes a generic point: the author's range within the genre of elegy, including epigram. The point is emphasized through starting with the final section of Callimachus' biggest work (on a small object, cf. 66.43–7), and proceeding to evoke (cf. 70) his book of epigrams.[4]

c unlike *a* has suggestions of an overall narrative, in theory moving from grief to love, then from (among other things) unhappiness in love to a happy ending. Whether this pattern within the book is also a temporal narrative may be thought far from clear. At all events, the narrative pattern is infringed by indications that happy endings are unlikely with Lesbia; the series of (separated) poems on love in *c2* conveys the narrator's inability to escape from his infatuation. They form a cumulative sequence; where there is antithesis, this only portrays fluctuation. The structure of *c2* thus expresses the lover's state of mind; the point is emphasized by the placing of the long, would-be closural, 76 early in *c2*. A dynamic movement in *c* is set against an idea of stagnant fixity.

The perspective of others bulks large in *c1*: Callimachus and his Lock, the door, Laodamia. *c2* is intensely focused on the perspective of the narrator, with his enemies as monsters and his beloved as mentally inaccessible. *a*, where only one poem exceeds 30 lines (10), is also concentrated on the narrator, with only a few exceptions (yacht (4), hymn to Diana (34); Septimius and Acme (45)). The long poems 61, 62, 63, 64 give much more place, within the *œuvre*, to other speakers; the narrator there is not connected with the details of the author's life. Laodamia in 68*b* is particularly akin to Ariadne in 64: narrative again provides the route to other perspectives, though 68*b* encloses the narrative within imagery about the narrator's

---

[4] For that book cf. Gutzwiller (1998), ch. 5; but a plurality of books is not impossible, cf. e.g. Athen. 10.412d, 414d, 415a: Posidippus ἐν Ἐπιγράμμασιν (120, 121, 143 AB), with no book number.

experience. Even *c*1 begins from him; its progressive implied narrative focuses on him. But there the plot about his emotional life also involves his activity as a poet. The love-objects Lesbia, and the lesser sub-plot Iuventius, form a focus for both *a* and *c*, which in that respect connect. This shaping through the *object* of emotion (cf. Antimachus' *Lyde*, Parthenius' *Arete*, Ticida) will offers an important structural element to later poets; in Catullus the objects of hatred and contempt also help to structure.

Ovid, *Amores* 3 may most usefully be considered next. The book seems to belong to a newly designed and simultaneously published series of books derived from an older series. The series as we have it resembles those of Gallus and Propertius (1–3), which were focused on the love of a single object. As in Propertius, the poems within each book, and the series of books itself, form an expressive and paratactic sequence. (The sense of accumulation in Propertius is heightened if his Book 2 is really two books.) Both the creativity of the writer and the absorption of the lover are displayed. For all the variety of incident and mood, the narrator is stuck in love, and there can be until the close of the series no decisive movement but only repetition and oscillation.

Amores 3 brings a different twist from the ending of Propertius 3: within the body of the book, love is presented paratactically and proves inescapable; but the external frame announces a resolve, after explicit generic struggle, to end with elegy. The book not only ends the series, but is separated from it at the start. There is thus in this book a narrative involving the narrator, with dynamic change, not simply an imperfective situation; the narrative gestures to the structure of a higher genre, tragedy. A world is broken out of, radically. The relation of *Amores* 3 to 2 and 1 involves antithesis as well as parataxis: as a *total* structure it contrasts with its predecessors. The internal antitheses of the book relate in various ways to the larger structure: within one poem (1), Elegy and Tragedy contend; the opposition of death and life (e.g. 9, 10) connects with genre and with poet; 11*b*'s revocation of 11*a*, which affects to end the affair, shows the impossibility of ending love-elegy, within its own world.

The limits and nature of the genre are played with extensively in the book. But the predominantly comic impact of the *Amores* makes the generic rationale of the whole series different from Propertius (for all Propertius' comic elements). The perspective of the narrator, though predominant, stands further from the reader's involvement. In this book other perspectives are made to enter, as in epic, by inset narrative (especially poems 6 and 10): the perspectives of god, woman, and goddess—the woman not in love. The length of the transgressive poem 6 has generic resonance itself, but in a complicated fashion: in the *Amores*' version of the genre length has marked the garrulity and inefficacy of the lover. The relation of love and length is again rewarding—all the more so as poems can be large expansions of love-epigrams. The pointed failure of the book to move into a Roman patriotic aetiology will highlight *Fasti* within the *œuvre*: that poem overtly takes just such a step. A crucial aspect for love-elegy, the nature of the love-objects and their relation to the amorous impetus of the series, undergoes in this book still further mystification and play. The book as a whole both sustains and undoes its genre and its series.

The books of Horace's *Odes* should be seen as a series, it was suggested. On the proposed chronology (not essential to seeing the series), the first three books appear at relatively short intervals, the fourth book ten years later. Books 1–3 and 1–4 both form series. These series should essentially be seen as paratactic. One side to this, as to paratactic arrangement within a book, is display of invention. Internally in Book 1 the author's fertility is highlighted by the range of metres and models; at the end of the third book, and in 4.3.13–24, the number of books is an implicit part of the larger achievement. But the paratactic sequence of the books also expresses the fixity which the narrator has attained: an imperfective narrative situation. After the vicissitudes of civil war, youthful love, and *Epodes*, he has now reached a state of quasi-philosophical tranquillity and country retirement. The restlessly active and political life of Alcaeus particularly contrasts (cf. esp. 1.32); so do the incessant movements and cares of his important addressees. The future ending of his own situation with perfective death is especially contemplated in Book 2.

The relationship with the paratactic books of love-elegy is especially intriguing. Horace goes further than Tibullus in changing his narrator's love-object not just within a book but constantly. The love-objects define the series of books only through their diversity. The continual change expresses, not painful fluctuations of emotion, but an untroubled hedonism, which escapes the turbulent storms of youthful lovers. The perpetual motion is only enhanced by the occasional profession of loyalty until death (one card that the ageing lover can offer, but an unexamined card): so 1.13.17–20, cf. 3.9.11–12, 24 (in 24 Lydia speaks). But the situation is ostensibly challenged by the idea that the narrator, now that youth is past, is going to end his life of love. This idea, announced in Book 1 (19.4 *finitis... amoribus*), is played with in Book 2. Book 3 offers a supposedly final, but unconvincing, realization (3.26, note lines 11–12; 27 follows, implying love). Book 4 resumes both love and ode-writing, and announces once again *meorum | finis amorum* (11.31–2, the phrase denoting Phyllis, who is implausibly said to be the last woman he will love (33–4)—and he has now included a boy, as the preceding poem stresses). The succession between *Odes* 3 and *Odes* 4 involves a marked interval in time, and thus a biological dynamic; but the narrator's emotional life is not changed. One may contrast the alteration between *Epodes* and *Odes* or indeed that between *Odes* 3 and *Epistles* 1. Like the *Aetia*, though in a very different respect, this movement between books is dynamic biologically but static mentally. As regards the narrator's literary achievement, however, the triumphant affirmation which closed Book 3 undergoes great expansion in Book 4.[5]

The perspective is very much focused on the narrator in all four books. Though we may surmise the reactions of girls and see something of addressees, the narrator is far the most vivid and interesting character, and it is his vision and experience that we explore.

Relationships between the books and within them are connected. It would be overstated to call the relation between the first three books one of thesis, antithesis, and synthesis, but Book 3 does join together the sterner and more Stoicizing colour of Book 2 with the more playful and Epicurean Book 1. In doing so it creates an internal antithesis within Book 3 (seen especially in the juncture of 3.6 and 3.7). This antithesis draws too on the relation of political and public with private, which is generally important in the internal shaping of the books. 1.11–12 and 37–8 form striking instances,

---

[5] The farewell in 27 can of course be seen as symbolic; but this does not remove the reversal of 26. And 27 also indicates that love is devious and inescapable, and minds complex.

heightened by the opposition of length and brevity; cf. also e.g.
3.25–6. The role and treatment of politics creates conspicuous
differences between the books; Book 4 here goes still further than
Book 3.

Metrically, we often see within the books the principle of variety;
this turns in Book 2 to a principle of alternation (alcaics and sapphics
alternate for much of the book), with some consecutive poems in the
same metre (13–15, 19–20, cf. in Book 1 16–17, 26–7, 34–5). These
last are massively taken up in the paratactic sequence of 3.1–6. Other
poems connected in both metre and content are 1.34–5 and 2.13–14
(cf. e.g. 2.6–7, 3.22–3, 4.8–9 for connected content and changed
metre). The *Epodes* moved from metrical parataxis (1–10) to variety.
The differences between the books of *Odes* in approach to metre
create variety between whole books.

One may certainly speak of an antithesis between the *Odes* and the
Epodes—roughly, the poetry of anger against the poetry of moderation. The narrator lost his dignity in the dynamic structure of the
Epodes, but not his emotionality. The *Satires* are left out of explicit
account in this shaping of a lyric life and *œuvre* (the *Epistles* can talk
about the *Odes* but not vice versa, just as satire can talk about epic
but not vice versa). The proportions—one book of *Epodes*, an accu-
mulating series for the *Odes*—confirm that the *Odes* are to present
the perfected and more important side of the narrator, and the more
ambitious creation.

The massive structure of the *Metamorphoses*, which was to have
been paired with an almost equally massive *Fasti*, opposes itself to the
smaller entities of Ovid's earlier love-poetry (cf. *Tr.* 1.1.117 and
3.14.19 *ter quinque uolumina* against the three of the deplorable
Ars). The size self-evidently marks and embodies the grand and
mock-grand scale to which the poet's *œuvre* is now rising. As a
cumulative series, the books and their number will have shown that
the work went far beyond ordinary metamorphosis poems; and this
literary ambition relates to the historical and metaphysical ambition
suggested by the continuous narrative. At the same time, rather as
with Apollonius, the scale on which love is treated arrests.

The structure has at least three elements: the paratactic form of
similar entities, that is stories with the same structure and ending (as
in the *Aetia*); the chronological form which joins the entities into a

supposedly single narrative (a different structure from *Aetia* 1 and 2); the books into which the continuous narrative is divided. The books form significant entities in their own right. Blurring of the books' boundaries underlines continuity, and matches the flow of hexameters as against end-stopped elegiacs; but it does not obliterate the essential division. If Phaethon is introduced just before the end of Book 1 (750–79), the contest of arms just before the end of Book 12 (620–8), the units remain visible, both actual book and 'long' book. The books can have an expressive structure: we have seen that Book 10, especially in its 'long' form, displays the poet's loss of power; Book 9 forcefully explores gender and suffering. Book 3 focuses and thematizes a concern of the whole poem: brevity.

Related perspectives are brought together, and strikingly different perspectives are confronted, by these books of epic narrative. So Actaeon (3.138–259) and Pentheus (3.511–733) frame Book 3 to be compared, after the opening narrative on Cadmus; in 8 Erysicthon (738–884) is clearly antithetical to Philemon and Baucis (618–724). (Erysicthon is not treated with sympathy, but his inner experience of hunger is drastically conveyed.) Perspective is especially shown through the great speeches and monologues: within books Scylla diverges from Althaea (speeches 8.44–80, 478–511), Hercules contrasts with Byblis, Byblis can be compared with Iphis (9.176–204; 474–516, cf. 530–63 (letter), 585–629; 726–63). Byblis and Myrrha (10.320–55) can be compared across their consecutive books. The difference from the single perspective of the *Amores* is striking, particularly since the subject-matter often connects; *Amores* 3.6, and the *Heroides*, complicate the picture. The uniting perspective of the narrator in the *Metamorphoses* is best seen not as a character's perspective, but as a poet's; it belongs to a whole text-world of scholarly and literary activity.[6]

Didactic poems bring us to a quite different use of books again. The Roman poets diverge, with Greek precedent, from the convention of the single book which continues into earlier Hellenistic didactic. This time, argument and exposition rather than narrative are the vital consideration—important as argument is in the *Amores* and intellectual activity in the *Metamorphoses*. The division into

---

[6] Cf. Hutchinson (forthcoming).

books imitates the intellectualism of prose structures; it also provides a focus for ostentatious poeticism. Each book fulfils its initial undertaking and is a complete account and part of a complete account: there is an intrinsic dynamic and perfective finality about the shaping.

The relationship of the separated books is full of point. Parataxis is a natural feature of instructive texts, and within books is constantly displayed by Manilius, visibly minimized in the *Georgics*. The series of books can also be seen as paratactic. Even in Virgil, achievement is suggested by the series displayed at *G.* 4.559–60, which takes up the opening 1.1–5 (cf. *te quoque* at 3.1, *hanc etiam partem* at 4.2, cf. e.g. Ov. *Tr.* 5.1.1–2). But the idea of antithesis is important too; it can be connected, as we have noticed, with the antithetical structures seen in some prose series of books. The books of the *Georgics* stand in contrast, to a certain degree, each with its neighbour's outlook. There are also contrasts in scale, and size of object: 3 deals with all animals, 4 with tiny bees. Comparably within 3 there is an internal opposition of dignity (3.284–93). More drastic are the antitheses provided by Ovid's amatory series: he frames such an antithesis in epic terms at the start of *Ars* 3 (1–4). Book 3 offers a reversal of perspective, within the battle of the sexes; the *Remedia* reverses the goal of *Ars* 1–3.[7]

Ars 3 offers a change of perspective such as we might rather have looked for in epic (cf. 3.1–6), and which we see at a subversive extreme in Apollonius' third and fourth books. Germane too is the expressively separate fourth book of the *Aeneid*, with its predominantly female perspective. There is a connection too, however, with the antithesis of male and female perspectives presented by the *Amores* and single *Heroides* as a pair of related works, like the *Metamorphoses* and *Fasti*. The emphatic presence of the narrator in

[7] In the poetic chronology, the *Remedia* can be supposed to posit an interval in time from *Ars*; thus a narrative involving the poet occurs on two levels (Cupid at the start, 1–40; critics in the middle, 361–98). Interesting for the ranking and connotations of animals are the encomia on horse and bull (the former implied to be grander): P. Oxy. 4647 (ii–iii AD), Liban. *Prog. Enc.* 8 (viii.267–73 Foerster), 'Nic. Soph.' (authorship uncertain) *Prog.* 8.3 (i.332–3 Walz); [Hermog.] *Prog.* 7.14–15 Rabe, *al.* The relation of bull's death and bees' birth at Liban. viii.273.8–11 and 'Nic. Soph.' i.333.26–9 is of interest for *Georgics* 3 and 4 (cf. Archel. *SH* 126, 127, Nic. *Alex.* 445–7, etc.).

the series *Ars* and *Remedia* marks a conspicuous difference from narrative epic—though the *Iliadic* narrator has considerable if less overt presence and the quasi-biographical aspects of the narrator in *Ars* and *Remedia* are fleeting (cf. e.g. *AA* 2.547–56, 3.663–8, *Rem.* 356, 499–502). The confidence of the narrator (sometimes deflated) displays a clear aspiration to differ from the *Amores*. The whole didactic series, probably including the *Medicamina*, forms a kind of move up within Ovid's elegiac *œuvre* into the non-narrative sort of epic. (The play involved is particularly notable in the rewriting of *Iliad* 1 at *Rem.* 465–86.) There are indeed touches of narrative, as in the movement from *Ars* 1 to 2 (advance of affair) and from *Ars* 1–3 to *Remedia*, and in the sexual climaxes of *Ars* 2 and 3. Actual mythical narrative also bulks large, as it had started to do in *Amores* 3. The *Metamorphoses* will take the *œuvre* to a further stage; the increase from relatively small numbers of books is crucial (contrast *Amores*, *Ars*, single *Heroides* (?), Nicander's *Metamorphoses*). The move from *Georgics* to *Aeneid* may be compared—and from *Epodes* to *Odes*.[8]

The treatment of groups and series of books in the Roman examples discussed may not be entirely the innovation of Roman rather than later Hellenistic poets: the books of didactic poetry, and the poems of love-elegy, counsel circumspection (p. 102). Nor should we forget poets before 60 BC: so Laevius would be an interesting figure for Catullus and Horace. Yet whatever the origins, the Roman examples show the inventiveness and generic exploration of the third-century Greek poets taken onwards. On the most external level, we see Catullus both condensing the range of poetry in elegiacs into a single book and creating two parallel books in elegiacs and 'lyric' metres; we see Horace going beyond a Callimachean recreation of epodes to a whole series of lyric books; we see Ovid's poem of metamorphosis apparently much expanding Greek metamorphosis poems; we see didactic poetry commonly enlarged into works in

---

[8] On the number of books in *Georgics* and *Aeneid*, cf. the section-headings of Holzberg (2006). Although elegiac didactic poems will not have been a startling novelty in Greek terms, the association of elegiacs and medical (or cosmetic) recipes is so strong that the *Medicamina* form the obvious starting-point or springboard for Ovid's elegiac didactic series. Cf. Eudemus *SH* 412A, Philo *SH* 690, Aglaias *SH* 18, Androm. *GDK*[2] LXII. The mock-medical *Remedia* looks back to the *Medicamina* (for the designation see *AA* 3.205–6, with R. K. Gibson's note).

several books; we see whole series of books devoted to sets of elegiac poems on love.

The notion of the *œuvre*, as seen in the Augustan poets, might take up the exploitation of the narrator's life seen specifically in the *Aetia*: Callimachus' poetic *œuvre* as a whole does not seem to depend for its meaning and interrelations on chronology and biographical sequence. Catullus' two books seem to be sharply focused on the same point of time, without the extension of a life; the importance of the *Aetia* in *c* may underline this point by contrast. The two books present, not a total *œuvre*, but perhaps a mini-*œuvre*, or condensed display of the relatively youthful author's talents. In Horace, however, the relation to a biological dynamic is very strong. Ovid's *œuvre* is less emphatically focused on biology; even the exile poems make relatively little use of his old age. But the sense of accumulation over time is weighty. The works are built in connected groups, which self-consciously rise in ambition (cf. *Fast.* 2.2–8, 4.3, 9–10, with *Tr.* 2.547–62); after this super-Virgilian achievement (cf. *Rem.* 395–6), the exile poetry is made to form a pathetic finale, returning to personal poetry, but of grief, not love. The exile was not of course the planned conclusion; but we have seen poets adapting their work under new impulses and circumstances, and like a skilled orator the poet can turn reality into affecting patterns.[9]

All these cases, including Catullus, show striking characterization of the narrator in relation to time as central to the force of the *œuvre* or mini-*œuvre* as an entity. Catullus writes other poems between *c.*59 and 47 BC; but the two books, by their temporal focus (contrast Posidippus) and by their emphasis on the experience and ethos of relatively young men in Rome, portray a personality very much

---

[9] More understanding of Posidippus' books would be welcome, not least for the place and force of 118 AB (the poet's old age and renown); the papyrus book, if a display of range, is less dramatically so than Catullus' *a* and *c*. On the supposed reference to the *Iambi* at the end of the *Aetia*, see ch. 2 n. 30. For old age in Ovid's exile poetry, see *Tr.* 4.1.71–4, 4.8; cf. and contrast *Pont.* 1.4.19–20; *Fast.* 2.5–8 *cum lusit … prima iuuenta*, etc., 4.9 *quae decuit primis sine crimine lusimus annis*; *Tr.* 2.339–40, 543–4, 5.1.7 *integer et laetus laeta et iuuenilia lusi. Tr.* 2.553–4 include the *Medea* among Ovid's grander works. They thus incorporate into a total pattern what seems from *Amores* 3.1 and 15 a different attempt to rise (like the *Metamorphoses* in a non-elegiac metre); this particular path was not followed beyond the *Medea*, as *Am.* 2.18.13–18 may humorously acknowledge.

bound up with the narrator's age in life—as that age is conceived in the late Republic. Age is crucial to the presentation over time of the narrator in Horace's *œuvre*, although the fuller conception of that *œuvre* (with hexameter poetry) already includes the outlook of contented good sense in the earliest book, *Satires* 1. In Ovid's *œuvre* the extension over time emphasizes alterations in the narrator-author's mood; it also highlights, however, the constancy of his wit and, at least as far as the *Fasti*, of his scepticism (the connected preludes to *Fasti* 1–4 bring out both change and fixity). This static element, and especially the pervading wit, has affinities with Callimachus' *œuvre*, to which the cohesive characterization and voice of the narrator are so vital. The *Aetia* add an explicit element of time; the stress on life-long dedication to poetry at Ov. *Tr.* 4.10.19–20, 117–20 points to Call. *Aet.* frr. 1–4 Massimilla. As usual, the relation of Hellenistic and Latin literature is both significant and complicated.[10]

   This epilogue may have done something to suggest how widely the question of book-form ramifies and how deeply it is rooted in critical issues. The different and interacting scales of structure indicate the challenge which this subject presents to see things newly. The importance of the subject is increasingly being recognized; but more knowledge and thought will make it bear more abundant fruit. This book attempts no more than a sort of start.

---

   [10] Cf. further perhaps Call. *H.* 3.136–41 with Ov. *Fast.* 4.7–8 (poetic constancy to Venus); Call. *Ia.* fr. 193.34–9 Pfeiffer with Ov. *Pont.* 4.2.45–6 (regret). The contexts of both Ovidian passages are also connected to *Aetia* frr. 1–4 Massimilla. For complications in the relation of Ovidian wit to Callimachus, cf. Hutchinson (1988), 77–82, (1993), 348–54; P. R. Hardie (2002c). Ovid's utilization of criticism (including eventually Augustus') in presenting his *œuvre* sometimes visibly draws on Callimachus; so *Rem.* 389 evokes Call. *Aet.* fr. 1.17 Massimilla (cf. 381–2; Hor. *Odes* 4.3.16). In Callimachus, unlike these poets, prose scholarship is part of the total *œuvre*, and makes an important contribution to the impact of the narrator. On Callimachus' narrator, see now Morrison (2007), ch. 3. Cat. 68a.15–20, assuming them to be part of *c*, place the narrator's life in time with complexity, and in a way that relates to the narrative of *c1* and *c*. Conceptions of youth in the late Republic need not involve ideological or political conflict between age-groups; cf. Isayev (2007).

Bibliography

Acosta-Hughes, B., and Stephens, S. (2002), 'Rereading Callimachus' *Aetia* Fragment 1', *CP* 97, 238–55.

——Kosmetatou, E., Baumbach, M. (edd.) (2004), *Labored in Papyrus Leaves: Perspectives on an Epigram Collection Attributed to Posidippus (P. Mil. Vogl. VIII 309)* (Cambridge, MA, and London).

Adams, J. N. (1982), *The Latin Sexual Vocabulary* (London).

Albrecht, M. von (2000), *Das Buch der Verwandlungen. Ovid-Interpretationen* (Düsseldorf and Zurich).

Alden, M. J. (2000), *Homer Beside Himself: Para-Narratives in the Iliad* (Oxford).

Alföldy G. (2000), 'Das neue Edikt des Augustus aus El Bierzo in Hispanien', *ZPE* 131, 177–205.

Anderson, R. D., Nisbet, R. G. M., Parsons, P. J. (1979), 'Elegiacs by Gallus from Qaṣr Ibrîm', *JRS* 69, 125–55.

Anderson, W. B. (1982), 'The Orpheus of Virgil and Ovid: *flebile nescio quid*', in J. Warden (ed.), *Orpheus: The Metamorphoses of a Myth* (Toronto, Buffalo, London), 25–50.

——(1989), 'The Artist's Limits in Ovid: Orpheus, Pygmalion, and Daedalus', *Syllecta Classica* 1, 1–11.

Argentieri, L. (1998), 'Epigramma e libro', *ZPE* 121, 1–20.

Arieti, J. (1990), 'Horatian Philosophy and the Regulus Ode (*Odes* 3.5)', *TAPA* 120, 209–20.

Arkenberg, J. S. (1993), 'Licinii Murenae, Terentii Varrones, and Varrones Murenae', *Historia* 42, 349–51.

Armstrong, R. (2005), *Ovid and his Love Poetry* (London).

Arweiler, A. (2003), *Cicero rhetor. Die* Partitiones oratoriae *und das Konzept des gelehrten Politikers*, Untersuchungen zur antiken Literatur und Geschichte 68 (Berlin and New York).

Asper, M. (1997), Onomata allotria. *Zur Genese, Struktur und Funktion poetologischer Metaphern bei Kallimachos*, Hermes Einzelschriften 75 (Stuttgart).

Asquith, H. (2005), 'From Genealogy to *Catalogue*: The Hellenistic Adaptation of the Hesiodic Catalogue Form', in Hunter (ed.) (2005*b*), 266–86.

Atallah, W. (1966), *Adonis dans la littérature et l'art grecs* (Paris).

Atherton, C. (ed.) (1998), *Form and Content in Didactic Poetry* (Bari).

Auhagen, U. (1999), *Der Monolog bei Ovid*, Scripta Oralia 119 (Tübingen).

Austin, C., and Bastianini, G. (2002), *Posidippi Pellaei quae supersunt omnia* (Milan).

—— and Olson, S. D. (2004), *Aristophanes*, Thesmophoriazusae: *Edited with Introduction and Commentary* (Oxford).

Axelson, B. (1945), *Unpoetische Wörter. Ein Beitrag zur Kenntnis der lateinischen Dichtersprache* (Lund).

Bader, B. (1973), 'Ein Afraniuspapyrus?', *ZPE* 12, 270–6.

Baezo Angulo, E. F. (1989), 'Ovidio, *Amores* III,7', *Faventia* 11, 25–58.

Baggermann, A. (1994), 'Lezen tot de laatste snik. Otto van Eck en zijn dagelijkse literatuur (1790–1798)', *Jaarboek voor Nederlandse Boekgeschiedenis* 1, 57–88.

Bailey, D. R. Shackleton (1996), *Onomasticon to Cicero's Treatises* (Stuttgart and Leipzig).

Bain, D. (1997), 'Salpe's παίγνια: Athenaeus 322a and Plin. *H.N.* 28.38', *CQ* 48, 262–8.

Baldini Moscadi, L. (1993), 'Caratteri paradigmatici e modelli letterari: Manilio e i *paranatellonta* dell'Aquarius', in Liuzzi (ed.) (1993), 79–94.

Barber, E. A., and Maas, P. (1950), 'Callimachea', *CQ* 44, 96.

Barchiesi, A. (1989), 'Voci e istanze narrative nelle *Metamorfosi* di Ovidio', *MD* 23, 55–97.

—— (1996), 'Poetry, Praise and Patronage: Simonides in Book 4 of Horace's *Odes*', *CA* 15, 5–47.

—— (1997), 'Endgames: Ovid's *Metamorphoses* 15 and *Fasti* 6', in D. H. Roberts, F. M. Dunn, D. Fowler (edd.), *Classical Closure: Reading the End in Greek and Latin Literature* (Princeton), 181–208.

—— (2000), 'Rituals in Ink: Horace on the Greek Lyric Tradition', in Depew and Obbink (edd.) (2000), 167–82.

—— (2001*a*), 'Horace and Iambos: The Poet as Literary Historian', in Cavarzere, Aloni, Barchiesi (edd.) (2001), 141–64.

—— (2001*b*), *Speaking Volumes: Narrative and Intertext in Ovid and Other Latin Poets* (London).

—— (2002), 'The Uniqueness of the *Carmen saeculare* and its Tradition', in Woodman and Feeney (edd.) (2002), 107–23.

—— (2005), 'The Search for the Perfect Book: A PS to the New Posidippus', in Gutzwiller (ed.) (2005), 320–42.

—— Rosati, G., Koch, L. (2007), *Ovidio*: Metamorfosi. *II (Libri III–IV)* (Milan).

Barns, J. (1950), 'A New Gnomologium: With Some Remarks on Gnomic Anthologies (I)', *CQ* 44, 126–37.

—— (1951), 'A New Gnomologium: With Some Remarks on Gnomic Anthologies, II', *CQ* 1, 1–20.

Barrett, A. A. (1972), 'Catullus 52 and the Consulship of Vatinius', *TAPA* 103, 23–38.

Barrett, W. S. (2007), *Greek Lyric, Tragedy, and Textual Criticism: Collected Papers. Assembled and Edited by M. L. West* (Oxford).

Bartman, E. (1999), *Portraits of Livia: Imaging the Imperial Woman in Augustan Rome* (Cambridge).

Bastianini, G. (2002), 'Frammento inedito di glossario a un testo poetico ellenistico', in Montanari and Lehnus (edd.) (2002), 271–5.

—— (2005), 'Postilla a PSI inv. 1923', in Ozbek (2005), 19–20.

—— and Gallazzi, C. (2001), *Posidippo di Pella. Epigrammi (P.Mil.Vogl. VIII 309)*, 2 vols. (Milan).

—— *et al.* (2004–), *Commentaris et lexica Graeca in papyris reperta (CLGP)* (Munich).

Batinski, E. E. (1990–1), 'Horace's Rehabilitation of Bacchus', *CW* 84, 361–78.

—— and Clarke, W. M. (1996), 'Word-Patterning in the Latin Hendecasyllable', *Latomus* 55, 63–77.

Battezzato, L. (2003), 'Song, Performance, and Text in the New Posidippus', *ZPE* 145, 31–43.

Battistoni, F. (2006), 'The Ancient *pinakes* from Tauromenion. Some New Readings', *ZPE* 157, 169–79.

Beard, M. (1986), 'Cicero and Divination: The Formation of a Latin Discourse', *JRS* 76, 33–46.

—— (2002), 'Ciceronian Correspondences: Making a Book Out of Letters', in T. P. Wiseman (ed.), *Classics in Progress: Essays on Ancient Greece and Rome* (Oxford), 103–44.

—— North, J., Price, S. (1998), *Religions of Rome*, 2 vols. (Cambridge).

Beck, J.-W. (1995), *'Lesbia' und 'Juventius': Zwei libelli im Corpus Catullianum*, Hypomnemata 111 (Göttingen).

Belfiore, E. S. (1992), *Tragic Pleasures: Aristotle on Plot and Emotion* (Princeton).

Bélis, A. (2004), 'Un papyrus musical inédit au Louvre', *CRAI* 1305–29.

Belling, H. (1903), *Studien über die Liederbücher des Horatius* (Berlin).

Ben, N. van der (1995/6), 'The meaning of ΓΝΩΜΑ', *Glotta* 73, 35–55.

Bernsdorff, H. (2002), 'Anmerkungen zum neuen Poseidipp (P. Mil. Vogl. VIII 309)', *Göttinger Forum für Altertumswissenschaft* 5, 32–7.

—— (2005), 'Offene Gedichtschlüsse', *ZPE* 153, 1–6.

—— (2007), '*P.Oxy.* 4711 and the poetry of Parthenius', *JHS* 127, 1–18.

Bernstein, F. (1998), *Ludi publici. Untersuchungen zur Entstehung und Entwicklung der öffentlichen Spiele im republikanischen Rom*, Historia Einzelschriften 119 (Stuttgart).

Berry, D. H. (1996), *Cicero: Pro P. Sulla Oratio* (Cambridge).

Bickenbach, M. (1999), *Von den Möglichkeiten einer 'inneren' Geschichte des Lesens* (Tübingen).

Billanovich, G. (1988), 'Il Catullo della cattedrale di Verona', in S. Krämer and M. Bernhard (edd.), *Scire litteras. Forschungen zum mittelalterlichen Geistesleben*, ABAW 99 (Munich), 35–57.

Bing, P. (1988), *The Well-Read Muse: Present and Past in Callimachus and the Hellenistic Poets*, Hypomnemata 90 (Göttingen).

——— (1993), 'Aratus and His Audiences', in Schiesaro, Mitsis, and Strauss Clay (edd.) (1993), 99–109.

——— (1997), 'Reconstructing Berenike's Lock', in G. W. Most (ed.), *Collecting Fragments. Fragmente sammeln* (Göttingen), 78–94.

Bingen, J., Cambier, G., Nachtergael, G. (edd.) (1975), *Le Monde grec. Pensée, littérature, histoire, documents. Hommages à Claire Préaux* (Brussels).

Birt, Th. (1876), *Ad historiam hexametri Latini symbola* (Diss. Bonn).

——— (1882), *Das antike Buchwesen in seinem Verhältniss zur Litteratur* (Berlin).

Blaak, J. (2004), *Geletterde levens. Dagelijks lezen en schrijven in de vroegmoderne tijd in Nederland 1624–1770* (Hilversum).

Boardman, J. (1990), 'Herakles Dodekathlos', *LIMC* v/1. 5–16.

Bömer, Fr. (1969–), *P. Ovidius Naso. Metamorphosen. Kommentar*, 8 vols. to date (Heidelberg; 8th vol. assembled by U. Schmitzer).

Bonadeo, A. (2002), 'Il pianto di Eco. Riflessioni sulla presenza dell'eco in alcune trasposizioni letterarie del *planctus*', *QUCC* 71, 133–45.

Booth, J. (1997), 'All in the Mind: Sickness in Catullus 76', in S. M. Braund and C. Gill (edd.), *The Passions in Roman Thought and Literature* (Cambridge), 150–68.

Bowersock, G. W. (1983), *Roman Arabia* (Harvard).

——— (1990), 'The Pontificate of Augustus', in Raaflaub and Toher (edd.) (1990), 380–94.

Bowie, E. L. (2001), 'Early Greek Iambic Poetry: The Importance of Narrative', in Cavarzere, Aloni, Barchiesi (edd.) (2001), 1–27.

Bowman, A. K., and Thomas, J. D. (1994), *The Vindolanda Writing-Tablets* (Tabulae Vindolandenses *II*) (London).

Boyd, B. W. (1997), *Ovid's Literary Loves: Influence and Innovation in the* Amores (Ann Arbor).

——— (ed.) (2002), *Brill's Companion to Ovid* (Leiden, Boston, Cologne).

Bradley, B. L. (1976), *Rainer Maria Rilkes Der neuen Gedichte anderer Teil. Entwicklungsstufen seiner Pariser Lyrik* (Bern and Munich).

Braswell, B. K. (1988), *A Commentary on the Fourth Pythian Ode of Pindar*, Texte und Kommentare 14 (Berlin).

Braund, S. M. (2002), *Latin Literature* (London and New York).

Bretzigheimer, G. (2001), *Ovids 'Amores'. Poetik in der Erotik* (Tübingen).

Brink, C. O. (1982), *Horace on Poetry.* Epistles *Book II: The Letters to Augustus and Florus* (Cambridge).

Brooks, P. (1984), *Reading for the Plot: Design and Intention in Narrative* (Oxford).

Broughton, T. R. S., and Patterson, M. L. (1951–86), *The Magistrates of the Roman Republic*, 3 vols. (New York and Atlanta).

Brown, C. G. (1997), 'Iambos', in D. E. Gerber (ed.), *A Companion to the Greek Lyric Poets*, Mnemosyne Suppl. 173 (Leiden, New York, Cologne), 11–88.

Brown, M. K. (2002), *The* Narratives *of Konon: Text, Translation and Commentary of the* Diegeseis, Beiträge zur Altertumskunde 163 (Leipzig).

Brown, R. (1991), '*Catonis nobile letum* and the List of Romans in Horace *Odes* 1.12', *Phoenix* 45, 326–40.

Bühler, W. (1960), *Die Europa des Moschos. Text, Übersetzung und Kommentar*, Hermes Einzelschriften 13 (Wiesbaden).

Bulloch, A. (2006), 'The Order and Structure of Callimachus' *Aetia* 3', *CQ* 56, 496–508.

Bülow-Jacobson, A. (1979), 'P. Haun. 6. An Inspection of the Original', *ZPE* 36, 91–100.

Burnikel, W. (1980), *Untersuchungen zur Struktur des Witzepigramms bei Lukillios und Martial*, Palingenesia 15 (Wiesbaden).

Burnyeat, M. F. (1996), 'Enthymeme: Aristotle on the Rationality of Rhetoric', in A. O. Rorty (ed.), *Essays on Aristotle's* Rhetoric (Berkeley and London), 88–115.

—— (2001), *A Map of* Metaphysics *Zeta* (Pittsburgh).

Burzacchini, G. (1976), 'Alc. 130b∼Hor. Carm. I 22', *QUCC* 22, 39–58.

—— (1985), 'Some Further Observations on Alcaeus fr. 130b Voigt', *PLLS* 5, 373–81.

Butrica, J. L. (1996), 'Hellenistic Erotic Elegy: The Evidence of the Papyri', *PLILS* 9, 297–322.

—— (1997), 'Editing Propertius', *CQ* 47, 176–208.

Cadili, L. (2001), *Viamque adfectat Olympo. Memoria ellenistica nelle 'Georgiche' di Virgilio* (Milan).

Cahoon, L. (1983), 'Juno's Chaste Festival and Ovid's Wanton Loves: *Amores* 3. 13', *CA* 2, 1–8.

Cahoon, L. (2005), 'Haunted Husbands: Orpheus's Song (Ovid, *Meta-morphoses* 10–11) in Light of Ted Hughes's *Birthday Letters*', in W. W. Batstone and G. Tissol (edd.), *Defining Genre and Gender in Latin Litera-ture: Essays Presented to William S. Anderson on his Seventy-fifth Birthday*, Lang Classical Studies 15 (New York, etc.), 239–67.

Cairns, F. (1970), 'Theocritus Idyll 10', *Hermes*, 38–44.

—— (1979), 'Self-Imitation within a Generic Framework: Ovid, *Amores* 2. 9 and 3. 11 and the *renuntiatio amoris*', in D. A. West and A. J. Woodman (edd.), *Creative Imitation and Latin Literature* (Cambridge), 121–41.

—— (1995*a*), 'Horace, *Odes* 3. 7: Elegy, Lyric, Myth, Learning, and Inter-pretation', in Harrison (ed.) (1995*b*), 65–98.

—— (1995*b*), 'Horace's First Roman Ode (3.1)', *PLILS* 8, 91–142.

Calasso, R. (1988), *Le nozze di Cadmo e Armonia* (Milan).

Callebat, L. (1982), 'La prose du "de architectura" de Vitruve', *ANRW* ii.30.1.696–722.

Cameron, A. (1968), 'The First Edition of Ovid's *Amores*', *CQ* 18, 320–33.

—— (1993), *The Greek Anthology from Meleager to Planudes* (Oxford).

—— (1995), *Callimachus and his Critics* (Princeton).

—— (2004), *Greek Mythography in the Roman World* (Oxford).

Campbell, D. A. (1982–93), *Greek Lyric, with an English Translation*, 5 vols. (Cambridge, MA, and London).

Campbell, M. (1981), *Echoes and Imitations of Early Epic in Apollonius Rhodius*, Mnemosyne Suppl. 72 (Leiden).

Canfora, L. (1974), *Conservazione e perdita dei classici* (Padua).

Capasso, M. (2003), *Il ritorno di Cornelio Gallo. Il papiro di Qaṣr Ibrîm venticinque anni dopo* (Naples).

Cape, R. W., Jr (2002), 'Cicero's Consular Speeches', in J. M. May (ed.), *Brill's Companion to Cicero: Oratory and Rhetoric* (Leiden, Boston, Cologne), 113–58.

Capomacchia, A. M. G. (1984), 'Il mito di Myrrha: aspetti del rapporto tra cultura classica e Oriente', in *Adonis. Relazioni del colloquio in Roma 22–23 maggio 1981* (Rome), 95–102.

Carey, C. (1986), 'Archilochus and Lycambes', *CQ* 36, 60–67.

Cartledge, P., and Spawforth, A. (2002), *Hellenistic and Roman Sparta: A Tale of Two Cities*² (London and New York).

Casson, L. (2001), *Libraries in the Ancient World* (New Haven and London).

Cavallo, G. (1983), *Libri scritture scribi a Ercolano. Introduzione allo studio dei materiali greci*, Cronache Ercolanesi 13 Suppl. 1 (Ercolano).

—— (1999), 'Between *volumen* and Codex: Reading in the Roman World', in Cavallo and Chartier (edd.) (1999), 64–90.

——and Chartier, R. (edd.) (1999), *A History of Reading in the West* (Oxford).

——Fedeli, P., Giardina, A. (edd.) (1989–91), *Lo spazio letterario di Roma antica*, 5 vols. (Rome).

Cavarzere, A., Aloni, A., Barchiesi, A. (edd.) (2001), *Iambic Ideas: Essays on a Poetic Tradition from Archaic Greece to the Late Roman Empire* (Lanham, etc.).

——and Bandini, F. (1992), *Orazio. Il libro degli* Epodi (Venice).

Chadwick, H. (2006), 'Some Ancient Anthologies and Florilegia, Pagan and Christian', *Studies on Ancient Christianity* (Aldershot and Burlington, VT), ch. 19.

Charpin, F. (1979–81), *Lucilius*. Satires, 3 vols. (Paris).

Chartier, R. (1994), *The Order of Books: Readers, Authors, and Libraries in Europe between the Fourteenth and Eighteenth Centuries* (Cambridge).

Cheney, P., and de Armas, F. (edd.) (2002), *European Literary Careers: the Author from Antiquity to the Renaissance*.

Christes, J. (1979), *Sklaven und Freigelassene als Grammatiker und Philologen im antiken Rom*, Forschungen zur antiken Sklaverei 10 (Wiesbaden).

Ciancio Rossetto (1993), 'Circus Maximus', *LTUR* i. 272–7.

Cichorius, C. (1922), *Römische Studien. Historisches epigraphisches literargeschichtliches aus vier Jahrhunderten Roms* (Berlin).

Citroni, M. (1995), *Poesia e lettori in Roma antica* (Bari).

Claes, P. (2002), Concatenatio Catulliana: *A New Reading of the* Carmina (Amsterdam).

Clare, R. J. (2002), *The Path of the Argo: Language, Imagery and Narrative in the* Argonautica *of Apollonius Rhodius* (Cambridge).

Clarke, M. L. (1955), 'The Hexameter in Greek Elegiacs', *CR* 5, 18.

——(1972), Horace, *Epistles* i. 13', *CR* 22, 157–9.

Clauss, J. J. (1993), *The Best of the Argonauts: The Redefinition of the Epic Hero in Book 1 of Apollonius'* Argonautica (Berkeley and Oxford).

——(1997), 'Conquest of the Mephistophelian Nausicaa: Medea's Role in Apollonius' Redefinition of the Epic Hero', in Clauss and Johnston (1997), 149–77.

——and Johnston, S. I. (edd.) (1997), *Medea*: Essays on Medea in Myth, Literature, Philosophy, and Art* (Princeton).

Clinton, K. (2003), 'Stages of Initiation in the Eleusinian and Samothracian Mysteries', in M. B. Cosmopoulos (ed.), *Greek Mysteries: The Archaeology and Ritual of Ancient Greek Secret Cults* (London and New York), 50–78.

Coarelli, F. (1993), 'Atrium Libertatis', *LTUR* i. 133–5.

Cody, J. V. (1976), *Horace and Callimachean Aesthetics*, Collection Latomus 147 (Brussels).

Coleman, J. (1996), *Public Reading and the Reading Public in Late Medieval England and France* (Cambridge).

Coleman, K. M. (1988), *Statius* Silvae *IV: Edited with an English Translation and Commentary* (Oxford).

Comella, A. (1986), *I materiali votivi di Falerii* (Rome).

Corretti, A. (1987), 'Civita Castellana', in G. Nenci, G. Vallet (edd.), *Bibliografia della colonizzazione greca in Italia e nelle isole tirreniche* v (Pisa, Rome), 323–68.

Costabile, F. (1984), 'Opere di oratoria politica e guidiziaria nella biblioteca della Villa dei Papiri: i *PHerc*. latini 1067 e 1475', *Atti del XVII Congresso Internazionale di Papirologia* (Naples), ii. 591–606.

Coste-Messelière, P. de la (1957), *Fouilles de Delphes* IV.4. *Sculptures du trésor des Athéniens* (Paris).

Courtney, E. (1988), 'Some Literary Jokes in Ovid's *Amores*', in N. Horsfall (ed.), Vir bonus discendi peritus: *Studies in Celebration of Otto Skutsch's Eightieth Birthday* BICS Suppl. 51 (London), 18–23.

—— (1996–7), 'Catullus' Yacht (or was it?)', *CJ* 99, 113–22.

—— (1995), *Musa Lapidaria: A Selection of Latin Verse Inscriptions* (Atlanta).

—— (2003), *The Fragmentary Latin Poets*[2] (Oxford).

Crane, G. (1986), 'Tithonus and the Prologue to Callimachus' *Aetia*', *ZPE* 66, 269–78.

Crawford, D. S. (1955), *Papyri Michaelidae: Being a Catalogue of the Greek and Latin Papyri, Tablets and Ostraca in the Library of Mr. G. A. Michaïlidis of Cairo* (Aberdeen).

Crawford, M. H. (ed.) (1996), *Roman Statutes*, 2 vols., *BICS* Supplement 64 (London).

Cribiore, R. (1996), *Writers, Teachers, and Students in Graeco-Roman Egypt*, American Studies in Papyrology 36 (Atlanta, GA).

—— (2001), *Gymnastics of the Mind: Greek Education in Hellenistic and Roman Egypt* (Princeton).

Cupaiuolo, F. (1965), *Studi sull'esametro di Catullo* (Naples).

Currie, B. (2002), 'Euthymus of Locri: A Case Study in Heroization in the Classical Period', *JHS* 122, 24–44.

Cuypers, M. P. (2004), 'Apollonius of Rhodes', in I. de Jong, R. Nünlist, A. Bowie (edd.), *Narrators, Narratees, and Narratives in Ancient Greek Literature*, Mnemosyne Suppl. 257 (Leiden and Boston), 43–62.

D'Alessio, G. B. (2004), 'Textual Fluctuations and Cosmic Streams: Ocean and Achelous', *JHS* 124, 16–37.

—— (2005), 'Osservazioni su PSI inv. 1923', in Ozbek (2005), 10–12.

Dällenbach, L. (1977), *Le Récit spéculaire. Essai sur la mise en abyme* (Paris).

Bibliography

275

Dalzell, A. (1955), 'C. Asinius Pollio and the Early History of Public Recitation at Rome', *Hermathena* 86, 20–8.

—— (1996), *The Criticism of Didactic Poetry: Essays on Lucretius, Virgil, and Ovid* (Toronto, Buffalo, London).

Damon, C. (1990), 'Poem Divisions, Paired Poems, and *Amores* 2. 9 and 3. 11', *TAPA* 120, 269–90.

Darnton, R. (1984), *The Great Cat Massacre and Other Episodes in French Cultural History* (New York).

Davies, M. (1991–), *Poetarum Melicorum Graecorum Fragmenta* (1 vol. to date, Oxford).

Davis, G. (1991), *Polyhymnia: The Rhetoric of Horatian Lyric Discourse* (Berkeley, Los Angeles, Oxford).

Davis, J. T. (1989), Fictus adulter. *Poet as actor in the* Amores (Amsterdam).

Davis, P. J. (2001), 'Horace, Augustus and the Secular Games', *Ramus* 30, 111–27.

—— (1999), 'Ovid's *Amores*: A Political Reading', *CP* 94, 431–49.

—— (2006), *Ovid and Augustus: A Political Reading of Ovid's Erotic Poems* (London).

De Lucia Brolli, M. A. (1991), *Civita Castellana. Il Museo Archeologico dell'Agro falisco* (Rome).

De Simone, G. F. (2006), 'VI 17 Insula Occidentalis 41', in M. Aoyagi and U. Pappalardo (edd.), *Pompeii (Regiones VI–VII). Insula Occidentalis* (Naples), 43–67.

DeBrohun, J. B. (2003), *Roman Propertius and the Reinvention of Elegy* (Ann Arbor).

Decker, W., and J.-P. Thuillier, J.-P. (2004), *Le Sport dans l'Antiquité. Égypte, Grèce et Rome* (Paris).

DeForest, M. M. (1994), *Apollonius' Argonautica: A Callimachean Epic*, Mnemosyne Suppl. 148 (Leiden).

Degani, H. (1991), *Hipponactis testimonia et fragmenta²* (Stuttgart and Leipzig).

Degrassi, A. (1965), *Inscriptiones Latinae Liberae Rei Publicae. Imagines* (Berlin).

Del Mastro, G. (2005), 'Riflessioni sui papiri latini ercolanesi', *Cronache Ercolanesi* 35, 183–94.

Demougin, S. (1998), *L'Ordre équestre sous les Julio-Claudiens* (LÉFR 108, Rome).

Depew, M., and Obbink, D. (edd.) (2000), *Matrices of Genre: Authors, Canons and Society* (Cambridge, MA).

Detienne, M. (1994), *The Gardens of Adonis: Spices in Greek Mythology*, tr. J. Lloyd (Princeton).

Dettmer, H. (1983), *Horace: A Study in Structure* (Hildesheim, Zurich, New York).

Deufert, M. (1996), *Pseudo-Lukrezisches im Lukrez. Die unechten Verse in Lukrezens 'De rerum natura'*, Untersuchungen zur antiken Literatur und Geschichte 48 (Berlin and New York).

——(2002), *Textgeschichte und Rezeption der plautinischen Komödien im Altertum*, Untersuchungen zur antiken Literatur und Geschichte 62 (Berlin and New York).

Devijver, H. (1976–93), *Prosopographia militiarum equestrium quae fuerunt ab Augusto ad Gallienum*, 5 vols. (Louvain).

Diederich, S. (2005), 'Das römische Agrarhandbuch als Medium der Selbstdarstellung', in Fögen (ed.) (2005), 271–88.

——(2007), *Römische Agrarhandbücher zwischen Fachwissenschaft, Literatur und Ideologie*, Untersuchungen zur antiken Literatur und Geschichte 88 (Berlin and New York).

Dietze, J. (1905), *Komposition und Quellenbenutzung in Ovids Metamorphosen* (Hamburg).

Diggle, J. (1970), *Euripides*, Phaethon: *Edited with Prolegomena and Commentary* (Cambridge).

Dihle, A. (1964), *Umstrittene Daten: Untersuchungen zum Auftreten der Griechen am Roten Meer* (Cologne).

Döpp, S. (1992), *Werke Ovids. Eine Einführung* (Munich).

Dorandi, T. (2000), 'Le commentaire dans la tradition papyrologique: quelques cas controversés', in M.-O. Goulet-Gazé (ed.), *Le Commentaire entre tradition et innovation* (Paris), 15–27.

Dover, K. J. (1989), *Greek Homosexuality* (Cambridge, MA).

Dräger, P. (2001), *Die Argonautika des Apollonios Rhodios. Das zweite Zorn-Epos der griechischen Literatur*, Beiträge zur Altertumskunde 158 (Munich and Leipzig).

Dué, C. (2002), *Homeric Variations on a Lament by Briseis* (Lanham, etc.).

Dueck, D. (2000), *Strabo of Amisia: A Greek Man of Letters in Augustan Rome* (London and New York).

Duhigg, J. (1971), 'The Elegiac Metre of Catullus', *Antichthon* 5, 57–67.

Dyck, A. R. (1996), *A Commentary on Cicero*, De Officiis (Ann Arbor).

——(2003), *Cicero*, De Natura Deorum, *Book I* (Cambridge).

Easterling, P. E. (1982), *Sophocles*: Trachiniae (Cambridge).

Ebert, J. (1974), 'Δηοσέβης', *ZPE* 13, 255–6.

Edwards, C. (1993), *The Politics of Immorality in Ancient Rome* (Cambridge).

Edwards, M. W. (1990), 'The Secret of Catullus 102', *Hermes* 118, 382–4.

Effe, B. (1977), *Dichtung und Lehre. Untersuchungen zur Typologie des antiken Lehrgedichts* (Munich).

—— (2003), 'Typologie und literarhistorischer Kontext: Zur Gattungsgeschichte des griechischen Lehrgedichts', in Horster and Reitz (edd.) (2003), 27–44.

Eisenstein, E. E. (2005), *The Printing Revolution in Early Modern Europe*² (Cambridge).

Elsner, J. (1996), 'Naturalism and the Erotics of the Gaze: Intimations of Narcissus', in N. B. Kampen (ed.), *Sexuality in Ancient Art* (Cambridge), 247–61.

Erbse, H. (1969–88), *Scholia in Homeri Iliadem (scholia vetera)*, 7 vols. (Berlin).

Fabian, Kl. (1992), *Callimaco. Aitia II* (Alessandria).

Fantham, E. (2001), 'Roman Elegy: Problems of Self-Definition, and Redirection', in E. A. Schmidt (ed.) (2001), 183–220.

—— (2004), *Ovid's* Metamorphoses (Oxford).

Fantuzzi, M., and Hunter, R. L. (2004), *Tradition and Innovation in Hellenistic Poetry* (Cambridge).

Farrell, J. (1991), *Virgil's* Georgics *and the Traditions of Ancient Epic: The Art of Allusion in Literary History* (Oxford).

—— (1998), 'Reading and Writing the *Heroides*', *HSCP* 98, 307–38.

—— (2002), 'Greek Lives and Roman Careers in the Classical *vita* Tradition', in Cheney and de Armas (edd.) (2002), 24–46.

Feeney, D. C. (1984), 'The Reconciliations of Juno', *CQ* 34, 179–94.

—— (1991), *The Gods in Epic: Poets and Critics of the Classical Tradition* (Oxford).

—— (1995), 'Horace and the Greek Lyric Poets', in Rudd (ed.) (1995), 41–63.

—— (1998), *Literature and Religion at Rome: Cultures, Contexts and Beliefs* (Cambridge).

—— (2005), 'The Beginnings of a Literature in Latin', *JRS* 95, 226–40.

—— (2007*a*), review of Gibson, Green, Sharrock (edd.) (2006), *Times Literary Supplement* (4 May), 8–9.

—— (2007*b*), *Caesar's Calendar: Ancient Time and the Beginnings of History* (Berkeley).

Feldherr, A. (1997), 'Metamorphosis and Sacrifice in Ovid's Theban Narrative', *MD* 38, 25–55.

Fergus, J. (2006), *Provincial Readers in Eighteenth-Century England* (Oxford).

Ferrari, F. [2004], 'Posidippus, the Milan Papyrus, and Some Hellenistic Anthologies', *Classics@* 1, 1–14 (see <http://chs.harvard.edu/chs/issue–1—posidippus>; made available by author (1 Aug. 2007); no longer accessible online, cf. <http: chs.harvard.edu/chs/issue–1—posidippus>.).

Fireman, G. D., McVay, T. E., Jr, and Flanagan, O. J. (edd.) (2003), *Narrative and Consciousness: Literature, Psychology, and the Brain* (Oxford).

Fitzgerald, W. (1995), *Catullan Provocations: Lyric Poetry and the Drama of Position* (Berkeley, Los Angeles, London).

Flemming, R. (1999), '*Quae corpore quaestum facit*: The Sexual Economy of Female Prostitution in the Roman Empire', *JRS* 89, 38–61.

Flint, K. (1993), *The Woman Reader: 1837–1914* (Oxford).

Floridi, L. (2007), *Stratone di Sardi. Epigrammi. Testo critico, traduzione e commento* (Alessandria).

Fögen, Th. (2000), *Patrii sermonis egestas. Einstellungen lateinischer Autoren zu ihrer Muttersprache*, Beiträge zur Altertumskunde 150 (Munich and Leipzig).

—— (ed.) (2005), *Antike Fachtexte* (Berlin).

Föllinger, S. (2005), 'Dialogische Elemente in der antiken Fachliteratur', in Fögen (ed.) (2005), 221–34.

Forbes Irving, P. M. C. (1990), *Metamorphosis in Greek Myths* (Oxford).

Forsyth, P. J. (1978–9), 'Order and Meaning in Catullus 97–9', *CW* 72, 403–8.

Fowler, D. P. (2000*a*), 'The Didactic Plot', in Depew and Obbink (edd.) (2000), 205–19.

—— (2000*b*), *Roman Constructions: Readings in Postmodern Latin* (Oxford).

Fowler, P. G. (1983), 'A Commentary on Part of Book Six of Lucretius *De Rerum Natura*' (D. Phil. thesis, Oxford).

Fowler, R. L. (2000), *Early Greek Mythography* i (Oxford).

Fränkel, H. (1977), *Die homerischen Gleichnisse*² (Göttingen).

Froning, H. (1992), 'La forma rappresentiva ciclica nell'arte classica', in R. Olmos (ed.), *Coloquio sobre Teseo y la copa de Aison* (Madrid), 131–54.

Fuhrer, Th. (1992), *Die Auseinandersetzung mit den Chorlyrikern in den Epinikien des Kallimachos* (Basle and Kassel).

—— (1994), 'The Question of Genre and Metre in Catullus' Polymetrics', *QUCC* 46, 95–108.

Fuhrmann, M. (1960), *Das systematische Lehrbuch. Ein Beitrag zur Geschichte der Wissenschaften in der Antike* (Göttingen).

Fulkerson, L. (2004), '*Omnia vincit amor*: Why the *Remedia* Fail', *CQ* 54, 211–23.

Gain, D. B. (1970), 'Gerbert and Manilius', *Latomus* 29, 128–32.

Gale, M. R. (ed.) (2004), *Latin Epic and Didactic Poetry: Genre, Tradition and Individuality* (Swansea).

—— (2005), '*Avia Pieridum loca*: Tradition and Innovation in Lucretius', in Horster and Reitz (edd.) (2005), 175–91.

Galinsky, G. K. (1972*a*), *The Herakles Theme: The Adaptations of the Hero in Literature from Homer to the Twentieth Century* (Oxford).

——(1972*b*), 'Hercules Ouidianus (Metamorphoses 9.1–272)', *WS* 6, 93–116.

Gallazzi, C. (1982), 'P. Narm. inv. 66.362: Vergilius, *Eclogae* VIII 53–62', *ZPE* 48, 75–8.

—— and Lehnus, L. (2001), 'Due nuovi frammenti delle Diegeseis. Approssimazioni al III libro degli Aitia di Callimaco', *ZPE* 137, 7–18.

Garezou, M.-X. (1994), 'Orpheus', *LIMC* vii/1.81–105.

Garvie, A. F. (1994), *Homer:* Odyssey *Books 6–8* (Cambridge).

Gauly, B. M. (1990), *Liebeserfahrungen: Zur Rolle des elegischen Ich in Ovids Amores* (Frankfurt).

Geiger, J. (1985), *Cornelius Nepos and Ancient Political Biography*, Historia Einzelschriften 47 (Stuttgart).

Gelzer, Th. (1992), 'Bemerkungen zu Catull c. 101', *MH* 49, 26–32.

Genette, G. (1987), *Seuils* (Paris).

Gerber, D. E. (1999), *Greek Iambic Poetry, from the Seventh to the Fifth Centuries B.C.* (Cambridge, MA, and London).

Gibson, B. K. (1995), 'Catullus 1.5–7', *CQ* 45, 569–73.

Gibson, R. K. (1998), 'Didactic Poetry as "Popular" Form: A Study of Imperatival Expressions in Latin Didactic Verse and Prose' (with response by A. Sharrock, 99–115), in Atherton (ed.) (1998), 67–98.

——(2000), 'Book Endings in Greek Poetry and *Ars Amatoria* 2 and 3', *Mnemosyne* 53, 588–91.

——(2003), *Ovid:* Ars Amatoria *Book 3* (Cambridge).

——(2007), *Excess and Restraint: Propertius, Horace, and Ovid's* Ars Amatoria, BICS Suppl. 89 (London).

—— Green, S. J., Sharrock, A. (edd.) (2006), *The Art of Love: Bimillennial Essays on Ovid's* Ars Amatoria *and* Remedia Amoris (Oxford).

Gildenhard, I., and Zissos, A. (2000), 'Ovid's Narcissus (*Met.* 3.339–510): Echoes of Oedipus', *AJP* 121, 129–47.

Giuliano, L. (2007), 'I segni nel *De ira* di Filodemo (*P Herc.* 182)', in J. Frösén, T. Purola, E. Salmenkivi (edd.), *Proceedings of the 24th International Congress of Papyrology: Helsinki, 1–7 August, 2004*, 2 vols. (Helsinki), i. 385–93.

Glei, R. (2004), 'Didactic Poetry', in *Brill's New Pauly* (Leiden and Boston), iv. 379–83.

Goldberg, S. M. (2005), *Constructing Literature in the Roman Republic: Poetry and its Reception* (Cambridge).

Goldhill, S. (1991), *The Poet's Voice: Essays on Poetics and Greek Literature* (Cambridge).

——(2002), *The Invention of Prose*, Greece and Rome New Surveys 32 (Oxford).

González, J. (1984), 'Tabula Siarensis, Fortunales Siarenses et municipia civium Romanorum', *ZPE* 55, 55–100.

Goold, G. P. (1965), '*Amatoria critica*', *HSCP* 69, 1–107.

——(1977), *Manilius*, Astronomica: *With an English Translation* (Cambridge, MA, and London).

——(1998), *M. Manilii Astronomica*² (Stuttgart and Leipzig).

Gorman, R. (2005), *The Socratic Method in the Dialogues of Cicero*, Palingenesia 86 (Stuttgart).

Gorrie, C. (2007), 'The Restoration of the Porticus Octaviae and Severan Imperial Policy', *G&R* 54, 1–17.

Gow, A. S. F. (1950), *Theocritus*, 2 vols. (Cambridge).

——and Page, D. L. (1965), *Hellenistic Epigrams*, 2 vols. (Cambridge).

————(1968), *Garland of Philip*, 2 vols. (Cambridge).

Grassmann, V. (1966), *Die erotischen Epoden des Horaz. Literarischer Hintergrund und sprachliche Tradition*, Zetemata 39 (Munich).

Gratwick, A. S. (1991), 'Catullus 1.10 and the Title of his *libellus*', *G&R* 38, 199–202.

——(2002), '*Vale, patrona uirgo*: The Text of Catullus 1.9', *CQ* 52, 305–20.

Graziosi, B. (2002), *Inventing Homer: The Early Reception of Epic* (Cambridge).

Griffin, J. (1980), review of Nisbet and Hubbard (1978), *JRS* 70, 182–5.

Griffiths, A. (2002), 'Just Where Do You Draw the Line?', in Woodman and Feeney (edd.) (2002), 65–79.

Gronewald, M. (1973), 'Ein Epigramm-Papyrus', *ZPE* 12, 92–8.

——and Daniel, R. W. (2004*a*), 'Ein neuer Sappho-Papyrus', *ZPE* 147, 1–8.

————(2004*b*) 'Nachtrag zum neuen Sappho-Papyrus', *ZPE* 149, 1–4.

————(2005), 'Lyrischer Text (Sappho-Papyrus)', *ZPE* 154, 7–11.

Gros, P. (1993), 'Apollo Palatinus', *LTUR* i. 54–7.

——(2006), *Vitruve et la tradition des traités d'architecture. Fabrica et raticinatio. Recueil d'études*, *CEFR* 366 (Rome).

Gross, N. P. (1975–6), 'Ovid, *Amores* 3. 11a and b: A Literary Mélange', *CJ* 71, 152–60.

——(1985), *Amatory Persuasion in Antiquity: Studies in Theory and Practice* (Newark, London, Toronto).

Grossardt, P. (2001), *Die Erzählung von Meleagros. Zur literarischen Entwicklung der kalydonischen Kultlegende*, Mnemosyne Suppl. 215 (Leiden, Boston, Cologne).

Guérard, O. (1925), 'Un nouveau papyrus de l'*Odyssée*', *Revue de l'Égypte Ancienne* 1, 88–131.

Gurd, S. (2007), 'Cicero and Editorial Revision', *CA* 26, 49–80.

Gutzwiller, K. J. (1981), *Studies in the Hellenistic Epyllion*, Beiträge zur klassischen Philologie 114 (Königstein).

—— (1995), 'Cleopatra's Ring', *GRBS* 36, 383–98.

—— (1996), 'The Evidence for Theocritean Poetry Books', in M. A. Harder, R. F. Regtuit, G. C. Wakker (edd.), *Theocritus*, Hellenistica Groningana 2 (Groningen), 119–48.

—— (1998), *Poetic Garlands: Hellenistic Epigrams in Context* (Berkeley, Los Angeles, London).

—— (ed.) (2005), *The New Posidippus: A Hellenistic Poetry Book* (Oxford).

Habinek, T. N. (1985), *The Colometry of Latin Prose*, University of California Publications, Classical Studies 25 (Berkeley and Los Angeles).

—— (1997), *The Politics of Latin Literature* (Princeton).

Hall, J. B. (1999), 'Critical Observations on the Text of Ovid's Amatory Works', in S. Morton Braund and R. Mayer (edd.), *Amor, Roma: Love and Latin Literature. Eleven Essays . . . presented to E. J. Kenney . . .*, PCPS Suppl. 22 (Cambridge), 94–103.

Hallett, J. P. (1997), 'Female Homoeroticism and the Denial of Roman Reality in Latin Literature', in Hallett and Skinner (edd.) (1997), 255–73.

—— and Skinner, M. B. (edd.) (1997), *Roman Sexualities* (Princeton).

Halleux, R., and Schamp, J. (1985), *Les Lapidaires grecs* (Paris).

Harder, M. A. (1985), *Euripides*, Kresphontes *and* Archelaos: *Introduction, Text and Commentary* (Leiden).

—— (1988), 'Callimachus and the Muses: Some Aspects of Narrative Technique in *Aetia* 1–2', *Prometheus* 14, 1–14.

—— (1990), 'Untrodden Paths: Where Do They Lead?', *HSCP* 93, 287–309.

—— (1993), 'Aspects of the Structure of Callimachus' *Aetia*', in M. A. Harder, R. F. Regtuit, G. C. Wakker (edd.), *Callimachus*, Hellenistica Groningana 1 (Groningen), 99–110.

—— (2002), review of Cameron (1995), *Mnemosyne* 55, 600–1.

—— (2003), 'The Invention of Past, Present and Future in Callimachus' *Aetia*', *Hermes* 131, 290–306.

—— Regtuit, R. F., Wakker, G. C. (edd.) (2000), *Apollonius Rhodius*, Hellenistica Groningana 4 (Leuven).

Hardie, A. (1983), *Statius and the* Silvae: *Poets, Patrons and Epideixis in the Graeco-Roman World* (Liverpool).

—— (2005), 'Sappho, the Muses and Life after Death', *ZPE* 154, 13–32.

Hardie, P. R. (1990), 'Ovid's Theban History: The First "Anti-*Aeneid*"?', *CQ* 40, 224–35.

—— (2002*a*), *Ovid's Poetics of Illusion* (Cambridge).

—— (ed.) (2002*b*), *The Cambridge Companion to Ovid* (Cambridge).

Hardie, P. R. (2002*c*), 'Ovid and Early Imperial Literature', in P. R. Hardie (ed.) (2002*b*), 34–45.

—— (2004), 'Ovidian Middles', in S. Kyriakidis and F. De Martino (edd.), *Middles in Latin Poetry* (Bari), 151–8.

—— Barchiesi, A., Hinds, S. (edd.) (1999), *Ovidian Transformations: Essays on the* Metamorphoses *and its Reception*, PCPS Suppl. 23 (Cambridge).

Harrauer, H. (1981), 'Epigrammincipit auf einem Papyrus aus dem 3. Jh. v. Chr. Ein Vorbericht', *Proceedings of XVI International Congress of Papyrologists* (Chico), 49–53.

Harrison, S. J. (1986), 'Philosophical Imagery in Horace, *Odes* 3.5', *CQ* 36, 502–7.

—— (1988), 'Horace, *Odes* 3.7: An Erotic *Odyssey*?', *CQ* 38, 186–92.

—— (1990*a*), 'Cicero's *De Temporibus Suis*: The Evidence Reconsidered', *Hermes* 118, 454–63.

—— (1990*b*), 'The Praise Singer: Horace, Censorinus and *Odes* 4.8', *JRS* 80, 31–43.

—— (1995*a*), 'Horace, Pindar, Iullus Antonius, and Augustus: *Odes* 4. 2', in Harrison (ed.) (1995*b*), 108–27.

—— (ed.) (1995*b*), *Homage to Horace: A Bimillenniary Celebration* (Oxford).

—— (1996), 'Mythological Incest: Catullus 88', *CQ* 46, 581–2.

—— (2001), 'Some Generic Problems in Horace's *Epodes*: or, On (Not) Being Archilochus', in Cavarzere, Aloni, Barchiesi (edd.) (2001), 165–86.

—— (2002), 'Ovid and Genre: Evolutions of an Elegist', in P. R. Hardie (ed.) (2002*b*), 79–94.

—— and Heyworth, S. J. (1998), 'Notes on the Text and Interpretation of Catullus', *PCPS* 85, 85–109.

Haselberger, L., Romano, D. G., Dumser, E. A. (2002), *Mapping Augustan Rome*, *JRA* Supplement 50 (Portsmouth, RI).

Hatzimichali, M. (2005), 'Greek Scholarship of the Early Imperial Period: Pamphilus of Alexandria' (D. Phil. thesis, Oxford).

Hazzard, R. A. (2000), *Imagination of a Monarchy: Studies in Ptolemaic Propaganda*, Phoenix Suppl. 37 (Toronto).

Heath, J. (1995–6), 'The *stupor* of Orpheus: Ovid's *Metamorphoses* 10.64–71', *CJ* 91, 353–70.

Heath, M. (1989), *Unity in Greek Poetics* (Oxford).

Heiden, B. (1998), 'The Placement of "Book Divisions" in the *Iliad*', *JHS* 118, 68–81.

Heinze, R. (1960), 'Ovids elegische Erzählung', *Vom Geist des Römertums. Ausgewählte Aufsätze*³ (Stuttgart), 308–403.

Helm, R. (1984), *Eusebius Werke 7. Die Chronik des Hieronymus*³ (Berlin).

Hemelrijk, E. A. (1999), *Matrona docta* (London).

Henderson, J. (1998), *Fighting for Rome: Poets and Caesars, History and Civil War* (Cambridge).

—— (1999), *Writing down Rome: Satire, Comedy, and other Offences in Latin Poetry* (Oxford).

—— (2002), 'A doo-dah-doo-dah-dey at the Races: Ovid *Amores* 3.2 and the Personal Politics of the *Circus Maximus*', *CA* 21, 41–65.

—— (2006), 'In Ovid with Bed (*Ars* 2 and 3)', in R. K. Gibson, Green, Sharrock (edd.) (2006), 77–95.

Henneböhl, R. (2005), '"*Stumm vor Schmerz ist die Lyra*": Der Gesang des Orpheus und die Entstehung der Liebeselegie. Zur Aussageabsicht des zehnten Buches der Metamorphosen Ovids', *Gymnasium* 112, 345–74.

Henry, W. B. (2005), '4711. Elegy (*Metamorphoses*?)', in N. Gonis *et al.* (edd.), *The Oxyrhynchus Papyri* lxix (London), 46–53.

Hershkowitz, D. (1999), 'The Creation of the Self in Ovid and Proust', in P. R. Hardie, Barchiesi, Hinds (edd.) (1999), 182–96.

Heslin, P. J. (1997), 'The Scansion of *Pharsalia* (Catullus 64.37; Statius, *Achilleis* 1.152; Calpurnius Siculus 4.101)', *CQ* 47, 588–93.

Heyworth, S. J. (1988), 'Horace's Second Epode', *AJP* 109, 71–85.

—— (1993), 'Horace's *Ibis*: On the Title, Unity, and Contents of the *Epodes*', *PLILS* 7 (1993) 85–96.

—— (1995), 'Dividing Poems', in O. Pecere and M. D. Reeve (edd.), *Formative Stages of Classical Traditions: Latin Texts from Antiquity to the Renaissance* (Spoleto), 117–48.

—— (2001), 'Catullian Iambics, Catullian *iambi*', in Cavarzere, Aloni, Barchiesi (edd.) (2001), 117–39.

Hezel, O. (1932), *Catull und das griechische Epigramm* (Stuttgart).

Hill, D. E. (1992), 'From Orpheus to Ass's Ears', in A. J. Woodman and J. Powell (edd.), *Author and Audience in Latin Literature* (Cambridge), 124–37.

Hinds, S. (1987), *The Metamorphosis of Persephone: Ovid and the Self-Conscious Muse* (Cambridge).

—— (1998), *Allusion and Intertext: Dynamics of Appropriation in Roman Poetry* (Cambridge).

Hirzel, R. (1895), *Der Dialog. Ein literarhistorischer Versuch*, 2 vols. (Leipzig).

Hollis, A. S. (1965), 'Some Fragments of Callimachus' *Hecale*', *CR* 15, 259–60.

—— (1976), 'Some Allusions to Earlier Hellenistic Poetry in Nonnus', *CQ* 26, 142–50.

—— (1977), *Ovid, Ars Amatoria Book I: Edited with an Introduction and Commentary* (Oxford).

Hollis, A. S. (1982), 'Teuthis and Callimachus, *Aetia* Book 1 (Lloyd-Jones and Parsons, *Supplementum Hellenisticum* 276)', *CQ* 32, 117–20.

—— (1990), *Callimachus*, Hecale: *Edited with an Introduction and Commentary* (Oxford).

—— (1991*a*), 'Callimachus fr. 535 Pfeiffer: Another Piece of *Hecale*?', *ZPE* 86, 14–16.

—— (1991*b*), 'Callimachus, *Hecale* fr. 36,2 H. = fr. 37 H.', *ZPE* 89, 25–6.

—— (1992), 'Attica in Hellenistic Poetry', *ZPE* 93, 1–15.

—— (1993), 'Callimachus, *Hecale* frs. 3–5 H.', *ZPE* 95, 45–7.

—— (1994), '*Supplementum Hellenisticum* 948–9, Callimachus, *Hecale*?', *ZPE* 100, 17–21.

—— (1996), 'Heroic Honours for Philetas?', *ZPE* 110, 56–62.

—— (1997*a*), 'The Beginning of Callimachus' *Hecale*', *ZPE* 115, 55–6.

—— (1997*b*), 'Three Possible Fragments of Callimachus' *Hecale* in Hesychius', *ZPE* 117, 47–9.

—— (1998*a*), 'Darkness on the Mountains: A Fragment of Callimachus' *Hecale*', *ZPE* 123, 72.

—— (1998*b*), 'Nicander and Lucretius', *PLILS* 10, 169–84.

—— (2000), 'Another Rare Epithet in Callimachus' *Hecale*?', *ZPE* 130, 16.

—— (2004), 'Hecale's Babies', *ZPE* 148, 115–16.

—— (2007), *Fragments of Roman Poetry: c.60 BC–AD 20* (Oxford).

Holzberg, N. (1990), 'Ovids Version der Ehebruchsnovelle von Ares und Aphrodite in der *Ars amatoria*' *WJA* 16, 137–52.

—— (1998*a*), '*Ter quinque volumina* as *carmen perpetuum*: The Division into Books in Ovid's *Metamorphoses*', *MD* 40, 77–98.

—— (1998*b*), *Ovid. Dichter und Werk*[2] (Munich).

—— (2000), 'Lesbia, the Poet, and the Two Faces of Sappho: "Womanufacture" in Catullus', *PCPS* 46, 28–44.

—— (2001), *Die römische Liebeselegie. Eine Einführung*[2] (Darmstadt).

—— (2002), *Catull. Der Dichter und sein erotisches Werk* (Munich).

—— (2006), *Vergil. Der Dichter und sein Werk* (Munich).

Hopkinson, N. (2000), *Ovid*, Metamorphoses *Book XIII* (Cambridge).

Horsfall, N. (1993), 'Empty Shelves on the Palatine', *G&R* 40, 58–67.

Horster, M., and Reitz, Ch. (edd.) (2003), *Antike Fachschriftsteller: Literarischer Diskurs und sozialer Kontext*, Palingenesia 80 (Stuttgart).

—— —— (edd.) (2005), *Wissensvermittlung in dichterischer Gestalt*, Palingenesia 85 (Stuttgart).

Hubbard, T. K. (2005), 'The Catullan *libelli* Revisited', *Philologus* 149, 253–77.

—— (2007), 'Theognis' *sphrêgis*: Aristocratic Speech and the Paradoxes of Writing', in C. Cooper (ed.), *Politics and Orality*, Mnemosyne Suppl. 280 (Leiden and Boston), 193–215.

Huber, I. (2001), 'Das Bild des Orpheus in der antiken Kunst', *Thetis* 8, 23–33.

Hübner, W. (1984), 'Manilius als Astrologe und Dichter', *ANRW* ii.32.1.126–320.

—— (1993), 'Manilio e Teucro di Babilonia', in Liuzzi (ed.) (1993), 21–40.

Humphrey, J. H. (1986), *Roman Circuses: Arenas for Chariot Racing* (London).

Hunter, R. L. (1989), *Apollonius of Rhodes*: Argonautica *Book III* (Cambridge).

—— (1993*a*), 'Callimachean Echoes in Catullus 65', *ZPE* 96, 179–82.

—— (1993*b*), *The* Argonautica *of Apollonius: Literary Studies* (Cambridge).

—— (1996), *Theocritus and the Archaeology of Greek Poetry* (Cambridge).

—— (2001), 'The Poetics of Narrative in the *Argonautica*', in T. D. Papanghelis and A. Rengakos (edd.), *A Companion to Apollonius Rhodius*, Mnemosyne Suppl. 217 (Leiden), 93–125.

—— (2005*a*), 'The Hesiodic *Catalogue* and Hellenistic Poetry', in Hunter (ed.) (2005*b*), 239–65.

—— (ed.) (2005*b*), *The Hesiodic* Catalogue of Women: *Constructions and Reconstructions* (Cambridge).

—— (2006), *The Shadow of Callimachus: Studies in the Reception of Hellenistic Poetry at Rome* (Cambridge).

Hutchinson, G. O. (1981), 'Notes on the New Gallus', *ZPE* 41, 37–42.

—— (1984), 'Propertius and the Unity of the Book', *JRS* 74, 99–106.

—— (1988), *Hellenistic Poetry* (Oxford).

—— (1992), review of Huys (1991), *CR* 42, 483–4.

—— (1993), *Latin Literature from Seneca to Juvenal: A Critical Study* (Oxford).

—— (1998), *Cicero's Correspondence: A Literary Study* (Oxford).

—— (1999), 'Sophocles and Time', in J. Griffin (ed.), *Sophocles Revisited: Essays Presented to Sir Hugh Lloyd-Jones* (Oxford), 47–72.

—— (2001*a*), *Greek Lyric Poetry: A Commentary on Selected Larger Pieces* (Oxford).

—— (2001*b*), 'The Date of *De Rerum Natura*', *CQ* 51, 150–62.

—— (2006*a*), 'The Metamorphosis of Metamorphosis: P. Oxy. 4711 and Ovid', *ZPE* 155, 71–84 [earlier version of ch. 9].

—— (2006*b*), *Propertius*, Elegies *Book IV* (Cambridge).

—— (forthcoming), 'Telling Tales: Ovid's *Metamorphoses* and Callimachus', in D. Obbink and R. B. Rutherford (edd.), *Culture in Pieces: The Proceedings of a Conference in Honour of Peter Parsons* (Oxford).

Huys, M. (1991), *Le Poème élégiaque hellénistique P. Brux. inv. 8934 et P. Sorb. inv. 2254* (Brussels).

Iannucci, A. (1998), 'Callimaco e la "discordia" degli ecisti di Zancle (Call. *Aet.* 2, 43, 73 Pfeiffer = P. Oxy. 2080 col. 2, 73)', *Sileno* 24, 173–9.

Immerwahr, H. (1966), *Form and Thought in Herodotus* (Cleveland).

Ioannidou, G. (1996), *Catalogue of Greek and Latin Literary Papyri in Berlin (P. Berol. inv. 21101–21299, 21911)*, Berliner Klassikertexte 9 (Mainz).

Isager, S. (1998), 'The Pride of Halicarnassus', *ZPE* 123, 1–23.

—— and Pedersen, P. (edd.) (2004), *The Salmakis inscription and Hellenistic Halicarnassus* (Odense).

Isayev, E. (2007), 'Unruly Youth? The Myth of Generation Conflict in Late Republican Rome', *Historia* 56, 1–13.

Jacobi, F. (1930), *ΠΑΝΤΕΣ ΘΕΟΙ* (Halle).

Jacobson, H. (2007), 'Horace *AP* 139: *parturient montes, nascetur ridiculus mus*', *MH* 64, 59–61.

Jacoby, F. (1961), 'Zur Entstehung der römischen Elegie', *Kleine philologische Schriften*, 2 vols. (Berlin), ii. 65–121.

—— et al. (1923–), *Fragmente der griechischen Historiker* (Berlin, etc.).

Jacques, J. M. (2002). *Nicandre. Œuvres* ii. Les Thériaques. *Fragments iologiques antérieurs à Nicandre* (Paris).

Jameson, S. (1968), 'Chronology of the Campaigns of Aelius Gallus and C. Petronius', *JRS* 58, 71–84.

Janan, M. (1988), 'The Book of Good Love? Design versus Desire in *Metamorphoses* 10', *Ramus* 17, 110–37.

—— (1991), ' "The Labyrinth and the Mirror": Incest and Influence in *Metamorphoses* 9', *Arethusa* 24, 239–56.

Janko, R. (1991), 'Philodemus' *On Poems* and Aristotle's *On Poets*', *Cronache Ercolanesi* 21, 5–64.

—— (2000), *Philodemus On Poems Book 1: Edited with Introduction, Translation, and Commentary* (Oxford).

Janson, T. (1964), *Latin Prose Prefaces: Studies in Literary Conventions* (Stockholm).

Jenkins, T. E. (2000), 'The Writing in (and of) Ovid's "Byblis" Episode', *HSCP* 100, 439–51.

Jocelyn, H. D. (1999), 'The Arrangement and the Language of Catullus' So-called *polymetra* with Special Reference to the Sequence 10–11–12', in J. N. Adams and R. G. Mayer (edd.), *Aspects of the Language of Latin Poetry*, PBA 93 (Oxford), 335–75.

Johns, A. (1995), *The Nature of the Book: Print and Knowledge in the Making* (Chicago and London).

Johnson, W. A. (2000), 'Towards a Sociology of Reading in Classical Antiquity', *AJP* 121, 593–627.

—— (2004), *Bookrolls and Scribes in Oxyrhynchus* (Toronto, Buffalo, London).

Jong, I. de (2001), *A Narratological Commentary on the* Odyssey (Cambridge).

Jourdain-Annequin, C., and Bonnet, C. (edd.) (1996), *Héraclès II. Les femmes et le féminin* (Brussels).

Kahil, L., and Jacquemin, A. (1988), 'Harpyiai', *LIMC* iv/1. 444–50.

Kalverkämper, H. (2005), 'Fachkommunikation zwischen Tradition und Innovation: Ein kulturhistorisches Phänomen der alten und modernen Gesellschaften', in Fögen (ed.) (2005), 319–61.

Kannicht, R. (2004), *Tragicorum Graecorum Fragmenta* v: *Euripides* (Göttingen).

Kassel, R. (1991*a*), 'Die Phalaeen des neuen hellenistischen Weihepigramms aus Pergamon', *Kleine Schriften* (Berlin and New York), 138–40.

—— (1991*b*), 'Dialoge mit Statuen', *Kleine Schriften* (Berlin and New York), 140–53.

Kaster, R. A. (1995), *C. Suetonius Tranquillus*, De Grammaticis et Rhetoribus: *Edited with a Translation, Introduction, and Commentary* (Oxford).

Keith, A. (2002), 'Sources and Genres in Ovid's *Metamorphoses* 1–5', in Boyd (ed.) (2002), 235–69.

Kellum, B. A. (1990), 'The City Adorned: Display at the *aedes Concordiae Augustae*', in Raaflaub and Toher (edd.) (1990), 276–307.

Kelly, A. (2007), 'Stesikhoros and Helen', *MH* 64, 1–21.

Kerkhecker, A. (1999), *Callimachus' Book of* Iambi (Oxford).

—— (2000), 'Zur internen Gattungsgeschichte der römischen Epik: das Beispiel Ennius', in E. A. Schmidt (ed.) (2001), 54–62.

Keul, M. (1989), *Liebe im Widerstreit. Interpretationen zu Ovids Amores und ihrem literarischen Hintergrund* (Frankfurt am Main).

Kidd, D. A. (1997), *Aratus*, Phaenomena: *Edited with Introduction, Translation and Commentary* (Cambridge).

Kienast, D. (1990), *Römische Kaisertabelle* (Darmstadt).

Kiessling, A. (1881), 'Horatius', in A. Kiessling and U. von Wilamowitz-Moellendorff (edd.), *Philologische Untersuchungen* 2 (Berlin), 48–122.

Kintgen, E. R. (1996), *Reading in Tudor England* (Pittsburgh).

Klementa, S. (1993), *Gelagerte Flußgötter des Späthellenismus und der römischen Kaiserzeit* (Cologne, Weimar, Vienna).

Kleve, K. (1989), 'Lucretius in Herculaneum', *Cronache Ercolanesi* 19, 5–27.

—— (1990), 'Ennius in Herculaneum', *Cronache Ercolanesi* 20, 5–16.

Kleve, K. (1994), 'An Approach to the Latin Papyri from Herculaneum', in *Storia, poesia e pensiero nel mondo antico. Studi in onore di Marcello Gigante* (Naples), 313–20.

—— (1996), 'How to Read an Illegible Papyrus. Towards an Edition of *PHerc.* 78, Caecilius Statius, *Obolostates sive Faenerator*', *Cronache Ercolanesi* 26, 5–14.

—— (2001), 'Caecilius Statius, The Money-Lender (PHerc. 78)', in I. Andorlini *et al.* (edd.), *Atti del XXII Congresso Internazionale di Papirologia* (Florence), ii. 725.

—— (2007), 'Lucretius' Book II in P.Herc. 395', in Palme (ed.) (2007), 347–54.

Knecht, A. (1972), *Gregor von Nazianz. Gegen die Putzsucht der Frauen* (Heidelberg).

Knight, V. (1995), *The Renewal of Epic: Responses to Homer in the* Argonautica *of Apollonius*, Mnemosyne Suppl. 152 (Leiden, New York, Cologne).

Knox, P. E. (1985), 'The Epilogue to the *Aetia*', *GRBS* 26, 59–65.

—— (1986), *Ovid's* Metamorphoses *and the Traditions of Augustan Poetry*, PCPS Suppl. 11 (Cambridge).

—— (1993), 'The Epilogue to the *Aetia*: An Epilogue', *ZPE* 96, 175–8.

—— (ed.) (2006), *Oxford Readings in* Ovid (Oxford).

Koenen, L. (1978), *The Cairo Codex of Menander: A Photographic Edition* (London).

Kondoleon, C. (2000), *Antioch: The Lost Ancient City* (Princeton; exhibition catalogue).

Korenjak, M. (1997), '*Τηλεκλείτη Ἀριάδνη*: Exemplum mit Folgen', *WS* 110, 19–25.

Kosmetatou, E., and Papalexandrou, N. (2003), 'Size Matters: Poseidippos and the Colossi', *ZPE* 143, 53–8.

Kraggerud, E. (1995), 'The Sixth Roman Ode of Horace: Its Date and Function', *SO* 70, 54–67.

Krevans, N. (1984), 'The Poet as Editor: Callimachus, Virgil, Horace, Propertius and the Development of the Poetic Book' (Diss. Princeton).

—— (1986), 'P. Oxy. 2258 B fr. 2: A Scholion to Callimachus' Victoria Berenices?', *ZPE* 65, 37–8.

—— (2000), 'On the Margins of Epic: The Foundation-Poems of Apollonius', in Harder, Regtuit, Wakker (edd.) (2000), 69–84.

Kroll, W. (1925), 'Lehrgedicht', *RE* 12, 1842–57.

Kruschwitz, P., and Schumacher, M. (2005), *Das vorklassische Lehrgedicht der Römer* (Heidelberg).

Kullmann, W., Althoff, J., Asper, M. (edd.) (1998), *Gattungen wissenschaftlicher Literatur in der Antike* (Tübingen).

Kurczyk, St. (2006), *Cicero und die Inszenierung der eigenen Vergangenheit. Autobiographisches Schreiben in der späten Römischen Republik* (Vienna).

Kyriakidis, S. (2006), 'Lucretius' *DRN* 1.926–50 and the Proem to Book 4', *CQ* 56, 606–10.

Lacey, N. (1995), '*Amores* 3. 12. 11–12: The Couplet that Forges a Deliberate Link between the *Amores* and the *Ars Amatoria*', *Eranos* 93, 24–9.

Langslow, D. R. (2000), *Medical Latin in the Roman Empire* (Oxford).

—— (2007), 'The *epistula* in Ancient Scientific and Technical Literature, with Special Reference to Medicine', in R. Morello and A. D. Morrison (edd.), *Ancient Letters: Classical and Late Antique Epistolography* (Oxford), 211–34.

Laser, S. (1955), 'ἄεθλος', *Lexikon des frühgriechischen Epos* (Göttingen), i. 151–2.

Lasserre, F. (1975), 'L'élégie de l'huître (P. Louvre inv. 7733 v° inéd.)', *QU* 19, 145–76.

Le Bonniec, H. (1958), *Le Culte de Cérès. Des origines à la fin de la République* (Paris).

—— (1980), 'La fête de Junon au pays des Falisques (Ovide, *Amores*, 3, 13)', in Thill (ed.) (1980), 233–44.

Leach, E. W. (1974), 'Ekphrasis and the Theme of Artistic Failure', *Ramus* 3, 102–42.

—— (1981), '*Georgics* 2 and the Poem', *Arethusa* 14, 35–48.

—— (2006), '*An gravius aliquid scribam*: Roman *seniores* write to *iuvenes*', *TAPA* 136, 246–67.

Lefèvre, E. (1995), 'Die Komposition von Horaz' erstem Oden-Buch', in L. Belloni, G. Milanese, A. Porro (edd.), *Studia classica Iohanni Tarditi oblata*, 2 vols. (Milan), 507–21.

Lefkowitz, M. (1981), *The Lives of the Greek Poets* (London).

Lehnus, L. (1995), 'Riflessioni cronologiche sull'ultimo Callimaco', *ZPE* 105, 6–12.

—— (1997), 'Ipotesi sul finale dell'*Ecale*', *ZPE* 117, 45–6.

—— (2003), 'Two Notes on Callimachean Fragments', *ZPE* 142, 31–3.

Leigh, M. (1998), 'Sophocles at Patavium (*fr.* 137 Radt)', *JHS* 118, 82–100.

Lenz, Fr. (1932–3), 'Ceresfest. Eine Studie zu Ovid Amores, 3, 10', *SIFC* 10, 299–313.

Levi, D. (1947), *Antioch Mosaic Pavements*, 2 vols. (Princeton and London).

Lévy, C. (1992), *Cicero Academicus. Recherches sur les* Académiques *et sur la philosophie cicéronienne*, CÉFR 162 (Rome).

Liberman, G. (1999), *Alcée. Fragments. Texte établi, traduit et annoté*, 2 vols. (Paris).

Lightfoot, J. L. (1999), *Parthenius of Nicaea, the Poetical Fragments and the Ἐρωτικὰ Παθήματα: Edited with Introduction and Commentaries* (Oxford).

Ling, R. (1997), *The Insula of the Menander at Pompeii* i: *The Structures* (Oxford).

Liuzzi, D. (ed.) (1993), *Manilio fra poesia e scienza. Atti del convegno: Lecce, 14–16 maggio 1992* (Galatina).

Livrea, E. (1979), 'Der Liller Kallimachos und die Mausefallen', *ZPE* 34, 37–42.

Lloyd-Jones, H. (1979), 'The Michigan List of Metamorphosed Persons', *ZPE* 35, 6.

—— (2005*a*), 'The Pride of Halicarnassus', *The Further Academic Papers of Sir Hugh Lloyd-Jones* (Oxford), 211–32.

—— (2005*b*), 'Notes on P.Mil.Vogl. VIII 309', *The Further Academic Papers of Sir Hugh Lloyd-Jones* (Oxford), 242–45.

Loewenstein, J. (1984), *Responsive Readings: Versions of Echo in Pastoral, Epic, and the Jonsonian Masque*, Yale Studies in English 192 (New Haven and London).

Loomis, J. W. (1972), *Studies in Catullan Verse: An Analysis of Word Types and Patterns in the Polymetra*, Mnemosyne Suppl. 24 (Leiden).

Lörcher, G. (1975), *Der Aufbau der drei Bücher von Ovids Amores*, Heuremata 3 (Amsterdam).

Loupiac, A. (1997), 'La trilogie d'Actium et l'*Épode IX* d'Horace: document historique ou carmen symposiacum', *REL* 75, 129–40.

Love, H. (1993), *Scribal Publication in Seventeenth-Century England* (Oxford).

Lowe, N. J. (2000), *The Classical Plot and the Invention of Western Narrative* (Cambridge).

Lowrie, M. (1993), 'Myrrha's Second Taboo, Ovid *Metamorphoses* 10.467–68', *CP* 88, 50–2.

—— (1995), 'A Parade of Lyric Predecessors: Horace *C.* 1.12–1.18', *Phoenix* 49, 33–48.

—— (1997), *Horace's Narrative Odes* (Oxford).

Ludwig, W. (1957), 'Zu Horaz, *C.* 2, 1–12', *Hermes* 85, 336–45.

—— (1961), 'Die Anordnung des vierten Horazischen Odenbuches', *MH* 18, 1–10.

Luppe, W. (2006*a*), 'Die Verwandlungssage der Asterie im P. Oxy. 4711', *Prometheus* 32, 55–6.

—— (2006*b*), 'Die Narkissos-Sage in P.Oxy. LXIX 4711', *APF* 52, 1–3.

—— (2007), review of N. Gonis *et al.* (edd.), *The Oxyrhynchus Papyri* lxix (London, 2005), *Gnomon* 79, 310–14.

Lyne, R. O. A. M. (1980), *The Latin Love Poets, from Catullus to Horace* (Oxford).

—— (1995), *Horace: Behind the Public Poetry* (Oxford).

—— (2007*a*), 'The Neoteric Poets', *Collected Papers on Latin Poetry* (Oxford), 60–84.

—— (2007*b*), 'Horace *Odes* Book 1 and the Alexandrian Edition of Alcaeus', *Collected Papers on Latin Poetry* (Oxford), 293–313.

—— (2007*c*), 'Structure and Allusion in Horace's Book of *Epodes*', *Collected Papers on Latin Poetry* (Oxford), 314–40.

Maas, P. (1973), 'Hephthemimeres im Hexameter des Kallimachos', *Kleine Schriften* (Munich), 92–3.

Macho, Th. (2002), 'Narziß und der Spiegel. Selbstrepräsentation in der Geschichte der Optik', in Renger (ed.) (2002), 13–25.

Mack, S. (1994–5), 'Teaching Ovid's Orpheus to Beginners', *CJ* 90, 279–85.

Macleod, C. W. (1982), *Homer: Iliad, Book XXIV* (Cambridge).

—— (1983*a*), 'Catullus 116', *Collected Essays* (Oxford), 181–6.

—— (1983*b*), 'The Artistry of Catullus 67', *Collected Essays* (Oxford), 187–95.

Maehler, H. (1982–97), *Die Lieder des Bakchylides*, 3 vols., Mnemosyne Suppl. 62 and 167 (Leiden).

—— (1987–9), *Pindari carmina cum fragmentis*, 2 vols. (Leipzig).

Magnani, M. (2007), 'Call. *Aet.* III fr. 64,9s. Pfeiffer e la *Sylloge Simonidea*', *ZPE* 159, 13–22.

Magnelli, E. (1995), 'Le norme del secondo piede dell'esametro nei poeti ellenistici e il comportamento della "parola metrica"', *MD* 35, 135–64.

—— (2002), 'Ancora sul nuovo Posidippo e la poesia latina: il "freddo letto"', *ZPE* 140, 15–16.

—— (2006), 'On the New Fragments of Greek Poetry from Oxyrhynchus', *ZPE* 158, 9–12.

Maltby, R. (1991), *A Dictionary of Ancient Latin Etymologies* (Leeds).

Maltomini, F. (2001), 'Nove epigrammi ellenistici rivisitati (PPetrie II 49b)', *ZPE* 134, 55–66.

Manakidou, F. (1995), 'Die Seher in den Argonautika des Apollonios Rhodios', *SIFC* 13, 190–208.

Mankin, D. (1995), *Horace: Epodes* (Cambridge).

Manuwald, B. (1975), 'Narcissus bei Konon und Ovid. (Zu Ovid, met. 3, 339–510)', *Hermes* 103, 349–72.

Marcovich, M. (1999–2002), *Diogenes Laertius. Vitae philosophorum*, 3 vols. (indices H. Gärtner) (Stuttgart and Leipzig).

Maresch, K. (1987), 'Anthologie: Anapästische Tetrameter (=TrGF II 646a) und Hexameter (Hymnus an Aphrodite) (Inv. 20270–4)', in M. Gronewald *et al.*, *Kölner Papyri (P. Köln)* vi (Opladen), 26–51.

Marincola, J. (1997), *Authority and Tradition in Ancient Historiography* (Cambridge).

Martin, A., and Primavesi, O. (1998), *L'Empédocle de Strasbourg (P. Strasb. fr. Inv. 1665–1666)* (Berlin).

Massimilla, G. (2005), 'Considerazioni su PSI inv. 1923', in Ozbek (2005), 13–18.

Mastronarde, D. (2002), *Euripides:* Medea (Cambridge).

Matthews, V. J. (1974), *Panyassis of Halikarnassos: Text and Commentary*, Mnemosyne Suppl. 33 (Leiden).

Mayer, R. G. (1990), 'The Epic of Lucretius', *PLLS* 6, 35–43.

—— (1994), *Horace,* Epistles *Book I* (Cambridge).

—— (2005), 'The Impractibility of Latin "Kunstprosa"', in T. Reinhardt, J. N. Adams, M. Lapidge (edd.), *Aspects of the Language of Latin Prose*, PBA 129 (Oxford), 195–210.

Mayerson, P. (1995), 'Aelius Gallus at Cleopatris (Suez) and on the Red Sea', *GRBS* 36, 17–24.

McDonnell, M. (1996), 'Writing, Copying, and Autograph Manuscripts in Ancient Rome', *CQ* 46, 469–92.

McGann, M. J. (1970), 'The Date of Tibullus' Death', *Latomus* 29, 774–80.

McGinn, T. A. J. (1998), *Prostitution, Sexuality, and the Law in Ancient Rome* (New York and Oxford).

McKenzie, D. F., *et al.* (1999–), *The Cambridge History of the Book in Britain* (Cambridge).

McKeown, J. C. (1987–), *Ovid:* Amores. Text, Prolegomena and Commentary, 3 vols. to date (Liverpool, Wolfeboro, Leeds).

McNamee, K. (1977), *Marginalia and Commentaries in Greek Literary Papyri* (Diss. Duke).

McNelis, C. (2003), 'Mourning Glory: Callimachus' *Hecale* and Heroic Honors', *MD* 50, 155–61.

Meillier, Cl. (1976), 'Callimaque (P.L. 76 d, 78 abc, 82, 84, 111 c), Stésichore (?) (P.L. 76 abc)', *Cahiers de recherches de l'Institut de Papyrologie et d'Égyptologie de Lille* 4, 255–360.

—— (1985), 'Extraits commentés d'Homère, *Odyssée*, 16 et 17: *P. Lille* inv. 83 + 134 + 93 b + 93 a + 114 t + 114 o + 87', in *Mélanges offerts à Jean Vercoutter* (Paris), 229–38.

Menci, G. (2004), 'Glossario a Callimaco?', in H. Harrauer and R. Pintaudi (edd.), *Gedenkschrift Ulrike Horak (P. Horak)*, 2 vols. (Florence), i. 19–31.

Merriam, C. U. (2001), *The Development of the Epyllion Genre through the Hellenistic and Roman Periods* (Lewiston and Lampeter).

Messeri, G. (2004), 'Osservazioni su alcuni gnomologi papiracei', in M. S. Funghi (ed.), *Aspetti di letteratura gnomica nel mondo antico* (Florence), 339–68.

Mette-Dittmann, A. (1991), *Die Ehegesetze des Augustus. Eine Untersuchung im Rahmen der Gesellschaftspolitik des Princeps*, Historia Einzelschriften 67 (Stuttgart).

Meyer, W. (1884), *Zur Geschichte des griechischen und lateinischen Hexameters*, SBAW 1884, Philos.-philol.-hist. Cl. 6 (Munich).

Miller, S. G. (2001), *Excavations at Nemea* II: *The Early Hellenistic Stadium* (London and Berkeley).

Miller, Th. (1997), *Die griechische Kolonisation im Spiegel literarischer Zeugnisse* (Tübingen).

Montanari, F., and Lehnus, M. (edd.) (2002), *Callimaque* (Entretiens Hardt 48, Geneva).

Moreau, A. (1994), *Le Mythe de Jason et Médée. Le Va-nu-pied et la sorcière* (Paris).

Morelli, A. M. (1994), 'Sul papiro di Ossirinco LIV 3723. Considerazioni sui caratteri dell'elegia ellenistica erotica alla luce dei nuovi ritrovamenti papiracei', *RFIC* 122, 385–421.

Morgan, Ll. (1999), *Patterns of Redemption in Virgil's* Georgics (Cambridge).

Morrison, A. D. (2007), *The Narrator in Archaic Greek and Hellenistic Poetry* (Cambridge).

Moscati, P. (1990), 'Nuove ricerche su Falerii veteres', in G. Maetzke (ed.), *La civiltà dei Falisci. Atti del XV Convegno di Studi Etruschi e Italici* (Florence), 141–71.

Most, G. (1981), 'On the Arrangement of Catullus' Carmina', *Philologus* 125, 109–25.

Mouritsen, H. (1998), *Italian Unification: A Study in Ancient and Modern Historiography*, BICS Suppl. 70 (London).

Müller, L. (1856), '*De Ovidi Amorum libris*', *Philologus* 11, 60–91.

Müller, R. W. (1964), *Rhetorische und syntaktische Interpunktion. Untersuchungen zur Pausenbezeichnung im antiken Latein* (Diss. Tübingen).

Munro, H. A. J. (1878), *Criticisms and Elucidations of Catullus* (Cambridge).

Murgatroyd, P. (2005), *Mythical and Legendary Narrative in Ovid's* Fasti, Mnemosyne Suppl. 263 (Leiden and Boston).

Murphy, T. (1998), 'Cicero's First Readers: Epistolary Evidence for the Dissemination of his Works', *CQ* 48, 492–505.

Mutschler, F.-H. (1974), 'Beobachtungen zur Gedichtanordnung in der ersten Odensammlung des Horaz', *RhM* 117, 109–32.

—— (1978), 'Kaufmannsliebe: Eine Interpretation der Horazode "Quid fles Asterie" (c. 3,7)', *SO* 53, 111–31.

Myers, K. S. (1994), *Ovid's Causes: Cosmogony and Aetiology in the* Metamorphoses (Ann Arbor).

Nagle, B. R. (1983), 'Byblis and Myrrha: Two Incest Narratives in the *Metamorphoses*', *CJ* 78, 301–15.

Naoumides, M. (1969), 'The Fragments of Greek Lexicography in the Papyri', in *Classical Studies Presented to Ben Edwin Perry* (Urbana, Illinois), 181–202.

Nappa, C. (1999), 'The Goat, the Gout, and the Girl: Catullus 69, 71, and 77', *Mnemosyne* 52, 266–76.

—— (2005), *Reading after Actium: Vergil's* Georgics, *Octavian, and Rome* (Ann Arbor).

Negri, M. (2004), *Pindaro ad Alessandria. Le edizioni e gli editori* (Brescia).

Neils, J. (1987), *The Youthful Deeds of Theseus* (Rome).

Nelis, D. (2001), *Vergil's* Aeneid *and the* Argonautica *of Apollonius Rhodius* (Leeds).

—— (2004), 'From Didactic to Epic: *Georgics* 2.458–3.48', in Gale (ed.) (2004), 73–107.

Nelis, J., and Woodford, S. (1994), 'Theseus', *LIMC* vii/1. 922–51.

Nesselrath, H.-G. (1992), *Ungeschehenes Geschehen. 'Beinahe-Episoden' im griechischen und römischen Epos von Homer bis zur Spätantike*, Beiträge zur Altertumskunde 27 (Stuttgart).

—— (2006), *Platon: Kritias. Übersetzung und Kommentar*, Platons Werke viii/4 (Göttingen).

Neudling, C. M. (1955), *A Prosopography to Catullus* (Oxford).

Newman, J. K. (1990), *Roman Catullus and the Modification of the Alexandrian Sensibility* (Hildesheim).

Newman, K. (1984), 'Myrrha's Revenge: Ovid and Shakespeare's Reluctant Adonis', *ICS* 9, 251–65.

Nicaise, S. (1980), 'Un conte de fées dans *Les Métamorphoses* d'Ovide (IX. 669–797). L'étrange histoire d'Iphis', *Les Études Classiques* 48, 67–71.

Nicholls, M. C. (2005), 'Roman Public Libraries' (D. Phil. thesis, Oxford).

Nicholson, J. (1996–7), 'Goats and Gout in Catullus 71', *CW* 90, 251–61.

Nikitinski, O. (1996), *Kallimachos-Studien*, Studien zur klassischen Philologie 98 (Frankfurt am Main).

Nikolopoulos, A. D. (2004), *Ovidius Polytropos. Metanarrative in Ovid's* Metamorphoses, Spudasmata 98 (Hildesheim, Zurich, New York).

Nisbet, R. G. M. (1995), *Collected Papers on Latin Literature* (Oxford).

—— (2007), 'Horace: Life and Chronology', in S. J. Harrison (ed.), *The Cambridge Companion to Horace* (Cambridge), 7–35.

—— and Hubbard, M. (1970), *A Commentary on Horace:* Odes Book I (Oxford).

——— (1978), *A Commentary on Horace: Odes Book II* (Oxford).

—— and Rudd, N. (2004), *A Commentary on Horace: Odes, Book III* (Oxford).

Nünlist, R. (2006), 'A Neglected *testimonium* on the Homeric Book-Division', *ZPE* 157, 47–9.

Nyberg, L. (1992), *Unity and Coherence: Studies in Apollonius Rhodius' Argonautica and the Alexandrian Epic Tradition* (Lund).

Obbink, D. (1996), *Philodemus,* On Piety, *Part 1: Critical Text with Commentary* (Oxford).

—— (2001), 'Le livre I du *De natura deorum* de Cicéron et le *De pietate* de Philodème' (with response by Cl. Auvray-Assayas 227–34), in Cl. Auvray-Assayas and D. Delattre (edd.), *Cicéron et Philodème. La polémique en philosophie* (Paris), 203–25.

—— (2003), '4648. Prose on Star-Signs quoting Homer, Hesiod, and Others', in N. Gonis, D. Obbink, P. J. Parsons (edd.), *The Oxyrhynchus Papyri* lxviii (London), 52–63.

—— (2004), 'Vergil's *De Pietate*: From *Ehoiae* to Allegory in Vergil, Philodemus, and Ovid', in D. Armstrong *et al.* (edd.), *Vergil, Philodemus, and the Augustans* (Austin), 175–209.

Oberleitner, G. (1985), *Geschnittene Steine. Die Prunkkameen der Wiener Antikensammlung* (Vienna, Cologne, Graz).

Ohly, K. (1928), *Stichometrische Untersuchungen* (Leipzig).

Oliensis, E. (1998), *Horace and the Rhetoric of Authority* (Cambridge).

Oliver, J. H, and Palmer, R. E. A. (1954), 'Text of the Tabula Hebana', *AJP* 75, 225–49.

Opsomer, Th. (2003), '*Referre aliter saepe solebat idem*: The Relation between Ovid's *Amores* and *Ars Amatoria*', in C. Deroux (ed.), *Studies in Latin Literature and Roman History* xi, Collection Latomus 272 (Brussels), 313–50.

Otis, B. (1970), *Ovid as an Epic Poet*² (Cambridge).

Ozbek, L. (2005), 'Callimachus, *Victoria Berenices* (?)', *Comunicazioni dell' Istituto Papirologico 'G. Vitelli'* 6, 3–20.

Page, D. L. (1955), *Sappho and Alcaeus* (Oxford).

—— (1962), *Poetae Melici Graeci* (Oxford).

—— (1974), *Supplementum Lyricis Graecis* (Oxford).

Pallotto, M. (1982), 'Costanti tematiche e variabili negli Amores di Ovidio. Appunti sulle elegie III 11 (10), 11b (11), 14', *Annali della Facoltà di Lettere e Filosofia dell'Università di Macerata* 15, 661–76.

Palme, B. (ed.) (2007), *Akten des 23. Internationalen Papyrologenkongresses. Wien, 22.–28. Juli 2001* (Papyrologica Vindobonensia 1, Vienna).

Papaioannou, S. (2003), 'Birds, Flames and Epic Closure in Ovid, *Metamorphoses* 13. 600–20 and 14. 568–80', *CQ* 53, 620–4.

Pardini, A. (1991), 'La ripartizione in libri dell'opera di Alceo', *RFIC* 119, 257–84.

Parise Bandoni, F. (2001), 'Narciso a Pompei nella Casa dei Quattro Stili', *MEFRA* 113, 787–98.

Parker, H. N. (1997), 'The Teratogenic Grid', in Hallett and Skinner (edd.) (1997), 47–65.

Parker, R. C. T. (2005), *Polytheism and Society at Athens* (Oxford).

Parkes, M. B. (1992), *Pause and Effect: An Introduction to the History of Punctuation in the West* (Aldershot).

Parsons, P. J. (1977), 'Callimachus: *Victoria Berenices*', *ZPE* 25, 44–50.

—— (1983), '3545–3552. Theocritus', in A. K. Bowman *et al.* (edd.), *The Oxyrhynchus Papyri* l (London), 100–34.

—— (1988), 'Eine neugefundene griechische Liebeselegie', *MH* 45, 65–74.

—— (1999), '4501, 4502. Epigrams: Nicarchus II?', in N. Gonis *et al.* (edd.), *The Oxyrhynchus Papyri* lxvi (London), 38–57.

—— (2002), 'Callimachus and the Hellenistic Epigram', in Montanari and Lehnus (edd.) (2002), 99–141.

—— (2007), *The City of the Sharp-nosed Fish: Greek Lives in Roman Egypt* (London).

Paschalis, M. (1994–5), 'Names and Death in Horace's *Odes*', *CW* 88, 181–90.

—— (ed.) (2002), *Horace and Greek Lyric Poetry*, Rethymnon Classical Studies 1 (Rethymnon).

Petersmann, H. (1990), '*Lucina Nixusque pares*. Die Geburtsgottheiten in Ovids Met. IX 294. Variationen eines mythologischen Motivs', *RhM* 133, 157–75.

Phelan, A. (1992), *Rilke*, Neue Gedichte (London).

Piazzi, L. (2005), *Lucrezio e i Presocratici. Un commento a* De rerum natura *1, 635–920* (Pisa).

Pietsch, Chr. (1999), *Die Argonautika des Apollonios von Rhodos. Untersuchungen zum Problem der einheitlichen Konzeption des Inhalts*, Hermes Einzelschriften 80 (Stuttgart).

Pintabone, D. T. (2002), 'Ovid's Iphis and Ianthe: When Girls Won't Be Girls', in N. S. Rabinowitz and L. Auanger (edd.), *Among Women: From the Homosocial to the Homoerotic in the Ancient World* (Austin), 256–85.

Platnauer, M. (1948), 'Elision of *atque* in Roman Poetry', *CQ* 42, 91–3.

Platthy, J. (1968), *Sources on the Earliest Greek Libraries, with the Testimonia* (Amsterdam).

Pöhlmann, E. (1973), 'Charakteristika des römischen Lehrgedichts', *ANRW* i.3, 813–901.

Pontani, F. (1999), 'The First Word of Callimachus' *Aitia*', *ZPE* 128, 57–9.

—— (2005), *Sguardi su Ulisse. La tradizione esegetica greca all'*Odissea (Rome).

Pordomingo, F. (1994), 'Sur les premières anthologies d'épigrammes sur papyrus', in A. Bülow-Jacobsen (ed.), *Proceedings of the 20th International Congress of Papyrologists, Copenhagen, 23–29 August, 1992* (Copenhagen), 326–31.

—— (1998), 'Les anthologies de *P. Tebt.* I 1 et 2', in I. Andorlini *et al.* (edd.), *Atti del XXII Congresso Internazionale di Papirologia* (Florence), ii. 1077–93.

—— (2007), 'Vers une caractérisation des anthologies sur papyrus', in Palme (ed.) (2007), 549–57.

Porro, A. (1994), *Vetera Alcaica. L'esegesi di Alceo dagli Alessandrini all'età imperiale* (Milan).

Porter, D. H. (1987), *Horace's Poetic Journey: A Reading of* Odes *1–3* (Princeton).

Powell, J. U. (1925), *Collectanea Alexandrina: Reliquiae Minores Aetatis Ptolemaicae, 323–146 A.C., Epicorum, Elegiacorum, Lyricorum, Ethicorum* (Oxford).

Privitera, T. (1989), 'Tib. 1, 1, 60 e Ov. *Amores* 3, 9, 58: la "Nemesi" incompiuta?', in G. Catanzaro, F. Santucci (edd.), *Tredici secoli di elegia latina* (Assisi), 307–10.

Pugliese Carratelli, G., and Baldassarre, I. (edd.) (1990–2003), *Pompei. Pitture e mosaici,* 11 vols. (Rome).

Pulleyn, S. (2000), *Homer,* Iliad *Book One: Edited with an Introduction, Translation, and Commentary* (Oxford).

Purcell, N. (1986), 'Livia and the Womanhood of Rome', *PCPS* 32, 78–105.

Putnam, M. C. J. (1973), 'Horace C. 3. 30: The Lyricist as Hero', *Ramus* 2, 1–19.

—— (1996), 'Horace's Arboreal Anniversary', *Ramus* 25, 27–38.

—— (2001), 'Ovid, Virgil and Myrrha's Metamorphic Exile', *Vergilius* 47, 171–93.

Quint, D. (1993), *Epic and Empire: Politics and Generic Form from Virgil to Milton* (Princeton).

Raaflaub, K. A., and Toher, M. (edd.) (1990), *Between Republic and Empire: Interpretations of Augustus and his Principate* (Berkeley, Los Angeles, London).

Rambaud, M. (1980), 'César et Catulle', in Thill (ed.) (1980), 37–50.

Rambaux, Cl. (1985), *Trois analyses de l'amour: Catulle, Poésies; Ovide, Les Amours; Apulée, Le conte de Psyché* (Paris), 141–76.

Ramírez de Verger, A. (1992), 'Elucidations on Ovid, *Amores* 3. 6. 1–22', *LCM* 17, 141–3.

Ranucci, G. (1976), 'Il primo monologo di Biblide. (Ovidio, *Metamorfosi* IX, vv. 474–516)', *Annali della Scuola Normale di Pisa* (*Classe di lettere e filosofia*) ser. 3, 6, 53–72.

Rauk, J. (1996–7), 'Time and History in Catullus 1', *CW* 90, 319–32.

Rawles, R. (2006*a*), 'Notes on the Interpretation of the "New Sappho"', *ZPE* 157, 1–7.

—— (2006*b*), 'Musical Notes on the New Anonymous Lyric Poem from Köln', *ZPE* 157, 8–13.

Rawson, E. (1985), *Intellectual Life in the Late Roman Republic* (London).

—— (1991), 'The Introduction of Logical Organization in Roman Prose Literature', *Roman Culture and Society: Collected Papers* (Oxford), 324–51.

Reed, J. D. (1997), *Bion of Smyrna, the Fragments and the* Adonis: *Edited with Introduction and Commentary* (Cambridge).

—— (2006), 'New Verses on Adonis', *ZPE* 158, 76–82.

Reitz, Ch. (2003), 'Dichtung und Wissenschaft', in Horster and Reitz (edd.) (2003), 61–71.

Rengakos, A. (2004), 'Die *Argonautika* und das "kyklische Gedicht"', in A. Bierl, A. Schmitt, A. Willi (edd.), *Antike Literatur in neuer Deutung. Festschrift für Joachim Latacz anläßlich seines 70. Geburtstages* (Munich and Leipzig), 277–304.

Renger, A.-B. (ed.) (2002), *Narcissus. Ein Mythos von der Antike bis zum Cyberspace* (Stuttgart and Weimar).

Renner, T. (1978), 'A Papyrus Dictionary of Metamorphoses', *HSCP* 82, 277–301.

Rich, J. W. (1990), *Cassius Dio: The Augustan Settlement (*Roman History *53–55.9)* (Warminster).

Richlin, A. (1992), *The Garden of Priapus: Sexuality and Aggression in Roman Humor*² (New York and Oxford).

Richmond, J. A. (1965), 'A Note on the Elision of Final *e* in Certain Particles used by Latin Poets', *Glotta* 43, 78–103.

Ricœur, P. (1983–5), *Temps et récit*, 3 vols. (Paris).

Rimell, V. (2006), *Ovid's Lovers: Desire, Difference, and the Poetic Imagination* (Cambridge).

Rix, H. (2002), *Sabellische Texte. Die Texte des Oskischen, Umbrischen und Südpikenischen* (Heidelberg).

Robert, L. (1967), 'Les épigrammes satiriques de Lucillius sur les athlètes. Parodie et réalités', in *L'Épigramme grecque*, Entretiens Hardt 14 (Geneva), 179–295.

Rohde, E. (1914), *Der griechische Roman und seine Vorläufer*³ (Leipzig).

Romano, E. (1979), *Struttura degli* Astronomica *di Manilio* (Palermo).

Rosati, G. (1983), *Narciso e Pigmalione. Illusione e spettacolo nelle* Metamorfosi *di Ovidio* (Florence).

——(2002), 'Narrative Techniques and Narrative Structures in the *Metamorphoses*', in Boyd (ed.) (2002), 271–304.

Ross, D. O., Jr, (1969), *Style and Tradition in Catullus* (Cambridge, MA).

Rossum-Steenbeek, M. van (1998), *Greek Readers' Digests? Studies on a
Selection of Subliterary Papyri*, Mnemosyne Suppl. 175 (Leiden, New
York, Cologne).

Rudd, N. (ed.) (1995), *Horace 2000, A Celebration. Essays for the Bimillen-
nium* (London).

——(2005), 'Echo and Narcissus: A Study in Duality', in *The Common
Spring: Essays on Latin and English Poetry* (Exeter), 69–74.

Rutherford, I. C. (2000), *Pindar's* Paeans: *A Reading of the Fragments, with a
Survey of the Genre* (Oxford).

Ryan, F. X. (1995), 'The Date of Catullus 52', *Eranos* 93, 113–21.

Salemme, C. (2000), *Introduzione agli* 'Astronomica' *di Manilio²* (Naples).

Salzman-Mitchell, P. B. (2005), *A Web of Fantasies: Gaze, Image, and Gender
in Ovid's* Metamorphoses (Baltimore).

Sammartano, R. (1998), Origines gentium Siciliae. *Ellanico, Antioco, Tuci-
dide* (Rome).

Sandbach, F. H. (1985), *Aristotle and the Stoics*, PCPS Suppl. 10 (Cambridge).

Santini, C. (1993), 'Connotazioni sociologiche in margine ai *paranatellonta*
maniliani', in Liuzzi (ed.) (1993), 109–26.

——(1999), 'Le notti di Mirra', in W. Schubert (ed.), *Ovid—Werk und
Wirkung. Festgabe für Michael von Albrecht zum 65. Geburtstag*, Studien
zur klassischen Philologie 100 (Frankfurt am Main, etc.), i. 467–76.

Santirocco, M. S. (1986), *Unity and Design in Horace's* Odes (Chapel Hill and
London).

Sbardella, L. (2000), *Filita. Testimonianze e frammenti poetici* (Rome).

Schachter, A. (1981–94), *Cults of Boiotia*, 4 vols., BICS Suppl. 38 (London).

Scheid, J. (1995), '*Graeco ritu*: A Typically Roman Way of Honoring the
Gods', *HSCP* 97, 15–31.

Scherf, J. (1996), *Untersuchungen zur antiken Veröffentlichung der Catullge-
dichte*, Spudasmata 61 (Hildesheim, Zurich, New York).

Schiesaro, A. (1994), 'The palingenesis of *De Rerum Natura*', *PCPS* 40,
81–107.

——(1996), 'Aratus' Myth of Dike', *MD* 37, 9–26.

——(2002), 'Ovid and the Professional Discourses of Scholarship, Religion,
Rhetoric', in P. R. Hardie (ed.) (2002*b*), 62–75.

——Mitsis, P., Strauss Clay, J. (edd.) (1993), *Mega Nepios. Il destinatario
nell' epos didascalico, MD* 31 (Pisa).

Schindler, C. (2000), *Untersuchungen zu den Gleichnissen im römischen Lehrgedicht: Lukrez. Vergil. Manilius*, Hypomnemata 129 (Göttingen).

Schmidt, E. A. (ed.) (2001), *L'Histoire littéraire immanente dans la poésie latine*, Entretiens Hardt 47 (Geneva).

Schmidt, J.-U. (2003), 'Die Blendung des Kyklopen und der Zorn des Poseidon. Zum Problem der Rechtfertigung der Irrfahrten des Odysseus und ihrer Bedeutung für das Anliegen des Odysseedichters', *WS* 116, 5–42.

Schmitz, Th. (1999), ' "I hate all common things": The Reader's Role in Callimachus' "Aetia" Prologue', *HSCP* 99, 151–78.

Schmitzer, U. (1994), '*Non modo militiae turbine factus eques*: Ovids Selbstbewußtsein und die Polemik gegen Horaz in der Elegie Am. 3,15', *Philologus* 138, 101–17.

Schneider, O. (1856), *Nicandrea. Theriaca et Alexipharmaca* (Leipzig).

Schneider, W. J. (1998), 'Hercules und das Horn des Achelous', *Eranos* 96, 108–113.

Schrijvers, P. H. (1976), 'O tragoedia tu labor aeternus. Étude sur l'élégie III,1 des Amores d'Ovide', in J. M. Bremer, S. L. Radt, C. J. Ruijgh (edd.), *Miscellanea tragica in honorem J. C. Kamerbeek* (Amsterdam).

Schröder, St. (2004), 'Skeptische Überlegungen zum Mailänder Epigrammpapyrus (P. Mil. Vogl. VIII 309)', *ZPE* 148, 29–73.

Schubart, W. (1911), *Papyri Graecae Berolinenses* (Bonn and Oxford).

Schulze, Ch. (2003), *Die pharmazeutische Fachliteratur in der Antike. Eine Einführung*[2] (Göttingen).

Schwindt, J. P. (1994), *Das Motiv der 'Tagesspanne'—Ein Beitrag zur Ästhetik der Zeitgestaltung im griechisch-römischen Drama*, Studien zur Geschichte und Kultur des Altertums 1. 9 (Paderborn, etc.).

Scognamiglio, E. (2005), 'I segni nel primo libro dell'opera di Filodemo *La richezza* (*PHerc*. 163)', *Cronache Ercolanesi* 35, 161–81.

Scott, W. (1885), *Fragmenta Herculanensia: A Descriptive Catalogue of the Oxford Copies of the Herculanean Rolls* (Oxford).

Seager, R. (1995), 'Horace and Augustus: Poetry and Politics', in Rudd (ed.) (1995), 23–40.

Sedley, D. N. (1998), *Lucretius and the Transformation of Greek Wisdom* (Cambridge).

Segal, C. P. (1969), *Landscape in Ovid's* Metamorphoses*: A Study in the Transformation of a Literary Symbol*, Hermes Einzelschriften 23 (Wiesbaden).

—— (1989), *Orpheus: The Myth of the Poet* (Baltimore and London).

—— (1998), 'Ovid's Metamorphic Bodies: Art, Gender, and Violence in the *Metamorphoses*', *Arion* 3rd ser. 5.3, 9–41.

—— (2001–2), 'Jupiter in Ovid's *Metamorphoses*', *Arion* 3rd ser. 9, 78–99.

Seider, R. (1972–8), *Paläographie der lateinischen Papyri*, 2 vols. (Stuttgart).

——(1982), 'Ein Heidelberger Fragment der Medea', *ZPE* 46, 33–6.

Seiler, M. A. (1997), Ποίησις ποιήσεως. *Alexandrinische Dichtung* κατὰ λεπτόν *in strukturaler und humanethologischer Deutung*, Beiträge zur Altertumskunde 102 (Stuttgart).

Selden, D. L. (1998), 'Alibis', *CA* 17, 289–420.

Sellwood, D. (1980), *An Introduction to the Coinage of Parthia*² (London).

Shackleton Bailey: *see under* Bailey.

Sharrock, A. (1994), *Seduction and Repetition in Ovid's* Ars Amatoria *2* (Oxford).

——(2000), 'Intratextuality: Texts, Parts, and (W)holes in Theory', in A. Sharrock and H. Morales (edd.), *Intratextuality: Greek and Roman Textual Relations* (Oxford), 1–39.

——(2006), 'Ovid and the Politics of Reading', in Knox (ed.) (2006), 238–61.

Shore, F. B. (1993), *Parthian Coins and History: Ten Dragons Against Rome* (Quarryville).

Sichtermann, H., and Koch, G. (1975), *Griechische Mythen auf römischen Sarkophagen* (Tübingen).

Sider, D. (1997), *The Epigrams of Philodemos: Introduction, Text, and Commentary* (New York and Oxford).

——(2005), *The Library of the Villa dei Papiri at Herculaneum* (Los Angeles).

——(2007), '*Sylloge Simonidea*', in J. Bruss and P. Bing (edd.), *The Brill Handbook to Hellenistic Greek Epigrams* (Leiden, Boston, Cologne), 113–30.

Simon, E. (1972), 'Aphrodite und Adonis—eine neuerworbene Pyxis in Würzburg', *AK* 15, 20–24.

Simonetta, B. (1976), 'Sulla monetazione di Fraate IV e di Tiridate II di Parthia', *Riv. It. di Numismatica* 23, 19–34.

Skinner, M. B. (1981), *Catullus' Passer: The Arrangement of the Book of Polymetric Poems* (Salem, New Hampshire).

Skinner, M. B. (2007), 'Authorial Arrangement of the Collection: Debate Past and Present', in M. B. Skinner (ed.), *A Companion to Catullus* (Malden and Oxford), 35–53.

Skutsch, O. (1969), 'Metrical Variations and Some Textual Problems in Catullus', *BICS* 16, 38–43.

Skydsgaard, J. E. (1968), *Varro the Scholar: Studies in the First Book of Varro's De Re Rustica* (Copenhagen).

Solin, H. (1968), 'Pompeiana', *Epigraphica* 30, 105–25.

Solodow, J. B. (1988), *The World of Ovid's* Metamorphoses (Chapel Hill and London).

Solodow, J. B. (1989), 'Forms of Literary Criticism in Catullus: Polymetric vs. Epigram', *CP* 84, 312–19.

Sommer, R. (1926), 'T. Pomponius Atticus und die Verbreitung von Ciceros Werken', *Hermes* 61, 389–422.

Spaeth, B. S. (1990), *The Roman Goddess Ceres* (Austin).

Spanoudakis, K. (2002), *Philitas of Cos*, Mnemosyne Suppl. 229 (Leiden, Boston, Cologne).

Spentzou, E. (2003), *Readers and Writers in Ovid's* Heroides: *Transgressions of Genre and Gender* (Oxford).

St Clair, W. (2004), *The Reading Nation in the Romantic Period* (Cambridge).

Starr, R. J. (1987), 'The Circulation of Literary Texts in the Roman World', *CQ* 37, 213–23.

Stephen, G. M. (1959), 'The coronis', *Scriptorium* 13, 3–14.

Strocka, V. M. (1981), 'Römische Bibliotheken', *Gymnasium* 88, 298–329.

—— (1993), 'Pompeji VI 17, 41: Ein Haus mit Privatbibliothek', *Röm. Mitt.* 100, 321–51.

Stroh, W. (1979), 'Ovids Liebeskunst und die Ehegesetze des Augustus', *Gymnasium* 86, 323–52.

Sumner, G. V. (1973), *The Orators in Cicero's* Brutus: *Prosopography and Chronology*, Phoenix Suppl. 11 (Toronto, 1973).

—— (1978), 'Varrones Murenae', *HSCP* 82, 187–99.

Susanetti, D. (1992), *Sinesio di Cirene. I sogni. Introduzione, traduzione e commento* (Bari).

Suter, A. (1989–90), 'Ovid, From Image to Narrative: *Amores* 1. 8 and 3. 6', *CW* 83, 15–20.

Swan, M. (1966), 'The Consular *Fasti* of 23 BC and the Conspiracy of Varro Murena', *HSCP* 71 (1966), 235–48.

Syme, R. (1958), *Tacitus*, 2 vols. (Oxford).

—— (1979), 'The Conquest of North-West Spain', *Roman Papers* ii (Oxford), 825–54.

—— (1986), *The Augustan Aristocracy* (Oxford).

—— (1991), 'Verona's Earliest Senators: Some Comparisons', *Roman Papers* vii (Oxford), 473–91.

Syndikus, H.-P. (1984–90), *Catull. Eine Interpretation*, 3 vols. (Darmstadt).

Tarditi, G. (1968), *Archiloco/Archilochus* (Rome).

Tarrant, R. J. (1989), 'The Reader as Author: Collaborative Interpolation in Latin Poetry', in J. N. Grant (ed.), *Editing Greek and Latin Texts* (New York), 121–62.

—— (2004), *P. Ovidi Nasonis Metamorphoses* (Oxford).

Taylor, J. H. (1970), '*Amores*, 3. 9: A Farewell to Elegy', *Latomus* 29, 474–77.

Theodorakopoulos, E. (1999), 'Closure and Transformations in Ovid's *Metamorphoses*', in P. R. Hardie, Barchiesi, Hinds (edd.) (1999), 142–62.

Thill, A. (ed.), *L'Élégie romaine. Enracinement—thèmes—diffusion* (Paris).

Thomas, E. (1969), 'Ovid at the Races', in J. Bibauw (ed.), *Hommages à M. Renard* i, Coll. Latomus 101 (Brussels), 710–24.

Thomas, M. (1998), 'Ovid's Orpheus: Immoral Lovers, Immortal Poets', *MD* 40, 99–109.

Thomas, R. (2003), 'Prose Performance Texts: *epideixis* and Written Publication in the Late Fifth and Early Fourth Centuries', in Yunis (ed.) (2003), 162–88.

Thomas, R. F. (1983), 'Callimachus, the *Victoria Berenices*, and Roman Poetry', *CQ* 33, 92–101.

—— (1987), 'Prose into Poetry: Tradition and Meaning in Vergil's *Georgics*', *HSCP* 91, 229–60.

—— (1988), *Virgil*, Georgics, 2 vols. (Cambridge).

—— (1999), *Reading Virgil and his Texts: Studies in Intertextuality* (Ann Arbor).

—— (2004), ' "Drownded in the Tide": The *nauagika* and Some "Problems" in Augustan Poetry', in Acosta-Hughes, Kosmetatou, Baumbach (edd.) (2004), 259–75.

Thompson, D'A. W. (1936), *A Glossary of Greek Birds*[2] (Oxford).

Thompson, D. J. (1987), 'Ptolemaios and The "Lighthouse": Greek Culture in the Memphite Serapeum', *PCPS* 33, 105–21.

Thomson, D. F. S. (1997), *Catullus: Edited with a Textual and Interpretative Commentary*, Phoenix Suppl. 34 (Toronto).

Toohey, P. (1996), *Epic Lessons: An Introduction to Ancient Didactic Poetry* (London).

Tracy, V. A. (1977), 'Dramatic Elements in Ovid's *Amores*', *Latomus* 36, 496–500.

Tränkle, H. (1963), 'Elegisches in Ovids Metamorphosen', *Hermes* 91, 459–76.

—— (1990), *Appendix Tibulliana, herausgegeben und kommentiert*, Texte und Kommentare 16 (Berlin and New York).

Treggiari, S. (1991), *Roman Marriage:* Iusti Coniuges *from the Time of Cicero to the Time of Ulpian* (Oxford).

Trépanier, S. (2004), *Empedocles: An Interpretation* (New York and London).

Tronchet, G. (1998), *La Métamorphose à l'œuvre. Recherches sur la poétique d'Ovide dans les* Métamorphoses (Louvain and Paris).

Tsantsanoglou, K. (2006), 'The Scholia on Alcman's *Partheneion*', Ἑλληνικά 56, 8–30.

Turner, E. G. (1977), *The Typology of the Early Codex* (Philadelphia).
—— (1987), *Greek Manuscripts of the Ancient World*², rev. P. J. Parsons, BICS Suppl. 46 (London).
Tuzet, H. (1987), *Mort et résurrection d'Adonis. Étude de l'évolution d'un mythe* (Paris).
Ullman, B. (1973), *Studies in the Italian Renaissance*² (Rome).
Van Sickle, J. (1980), 'The Book-Roll and Some Conventions of the Poetic Book', *Arethusa* 13, 13–32.
Vardi, A. D., 'An Anthology of Early Latin Epigrams? A Ghost Reconsidered', *CQ* 50 (2000), 148–54.
Vieillefond, J.-R. (1992), *Aristénète. Lettres d'amour. Texte établi et traduit* (Paris).
Viscogliosi, A. (1999), 'Porticus Octaviae', *LTUR* iv. 141–5.
Visser, E. (1997), *Homers Katalog der Schiffe* (Stuttgart and Leipzig).
Vogt-Spira, G. (2002), 'Der Blick und die Stimme: Ovids Narziß- und Echomythos im Kontext römischer Anthropologie', in Renger (ed.) (2002), 27–40.
Voigt, E.-M. (1971), *Sappho et Alcaeus. Fragmenta* (Amsterdam).
Volk, K. (2002), *The Poetics of Latin Didactic: Lucretius, Vergil, Ovid, Manilius* (Oxford).
—— (2005), '*Aetna* oder Wie man ein Lehrgedicht schreibt', in N. Holzberg (ed.), *Die* Appendix Vergiliana. *Pseudepigraphen im literarischen Kontext*, Classica Monacensia 30 (Tübingen), 68–90.
Vox, O. (2000), 'Sul genere grammaticale della Chioma di Berenice', *MD* 44, 175–81.
Walbank, F. W. (1957–79), *A Historical Commentary on Polybius*, 3 vols. (Oxford).
—— (1972), *Polybius* (Berkeley, Los Angeles, London).
Waller, P. (2006), *Writers, Readers, and Reputations: Literary Life in Britain 1870–1918* (Oxford).
Watson, L. C. (1983), 'Problems in *Epode* 11', *CQ* 33, 229–38.
—— (1991), *Arae: The Curse Poetry of Antiquity* (Leeds).
—— (2003), *A Commentary on Horace's* Epodes (Oxford).
Weil, H. (1879), *Un papyrus inédit. Nouveaux fragments d'Euripide et d'autres poètes grecs* (Paris).
Weinlich, B. (1999), *Ovids Amores: Gedichtfolge und Handlungsablauf*, Beiträge zur Altertumskunde 128 (Stuttgart and Leipzig).
West, D. A. (1957), 'The Metre of Catullus' Elegiacs', *CQ* 7, 98–102.
—— (1998), *Horace*, Odes II: Vatis Amici (Oxford).
West, M. L. (1974), *Studies in Greek Elegy and Iambus* (Berlin and New York).

—— (1978), *Hesiod*, Works and Days: *Edited with Prolegomena and Commentary* (Oxford).

—— (1983), *Greek Metre* (Oxford).

—— (1989), *Iambi et Elegi Graeci ante Alexandrum Cantati*², 2 vols. (Oxford).

—— (1997), *The East Face of Helicon: West Asiatic Elements in Greek Poetry and Myth* (Oxford).

—— (1998–2000), *Homeri Ilias*, 2 vols. (Stuttgart, Leipzig, Munich).

—— (1999), 'The Invention of Homer', *CQ* 49, 364–82.

—— (2001), *Studies in the Text and Transmission of the* Iliad (Leipzig and Munich).

—— (2003*a*), *Greek Epic Fragments from the Seventh to the Fifth Century B.C.* (Cambridge, MA, and London).

—— (2003*b*), '*Iliad* and *Aethiopis*', *CQ* 53, 1–14.

—— (2005), 'The New Sappho', *ZPE* 151, 1–9.

—— (2007), *Indo-European Poetry and Myth* (Oxford).

West, S. R. (1963), '*Reclamantes* in Greek Papyri', *Scriptorium* 17, 314–15.

—— (1967), *The Ptolemaic Papyri of Homer*, Papyrologica Coloniensia 3 (Cologne and Opladen).

—— (1985), 'Venus Observed? A Note on Callimachus, fr. 110', *CQ* 35, 61–6.

—— (1998), 'Whose Baby? A Note on P. Oxy. 744', *ZPE* 121, 167–72.

Wheeler, S. M. (1999), *A Discourse of Wonders: Audience and Performance in Ovid's* Metamorphoses (Philadelphia).

—— (2000), *Narrative Dynamics in Ovid's* Metamorphoses, Classica Monacensia 20 (Tübingen).

Whitehead, D. and Blyth, P. H. (2004), *Athenaeus Mechanicus*, On Machines (Περὶ Μηχανημάτων): *Translated with Introduction and Commentary*, Historia Einzelschriften 182 (Stuttgart).

Wilkinson, L. P. (1969), *The* Georgics *of Virgil: A Critical Survey* (Cambridge).

Wille, G. (1984), 'Zum künstlerischen Aufbau von Ovids Amores', in F. J. Oroz Arizcuren (ed.), *Navicula Tubingensis: studia in honorem Antonii A. Tovar* (Tübingen), 389–423.

Williams, C. A. (1999), *Roman Homosexuality: Ideologies of Masculinity in Classical Antiquity* (New York and Oxford).

Williams, F. (2003), 'The Hands of Death: Ovid *Amores* 3. 9. 20', *AJP* 124, 225–34.

Wilson, J. R. (1979), '*ΚΑΙ ΚΕ ΤΙΣ ΩΔ' ΕΡΕΕΙ*: An Homeric Device in Greek Literature', *ICS* 4, 1–15.

Wimmel, W. (1993), *Die Bacchus-Ode C. 3,25 des Horaz*, AAWM 1993.11 (Mainz and Stuttgart).

Wingo, E. O. (1972), *Latin Punctuation in the Classical Age* (Mouton).

Wiseman, T. P. (1969), *Catullan Questions* (Leicester).

—— (1987), 'The Masters of Sirmio', *Roman Studies, Literary and Historical* (Liverpool), 307–72.

Wissowa, G. (1912), *Religion und Kultus der Römer* (Munich).

Wöhrle, G. (1998), 'Bemerkungen zur lehrhaften Dichtung zwischen Empedokles und Arat', in Kullmann, Althoff, Asper (edd.) (1998), 279–86.

Wonterghem, F. van (1984), *Superaequum, Corfinium, Sulmo (Forma Italiae, Regio IV.i)* (Florence).

Woodman, A. J. (1975), 'Questions of Date, Genre, and Style in Velleius: Some Literary Answers', *CQ* 25, 272–306.

—— (1983), *Velleius Paterculus: The Caesarian and Augustan Narrative (2.41–93), Edited with a Commentary* (Cambridge).

—— (2002), '*Biformis uates*: The *Odes*, Catullus and Greek Lyric', in Woodman and Feeney (edd.) (2002), 53–64.

—— (2003), 'Poems to Historians: Catullus 1 and Horace, *Odes* 2.1', in D. Braund and C. Gill (edd.), *Myth, History and Culture in Republican Rome: Studies in Honour of T. P. Wiseman* (Exeter), 191–216.

—— and Feeney, D. C. (edd.) (2002), *Traditions and Contexts in the Poetry of Horace* (Cambridge).

Woudhuysen, H. R. (1996), *Sir Philip Sidney and the Circulation of Manuscripts 1558–1640* (Oxford).

Wray, D. (2000), 'Apollonius' Masterplot: Narrative Strategy in *Argonautica* 1', in Harder, Regtuit, Wakker (edd.) (2000), 239–65.

—— (2001), *Catullus and the Poetics of Roman Manhood* (Cambridge).

Wyke, M. (2002), *The Roman Mistress: Ancient and Modern Representations* (Oxford).

Wyß, B. (1983), 'Gregor II (Gregor von Nazianz)', *RAC* 12, 793–683.

Yunis, H. (ed.) (2003), *Written Texts and the Rise of Literate Culture in Ancient Greece* (Cambridge).

Zanker, P. (1966), '"Iste ego sum". Der naive und der bewußte Narziß', *Bonner Jahrbücher* 166, 152–70.

—— (1988), *The Power of Images in the Age of Augustus*, tr. A. Shapiro (Ann Arbor).

Zehnacker, H. (1995), 'Horaz, carmen III 27', *RhM* 138, 68–82.

Zetzel, J. E. G. (1981), 'On the Opening of Callimachus, *Aetia* II', *ZPE* 42, 31–3.

Zicàri, M. (1964), 'Some Metrical and Prosodical Features of Catullus' Poetry', *Phoenix* 18, 193–205.

Ziegler, K. (1952), 'Polybios (1)', *RE* xxi. 1440–578.

Zwierlein, O. (1999), *Die Ovid- und Vergil-Revision in tiberischer Zeit* i. *Prolegomena* (Berlin and New York).

Zwierlein-Diehl, E. (1973–91), *Die antiken Gemmen des Kunsthistorischen Museums in Wien*, 3 vols. (Munich).

Index of Passages Discussed

Entities the size of a papyrus roll or more (e.g. Callimachus, Aetia Book 3) normally appear in the General Index

General Index

Accius, scholarly activity of 21
actus 249
Adonis 212–15
Aeetes:
  in Apollonius 84
  in Callimachus 56
Aelius Gallus 139–40
ἄεθλος 77–9
age and youth:
  in Apollonius 82
  in Callimachus 53–4
  and Catullus 265–6
  in Horace 152, 170
  and Horace's *œuvre* 260–1,
    265–6
  and Ovid's *œuvre* 265
Alcaeus:
  and Archilochus 167
  arrangement of poems 167
  popularity of 167
  see also Horace: and Alcaeus
Alexandria 59, 125
Alfieri 222 n. 34
allegory 151 n. 49, 168 n. 18
Anacreon 2
  see also Horace: and Anacreon
animals, connotations of 263 n. 7
'anthologies' 5–15, 110–11, 209
  Latin 31
  and readers 14–15
  and symposium? 12
Antimachus 258
antithetical structure 252–8, 260–3
  in arrangement of books 236,
    239, 244–5, 252

in arrangement of poems 179–80
Antoninus Liberalis 207, 210
Anubion 207 n. 10, 229
apices 22
Apollonius of Citium 230, 233
Apollonius of Perga 4, 230, 241
Apollonius Rhodius:
  ἄεθλοι in 77–9, 86–7, 255
  Argonautica short 66
  age in 82–3
  Books 1 and 2: 80–6, 252; Books
    3 and 4: 45, 86–8
  books distinct 79
  bulls 80
  division in 4, 81–2
  and Euripides 85
  gender in 79–81, 255
  and *Iliad* 78, 80, 82–3, 85–6,
    88, 89
  Jason in 86–8
  ktisis-poems 255 n. 3
  Medea in 86–9
  multiple perspectives in 83–5, 86
  and *Odyssey* 77, 78, 82, 84, 89
  paratactic structure in 77, 80, 86
  scale on which love treated 261
  structure 208
  structuring elements in 80–1
  and tragedy 81, 85
Aratus:
  avoids planets 241
  commentaries on 18
  and Callimachus 62
  and Hesiod 62, 228–9
  and Lucretius 235

Horace (*cont.*)
  C. 4: and *C.* 1–3: 28, 176; date
    of 136 n. 14; and lyric
    tradition 174–6; politics
    in 261; structure 161, 174–6
  Canidia in 145, 166
  Cantabrians in 141–2
  Carmen 174
  and Catullus 149, 152, 153
  datable references in 138–44
  enjambement after
    prepositives 134–5
  Epicureanism in 152, 158–9
  and epinician 175
  Epistles and *Odes* 261
  Epistles 2: 148–9
  Epodes 132, 134, 150, 163–6;
    and fables 164; metre
    in 163–6; and
    narrative 164–5; narrator
    in 165–6; and *Odes* 149, 150,
    167–8, 169, 261, 264
  and Hipponax 163–6
  love-objects in 137, 156 n. 60,
    259–60
  lyric tradition in 149–50, 153,
    156–7, 167–76
  Maecenas in 136, 145, 165
  Marcelli in 139
  metre need not change between
    poems 135 n. 13
  and mime 164
  narrator in 165–6, 167–8, 172,
    173, 175–6
  number of poems in books 135
  Parthians in 139, 140–3
  and Pindar 173, 174, 175
  and Sappho 150, 152, 153, 157,
    167–76
  sapphic stanza in 133–4, 153

  Satires: Book 1: 104; Book 2: 148;
    and Lucilius 162; ignored in
    Odes 261; outlook in 266
  Sestius in 138, 139 n. 21
  and Simonides 153, 170, 172,
    174, 175
  and Stesichorus 168
  Stoicism in 154, 158
  storms and sailing in 151 n. 50
  temples in 142
  trees in 136, 153–4
  Virgil in 151, 152
Hyacinthus 214

iambus, fables in 164
Ilia 187–8
immortality and love 96–7
impotence of narrator 181, 165, 188
intercolumn 17
interpuncts 21–2, 24
intertextuality 101–2
  Hellenistic, with earlier
    poetry 163
  in inscription 29
  of Latin poetry with Greek ch. 4
    (esp. 101–2), ch. 5, ch. 7 (esp.
    162–3), ch. 9
invitations 48
Irigaray, L. 127 n. 51

joke-books 124 n. 42, 125, 126

Kleophrades Painter 83 n. 37
knowledge, types of 46–7

Laevius 27, 264
lectional aids 15, 17
Leges Iuliae 185–6
Leto 217
libraries 34–7